# 15th Nordic Conference of Computational Linguistics (NODALIDA 2005)

Joensuu, Finland
20 – 21 May 2005

**Editor:**

**Stefan Werner**

ISBN: 978-1-5108-3518-4

# NODALIDA2005

Ling@JoY 1

Ling@JoY :
University of Joensuu electronic publications
in linguistics and language technology;
n:o 1
ISBN 952-458-771-8
ISSN 1796-1114

# Proceedings of the 15th NODALIDA conference, Joensuu 2005

## Edited by Stefan Werner

JOENSUUN YLIOPISTO
JOENSUU 20006

# Contents

# Preface

The 15<sup>th</sup> Nordic Conference of Computational Linguistics—better known as NODALIDA—was held on May 20 and 21, 2005 at the University of Joensuu in Eastern Finland. Several related events also took place in Joensuu during the days leading up to NODALIDA, most notably the final seminar of the NorFA- (now NordForsk) funded Nordic language technology research program.

Over 120 participants registered for NODALIDA 2005 and every other also presented their work at the conference which offered 31 papers and 29 posters on many different aspects of language and speech technology, in addition to three invited lectures. For more information, please refer to the conference web site which will remain available at `http://ling.joensuu.fi/nodalida2005/`. This electronic proceedings volume contains 27 articles based on NODALIDA presentations.

I would like to express my sincere thanks to all conference participants as well as my special gratitude to those who made it possible at all to have NODALIDA at Joensuu University, in particular Kimmo Koskenniemi and Jussi Niemi. I would also like to take the opportunity to thank the members of our International Program Committee for their very valuable work and their kind assistance. Thanks of course also go to the session chairs and to all local helpers. Finally, let me acknowledge the financial support received from the Academy of Finland.

In the plenary session following Kimmo Koskenniemi's talk on *Past, present and future of language technology in the Nordic area* several interesting ideas for future Nordic and Baltic cooperation were discussed; a short summary can be found at the site of the Language Technology Documentation Centre in Finland (FiLT). One of the decisions made was to accept the University of Tartu's offer to host the 16<sup>th</sup> NODALIDA in the spring of 2007.

Joensuu, April 13, 2006
Stefan Werner

# Robust stochastic parsing: comparing and combining two approaches for processing extra-grammatical sentences


**Marita Ailomaa**[1] and **Vladimír Kadlec**[2]
and **Martin Rajman**[1] and **Jean-Cédric Chappelier**[1]
[1]Artificial Intelligence Laboratory (LIA)
Ecole Polytechnique Fédérale de Lausanne (EPFL)
1015 Lausanne, Switzerland
[2] Faculty of Informatics, Masaryk University
Botanická 68a, 602 00 Brno, Czech Republic
{marita.ailomaa,jean-cedric.chappelier,martin.rajman}@epfl.ch,
xkadlec@fi.muni.cz


## Abstract


This paper compares two techniques for robust parsing of extra-grammatical natural language. Both are based on well-known approaches; one selects the optimal combination of partial analyses, the other relaxes grammar rules. Both techniques use a stochastic parser to select the "best" solution among multiple analyses. Experimental results show that regardless of the grammar, the best results are obtained by sequentially combining the two techniques, by first relaxing the rules and only when that fails by then selecting a combination of partial analyses.


## 1 Introduction

Formal grammars are often used in NLP applications to describe well-formed sentences. But when used in practice, the grammars usually describe only a subset of a NL, and in addition NL sentences are not always well-formed, especially in speech recognition applications. NLP applications that rely exclusively on such grammars cannot be practically used in a large scale because of the large fraction of sentences that will receive no analysis at all. This problem is called undergeneration and has given birth to a field called robust parsing, where the goal is to find domain-independent and practical parsing technique that returns a correct or usefully "close" analysis for almost all (say 90%) of the input sentences (Carroll and Briscoe, 1996). In order to achieve such a high performance, one has to handle not only the problems of undergeneration but also the increased ambiguity which is usually a consequence of the robustification of the parser.

In previous work, a variety of approaches have been proposed to robustly handle natural language. Some techniques are based on modifying the input sentence, for example by removing words that disturb the fluency (Bear et al., 1992; Heeman and Allen, 1994), more recent approaches are based on selecting the right sequence of partial analyses (Worm and Rupp, 1998; van Noord et al., 1999). Minimum Distance Parsing is a third approach based on relaxing the formal grammar, allowing rules to be modified by insertions, deletions and substitutions (Hipp, 1992). For most of the approaches it is important to make the distinction between ungrammaticality and extra-grammaticality. Ungrammatical sentences contain speech errors, hesitations etc. while extra-grammatical sentences are linguistically correct sentences that are not covered by the grammar.

This paper presents two approaches that focus on extra-grammatical sentences. The first approach is based on the selection of a most optimal coverage with partial analyses and the second on controlled grammar rule relaxation. The aim of the paper is to compare these two approaches and to investigate if they present differences in behavior when given the same grammar and the same test data.

The rest of the paper is divided into five sections. Section 2 describes the notion of coverage and defines the most probable optimal maximum coverage; section 3 presents the rule-relaxation technique and introduces the con-

1

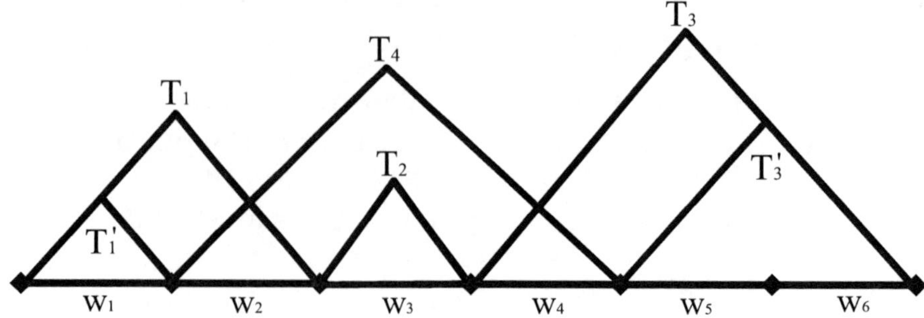

Figure 1: Partial derivation trees. Some of them (e.g. $T_1, T_2, T_3$ and $T_1', T_4, T_3'$) can be composed into a coverage.

cept of "holes". In section 4 the data and methodology for the experiments are presented and section 5 gives a summary of the results. Finally, in section 6 we give a brief conclusion and outline the direction for future work.

## 2 Selecting the most probable optimal maximum coverage

This section briefly describes the first approach to robust parsing that we tested in our comparative experiments. It is based on selecting partial analyses and gluing them together into an artificial full tree (Kadlec et al., 2005). This technique provides at least one analysis for all input sentences (in the most trivial case, a set of lexical trees).

To describe the technique we will start with the notion of coverage. For any given grammar G and any given input sentence, a coverage is a sequence of non-overlapping, possibly partial derivation trees that cover the whole input. Since the derivation trees can overlap fully or partially, there can be several distinct coverages for the same input sentence.

A maximum coverage is one that consists of maximum derivation trees, i.e. trees that are not subtrees of other ones covering the same subsequence. If a sentence can be analyzed by a single parse tree, the number of maximum coverages is the same as the number of complete parse trees.

Provided that a quality measure is available for coverages, an optimal maximum coverage (OMC) is then a maximum coverage with the highest quality among all maximum coverages derived for the given input sentence. In our experiments, we use a quality measure that favors a coverage with partial analyses of largest average width.

If the used grammar and parsing algorithm can be probabilized, the most probable OMC is the one that is associated with the highest probability. Finding the most probable OMC for stochastic context-free grammars can easily be achieved using a usual bottom-up chart parser (Chappelier and Rajman, 1998).

## 3 Deriving trees with holes

Our second approach to robust parsing is based on the assumption that extra-grammatical sentences are structurally similar to sentences that the grammar is able to describe. The underlying idea is that, in the case of a rule-based parser, the reason why the parser fails to analyze a given (extra-grammatical) sentence is that one or several rules are missing in the grammar. If a rule relaxation mechanism is available (i.e. a mechanism that can derive additional rules from the ones present in the grammar), it can be used to cope with situations where rules are missing, and in this case, the goal of the robust parser is to derive a full tree where the subtrees corresponding to the used relaxed rules are represented as "holes". (See figure 3).

The main difficulty with this approach is to determine how the hole should be derived. Simple rules allowing holes at any position in the tree are too general and will produce a high number of unacceptable analyses.

In addition we observed that it is more likely that a missing rule corresponds to a syntactic category that frequently appears as rule left hand side in the grammar (Ailomaa, 2004).

---

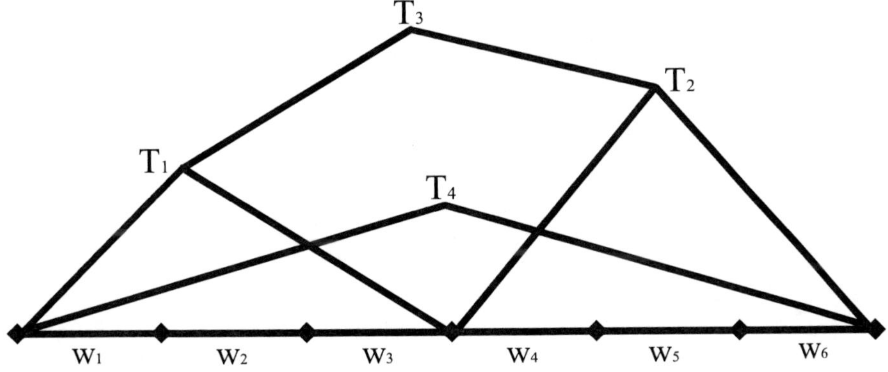

Figure 2: An illustration of maximum coverage. $C_1 = (T_3)$ and $C2 = (T_4)$ are m-coverages but $C_3 = (T_1, T_2)$ is not.

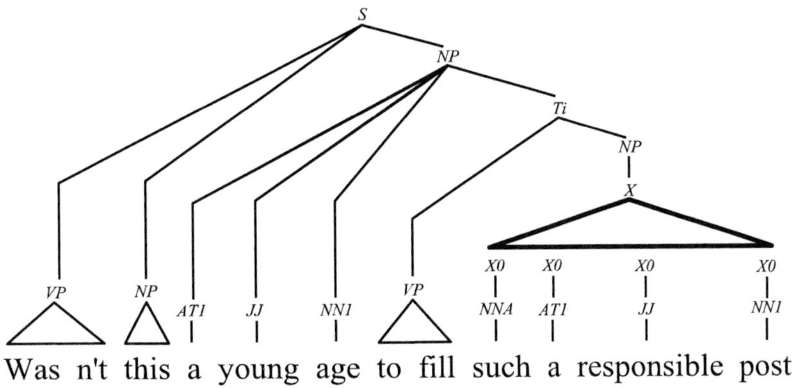



Figure 3: A tree with a hole representing a missing $NP$ rule $NP \rightarrow NNA \ AT1 \ JJ \ NN1$.

Indeed, the higher the number of such rules is, the higher is the variety of possible constructions for the given category and therefore the higher is the probability that some of these constructions are missing in the grammar. NP, VP and S are examples of syntactic categories that are heavily represented in grammars, whereas PPs are not. Consequently, a hole is more likely to have a root of category NP, VP or S than for example PP.

The second issue is how to produce a hole with appropriate leaves. Here we use the principle called Minimum Distance Parsing which has been used in earlier robust parsing applications (Hipp, 1992). The idea is to relax rules in the grammar by inserting, deleting or substituting elements in their right hand side (RHS). Derivation trees are ranked by the number of modifications that have been applied to achieve a complete analysis. The problem is that when all the rules are allowed to be relaxed the number of analyses increases dramatically. It becomes difficult to select a good analysis among all the unacceptable ones. Therefore, in its unconstrained form, the method works well only for small grammars (Rosé and Lavie, 2001).

Our solution to the problem is to make restrictions on how the rules can be relaxed. We used two types of restrictions. The first one defines which one of the rules that are allowed to be relaxed. As we previously mentioned, some rules are more likely to be missing in the grammar than others, so we select the ones that correspond to syntactic categories heavily represented in the grammar. It means that we still have a large number of solutions, but they are more likely to be the good ones. The second restriction defines how the rules should be relaxed. In a preliminary test we observed that the most frequent modification that produced the missing rule was insertion. Therefore we limit the relaxation to only this type of modification. The inserted element is hereafter referred to as a filler.

A further refinement of the algorithm is to specify where in the RHS of a rule the filler can appear and what syntactic category that filler is allowed to have. These two restrictions are linguistically motivated. Most phrases are constructed according to a general pattern, e.g. in English NPs are composed of determiners, adjectives and other elements followed by a head, typically a noun, and some complements, e.g. PPs. Finite-state parsing (Ait-Mokhtar and Chanod, 1997) is an example of how such patterns have been successfully used to implement general-purpose robust parsers. In our approach, the elements in the RHS of a rule are considered as belonging to one of three types: (1) elements preceding the head, (2) the head itself, and (3) elements following the head. The reason for this distinction is that, again in English, there are syntactic categories that frequently occur in one part of the phrase but not in another. PPs for instance are often complements of NPs but are less likely to occur before the head. The decision of inserting or not a filler into a RHS is therefore a matter of deciding whether the syntactic category of the filler is appropriate, i.e. whether there is a rule in the grammar in which the category appears in the correct position with respect to the head. As an example, assume that we have a simple grammar with the following NP rules (The head is indicated with underlined syntactic categories):

$$R1 : NP \rightarrow ADJ \ \underline{N}$$
$$R2 : NP \rightarrow POS \ \underline{N}$$

According to this grammar "successful brothers" and "your brother" are syntactically correct NPs while "your successful brother" is not. In order to parse the last one, some NP rule needs to be relaxed. We select the second one, R2 (though both are possible candidates). If the filler that needs to be inserted is ADJ (in this case "successful"), then the relaxed NP rule is expressed as:

$$R3 : {}^{\sim}NP \rightarrow POS^{@} \ ADJ_{filler} \ \underline{N^{@}}$$

We use the category $^{\sim}NP$ instead of NP to distinguish relaxed rules from initial ones, the "filler" subscripts to identify the fillers in the RHS in the relaxed rule, and the @ to label the

|  | ATIS | Susanne |
|---|---|---|
| Sentences | 1,381 | 3,981 |
| CF rules | 1,029 | 8,810 |
| Non-terminals | 40 | 469 |
| Terminals | 1,167 | 10,247 |
| PoS tags | 38 | 122 |
| Average sentence length | 12,5 | 12,9 |
| Av. nb of CF rules/sent | 23,3 | 23,8 |
| Max depth | 17 | 17 |

Table 1: Some characteristics of the two corpora used for the experiments

original RHS elements. The decision of allowing an insertion of an ADJ as filler is based on whether ADJ is a possible element before the head or not. Since there is a rule in the grammar where an ADJ exists before the head (R1), the insertion is appropriate.

## 4 Data and methodology

The goal of this paper is to compare the two robust parsing approaches described in Section 2 and 3 and to analyze differences in their behavior. In both approaches the sentences are parsed with a probabilistic CFG, which means that the produced analyses have probabilistic scores that allow the selection of the most probable one (or ones).

The probabilistic grammar is extracted and trained from a treebank, which contains parsed sentences representative of the type of sentences that the parser should be able to handle. In our comparative tests we use subsets of two treebanks, ATIS and Susanne, which have very different characteristics (Marcus et al., 1994).

The purpose is to study if the characteristics of the grammar have some impact on the performance of the robust parsing techniques measured in terms of accuracy and coverage. Some of the possible characteristics are given in Table 1.

In addition, we also considered characteristics such as the number and syntactic category of rules that are missing in the grammar to describe the test sentence.

Concretely each treebank is divided into a learning set and a test set. The learning set is used for producing the grammar with which the test set is then parsed. The division is done in such a way that around 10% of the sentences in the test set are not covered by the grammar.

These sentences represent the "true" test set for our experiments, as we only want to process the sentences that the initial grammar fails to describe.

Once the test sentences have been processed with each of the two robust techniques, the most probable analysis is manually characterized as good, acceptable or bad. The categorization is based on the comparison of the produced parse tree with the reference one that can be extracted out of the treebank. A good analysis has a close match to the reference tree; an acceptable one can have some more substantial differences with respect to the phrase segmentation but has to correspond to a useful semantic interpretation. A bad analysis corresponds to an incorrect segmentation that cannot lead to any useful semantic interpretation. Notice that it may be argued that the definition of a "useful" semantic analysis might not be decidable only by observing the syntactic tree. Although we found this to be a quite usable hypothesis during our experiments, some more objective procedure should be defined. In a concrete application, the usefulness might for example be determined by the next actions that the system performs based on the received syntactic analysis. Therefore, from this point of view, the results that we obtain have to be considered as preliminary and a future step is to integrate the implemented techniques in some application, e.g. an automatic translator, and to compare the results.

## 5  Experimental results

This section presents the experimental results of the two robust parsing techniques described in section 2 and 3, using the methodology described in section 4. The number of test sentences is not the same for the two corpora, 89 for ATIS and 250 for Susanne, due to the size and characteristics of each corpus. We parsed the sentences first with technique 1 and technique 2 separately and then with a combined approach where we started with the rule-relaxation technique and only when that failed selected the most probable OMC. All the sentences from ATIS were parsed and analyzed by hand; from Susanne a subset consisting of 134 sentences was chosen. The results of the robust parsing are presented in table 2.

When observing only the number of good analyses, one can see that for both grammars technique 2 performs better than technique 1. But when including all analyses, there is a difference related to the grammars. With ATIS, technique 1 provides acceptable analyses in the majority of cases whereas technique 2 badly suffers from undergeneration. With Susanne, technique 1 produces bad analyses for more than half of the test sentences; on the other hand technique 2 has a good coverage and overall better results than technique 1.

One indicator to why the techniques produce bad analyses, or no analysis at all, is that in more than half of the cases, three or more rules are missing in the grammar to derive the reference tree.

For technique 2 the undergeneration can be explained by the characteristics of the two grammars. ATIS is a very homogeneous corpus, which means that the same rules appear often. A division of 10% learning set and 90% test set was necessary to achieve the desired level of undergeneration ($\simeq 10\%$). With such a small learning corpus, the extracted grammar will have very few rules. There-fore the lists of possible fillers and rules that can be relaxed become very small. (Notice that we refer to two cases of undergeneration; the one mentioned here relates to the preparation of the data for the tests. The other case is when we speak of the results received from the robust parser).

Susanne suffers from the opposite problem. The corpus is very heterogeneous, and the learning set has to be larger in order to keep the undergeneration down to $\simeq 10\%$. The lists of possible fillers and rules to relax are long, but for a sentence that has no analysis, the missing rule is often of some other category than the ones heavily represented in the grammar (NP, VP or S). This is because the number of non-terminals in the corpus is large (469) compared to ATIS (40), and that 77% of the rules appear only once in the corpus.

Here we need to consider if the restrictions we applied on the relaxation of rules are too strong. It is possible that different types of restrictions are appropriate for different types of grammars. Some more experimenting is needed to decide how the change of flexibility in the algorithm affects coverage and accuracy.

Sentences for which the indicators mentioned above do not apply but which nevertheless have bad analyses, the main explanation

|              | Good (%) | Acceptable (%) | Bad (%) | No analysis (%) |
|--------------|----------|----------------|---------|-----------------|
| **ATIS corpus** |       |                |         |                 |
| Technique 1  | 10       | 60             | 30      | 0               |
| Technique 2  | 24       | 36             | 9       | 31              |
| Technique 1+2| 27       | 58             | 16      | 0               |
| **Susanne corpus** |    |                |         |                 |
| Technique 1  | 16       | 29             | 55      | 0               |
| Technique 2  | 40       | 17             | 33      | 10              |
| Technique 1+2| 41       | 22             | 37      | 0               |

Table 2: Experimental results. Percentage of good, acceptable and bad analyses with technique 1 (optimal coverage), technique 2 (tree with holes) and with the combined approach.

is that the probabilistically best analysis is not the linguistically best one. This is a non-trivial problem related to all types of natural language parsing, not only for robust parsers.

In short, we conclude that technique 2 is more accurate than technique 1 but cannot stand alone as a robust parser, not being able to provide full coverage. In particular it tends to be less suitable for simple grammars describing small variation of syntactic structures. What we can state is that when the sentences are processed sequentially with both techniques, the advantage of each approach is taken into account and the performance is better than when either technique stands alone.

## 6  Conclusions

The aim of this paper was to compare two robust parsing techniques based on different principles. The method we chose was to provide them with the same grammar and test data and to analyze differences in performance. Experimental results show that a combination of the techniques gives a better performance than each technique alone, because the first one guarantees full coverage while the second has a higher accuracy. The richness of the syntactic structures defined in the grammar tends to have some impact on the performance in the second approach but less on the first one. This can be linked to the restrictions in technique 2 that were chosen for the relaxation of the grammar rules. These restrictions were based on observations of a relatively small set of extra-grammatical sentences and cannot be considered as final.

A future experiment is to test different levels of flexibility for technique 2 and to see how this affects accuracy and coverage. Another im-

portant issue is to integrate the parsing techniques into some target application so that we have more realistic ways of measuring the usefulness of the produced robust analyses.

As a final remark, we would like to point out that this paper has addressed the problem of extra-grammaticality but did not address ungrammaticality, which is an equally important phenomenon in robust parsing, particularly if the target application deals with spoken language.

## References

Marita Ailomaa. 2004. Two approaches to robust stochastic parsing. Master's thesis, Ecole Polytechnique Federale de Lausanne (EPFL), Lausanne, Switzerland.

Salah Ait-Mokhtar and Jean-Pierre Chanod. 1997. Incremental finite-state parsing. In *Proceedings of the ANLP97*, pages 72–79, Washington.

John Bear, John Dowding, and Elizabeth Shriberg. 1992. Integrating multiple knowledge sources for the detection and correction of repairs in human-computer dialogue. In *Proceedings of the 30th ACL*, pages 56–63, Newark, Delaware.

John Carroll and Ted Briscoe. 1996. Robust parsing — a brief overview. In John Carroll, editor, *Proceedings of the Workshop on Robust Parsing at the 8th European Summer School in Logic, Language and Information (ESSLLI'96), Report CSRP 435*, pages 1–7, COGS, University of Sussex.

J.-C. Chappelier and M. Rajman. 1998. A generalized cyk algorithm for parsing stochastic cfg. In *TAPD98 Workshop*, pages 133–137, Paris, France.

Peter A. Heeman and James F. Allen. 1994. Detecting and correcting speech repairs. In *Proceedings of the 32th ACL*, pages 295–302, Las Cruces, New Mexico.

Dwayne R. Hipp. 1992. *Design and development of spoken natural language dialog parsing systems*. Ph.D. thesis, Duke University.

Vladimír Kadlec, Marita Ailomaa, Jean-Cedric Chappelier, and Martin Rajman. 2005. Robust stochastic parsing using optimal maximum coverage. In *Proc. of International Conference on Recent Advances in Natural Language Processing (RANLP)*, pages 258–263, Borovets, Bulgaria.

Michell P. Marcus, Beatrice Santorini, and Mary Ann Marcinkiewicz. 1994. Building a large annotated corpus of english: The penn treebank. *Computational Linguistics*, 19(2):313–330.

C. Rosé and A. Lavie. 2001. Balancing robustness and efficiency in unification-augmented contextfree parsers for large practical applications. In G. van Noord and J. C. Junqua, editors, *Robustness in Language and Speech Technology*. Kluwer Academic Press.

Gertjan van Noord, Gosse Bouma, Rob Koeling, and Mark-Jan Nederhof. 1999. Robust grammatical analysis for spoken dialogue systems. *Natural Language Engineering*, 5(1):45–93.

Karsten L. Worm and C. J. Rupp. 1998. Towards robust understanding of speech by combination of partial analyses. In *Proceedings of the 13th Biennial European Conference on Artificial Intelligence (ECAI'98), August 23-28*, pages 190–194, Brighton, UK.

# A new semantic similarity measure evaluated in word sense disambiguation

**Ergin Altintas**
Naval Science and Eng. Inst.
Turkish Naval Academy
PK 34492 Tuzla, Istanbul
ealtintas@dho.edu.tr

**Elif Karsligil**
Computer Eng. Dep.
Yildiz Technical University
PK 34349 Yildiz, Istanbul
elif@ce.yildiz.edu.tr

**Vedat Coskun**
Naval Science and Eng. Inst.
Turkish Naval Academy
PK 34492 Tuzla, Istanbul
vedatcoskun@dho.edu.tr

## Abstract

In this paper, a new conceptual hierarchy based semantic similarity measure is presented, and it is evaluated in word sense disambiguation using a well known algorithm which is called Maximum Relatedness Disambiguation. In this study, WordNet's conceptual hierarchy is utilized as the data source, but the methods presented are suitable to other resources.

## 1  Introduction

Semantic similarity is an important topic in natural language processing (NLP). It has also been subject to studies in Cognitive Science and Artificial Intelligence. Application areas of semantic similarity include word sense disambiguation (WSD), information retrieval, malapropism detection etc.

It is easy for humans to say if one word is more similar to a given word than another. For example, we can easily say that *cruiser* is more similar to *destroyer* than *spoon* is. In fact, semantic similarity is a kind of semantic relatedness defining a resemblance.

There are mainly two approaches to semantic similarity. First approach is making use of a large corpus and gathering statistical data from this corpus to estimate a score of semantic similarity. Second approach makes use of the relations and the hierarchy of a thesaurus, which is generally a hand-crafted lexical database such as WordNet (Fellbaum, 1998). As in many other NLP studies, hybrid approaches that make benefit from both techniques also exist in semantic similarity.

There is not many ways to evaluate a semantic similarity measure. You may check the correlation between your results and human judg-ments, or else you may select an application area of semantic similarity, and you compare your similarity measure with others according to the success rates in that application area.

In this study we have chosen the second method as our evaluation method, and WSD as our application area to practice our similarity measure and compare our results with the others'.

WSD is one of the most critical and widely studied NLP tasks, which is used in order to increase the success rates of NLP applications like translation, information retrieval etc. WSD can be defined as the process of selecting the correct or intended sense of a word, occurring in a specific context. The set of candidate senses are generally available from a lexical database.

The main idea behind our evaluation approach is: The success rate of WSD should increase as the similarity measure's performance gets better.

The remainder of this paper is organized as follows: We discussed the related work in Section 2. Our similarity measure and the WSD algorithm that we have used in this study are described in Section 3. The performance of our measure is evaluated, and compared to others in Section 4. Some discussion topics are probed in Section 5, and the paper is concluded in Section 6.

## 2  Related work

To quantify the concept of similarity between words, some ideas have been put forth by researchers, most of which rely heavily on the knowledge available in lexical knowledge bases like WordNet. First studies in this area date back to Quilian's semantic memory model (Quilian, 1968) where the number of hops between nodes of concepts in the hierarchical network specifies the similarity or difference of concepts.

Wu and Palmer's semantic similarity measure (WUP) was based on the path length between concepts located in a taxonomy (Wu and Palmer, 1994), which is defined as:

$$sim_{wup}(c_1, c_2) = max\left(\frac{2*depth(lcs(c_1,c_2))}{len(c_1,c_2)+2*depth(lcs(c_1,c_2))}\right)$$

Resnik introduced a new factor of relatedness (Resnik, 1995) called information content (IC), which is defined as:

$$IC_{res}(c) = -logP(c)$$

Similarity measures of Resnik (RES) (Resnik, 1995), Jiang and Conrath (JCN) (Jiang and Conrath, 1997) and Lin (LIN) (Lin, 1998) all relies on the IC values assigned to the concepts in an *is-a hierarchy*, but their usage of IC has little differences:

$$sim_{res}(c_1, c_2) = IC\left(lcs(c_1, c_2)\right)$$
$$rel_{jcn}(c_1, c_2) = \frac{1}{IC(c_1)+IC(c_2)-2*IC(lcs(c_1,c_2))}$$
$$rel_{LIN}(c_1, c_2) = \frac{2*IC(lcs(c_1,c_2))}{IC(c_1)+IC(c_2)}$$

Using a different approach Hirst G. and St-Onge assigns relatedness scores to words instead of word senses. They set different weights for different kinds of links in a semantic network, and uses those weights for *edge counting* (Hirst and St-Onge, 1997).

The similarity measure of Leacock and Chodorow (LCH) is based on the shortest path length between two concepts in an *is-a hierarchy* (Leacock et al., 1998). The formulation is as follows:

$$sim_{lch}(c_1, c_2) = max\left(-log\frac{ShortestLen(c_1,c_2)}{2*TaxonomyDepth}\right)$$

## 3 Algorithms

### 3.1 Maximum Relatedness Disambiguation

In this study we have used a relatively simple algorithm named *Maximum Relatedness Disambiguation* which is sometimes also called as the *Adapted Lesk Algorithm* (Pedersen et al., 2003). This algorithm uses a quantitative measure of relatedness (hence similarity) between word senses as a measure to disambiguate them in a context.

In this algorithm, it is assumed that, the senses having higher similarity values with the senses of other words in the context, are more likely to be the intended sense. This assumption is the key of this algorithm to determine the intended sense of a target word occuring in a context.

1: Select a window of n-word size context that contains the target word in the middle.
2: Identify candidate senses of each word in the context.
3: **for** each candidate sense of the target word **do**
4:  Measure the relatedness of the candidate sense of the target word to those of the surrounding words in the context.
5:  Sum the relatedness scores for each combination of senses.
6:  Assign this sum to the candidate sense of the target word.
7: **end for**
8: Select the candidate sense that has the highest score of relatedness.

In short, this algorithm assigns a target word, the sense that is most related (or similar) to the senses of its neighboring words. We have used this algorithm in order to evaluate our similarity measure, hence similarity is also a kind of relation.

### 3.2 Our similarity approach

We propose a new model based on the hierarchical structure of taxonomies, with which we tried to improve over LCH. We assume that WordNet's taxonomic structure is well organized in a meaningful way, so that the leaf nodes of the taxonomies are the most specific concepts in the hierarchy, and as we go up to the roots the specificity of concepts decreases. For noun taxonomies, one can also say that the root nodes are the most abstract ones, and as we go down to leafs, concreteness of the nodes increases.

We argue that, *concreteness* and *abstractness* are attributes of concepts which can help us improve our estimations when calculating similarity of concepts. Let's assume that we have three concepts $c_1$, $c_2$, $c_3$ and the shortest path length between $c_1$ and $c_2$ and the shortest path length between $c_1$ and $c_3$ is equal to 7.

In this case, according to the $sim_{lch}$ formula, similarity of $c_1$ and $c_2$ is the same as similarity of $c_1$ and $c_3$. So, if we use $sim_{lch}$ as the similarity measure for WSD, we will not be able to differentiate between $c_2$ and $c_3$. Let's assume that, $c_1$ is a leaf node and:

$$Depth(c_1) = 5, ClusterDepth(c_1) = 5,$$
$$Depth(c_2) = 7, ClusterDepth(c_2) = 8,$$
$$Depth(c_3) = 4, ClusterDepth(c_3) = 8.$$

By *ClusterDepth* we mean the depth of the

deepest node in a cluster. If we define the specificity of a concept using the hierarchical place in its local cluster as:

$$Spec(c) = \frac{Depth(c)}{ClusterDepth(c)}$$

Which will always be in the range $[0..1]$. Then we can calculate the specificity of these concepts as:

$$Spec(c_1) = 5/5 = 1$$
$$Spec(c_2) = 7/8 = 0.875$$
$$Spec(c_3) = 4/8 = 0.5$$

Then according to these specificity values, we may say that $c_2$ is nearly as specific as $c_1$ but $c_3$ is not. So, we can say that $c_2$ should be more similar to $c_1$, than $c_3$.

If we formularize our similarity measure, it has two components *LenFactor* and *SpecFactor* which are defined as:

$$LenFactor = \frac{ShortestLen(c_1,c_2)}{2.TaxonomyDepth}$$
$$SpecFactor = abs(Spec(c_1) - Spec(c_2))$$

and our similarity measure is defined as follows:

$$sim_{our}(c_1, c_2) = \frac{1}{1+LenFactor+SpecFactor}$$

If we assume *SpecFactor* to be zero in all cases, our measure behaves just like the LCH measure. So, we can easily say that the differentiator (from LCH) in our measure is the *SpecFactor*.

## 4   Evaluation

When a similarity measure for English is to be evaluated, it is usually compared to Miller & Charles' results (Miller and Charles, 1991) using correlation. Usually, the senses giving the maximum similarity score are considered to estimate a similarity score between two polysemous words, and this approach tends to give the best correlation values with Miller & Charles' results (Yang and Powers, 2005). But there is a possibility that the chosen senses (by the human judges) may not be the most similar ones, even though the estimated similarity score may be in correlation with the human judgments. In Miller & Charles' study the sense pairs chosen by the human judges were not explicitly stated. So, there is no easy way to discover if the senses selected by our algorithm are the same as the senses chosen by the human judges. Because of this, we didn't use this method of evaluation in our study.

Another way of evaluation is to analyze the similarity measures theoretically, but this may not be sufficient or practical for every case.

The approach which we have chosen, is to evaluate the similarity measures with respect to their performance within a particular NLP application (Budanitsky, 2001).

We did WSD experiments using the noun data of English lexical sample task of Senseval-2. Each instance was made up of three or four sentences containing a single tagged target word.

To access WordNet, we have used a Perl interface called WordNet::QueryData (Rennie, 2000), to compare our results with the existing measures, we have used the WordNet::Similarity package   (Pedersen et al., 2004). We adopted our measure compatible to the WordNet::Similarity modules so that it can be published in the next release of the package.

Since taxonomies other than the noun taxonomy are very shallow in WordNet, we take only nouns as our target for disambiguation. We didn't PoS tag our input text, instead we used the approach in (Patwardhan et al., 2002), selecting the nearest words to our target word into our context, which have noun forms in WordNet, regardless of if they are used as a noun or not. Our results can be seen in Table 1.

| Measure | Precision | Recall |
|---|---|---|
| RES | 0.295 | 0.83 |
| LCH | 0.316 | 0.97 |
| WUP | 0.331 | 0.97 |
| LIN | 0.380 | 0.58 |
| JCN | 0.305 | 0.72 |
| Our Measure | 0.347 | 0.97 |

Table 1: Disambiguation results.

Our precision has %9.8 relative improvement over the LCH measure, %17.6 relative improvement over the RES measure, and %4.8 relative improvement over the WUP measure. Our recall is the same as the LCH and the WUP measures, which are also path-length based measures. The LIN measure has a better precision (relatively %9.5) than Our's, but the recall rate of the LIN measure is much lower (relatively %59.7).

## 5   Discussion

Although our precision rate is higher than the others, we think it is still smaller than what is needed. It seems that unnecessarily subtle distinction of senses in WordNet and the strict relation structure of WordNet are the cause for this. There are some techniques to overcome this problem, which we plan to work on, in the future.

In our similarity approach all the leaf nodes have a specificity value of 1, but some leaf nodes in WordNet like *something* and *anything* are not as specific as their place in the hierarchy indicates. Although this kind of words are not too many, they can be identified manually, and filtered using a stop word list.

It should be noted that, a similarity measure may perform better than the other measures in a specific application area, but it may perform poor in some other application areas.

## 6  Conclusion

In this paper, we have introduced a new word sense similarity measure, and evaluated it in the WSD application area of NLP. We have only used a concept hierarchy. So, there is no sparse data problem in our approach.

All the source code and data used and developed in this study, can be downloaded from the author's web site[1].

## References


Alexander Budanitsky. 2001. Semantic distance in wordnet: An experimental, application-oriented evaluation of five measures.

Christiane D. Fellbaum. 1998. *WordNet: An electronic lexical database*. MIT Press, Cambridge, MA.

Graeme Hirst and David St-Onge. 1997. Lexical chains as representation of context for the detection and correction malapropisms.

Jay J. Jiang and David W. Conrath. 1997. Semantic similarity based on corpus statistics and lexical taxonomy. In *Proceedings of International Conference on Research in Computational Linguistics*.

Claudia Leacock, Martin Chodorow, and George A. Miller. 1998. Combining local context and wordnet similarity for word sense identification. *WordNet: An electronic lexical database*, pages 265–283.

Dekang Lin. 1998. An information-theoretic definition of similarity. In *Proc. 15th International Conf. on Machine Learning*, pages 296–304. Morgan Kaufmann, San Francisco, CA.

George A. Miller and Walter G. Charles. 1991. Contextual correlates of semantic similarity. *Language and Cognitive Process*, pages 1–28.

Siddharth Patwardhan, Satanjeev Banerjee, and Ted Pedersen. 2002. Using semantic relatedness for word sense disambiguation. In *Proceedings of the Fourth International Conference on Intelligent Text Processing and Computational Linguistics*. Mexico City.

Ted Pedersen, Satanjeev Banerjee, and Siddharth Patwardhan. 2003. Maximizing semantic relatedness to perform word sense disambiguation. *Preprint submitted to Elsevier Science*.

Ted Pedersen, Siddharth Patwardhan, and Jason Michelizzi. 2004. WordNet::Similarity - measuring relatedness of concepts. *Proceedings of the Nineteenth National Conference on Artificial Intelligence (AAAI-04)*, pages 1024–1025.

M.Ross Quilian. 1968. Semantic memory. *Semantic Information Processing*, pages 216–270.

Jason Rennie. 2000. WordNet::QueryData: a Perl module for accessing the WordNet database. http://people.csail.mit.edu/~jrennie/WordNet.

Philip Resnik. 1995. Using information content to evaluate semantic similarity in a taxonomy. In *IJCAI*, pages 448–453.

Zhibiao Wu and Martha Palmer. 1994. Verb semantics and lexical selection. In *32nd. Annual Meeting of the Association for Computational Linguistics*, pages 133 –138, New Mexico State University, Las Cruces, New Mexico.

Dongqiang Yang and David M. W. Powers. 2005. Measuring semantic similarity in the taxonomy of wordnet. In *ACSC*, pages 315–322.


---

[1] Http://www.ergin.altintas.org

# Reformulations of Finnish questions for question answering

**Lili Aunimo and Reeta Kuuskoski**
Department of Computer Science
University of Helsinki
P.O. Box 68
FI-00014 University of Helsinki
aunimo|rkuuskos@cs.helsinki.fi

## Abstract

This paper presents a series of experiments that were performed with a dataset of Finnish question reformulations. The goal of the experiments was to determine whether some reformulations are easier for a question answering system to deal with than others, and if so, how easy it is to transform a question into that form. A question answering system typically consists of several independent modules that are arranged into a pipeline architecture. In order to determine if some reformulations are easier for a question answering system to deal with, the performance of the question classifier component was analyzed. The experiments show that different question reformulations do affect the performance of the classifier significantly. However, the automatic transformation of a question into another form seems difficult.

## 1 Introduction

Question reformulations (or variants) are questions that have the same semantic content, i.e. that can be answered with the same answer, but whose form is different. Eight different reformulations of the same question from the TREC [1]-9 QA Track (Voorhees, 2000) question dataset [2] are listed in the following:

1. Name a film in which Jude Law acted.

2. Jude Law was in what movie?

---

[1] Text REtrieval Conference, http://trec.nist.gov

[2] The question reformulations data is available at: http://trec.nist.gov/data/qa/T9_QAdata/variants.key

3. Jude Law acted in which film?

4. What is a film starring Jude Law?

5. What film was Jude Law in?

6. What film or films has Jude Law appeared in?

As can be seen from the above reformulation examples, the differences between the questions can be syntactic or lexical. For example, question 2 has the word *movie* and question 3 the word *film*, and question 2 and question 5 have different word orders. Determining what is a question reformulation is not straightforward, because the set of all possible answers to a question is not always the same for different reformulations even though they do have at least one common answer (Voorhees, 2000). For example, among the above questions, question 6 accepts for answer in addition to a single movie name also a list of movie names. Thus, we define question reformulations as being a set of questions that have at least one similar answer.

There may exist similarity across questions with different semantic content that can be used in automatically generating or analyzing question reformulations. For example, if we can analyze the example questions above, we could also analyze the reformulations for the question *Name a film in which Woody Allen acted.* and for questions dealing with any other actor. We could also analyze the reformulations for the question *Name a play in which Jude Law acted.* and for questions dealing with any other things in which people act, such as a scene or TV-series. We call this a *similarity class*. The similarity class of the above example could be denoted by the verb based template *PERSON act in ACTED_THING*. The verb based templates of the similarity classes can be seen as semantic frames (see e.g. (Baker et al., 1998)).

Question answering (QA) systems are information access systems that receive as input a natural language question and that produce as output the answer. QA systems can be classified according to the type of data from which the answers are extracted. Text based QA systems extract the answer from plain text documents, FAQ (Frequently Asked Questions) based systems extract the answer from a dataset of question-answer pairs, and structure based systems extract the answer from a relational database or from a semistructured data repository such as text containing XML or HTML markup. Text based QA systems are the ones that have attracted most attention in the research community over the last years. A text based system typically consists of a pipeline architecture containing a question processing module, a document processing module and an answer extraction and formulation module (Harabagiu and Moldovan, 2003). One of the most important tasks of the question processing module is to determine the expected answer type of the question.

Text based QA systems have been systematically evaluated in evaluation campaigns such as the TREC, CLEF [3], NTCIR [4] and EQUER (Ayache, 2005). The evaluation datasets created in the above campaigns have had a significant impact in directing the research on QA systems. Some of the evaluation campaigns have had datasets consisting of question reformulations. In TREC-9, there were 54 questions, which all had from two to eight reformulations (Harabagiu et al., 2001). The total number of reformulations was 243. In the domain independent task of EQUER, 100 out of the total of 500 questions were reformulations, and in the domain specific task, 50 out of 200 were reformulations (Ayache, 2005).

In FAQ based QA systems, the main answering technique consists in measuring the similarity between a new question and the old ones and returning the answer that has been given to the old question that is most similar with the new one (Burke et al., 1997; Aunimo et al., 2003). In this kind of systems, the techniques for recognizing question reformulations are especially important.

---

[3]Cross-Language Evaluation Forum, http://www.clef-campaign.org
[4]NII-NACSIS Test Collection for IR Systems, http://research.nii.ac.jp/ntcir/workshop

Question reformulations for English have been extensively studied in the field of QA because not only users tend to express the same information need as a different natural language question (Aunimo et al., 2003), but also because there are a variety of similarity classes among questions whose identification would lead to better question analysis results. However, only very little work has been done for processing question reformulations for QA in other languages than English. To the best of our knowledge, this paper presents the first experiments on question reformulations for Finnish questions.

Question reformulations in QA systems have been approached in two different ways. The first approach is to measure the similarity between questions, and the second approach is to generate reformulations for questions (Hermjakob et al., 2002). In order to measure the similarity between questions, many different similarity metrics have been developed (see e.g. (Harabagiu et al., 2001; Burke et al., 1997; Aunimo et al., 2003)). One of the approaches even transforms the questions into a completely different form, the semantic case frame representation, before measuring similarity between them (Tomuro, 2003).

Our approach can be seen as as a hybrid approach combining elements from the above mentioned question reformulations generation (Hermjakob et al., 2002) and semantic case frame generation (Tomuro, 2003) approaches. In our approach, questions are not transformed into an abstract semantic representation (as in the case frame generation approach), but into one real reformulation (like in the question reformulations generation approach) that is called the canonical reformulation. However, our approach differs from the questions reformulations generation approach in that we only produce at most one reformulation for a given question, which is called the canonical reformulation. In addition, the canonical question reformulations are real questions, while some reformulations of the reformulations generation approach are closer to answer reformulations than question reformulations.

The rest of the paper is organized as follows: Section 2 describes the question reformulations dataset that is used in the experiments. In Section 3, the method for determining the canoni-

---

Aunimo & Kuuskoski: *Reformulations of Finnish questions for question answering*

cal (or centroid or best) reformulation for each question is presented. Section 4 presents the question classification method that is used to asses the effect of different question reformulations to QA. Section 5 describes the different transformations that are needed to transform a question variant into the canonical form. Finally, Section 6 presents the results of the experiments and an analysis.

## 2 The question variant data

The question variants dataset[5] consists of 200 Finnish questions from the Multieight-04 Corpus (Magnini et al., 2005) and of three variants for each question. Each question variant in the dataset was translated from English by a single translator who worked independently and without having seen the other variants. The variants may be similar or different with each other. As can be seen from Figure 1, there are 59 questions where all variants are different from each other, 46 with one or two pairs of similar variants, 55 with three similar variants and 40 questions where all four variants are similar. The dotted line in the column illustrating the 46 questions that have two similar variants shows the number of questions containing two pairs of similar variants (5) and the number of questions containing only one pair of similar variants (41).

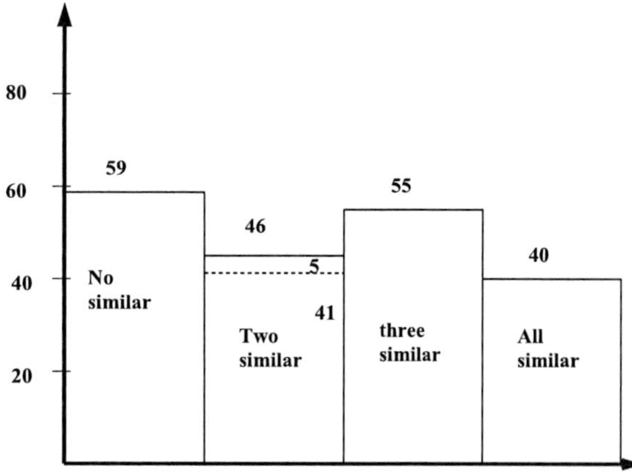


Figure 1: Number of questions with no similar variants, two similar variants, three similar variants and four similar variants.

---

[5]The question variants dataset is available at http://www.cs.helsinki.fi/research/doremi/interests/ QAResources.shtml

## 3 Distance between question variants

The distance between two question variants, $v_i$ and $v_j$, is measured using their edit distance (Wagner and Fischer, 1974) $d$, which is the minimum cost sequence of edit operations needed to change one variant into the other. The edit operations are insertion, deletion and substitution, and each of them is assigned a cost of 1. In order to be able to compare the edit distances with each other, they are normalized between 0 and 1. In the case where the cost of substitution is 1, the normalization is achieved by dividing the distance by the length of the longer string, more formally:

$$d_{normalized}(v_i, v_j) = \frac{d(v_i, v_j)}{max(|v_i|, |v_j|)},$$

where $d_{normalized}$ denotes the normalized distance $d$, and $v_i$ and $v_j$ are the question variants. As the basic unit of edit distance operations, both words and single characters are used, as will be explained in detail later in this section.

The centroid of each question variant set is the variant which is closest to all other variants. More formally, it is

$$i^* = arg \min_i \sum_{j=0}^{n} d(v_i, v_j),$$

where $n$ is the total number of variants for a question. The centroid variant id $i^*$ is thus the variant id whose sum of distances from all the other variants is the smallest.

For the experiments described in section 6, also the set of the most different variants was created. The most different variant, which is called the *worst* variant, is calculated in the same way as the centroid except that instead of taking the variant with the smallest sum of distances to all other variants, the variant with the biggest sum is taken. More formally, the worst variant id $i'$ is calculated as:

$$i' = arg \max_i \sum_{j=0}^{n} d(v_i, v_j).$$

Table 1 gives an example of four different question variants and of the sums of their distances from the other variants. Both word and character based distance sums are given. As can be seen from the table, variant 1 is the centroid if word based distance is used and variant

---

| Id | Question variants | Sum of Distances | |
|---|---|---|---|
| | | Word | Char |
| 1 | Kuinka monta asukasta on Etelä-Afrikassa? | 2.2 | 1.56 |
| 2 | Mikä on Etelä-Afrikan väkiluku? | 3 | 1.87 |
| 3 | Paljonko Etelä-Afrikassa on asukkaita? | 2.8 | 1.89 |
| 4 | Kuinka monta asukasta Etelä-Afrikassa on? | 2.4 | 1.44 |

Table 1: Question variants and sums of their normalized distances from the other variants.

4 is the centroid if the character based distance is used. Variant 2 is the worst variant according to the word based distance and variant 3 according to the character based distance.

In some cases, the above described method does not yield a unique centroid or worst variant. In such cases, the edit distance for the variants having the same score is calculated based on words or characters - depending on which one was used in the first phase. (If it was words in the first phase, characters is used in the second phase, and vice versa.) If no unique centroid or worst variant is still not obtained, it is determined manually.

The principles guiding the manual selection are based on the set of automatically selected centroids. For instance, if the case morphemes of an abbreviation denoting an organization are separated with a colon in the automatically generated set, the manual selections apply the same rule. For example, NATO:lle would be selected instead of NATOlle. If the decision cannot be taken based on the automatically generated set of centroids, the linguistic instinct of the human expert is followed.

## 4 Question classification

Question classification means the classification of natural language questions according to the expected answer type of the question. In the experiments described in Subsection 6.2, the set of nine question classes listed in Table 2 are used. The classes are taken directly from the Multieight-04 Corpus (Magnini et al., 2005). The table also shows the frequencies of the classes in the dataset that is used in the experiments presented in this paper.

The question classifier used in the experiments is the C4.5 decision tree classifier (Quinlan, 1993). The nodes of the tree are tests for attribute values that are extracted from the questions. A decision tree classifier is a natural choice when dealing with *nominal data*, i.e. data where the instance descriptions are

| Class | # |
|---|---|
| TIME | 30 |
| LOCATION | 26 |
| MANNER | 17 |
| PERSON | 27 |
| ORGANIZATION | 25 |
| MEASURE | 20 |
| DEF_ORGANIZATION | 11 |
| OTHER | 35 |
| DEF_PERSON | 9 |
| $\sum$ | 200 |

Table 2: Question class frequencies of the 200 Finnish questions in the Multieight-04 Corpus (Magnini et al., 2005).

discrete and don't have any natural notion of similarity or ordering. For example, the attribute named *first* may take the values *Kuka* and *Mikä*. These values have no order relation. Nominal data is often represented as a list of attribute-value pairs. Another benefit of using a decision tree classifier is its interpretability. It is straightforward to render the information it contains as logical expressions.

In order to be able to induce a question classifier from the question data and to be able to apply the classifier to unseen questions, the questions have to be transformed into lists of attribute-value pairs. This transformation is not at all straightforward and the choice of attributes and values has a significant effect on classifier accuracy (Aunimo, 2005). The impact of attribute or feature selection is significant also when performing question classification with other classifiers than C4.5 (see e.g. (Suzuki et al., 2003; Li et al., 2004)). The attribute set and the transformation of questions into lists of attribute-value pairs is described in the following.

The attribute set contains six attributes: *first*, *second*, *third*, *fourth*, *fifth* and *last* word. As the names of the attributes suggest, they are derived from the first, second, third, fourth, fifth and last words of the question. Punctuation is treated in the same way as any word. If the question contains less than six words, the missing word attributes are given the value *NIL*. However, each question has to contain at least two words. Table 3 lists the attributes, their type, the five most common attribute values in the question variants dataset with their frequencies and the total number of possible values for each attribute in the dataset. The type of the first attribute is *plain word*, which means that the first word of the question is taken as such. The type of the second and last word is *lemmatized word*, which means that the lemmatized form of the word is used. For lemmatizing, the Functional Dependency parser from Connexor[6] was used. The type of the third, fourth and fifth words is *POS or lemmatized word*, which means that for open word classes (noun, verb, adjective, adverb) and numerals, the part of speech (POS) is used and for the rest of the word classes the lemmatized word form is used. All attribute values can be symbols for punctuation, such as quotation mark, comma, etc. An example: The question *Minä vuonna Thomas Mann sai Nobelin palkinnon?*[7] is transformed into the following list of attribute-value pairs: *first=Minä, second=vuosi, third=noun, fourth=noun, fifth=verb, last=palkinto*. The class of the question is *TIME*.

## 5　Question transformations

The question variants were examined and classified based on their differences from the centroid. 27 different transformation classes were found. They are listed in Table 4. Examples of the classes are given in Table 5. The classes are described in detail in the following text.

The transformation categories are divided into subclasses, and the POS of the altering term is inside brackets. `lex` classes are those transformations that are achieved by lexical changes. For instance, `lex(n)` means that a noun has been replaced by another noun, its lexical variant. This is the case in variant v3 of question 168 (or Q168/v3) in Table 5, where the noun *isku* of the centroid has been replaced with its lexical variant *hyökkäys*.

Morphological changes are categorized into the class `morph`. `morph(v)` typically denotes

a change in the tense of a verb (for instance imperfect is replaced by perfect) or mode (active replaced by passive). The class `morph(n)` is recorded when a common noun is subject to a morphological alternation. This happens in Q168/v3, where the case of the noun *metroasema* changes.

The class `pos` refers to those alternations where the POS of a word changes, but the base word remains the same. An example of this is in in Q22/v4, where the adjective *skotlantilainen* has been replaced by the inessive form of the proper noun *Skotlanti*, yielding *Skotlannissa*. This transformation is classified as (`pos(n/a)`). When both the POS and the base word are different, the transformation is classified `lexpos`.

Some transformations are of conventional type, and belong to class `conv`. For instance, changes that reflect the source language of the translation are of class `conv(trans)`. Conventions that deal with the way in which abbreviations are written belong to class `conv(abbr)`. In Q24/v4 , the non-capital letter in the beginning of the name of the mosque produces `conv(case)`, and the existence of the hyphen `conv(ortograph)`.

The transformations listed in the column `other` in Table 4 do not belong to the above mentioned subclasses. When the specificity differs, the transformation is of type `spec`, the difference in the order of the terms belongs to class `order`. Examples of these transformations can be seen in Q22/v4, where the specifying noun *kieltä* is missing from the canonical form, and the noun *Skotlannissa* appears after the verb.

The changes in the case of proper noun modifiers are categorized into their own classes. The selection of a genitive attribute instead of the locative form of a proper noun signifying a location is of class (`genattr/locative`). An example of this is Q168/v3, where in the centroid, the locative form *Pariisissa* is used, whereas in the variant, the location is expressed using the genitive attribute.

When the syntactic structure differs due to the selection of the word that bears the contents of the question, the transformation is of class `struct`. This is the case in Q22/v3, for instance, where the verb is very general, *on*, and the essential meaning is contained in the attributes of the noun: *gaelia puhuvia ihmisiä*; in the corresponding centroid (Q22/c) the con-

---

[6]http://www.connexor.com

[7]What year was Thomas Mann awarded the Nobel Prize?

| Name | Type | Example Values and their frequencies | # |
|---|---|---|---|
| first | plain word | Mikä (152), Kuka (121), Missä (80), Kuinka (75), Milloin (69) | 23 |
| second | lemmatized word | olla (219), moni (49), vuosi (41), jokin (37), maa (13) | 168 |
| third | POS or lemmatized word | noun (415), NIL (207), verb (107), adjective (53), quotation mark (3) | 14 |
| fourth | POS or lemmatized word | NIL (411), noun (217), verb (78), adjective (49), quotation mark (15) | 10 |
| fifth | POS or lemmatized word | NIL (593), noun (118), verb (36), adjective (25), quotation mark (13) | 8 |
| last | lemmatized word | olla (57), nimi (33), kuolla (21), quotation mark (15), tehdä (14) | 261 |

Table 3: The set of six attributes used in question classification. For each attribute, the table lists its name, type, five most common values with their frequencies and the total number of possible values.

| lexical | | morphological | | pos | | convention | | other | |
|---|---|---|---|---|---|---|---|---|---|
| lex(n) | 76 | morph(n) | 34 | pos(n/a) | 6 | conv(ortograph) | 23 | order | 89 |
| lex(v) | 74 | morph(v) | 25 | pos(n/v) | 1 | conv(trans) | 23 | spec | 45 |
| lex(q) | 28 | morph(q) | 10 | | | conv(case) | 18 | struct | 19 |
| lex(a) | 8 | morph(a) | 3 | | | conv(abbr) | 5 | nounattr/genattr | 9 |
| lex(part) | 4 | morph(pron) | 3 | | | conv(accent) | 2 | genattr/locative | 8 |
| lex(postpos) | 4 | | | | | | | meaning | 4 |
| lex(pron) | 1 | | | | | | | add(adverb) | 1 |
| lexpos(n/a) | | | 1 | | | | | | |

Table 4: The question transformation classes and their frequencies in the question variants dataset.

tents are expressed in the verb and its attributes: *puhuu gaelia*. Similarly, in Q168/v1 the verb *iskettiin* contains the meaning, but in the centroid, it is in the noun acting as the object of the sentence, *isku*.

Class meaning is used when the semantics of the two questions differ, as can happen when the translators have interpreted the original English question differently. The interpolation of an additional word results a transformation of class add.

In general, the difference between two variants can consist of multiple concurrent transformations. The transformation classes struct and meaning, however, occur alone. When there is a fundamental difference in either the semantics or the syntax of the variants, no alternations on the surface level are recorded.

Basically, one question transformation can consist of multiple simple alternations. For example, the selection of a synonymous verb can cause multiple modifications to the morphology of the other words due to government, i.e. different verbs require different cases from their dependents. This influence has been ignored in the categorization of the transforma-

tion, and recorded solely by the transformation class morph(v).

## 6 Results and analysis

### 6.1 Distances between question reformulations

The datasets of question centroids, or *best* questions, and of the *worst* questions were created using the metrics described in Section 3. Both word and character based metrics were applied to the data, and thus two different datasets for *best* and *worst* were created. Among the *best* variants calculated using first the word based distance and then, if needed, the character based distance, only 6 variants out of 200 were different from the ones obtained by only calculating the character based distance. The names of these two datasets are *Best WordChar* and *Best Char*, respectively. Among the *worst* variants, 28 out of 200 questions were different in the datasets *Worst WordChar* and *Worst Char*. When using the character based distance, only human judgments were used in order to select the best or worst variant among equally scored variants, because us-

---

Aunimo & Kuuskoski: *Reformulations of Finnish questions for question answering*

| | Question | Transformations |
|---|---|---|
| o | **Q22: How many people speak Gaelic in Scotland?** | |
| c | *Kuinka moni skotlantilainen puhuu gaelia?* | |
| v1-v2 | how many ScottishNOM speakS3 GaelicPART<br>Kuinka moni skotlantilainen puhuu gaelia? | - |
| v3 | how much PART(Gaelic speaking people) INESS existS3<br>Kuinka paljon gaelia puhuvia ihmisiä Skotlannissa on? | struct |
| v4 | how many speakS3 GaelicGEN languagePART INESS<br>Kuinka moni puhuu gaelin kieltä Skotlannissa? | pos(n/a)<br>order spec |
| o | **Q24: Where is the Al Aqsa Mosque?** | |
| c | *Missä on Al Aqsa -moskeija?* | |
| v1-v3 | where beS3 NOM mosque<br>Missä on Al Aqsa -moskeija? | - |
| v4 | where beS3 GEN mosque<br>Missä on al-Aqsan moskeija? | conv(case)<br>conv(ortograph)<br>nounattr/genattr |
| o | **Q168: When did the attack at the Saint-Michel underground station in Paris occur?** | |
| c | *Milloin tapahtui isku Saint-Michelin metroasemalle Pariisissa* | |
| v1 | when GEN GEN<br>Milloin Pariisin Saint-Michelin<br>metro_stationALL attackIMP_PASS<br>metroasemalle iskettiin? | struct |
| v2 | when happenIMP_S3 attackNOM GEN<br>Milloin tapahtui isku Saint-Michelin<br>metro_stationALL INESS<br>metroasemalle Pariisissa? | - |
| v3 | when happenIMP_S3 GEN GEN<br>Milloin tapahtui Pariisin Saint-Michelin<br>metro_stationGEN attackNOM<br>metroaseman hyökkäys? | lex(n) morph(n)<br>genattr/locative<br>2×order |
| v4 | when attackNOM GEN metroGEN stationALL<br>Milloin isku Saint-Michelin maanalaisen asemalle<br>INESS happenIMP_S3<br>Pariisissa tapahtui? | lex(n) order |

Table 5: The question variants for questions 22, 24 and 168 in the question variant dataset. The original question (o), the canonical form, or centroid, (c) and the variants (v1-v4) with their transformations. When there are no tranformations, the variant equals the centroid of the variant set.

ing the word based distance did not distinguish among the variants in any of the cases in the data. All in all, there were six questions in the dataset whose best and worst variants had to be determined manually. Five of these could be determined following the automatically made choices, and only one case was determined using the intuition of the human expert.

## 6.2 Classification of question reformulations

The extent to which different question reformulations affect the accuracy of question classification was investigated by evaluating the performance of a classifier using different question reformulation datasets. The different datasets are listed in Table 6 in the column named *Dataset Name*. The creation of the datasets

*Best WordChar*, *Best Char*, *Worst WordChar* and *Worst Char* was explained in Section 3. The dataset *Mixed* is a dataset containing 50 randomly selected different questions from each variant set. The datasets *Variant 1, 2, 3 and 4* only contain questions created by one author. The dataset *All* consists of all question variants. The results table reports the accuracy of the classifier both on training data and on unseen data. The accuracy of the classifier on training data is given because it illustrates how well the features selected can classify the data at hand. The results obtained by testing the classifier with unseen data naturally give a more realistic picture of the performance of the classifier. These results were obtained by 10-fold cross-validation (see e.g. (Duda et al., 2001), page 483). The accuracy on unseen data for the dataset *All* has two figures, 86.4 and 70.8, in parentheses. The different figures are obtained by using a different sampling in the creation of the training and test sets. The higher accuracy is obtained when the different variants of the same questions appear in both the training and test datasets. The lower accuracy is obtained when all variants of a specific question have to appear in either the training set or the test set, but not in both.

| Dataset Name | Accuracy in % | |
|---|---|---|
| | training data | unseen data |
| **Datasets of 200 questions** | | |
| Best WordChar | 80.8 | 75.0 |
| Best Char | 80.8 | 75.0 |
| Worst WordChar | 77.9 | 68.5 |
| Worst Char | 77.9 | 70.0 |
| Mixed | 79.1 | 70.6 |
| Variant 1 | 75.5 | 71.5 |
| Variant 2 | 80.8 | 73.0 |
| Variant 3 | 80.2 | 73.5 |
| Variant 4 | 78.8 | 72.0 |
| **Dataset of 800 questions** | | |
| All | 90.9 | 86.4 (70.8) |

Table 6: Accuracy of classifiers inducted from different datasets. Classification accuracy is reported both on training data and on unseen data.

Analysis of the classification results shows that different question reformulations do make a significant difference in the accuracy of a decision tree classifier that uses the features described in Section 4. Among the datasets of 200 questions, the highest classification accuracy, 75,0%, was achieved using the datasets *Best WordChar* and *Best Char* that consist of the centroid of each question. The lowest classification accuracy, 68,5%, was achieved using the dataset *Worst WordChar*. The classification accuracies of the datasets consisting of questions produced by a sole author (*Variants 1 , 2, 3 and 4*) are higher than that of the dataset that contains a mixture of variants from all four authors (*Mixed*). This shows that the authors have some author specific traits that have been captured by the classification features. However, the fact that the centroid datasets have a higher classification accuracy than any of the author specific datasets shows that all centroids are somehow more similar with each other than the questions created by the same author.

## 6.3 Question transformations and the dataset

As can be seen from Table 4, lexical variations and different ordering of words are the most frequent transformation classes in the dataset. In addition, the transformations related to conventions are very common. Some translator specific features can be seen from the data. For instance, the translator of variant set number four prefers placing the verb as the last item in the question, while the other translators generally use the question word - verb - noun pattern. For this reason, there are 14 questions where all the other variants are equal, but the translation done by the fourth translator differs by one transformation of class order. Also orthographic and translation conventions tend to be author specific.

The differences between variants vary significantly. Some of them consist only of one transformation, while others have multiple transformations. Even though there is the same amount of transformations, the complexity of different transformations is not equal.

The taxonomy of the transformation classes described in this paper is created through a data driven approach and as such, is based on a specific data set. It is suitable for the given data, but it is not certain that it can be generalized to other collections of data. A question paraphrasing taxonomy with only six classes has been constructed (Tomuro, 2003), and the classes cannot be straightforwardly mapped into our system.

## 7 Conclusion

This paper presents the first experiments with Finnish question reformulations. In order to study the different reformulations of natural language questions that arise spontaneously, a question variants dataset was created. The effect of different reformulations of the same question on the performance of a question answering system was evaluated by creating ten different question datasets and by measuring the accuracy of the question classifier component of a question answering system using each of the datasets. Among the different question reformulation datasets created is the set of canonical reformulations. In order to create this dataset, a similarity metric between question reformulations was devised. The experiments show that the question classification accuracy is 75% when the canonical reformulations set is used, but only 70.6% when a mixed dataset reflecting a realistic set of incoming questions to a question answering system is used. Thus, the performance of the question processing component and most likely also the performance of the whole question answering system would improve if the incoming questions were first transformed into a canonical form.

The next step in the research that is presented in the paper consists in analyzing the different transformations that are needed in order to transform a question reformulation into a canonical form. Based on a careful study of the question reformulations dataset, a set of 27 transformation classes were defined. The analysis of these transformations shows that the automatic transformation of a question reformulation into a canonical form, or even the automatic recognition of questions that already are in canonical form would be very challenging. However, research has been done on transforming English question reformulations into a canonical form, and this research indicates that further research on Finnish question reformulations is needed in order to determine the feasibility of transforming Finnish questions into a canonical form. The work presented in this paper constitutes a starting point for this further research, and it already shows that various types of question reformulations spontaneously arise and that their effect on the performance of the question analysis component of a question answering system is significant.

# References


Lili Aunimo, Oskari Heinonen, Reeta Kuuskoski, Juha Makkonen, Renaud Petit, and Otso Virtanen. 2003. Question answering system for incomplete and noisy data: Methods and measures for its evaluation. In *Proceedings of the 25th European Conference on Information Retrieval Research (ECIR 2003)*, pages 193 – 206, Pisa, Italy.

Lili Aunimo. 2005. A typology and feature set for questions. In *Proceedings of the Workshop on Knowledge and Reasoning for Answering Questions held in conjunction with the 19th International Joint Conference on Artificial Intelligence*, Edinburgh, United Kindom, August.

Christelle Ayache. 2005. Campagne evalda/equer, evaluation en question réponse. Technical report, ELDA - Evaluations and Language resources Distribution Agency.

Collin Baker, Charles Fillmore, and John Lowe. 1998. The Berkeley FrameNet project. In *Proceedings of the 17th International Conference on Computational Linguistics and 36th Annual Meeting of the Association for Computational Linguistics (COLING-ACL)*, Montreal, Canada, August.

R. Burke, K. Hammond, V. Kulyukin, S. Lytinen, N. Tomuro, and S. Schoenberg. 1997. Question answering from frequently asked question files: Experiences with the faqfinder system. *AI Magazine*, 18(2):57–66.

Richard O. Duda, Peter E. Hart, and David G. Stork. 2001. *Pattern Classification*. Wiley-Interscience.

Sanda Harabagiu and Dan Moldovan. 2003. Question answering. In Ruslan Mitkov, editor, *Computational Linguistics*. Oxford University Press.

Sanda M. Harabagiu, Dan I. Moldovan, Marius Paşca, Rada Mihalcea, Mihai Surdeanu, Răzvan C. Bunescu, Roxana Gîrju, Vasile Rus, and Paul Morărescu. 2001. The role of lexico-semantic feedback in open-domain textual question-answering. In *Proceedings of the 39th Meeting of the Association for Computational Linguistics*, pages 274–281.

Ulf Hermjakob, Abdessamad Echihabi, and Daniel Marcu. 2002. Natural language based reformulation resource and web exploitation for question answering. In Ellen M. Voorhees and Lori P. Buckland, editors, *Proceedings of TREC-2002*, Gaithersburg, Maryland, November. Department of Commerce, National Institute of Standards and Technology.

Xin Li, Dan Roth, and Kevin Small. 2004. The role of semantic information in learning question classifiers. In *Proceedings of the 1st International Joint Conference on Natural Language Processing*, Hainan Island, China.

B. Magnini, A. Vallin, C. Ayache, G. Erbach, A. Peñas, M. de Rijke, P. Rocha, K. Simov, and R. Sutcliffe. 2005. Overview of the CLEF 2004 Multilingual Question Answering Track. In C. Peters, P. D. Clough, G. J. F. Jones, J. Gonzalo, M. Kluck, and B. Magnini, editors, *Multilingual Information Access for Text, Speech and Images: Results of the Fifth CLEF Evaluation Campaign*, volume 3491 of *Lecture Notes in Computer Science*. Springer Verlag.

J. Ross Quinlan. 1993. *C4.5: Programs for Machine Learning.* Morgan Kaufmann, San Francisco, CA.

Jun Suzuki, Hirotoshi Taira, Yutaka Sasaki, and Eisaku Maeda. 2003. Question classification using HDAG kernel. In *Proceedings of the Workshop on Multilingual Summarization and Question Answering, held in conjunction with the 41th Annual Meeting of the Association for Computational Linguistics.*, Sapporo, Japan.

Noriko Tomuro. 2003. Interrogative reformulation patterns and acquisition of question paraphrases. In *Proceedings of the International Workshop on Paraphrasing Workshop , held in conjunction with the 41th Annual Meeting of the Association for Computational Linguistics.*, Sapporo, Japan.

Ellen M. Voorhees. 2000. Overwiew of the TREC-9 Question Answering Track. In Ellen M. Voorhees and Donna K. Harman, editors, *Proceedings of TREC-9*, Gaithersburg, Maryland, November. Department of Commerce, National Institute of Standards and Technology.

Robert A. Wagner and Michael J. Fischer. 1974. The string-to-string correction problem. *Journal of the Association for Computing Machinery*, 21(1):168–173.

# Dictionary acquisition using
# parallel text and co-occurrence statistics


**Chris Biemann** and **Uwe Quasthoff**

NLP department

University of Leipzig

Augustusplatz 10-11

D-04109 Leipzig

{biem,quasthoff}@informatik.uni-leipzig.de


## Abstract


We present a simple and efficient approach for deriving bilingual dictionaries from sentence-aligned parallel text by extending the notion of co-occurrences to a cross-lingual setting. Dictionaries are evaluated against gold standards and manually; the analysis accounts for frequency and corpus size effects.


## 1  Introduction

While more and more parallel text resources become available due to common regulations amongst different countries and the internationalization of markets, there is a need for translational lexicons that can keep pace with the daily creation of new terminology. The standard procedure amongst the Machine Translation Community to extract translation pairs from sentence-aligned parallel corpora can be outlined as follows (cf. (Melamed, 1996), (Moore, 2001) for an overview):

1. Define a measure which yields association scores between words of different languages

2. Calculate the association scores between all possible pairs

3. To obtain translations for a given word, sort its trans-lingual associations by score and take the top N or apply a threshold.

The crucial choice in the first step is to define a well-suited measure, the problem in step two is the effectiveness of the calculation, and in the last step the challenge is to cut the list at the right point.

In (Melamed, 1996), the problem of selecting inappropriate translations due to indirect associations is addressed: When e.g. *European* and *Council* often occur together in one language (here English) and *Europæiske* and *Råd* in the translation (here Danish), the measure yields a high association score between *Council* and *Europæiske* which is unwanted. He proposes a re-estimation method to alleviate this problem at the cost of long computation times. Other approaches like e.g. (Moore, 2001) or (Lee and Chang, 1993) rely on language-dependent resources like taggers, parsers or transliteration modules or use string similarity for preferring cognates.

We present an approach that is especially suited for large data sets, as it scales well with the corpus size - processing time is about 2 hours for a bilingual resource with about 28 million tokens in each language. Further, it does not make any assumptions on the languages and is therefore also suited for languages that are by no means close in terms of edit distance or character set (for languages without whitespace like Chinese and Japanese, a segmentation step is assumed in the pre-processing). We argue that a language independent approach like ours is a good baseline where more problem-specific methods (like using edit distances for cognates) can build upon.

Usually, co-occurrence statistics is used for large monolingual texts. It returns pairs of words that significantly often occur together within a predefined window. Implementations differ in the significance measure and the window size used. For our experiments, we use a log-likelihood-measure (which has been noticed to be adequate for the translation relation, see e.g (Tufiş, 2002)) and sentences as windows. This approach has proved to return pairs of semantically related words similar to human associations, cf. (Biemann et al., 2004).

For dictionary acquisition, we slightly modify the setting: Starting from a parallel corpus, we build a corpus containing bilingual *bi-sentences* built from pairs of aligned sentences. For technical reasons, we add language information to each word. Next, the co-occurrence statistics returns pairs of words which significantly often occur together in such bi-sentences. Here we consider only pairs of words having different language tags. Hence, for a given word we get an ordered list of translation candidates.

## 2  Methodology

Following the methodology of (Biemann et al., 2004), we adopt the machinery to compute co-occurrences of monolingual corpora (see *http://corpora.informatik.uni-leipzig.de* for co-occurrences in different languages) for the extraction of translation candidates: We mark the words in a bilingual sentence pair by source language and only regard co-occurrences between words of different languages. We call these significant trans-lingual associations *trans-co-occurrences*.

For two words $A$ and $B$ of different languages, each occurring $a$, $b$ times in the corpus of bi-sentences and together in $k$ of $n$ bi-sentences in total, we compute the significance $sig(A,B)$ of their trans-co-occurrence as follows:

$$sig(A,B) = \frac{\lambda - k\log\lambda + \log k!}{\log n} \text{ with } \lambda = \frac{ab}{n}.$$

To illustrate the necessary preprocessing, we give some examples for German-English bi-sentences as used in our experiments, words are marked by language:

- Die@de drogenfreie@de Gesellschaft@de wird@de es@de aber@de nie@de geben@de .@de But@en there@en never@en will@en be@en a@en drug-free@en society@en .@en

- Unsere@de Gesellschaft@de neigt@de leider@de dazu@de ,@de Gesetze@de zu@de umgehen@de .@de Unfortunately@en ,@en our@en society@en is@en inclined@en to@en skirt@en round@en the@en law@en .@en

- Zum@de Glück@de kommt@de das@de in@de einer@de demokratischen@de Gesellschaft@de selten@de vor@de .@de Fortunately@en ,@en in@en a@en democratic@en society@en this@en is@en rare@en .@en

- Ich@de sprach@de vom@de Paradoxon@de unserer@de Gesellschaft@de .@de I@en mentioned@en what@en is@en paradoxical@en in@en society@en .@en

In all pairs, *Gesellschaft@de* and *society@en* occur. Exactly this is used by the trans-co-occurrence calculation mechanism to produce the following top-ranked translation candidates:

- **Gesellschaft@de**: society@en (12082), social@en (342), our@en (274), in@en (237), societies@en (226), Society@en (187), women@en (183), as@en a@en whole@en (182), of@en our@en (168), open@en society@en (165)

- **society@en**: Gesellschaft@de (12082), unserer@de (466), einer@de (379), gesellschaftlichen@de (328), Wissensgesellschaft@de (312), Menschen@de (233), gesellschaftliche@de (219), Frauen@de (213), Zivilgesellschaft@de (179), Gesellschaften@de (173)

Note the large difference in significance between the first and all the other translation candidates. The significance values only have a local meaning: there is no global threshold for deciding whether candidates are good or bad, but within a ranked list of translation candidates for one word, they in fact tell the chaff from the wheat. To illustrate what happens if words have several possible translations, the following example lists candidates whose significance values do not differ considerably:

- **kaum@de**: hardly@en (825), scarcely@en (470), little@en (362), barely@en (278), hardly@en any@en (254), very@en little@en (186), almost@en (88), difficult@en (68), unlikely@en (63), virtually@en (53), scarcely@en any@en (51), impossible@en (47), or@en no@en (40), there@en is@en (38), hardly@en ever@en (37), any@en (32), hardly@en anything@en (32), surprising@en (31), hardly@en a@en (29), hard@en (28), ...

- **hardly@en**: kaum@de (825), wohl@de kaum@de (138), schwerlich@de (64), nicht@de (51), verwunderlich@de (43), kann@de (37), wenig@de (37), wundern@de (25), man@de (21), dürfte@de (17), gar@de nicht@de (17), auch@de nicht@de (16), gerade@de (16), überrascht@de (15), fast@de (14), überraschen@de (14), praktisch@de (13), ist@de (12), schlecht@de (12), verwundern@de (12), ...

Note that the methods produces a much longer list of candidates. Our machinery can deal with multi-words in a way that multi-words that are known beforehand can be treated as single units. For our experiments, we added multi-words that could be found in our evaluation dictionaries, e.g. "hardly any" in the examples above. To replace these manual resources, any approach for extracting collocations, e.g. (Smadia, 1993), could be applied in preprocessing; we did not undertake such efforts, which might be subject to further research.

## 3 Experiments

### 3.1 Data and resources

For evaluating our approach we use the multilingual, sentence-aligned Europarl Corpus (Koehn, 2002) available within the OPUS collection (*http://logos.uio.no/opus/*). The corpus consists of transcribed and translated parliament speeches of the EU parliament and covers a variety of topics. In each of the 11 languages, there are about 1 million sentences totalling about 28 million words. The corpus was neither tagged nor lemmatized.

Using machine-readable dictionaries for judging the quality of the obtained dictionary has a number of deficiencies. First of all, dictionaries are never complete, which leads to misjudging translations which might be correct, but not found in the dictionary. Second, a general-purpose dictionary might not suit domain-specific translations of the actual corpus. Third, if processing full forms, an automatic approach might give results in inflected form that cannot be found in a base-form dictionary, and lemmatizers or stemmers are not widely available for many of the European languages. Further, the differences between languages w.r.t compounding may lead to confusion in automatic evaluation. The results presented here can therefore only account for a lower bound of precision.

Comparing evaluations within different works is difficult. Many researchers lemmatize the corpus, some remove function words and some use word class information. What is considered correct or not for this task is also differing. In (Melamed, 1996), three kinds of 'correct' translations are given: pairs that are proper translations in *at least one context*, pairs that can be translations but have different parts of speech and pairs where one word is a possible part of the translation of another. Of course, this metric is much more relaxed then ours (which should not belittle his impressive results) and accepts entries you will never find in published dictionaries. Nevertheless, these entries are useful for machine translation or word alignment, see section 4 for an example.

### 3.2 Evaluation

We obtained machine-readable dictionaries from Freelang (*http://www.freelang.net*). Additionally we asked persons with very good knowledge of the respective language pair to judge the results without giving them contexts. Due to availability of personal and dictionary resources, we tested our approach on the language pairs English-Danish, English-Dutch, English-Finnish, English-German, English-Italian, English-Portuguese and English-Swedish. Depending on the language, the method proposes at least three translation candidates for 34%-51% of total word types, which translates into 83%-89% coverage on tokens. For German-English, we used a larger dictionary in order to directly compare our approach to (Sahlgren, 2004), who uses random indexing instead of co-occurrence analysis but operates on the same data otherwise.

To alleviate the problem of full forms in the corpus as opposed to base forms in the dictionary to some extend, we use the following similarity measure: The similarity between two strings (words) $V$ and $W$ is defined as the number of similar prefix letters divided through the length of the longest string:

$$pfm(V, W) = \frac{\text{length of common prefix of } V \text{ and } W}{\max(length(v), length(W))}.$$

Although this measure is somewhat crude, it gives hints on how many correct, but inflected translations could be extracted. For evaluation,

---

we checked the first three translation candidates for exact match (=1) and prefix match $\geq 0.6$. This threshold produces almost no errors and takes flexations and sometimes part-of-speech change into account. It however does not capture Finnish case endings in all cases.

Table 3 in the appendix shows a randomly selected sample from the English-German data together with the maximum prefix match between the trans-co-occurrence candidates and the translations in the dictionary.

Table 1 contains precision values in % for all words that could be found in the dictionary for the first three translation candidates. Both translation directions are combined into one value.

| language pair | 1st candidate | | | 2nd candidate | | |
|---|---|---|---|---|---|---|
| mode | corr. | part | both | corr. | part | both |
| de-en | 64.5 | 19.6 | 84.1 | 25.5 | 22.4 | 47.9 |
| en-de | 52.8 | 26.4 | 79.2 | 35.9 | 25.5 | 61.4 |
| da-en | 55.5 | 21.8 | 77.3 | 12.7 | 18.2 | 30.9 |
| en-da | 56.8 | 27.0 | 83.8 | 27.9 | 25.2 | 53.1 |
| sv-en | 64.9 | 15.3 | 80.2 | 15.3 | 17.1 | 32.4 |
| en-sv | 67.6 | 13.5 | 80.1 | 36.0 | 10.8 | 46.8 |
| nl-en | 51.1 | 29.1 | 80.2 | 29.2 | 27.7 | 56.9 |
| en-nl | 56.6 | 18.9 | 75.5 | 32.0 | 24.5 | 56.5 |

Table 2: Precision in manual evaluation for first and second candidate in %

### 3.3 Influence of frequency

As has been previously observed, precision of translation pairs is dependent on word frequency. (Sahlgren, 2004) uses co-occurrence information as well but reduces complexity by random indexing and stemming. He describes experiments for English-German with the same corpus and evaluates against the same large dictionary (*http://dict.tu-chemnitz.de/*). Intuitively, the more frequent a word is, the more reliable is the data for it, which should lead to higher results. The effect of using random indexing hence seems to prefer a certain frequency region, as Sahlgren obtained peak values in the absolute frequency range of 1000-5000.

| language pair | 1st candidate | | 2nd candidate | | 3rd candidate | | 1st, 2nd or 3rd cand. | |
|---|---|---|---|---|---|---|---|---|
| prefix match | =1 | $\geq$0.6 | =1 | $\geq$0.6 | =1 | $\geq$0.6 | =1 | $\geq$0.6 |
| en-sv | 44.7 | 57.7 | 16.8 | 32.8 | 8.4 | 20.2 | 64.1 | 72.0 |
| en-it | 52.0 | 61.5 | 14.3 | 29.3 | 7.1 | 19.0 | 66.4 | 73.3 |
| en-pt | 56.6 | 66.7 | 12.8 | 27.3 | 6.4 | 17.4 | 70.6 | 78.7 |
| en-nl | 47.3 | 57.0 | 14.2 | 24.9 | 7.9 | 15.6 | 62.4 | 69.2 |
| en-de | 52.6 | 61.4 | 16.4 | 31.2 | 9.0 | 20.0 | 68.2 | 75.1 |
| en-da | 50.9 | 61.6 | 15.1 | 29.3 | 7.3 | 26.0 | 67.7 | 74.3 |
| en-fi | 34.9 | 51.3 | 17.3 | 34.26 | 10.4 | 25.9 | 52.0 | 65.9 |
| total | 46.1 | 58.0 | 15.8 | 30.9 | 8.6 | 21.2 | 62.2 | 71.3 |

Table 1: Dictionary precision for top-3 translation candidates in %

For manual evaluation, we presented about 200 randomly selected words for each pair and let our language experts chose amongst correct, partially (part of a correct multiword, e.g. "Richter" instead of "Bundesrichter") and wrong. Table 2 depicts the results of manual evaluation.

As expected, results of manual evaluation are higher than comparing to electronic dictionaries. Results demonstrate that our approach works in a language-independent fashion. Moreover, results for the first candidate are much higher than for the second, indicating that the association measure is appropriate.
For the remainder, we use German-English to determine the influence of word frequency and corpus size.

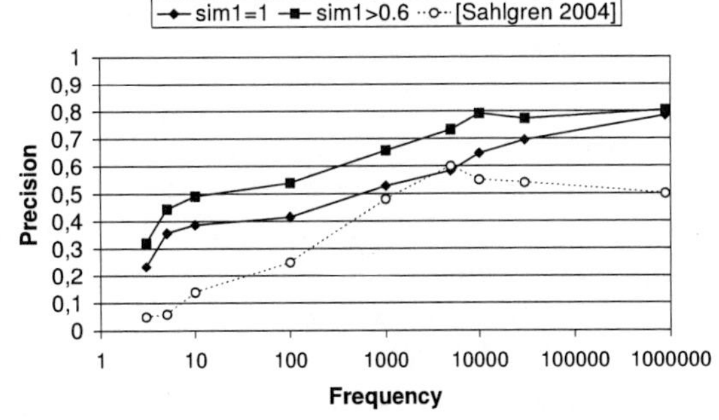


Figure 1: Dictionary precision for different frequency bands for English-German in comparison to (Sahlgren, 2004).

Our approach obtains a higher precision for

all frequency bands, higher frequency leads to a higher precision, as figure 1 shows. Further, our method does not require brittle parameter tuning and does not introduce random.

### 3.4 Influence of corpus size

Another question we try to answer is the influence of corpus size. Of course, more parallel data means more evidence, so better results can be expected. But how little is necessary to start the process and what quality can we expect using much smaller parallel corpora?

We conducted experiments with English-German and gradually increased the number of parallel sentences from 500 to 1 million. The number of words, for which at least one trans-co-occurrence exists, grows a little less than linear in corpus size, as figure 2 indicates. This is the same progression as the total amount of word types.

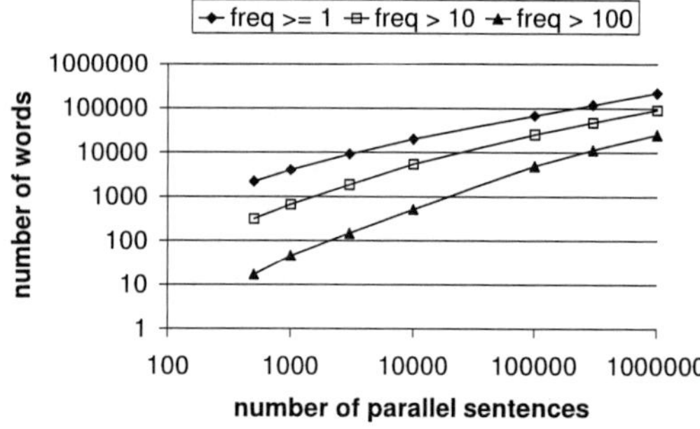

**Number of words that have trans-co-occurrences for different frequencies**



Figure 2: Number of words with trans-co-occurrences of different frequencies depending on corpus size

To measure whether corpus size influences the dictionary precision at absolute frequency count labels, we evaluated words of different frequency bands in our corpora of different sizes. We only took the highest-ranked trans-co-occurrence into account and accepted a translation as correct if a dictionary entry with prefix match $\geq 0.6$ existed.The results as depicted in figure 3 indicate that precision is merely dependent on absolute frequency and not whole corpus size. The lower performance for the highest frequency band available in small corpora can be explained by the impossibility to give 1:1 equivalences of function words (e.g. (Catizone

et al., 1989) give an example where German *auf* translates at least into English *for, in* or *on*). As these words constitute the topmost entries in a word list ordered descending by frequency, they deteriorate evaluation results if not many other words in the same frequency class are considered.

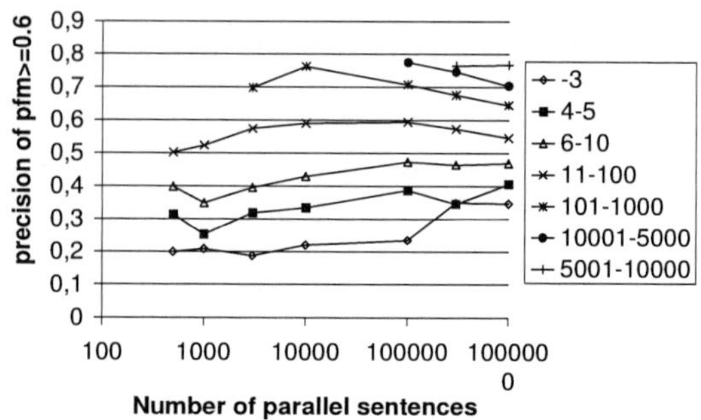

**Dictionary precision for different corpus sizes and frequency bands**



Figure 3: Dictionary precision for different corpus sizes and frequency bands containing at least 100 words

Another factor that might influence precision in dictionary acquisition is the (average) length of an aligned unit. Where we used the comparably long sentences of Europarl (about 28 words per unit), there exist versions of the Hansards corpus (as e.g. used by (Melamed, 1996)) that are aligned on a sub-sentence level in units of about 16 words.

## 4   Word alignment

The ordered list of translation candidates per word can be used for word-to-word alignment of sentence-aligned corpora as follows: Given a sentence pair of L1 and L2, all words of L1 are linked to the word in L2 that can be found on the highest rank in the candidate list. In this way, even rare translations can be aligned, as the example in figure 4 shows: German *stellt* (usually English *puts*) and English *provides* (usually German *beliefert, beschafft*) are correctly linked, although *stellt* is ranked at position 15 in the candidate list for "provides". High frequency words as well as numbers are omitted in alignment.

In figure 5, another example demonstrating our approach's capability to do word alignment

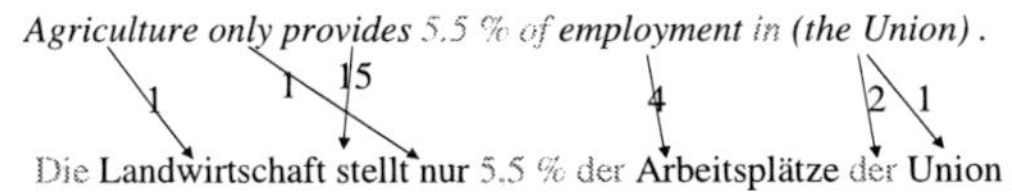


Figure 4: Grey words are not aligned, grey arrows indicate multiple alignments to the same word type. Numbers on arrows indicate the rank of the trans-co-occurrence. For a larger example, see figure 5.

for long parallel units is depicted. It indicates that we can handle scrambling of word order naturally: In the first line in figure 5, the verb *setzen* int the final position of the clause is aligned to *setting* at third position. A simple heuristic could avoid multiple alignments of several determiners, as can be observed between a and *ein, eine, einen*. Finding several high-ranked trans-co-occurrences adjacent to each other (as with *Inkrafttreten* and *entry into force*) gives rise to the detection of multi-word units and their alignment. This breaks the 1:1 mapping assumption, which is especially not met when languages forming one-word compounds are involved. A more elaborate evaluation of this method on the word alignment of Bible texts can be found in (Cysouw et al., forthcoming).

## 5   Conclusion and future work

Co-occurrence statistics have proved to be useful to find translation pairs using parallel text, especially aligned sentences. Moreover, the need for large parallel texts is shown to extract large vocabularies. The next and more complicated question is to get rid of the sentence alignment and use only nearly parallel text. Here we have to replace the above bi-sentences by bi-texts an to calculate co-occurrences at bi-text level. While such texts are available at large scale (for instance, the multilingual Reuters corpus or multilingual web sites, see (Resnik and Smith, 2003)), processing is much more complex because it is quadratic in the length of the bilingual objects (i.e. texts instead of sentences). Further, longer units introduce more noise in the process.

## 6   Acknowledgements

The authors would like to thank Philipp Koehn for the preparation of the Europarl corpus and Wibke Kuhn, Ronny Melz and Pauliina Svensk for helping us with the manual evaluation.

## References

Chris Biemann, Stefan Bordag, Gerhard Heyer, Uwe Quasthoff, and Christian Wolff. 2004. Language-independent methods for compiling monolingual lexical data. In *Proceedings of CicLING 2004, Seoul, Korea and Springer LNCS 2945 Springer Verlag Berlin Heidelberg*, pages 215–228.

R. Catizone, G. Russel, and S. Warwick. 1989. Deriving translation data from bilingual texts. In *Proceedings of the First International Lexical Acquisition Workshop, Detroit, USA*.

Michael Cysouw, Chris Biemann, and Matthias Ongyerth. forthcoming. Using strong's numbers in the bible to test an automatic alignment of parallel texts. *In: Michael Cysouw and Bernhard Wälchli (eds.) Parallel Texts: Using translational equivalents in linguistic typology. Special issue of Sprachtypologie und Universalienforschung.*

Philipp Koehn. 2002. Europarl: A multilingual corpus for evaluation of machine translation (unpublished manuscript).

Chun-Jen Lee and Jason S. Chang. 1993. Acquisition of english-chinese transliterated word pairs from parallel-aligned texts using a statistical machine transliteration model. In *HLT-NAACL 2003 Workshop: Building and Using Parallel Texts, Data Driven Machine Translation and Beyond, Edmonton*, pages 96–103.

I. Melamed. 1996. Automatic construction of clean broad-coverage translation lexicons. In *Proceedings of the 2nd Conference of the Association for Machine Translation in the Americas, Montreal, Canada*.

Robert C. Moore. 2001. Towards a simple and accurate statistical approach to learning translation relationships among words. In *Workshop on Data-driven Machine Translation, 39th Annual Meeting and 10th Conference of the EACL, Toulouse, France*, pages 79–86.

P. Resnik and N.A. Smith. 2003. The web as a parallel corpus. *Computational Linguistics*, 29(3):349–380.

Magnus Sahlgren. 2004. Automatic bilingual lexicon acquisition using random indexing of aligned bilingual data. In *Proceedings of LREC-2004, Lisbon, Portugal*.

Frank Smadia. 1993. Retrieving collocations from text: Xtract. *Computational Linguistics,* 19(1).

Dan Tufiş. 2002. A cheap and fast way to build useful translation lexicons. In *Proceedings of the 19th International Conference on Computational Linguistics COLING-02,Taipei, Taiwan.*

| word | cand.1 | pfm1 | cand.2 | pfm2 | cand.3 | pfm3 |
|---|---|---|---|---|---|---|
| acute | **akuten** | 0.66 | **akute** | 0.8 | **akuter** | 0.66 |
| absolutely essential | *absolut* | 0 | *unbedingt* | 0.166 | **unbedingt notwendig** | 0.1 |
| essential | **wesentlichen** | 0.83 | **wesentliche** | 0.909 | ist | 0 |
| office | **Büro** | 1 | **Amt** | 1 | **Büros** | 0.8 |
| pollutants | **Schadstoffe** | 1 | **Schadstoffen** | 0.916 | Emission | 0 |
| expertise | **Fachwissen** | 0 | **Sachverstand** | 1 | **Sachkenntnis** | 1 |
| prescribed | **vorgeschrieben** | 1 | **vorgeschriebenen** | 0.875 | **vorgeschriebene** | 0.93 |
| means | **bedeutet** | 1 | **Mittel** | 1 | heisst | 0.09 |
| industrial goods | **Industriewaren** | 0.64 | *gewerbliche* | 0 | *Erzeugnisse* | 0 |
| bill | *Gesetzentwurf* | 0.15 | *Gesetzesentwurf* | 0.133 | **Rechnung** | 1 |
| approach | **Ansatz** | 1 | Konzept | 0 | **Vorgehensweise** | 0 |
| audit | *Prüefung* | 0 | **Audit** | 1 | **Rechnungsprüfung** | 1 |

Table 3: Top three candidates for German-English sample with prefix match scores. Manually judged correct translations are marked in **bold**, part of translations *in italics*. Note the disagreement between automatic and manual evaluation.

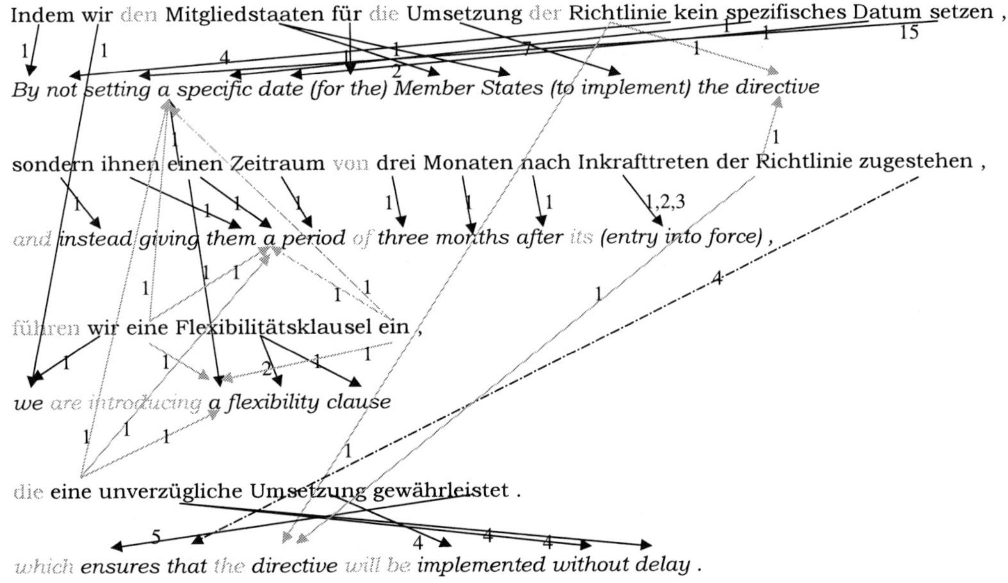


Figure 5: Second example for word alignment. Grey words are not aligned, grey arrows indicate multiple alignments to the same word type. Numbers on arrows indicate the rank of the trans-co-occurrence. The dashed arrow marks an alignment error. the only content word pair which is not aligned is the particle verb *führen .. ein* to its equivalent *introducing*.

---

# The influence of written task descriptions in Wizard of Oz experiments

**Heidi Brøseth**
Department of Language
and Communication Studies
Norwegian University of
Science and Technology
NO-7491 Trondheim
broseth@hf.ntnu.no

## Abstract

In this paper we investigate an assertion made by Richards and Underwood (1985), who claim that people interacting with a spoken information retrieval system, structure their information in such a uniform manner that this regularity can be used to enhance the performance of the dialog system. We put forward the possibility that this uniform ordering of information might be due to the design of the written task descriptions used in Wizard of Oz experiments.

## 1 Introduction

As noted in for instance Richards and Underwood (1985), Jönsson and Dahlbäck (1988) and Wooffitt et al. (1997), people tend to behave differently when interacting with a machine as opposed to a human being. These differences are found in various aspects of the dialog, such as the type of request formulation, the frequency of response token, the use of greetings and the organization of the opening and closing sequences, to mention a few. As a consequence of these findings, so-called Wizard of Oz experiments (abbrev. WOZ) are widely used for collecting data about how people interact with computer systems. In a Wizard of Oz experiment the subjects are led to believe that they are interacting with a computer when they are in fact interacting with a human being (a wizard). The wizard can act as a speech synthesizer, speech recognizer, and/or perform various tasks which will eventually be performed by the future system. It is vital that the subjects really think they are communicating with an implemented system in order to obtain reliable data concerning human-computer interaction. The findings in WOZ experiments can serve as an important guide in further development and design of the system (Dahlbäck et al., 1993).

In this paper we investigate the methodology used in WOZ experiments to see how various factors can influence the results. We will start by introducing the experiment done by Richards and Underwood (1985). Then a similar experiment performed in Trondheim will be presented. The results from this experiment will serve as our stance for questioning the claim made in Richards and Underwood (1985). We will also use data material from human-human dialogs to support our claim.

## 2 Richards and Underwood (1985): significant regularity in the user utterances

The domain for Richards and Underwood's (1985) experiment was train tables. 48 subjects were asked to carry out 6 inquiry tasks concerning these train tables via the phone. Richards and Underwood (1985) claim that the participants in their WOZ experiment rendered the information to the system in the following order: 1) place of departure, 2) place of arrival, 3) day and 4) approximate time of travel. They also investigated how the participants responded to different introductory messages. The conclusion was: "_In all cases the finding was sufficiently well established to provide for a potentially useful means of improving recognition accuracy by allowing recognition probabilities to be appropriately weighted_" (217:1985). This conclusion seems very promising, but there is an important aspect of this experiment to be accounted for. Richards and Underwood (1985) mention that the information necessary to perform the request in the WOZ experiment was included in a written task description given to the participants. Unfortunately, they do not give any examples of such a description. The possible influence that these could yield on the results was neither investigated nor discussed in the paper. It is reasonable to ask whether the regularity in information structure reported by Richards and Underwood (1985) is really caused by a spontaneous and natural way of asking about traveling, or perhaps this uniform ordering of information could be caused by the written task description given to the participants. In order to shed some light on this question, we will present some interesting findings in the Trondheim WOZ experiment, as well as some results from the recorded human-human dialogs.

## 3    The Trondheim WOZ experi-ment

The Trondheim WOZ experiment (abbrev. TWOZ) is within the domain of bus information, and it was conducted in 2003/2004 (Johnsen et al., 2003). The TWOZ is part of the BRAGE[1]-project, and the aim is to develop a mixed-initiative spoken dialog system. The system was built on an existing written query system called BussTUC (Amble, 2000), i.e. a speech interface and a dialog manager were added. The wizard's task was to act as a "perfect speech recognizer". All other tasks were performed by the BussTUC system, the dialog manager and speech synthesis. 64 participants made 3 phone calls asking about bus

---

[1] BRAGE is an acronym for Brukergrensesnitt for naturlig tale (User interface for natural speech).

information resulting in 192 inquiries. The data material consists of 455 user turns (4063 tokens). The participants were either students or staff at Norwegian University of Science and Technology (NTNU).

As already mentioned, the experiment performed by Richards and Underwood (1985) concerned train tables, hence the domains in the two experiments are comparable to a great extent. Both WOZ experiments were conducted via telephone, and written task descriptions containing different scenarios were given to the participants beforehand. In the TWOZ experiment the descriptions also informed that there were no restrictions regarding the actual spoken formulation of the inquiries.

### 3.1    Scenario groups

The scenarios were divided into five main groups which gave slightly different instructions to the participants.

Group A
The participants should include all information given in the scenario in one utterance, like in a query system.
Example of scenario from which the user should formulate a request to the system:
_Place of departure: Munkvoll_
_Place of arrival: Kalvskinnet_
_Time: On Monday. You want to arrive at 16:00._

Group B
The participants should divide their inquiry in several utterances.
Example of scenario from which the user should formulate a request to the system:
_Place of departure: Hospitalkirka_
_Place of arrival: Fagerheim_
_Time: You want to leave after 13 o'clock._

Group C
The scenario consisted of a short narrative which should be the basis for the inquiry.
Example of scenario:
_You are working at Dragvoll and wish to go to a football match at Lerkendal. The game starts at 21:00 but you want to be there in due time to meet some old friends and enjoy the supporter band before the match._

---

Group D
The participant should alter parts of their original inquiry after receiving an answer from the dialog system.
Example of scenario:
*Formulate an inquiry that contains the following information:*
*Place of departure: Lade*
*Place of arrival: Saupstad*
*Time: Tomorrow, after 14:30*
*You are not satisfied with the answer and ask a question about a later bus.*

Group E
The participants were allowed to ask freely.
*You should freely formulate an inquiry about bus schedules in Trondheim. Beforehand, consider what information you seek. Remember that you can ask questions about only one bus schedule. You don't have to reveal all the information in your inquiry at once.*

## 3.2   Scenario information ordering

An investigation of the written task descriptions in the TWOZ experiment showed that except from Group E, and two occurrences in group C, all the information that the participants should use in their inquiry, were presented to the participants in the following order:

1) place of departure 2) place of arrival 3) time of travel.

## 3.3   Information categories

The language data obtained in the TWOZ experiment was then divided into four main information categories, based on semantic content that was regarded as vital information to the future dialog system.

   a.  Main category PLACE contains subcategories DEPARTURE and ARRIVAL.
   b.  Main category TIME contains subcategories EXACT TIME, PERIOD, INDICATION OF TIME.
   c.  Main category DAY contains subcategories D(AY)-SPECIFIC, D(AY)- RELATIVE and DAYS.
   d.  Main category BUS contains subcategories X(BUS), BUS NUMBER, X(BUS NUMBER)[2].

Category (a) contains references to places, usually names of bus stops[3]. Example of the two subcategories in (a) are given in the following.

*Jeg skal fra Fiolsvingen til Ugla.*
  "I am going [from Fiolsvingen] [to Ugla]."
      [DEPARTURE]     [ARRIVAL]

Category (b) includes phrases referring to the exact time of the day. These are labeled EXACT TIME. References to parts of the day, such as morning, evening, early or late are assembled in PERIOD. Temporal expressions like *as soon as possible* and *now* are gathered in subcategory INDICATION OF TIME. Category (c) contains phrases referring to days like *today* and *tomorrow*, labeled DAY RELATIVE. All seven proper names like *Monday, Tuesday,* etc. are in the subcategory DAY SPECIFIC. The use of the phrases *weekends* and *weekdays* are assembled in subcategory DAYS. Examples of the subcategories in (b) and (c) are given in the following.

*Jeg skal være på Lade halv ti på lørdag.*
  "I ought to be at Lade [half ten] [on Saturday]."
      [EXACT TIME][D-SPECIFIC].

*Når går første buss fra Ila i morgen tidlig?*
  "When does the first bus leave from Ila [tomorrow] [early]?"
  [D-RELATIVE][PERIOD].

*Jeg vil til Være så fort som mulig.*
  "I want to go to Være [as soon as possible]."

---

[2] The categories Bus number and X(Bus number) were not found in the TWOZ material, hence the examples are from the human-human dialogs.
[3] In this paper, the terms DEPARTURE and ARRIVAL are exclusively used for referring to localities.

---

[INDICATION OF TIME]

*Når går siste buss til Lade i helgene?*
"When does the last bus to Lade leave
[in weekends]?"
[DAYS]

Category (d) includes references to buses, i.e.
phrases like *first/last/next bus* or *bus number
four*, as in the following examples.

*Når går neste buss til Studenterhytta?*
"When does the [next bus] to
Studenterhytta leave?"
[X(BUS)]

*Jeg vil vite når 46eren går fra Tiller.*
"I want know when [the 46] leaves from
Tiller."
[BUS NUMBER]

*Jeg vil vite når neste 24 går fra Tunga.*
"I want know when [next 24] leaves
from Tunga."
[X(BUS NUMBER)]

The categories described above were then
plotted according to where they were located
in the opening sequence relative to the other
categories. The opening sequence equals the
subjects' first turn in the dialog.

We will not go into details about all the
subcategories in all the main groups since this
is not relevant for this paper. The investigation
was limited to the categories (a) and (d),
namely DEPARTURE, ARRIVAL and BUS. This
selection was based on Richards and
Underwood's claim that the distribution of
place of departure as the first piece of
information and place of arrival as the second
was so significant that is could be used to
enhance the performance of the system. The
category BUS is selected due to some
interesting patterns emerging when comparing
the TWOZ material with a corpus containing
106 human-human dialogs (abbrev. H-H).

## 4    The results

### 4.1    Dispersion of Departure-Arrival in the TWOZ experiment

The categories DEPARTURE and ARRIVAL are the
overall most frequently used categories in the
opening sequence, cf. Figure 1.

*Figure 1: Dispersion of departure-arrival in the
opening sequence in the TWOZ material.*

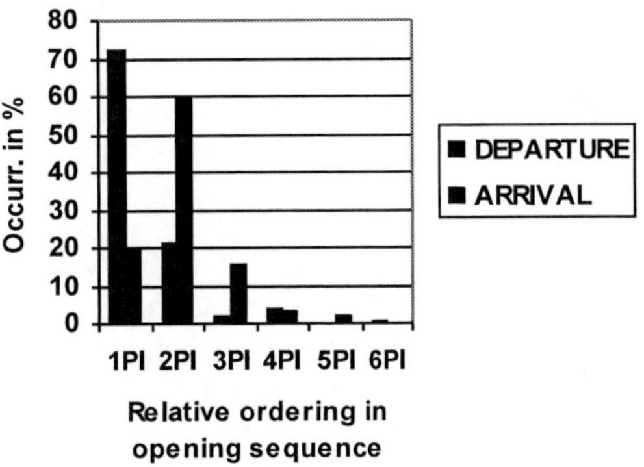


Figure 1 clearly shows that DEPARTURE is most
frequently used as the first piece of
information (abbrev. 1PI) with 72% of the
occurrences of DEPARTURE emerging in this
position. Only 21% of the occurrences of
category DEPARTURE occur as the second piece of
information (abbrev. 2PI). (The remaining 7%
are divided amongst the remaining positions in
the utterance.) As we can see, the difference
between DEPARTURE as the 1PI and the 2PI is
clearly significant.

Occurrences of the ARRIVAL, on the other
hand, emerge more frequently as the 2PI with
59% in contrast with 21% as the 1PI. (15% of
ARRIVAL is found as the 3PI.)

The picture rising from the TWOZ
experiment largely coincides with the findings
in Richards and Underwood (1985), and could
be taken as supportive evidence to their claim.
However, there is one important issue to be
noted. As mentioned in section 3.2, there is a
uniform ordering of the written task
descriptions given to the participants, and the
ordering of DEPARTURE and ARRIVAL illustrated in

---

Figure 1 coincides with the ordering of information categories found in the descriptions. In other words, the strong tendency for subcategory DEPARTURE to occur as the 1PI in the opening sequence may be due to influence from the written task description. The occurrences of ARRIVAL crowding together in the 2PI do also follow the pattern from the task description. Thus, the ordering of DEPARTURE and ARRIVAL might not be a result of human beings spontaneously presenting their inquiries about travels in a particular order, but might be due to influence from the written task descriptions.

## 4.2 Dispersion of Departure-Arrival in the human-human dialogs

A collection of H-H dialogs were recorded at the manual bus information service in Trondheim in 1996. This service is public available and the H-H dialogs consist of a randomly chosen sample of 106 phone calls. The callers did not get any instructions or information before their inquiries.

The observation described in 4.1 does not prove the hypothesis that written task descriptions influence the participants in a WOZ experiment, since the congruent tendency of ordering information in both the TWOZ experiment and Richards and Underwood's experiment (1985) can also be interpreted as a natural inclination for humans to structure these kinds of inquiries in a specific way. In order to test the above hypothesis, we compared the TWOZ material with the H-H dialogs to see if the same regularity in the information pattern was found here. If humans prefer to order their inquiry in a specific way when asking about traveling, we should expect the same pattern to emerge here as in the TWOZ experiment. Figure 2 shows the occurrences of DEPARTURE and ARRIVAL in the H-H dialogs.

*Figure 2: Distribution of Departure-Arrival in the opening sequence in the H-H dialogs.*

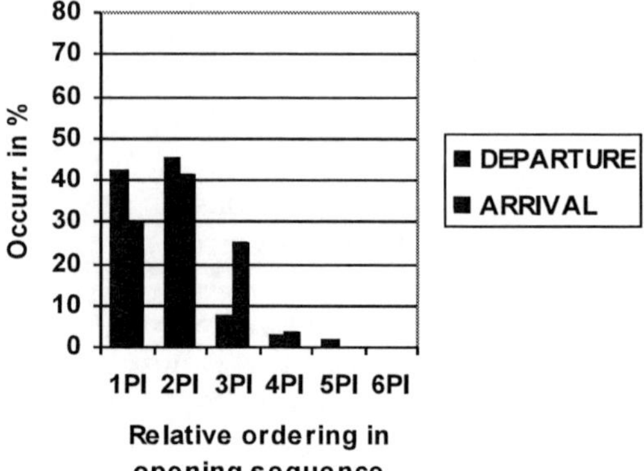


The categories DEPARTURE and ARRIVAL are still the overall most frequently used categories, but the data material shows a rather different distribution. DEPARTURE is now slightly more frequent as the 2PI (42% vs. 45%), and do not follow the pattern discovered in Figure 1 (72% vs. 21%). DEPARTURE is now actually more common than ARRIVAL both as the 1PI and the 2PI. ARRIVAL is still most frequently found as the 2PI compared to its occurrences in the 1PI, but the difference which was 38% in the TWOZ is now decreased to 11%. Both the TWOZ material and the H-H dialogs display a predominance of ARRIVAL as the 3PI. Figure 2 weakens the hypothesis that humans tend to follow a "pre-established" ordering when inquiring about time tables since the regularity in the H-H dialogs is not the same as shown in Figure 1. The findings in Figure 2 can also support the hypothesis that written task descriptions influence the inquiries made in a WOZ experiment. The callers in the H-H dialogs did not have any user instructions on how to conduct an inquiry, and this might have caused a greater diversity in the dispersion of the ordering of the information in these dialogs.

## 4.3 Frequency of information categories

In addition to investigate the dispersion of the categories DEPARTURE and ARRIVAL in the TWOZ and the H-H dialogs, we looked at the overall frequency of the various categories in the opening sequence. This investigation yielded some interesting insights particularly eye-

---

catching with respect to the category Bus. Figure 3 shows the overall frequency in opening sequence in the TWOZ material and H-H material.

_Figure 3: The overall frequency of information categories in the opening sequence in the TWOZ and the H-H dialogs._

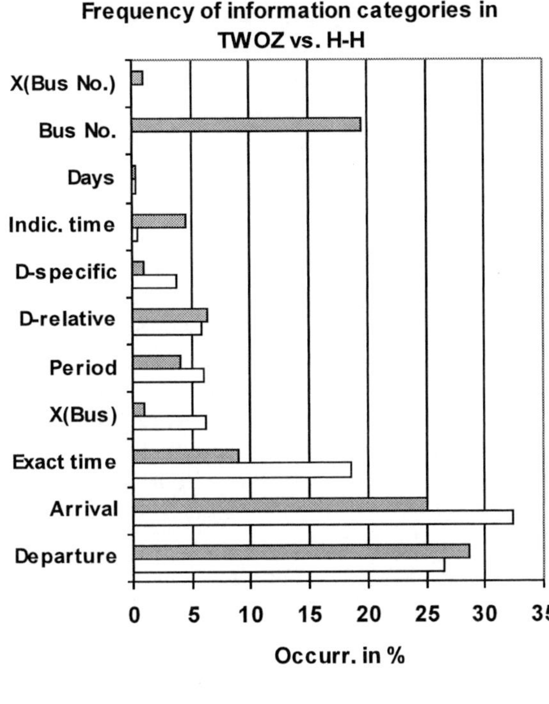


There is a noticeable difference in the use of the category EXACT TIME which is twice as common in the TWOZ material as in the H-H material. Questions about X(Bus) show a similar tendency. This category amounts to only 0.9% of the information categories in the H-H, while it is the forth most frequent category in the TWOZ material with 6.2%. DAY SPECIFIC is also more frequently used in the TWOZ material than in the H-H material. The opposite tendency is found in the categories INDICATION OF TIME, and BUS NUMBER/X(BUS NUMBER) which is more frequent in the H-H. The most eye-catching difference is use of the category BUS NUMBERS which is the third most frequent category in the H-H dialogs (almost as frequent as ARRIVAL) but <u>non-existing</u> in the TWOZ material. This striking difference is extremely

odd considering that the domain of both corpora is the very same bus schedules in Trondheim. If the use of BUS NUMBER is the third most frequently used category in the H-H dialogs, why are there zero occurrences in the TWOZ material? The difference can be explained if we again look at the written task description given to the participants. The possibility of using bus number as a strategy to obtain information was not described neither exemplified in any of the scenarios, and it is reasonable to claim that this is why the bus numbers are absent in the TWOZ dialogs[4].

The fact that occurrences of the category BUS NUMBER was so frequent in the H-H dialogs while never used in the opening sequence in the TWOZ dialogs sustains our claim that written task descriptions do influence participants in a WOZ experiment.

## 5   Rigid structure restricted to computer-oriented talk?

As mentioned in the introduction, people behave differently when interacting with a computer. Further investigation might show that people actually order their inquiries in a much more rigid and uniform manner when the interlocutor is a computer, but as long as we do not have any human-computer dialogs unaffected by written tasks descriptions, we cannot pin down the actual cause for the rigid order of information categories. In order to support or dismiss the hypothesis that written task descriptions can yield misleading data, one must perform another experiment without the ready-made scenarios given to the participants in forehand. Unfortunately, the results from the scenario in group E in the TWOZ experiment would not give us any pointer with regard to this matter because the participants first performed two inquiries that

---

[4] If we extend the investigation of the categories beyond the opening sequence, there are three occurrences of bus numbers in TWOZ material. They occur when the participants are unsatisfied with the answer from the dialog system, and utter for instance: "But what about bus number four? I know that this bus also arrives at..." This indicates that the possibility of using bus numbers is known to at least some of the participants. Still they do not use this strategy in the opening sequence.

were based on structured schemas. Not until their third call could the participants ask freely. Consequently, the participants conducted two inquiries based on Group A-D before carrying out the scenario described in Group E. As noted by Thomson (1980), users interacting with a computer tend to follow what she calls a "success strategy". This means that the users repeat the same type of request if they have experienced that this particular way of interacting with the computer functions well. It is plausible that the participants in the TWOZ experiment had already learned how to successfully communicate with the system when they performed their last and unrestricted inquiry. If so, the unrestricted dialogs would pattern with the restricted one due to the influence from the previously executed inquiries. As a matter of fact, the dialogs based on the unrestricted inquiry show exactly the same ordering of information, namely departure, arrival and time.

## 6   Conclusion

Our investigation of the Trondheim Wizard of Oz- experiment (TWOZ) agrees with the findings in Richards and Underwood (1985) in that people render their information request in a uniform and strict manner. However, we have questioned whether the ordering is actually a natural way of asking about time tables, or rather follows from written task descriptions given to the participants before the experiment. Both Richards and Underwood and the TWOZ experiment made use of such written task descriptions. An investigation of these task descriptions in the TWOZ experiment showed that the categories were presented in the same order in practically every scenario, and that this order was congruent with the order of the categories found in the opening sequence in the TWOZ dialogs.

A comparison with human-human dialogs that were not influenced by any written task descriptions, did not display the same striking distribution difference with regard to DEPARTURE as the first piece of information (1PI) and ARRIVAL as the second piece of information (2PI). This supports our suspicion that written task

descriptions may influence the result in a WOZ experiment.

The eye-catching difference in the use of bus numbers is also an argument for sustaining that written task descriptions do influence the results in a Wizard of Oz experiment. We found that occurrences of the category BUS NUMBER was the third most frequently used category in the human-human dialogs, while non-existing in the TWOZ material. An investigation of the written task description in the TWOZ experiment showed that the category BUS NUMBER were not presented as a possible strategy to obtain information about bus schedules.

Unfortunately, our data contains no examples of human-computer dialogs not influenced by any written task description. Further investigation is necessary to see whether the differences between the findings in the TWOZ and the H-H dialogs nevertheless can be explained by a tendency to perform the inquiry in a more structured way when interacting with a computer. To completely dismiss or confirm this hypothesis another experiment must be performed, but without the ready-made scenarios.

Based on our findings, it is questionable whether the pattern of information structure found in the TWOZ experiment, or other WOZ experiments based on similar written task descriptions, can be used as a reliable source for improvement of performance in a dialog system. A possible improvement of the written task descriptions avoiding some of the problems addressed in this paper would be to present the information in a more haphazard way.

Even though our findings are not devastating to Richards and Underwood's (1985) claim about a statistically significant regularity in the ordering of information, it makes it less plausible that this ordering will be prominent enough to be of considerable aid in enhancing the performance of a future dialog system.

In addition, our study raises some methodological issues in the use of WOZ experiments in dialog system development. If the participants are as influenced by the written task description as it might seem from our findings, the design of these written task

---

Brøseth: *Written task descriptions in Wizard of Oz experiments*

descriptions should be given much more consideration than previously acknowledged

## References


Tore Amble. 2000. BussTUC – a natural language bus route oracle. *ANLP-NAACL 2000- 6ᵗʰ Applied natural language conference*, Seattle. PDF-file: http://acl.ldc.upenn.edu/A/A00/A00-1001.pdf

Nils Dahlbäck, Arne Jönsson and Lars Ahrenberg. 1993. Wizard of Oz studies – why and how. *Proceedings of the 1ˢᵗ international conference on intelligent user interfaces*, 193-200. Orlando.

Magne H. Johnsen, Tore Amble and Erik Harborg. 2003. A Norwegian Spoken Dialog System for Bus Travel Information – Alternative Dialog Structures and Evaluation of a System Driven Version. *Teletronikk* 2:126-31.

Arne Jönsson and Nils Dahlbäck. 1988. Talking to a computer is not like talking to your best friend. *Proceedings in the First Scandinavian Conference on Artificial Intelligence*, 53-68, Tromsø.

M.A. Richards and K.M. Underwood. 1984. Talking to machines: how are people naturally inclined to speak. *Contemporary Ergonomics*, 62-7, (ed.) Megaw. Taylor&Francis, London.

M.A. Richards and K.M. Underwood. 1985. How should people and computers speak to each other?. *INTERACT'84*, 215-18, Elsevier Science Publisher, Amsterdam.

Bozena Henisz Thomson. 1980. Linguistic analysis of natural language communication with computers. *Proceedings of the 3ʳᵈ International Conference of Computational Linguistics*, Tokyo.

Robin Wooffitt, Norman M. Fraser, Nigel Gilbert and Scott McGlashan. 1997. *Humans, Computers and Wizards. Analysing human (simulated) computer interaction*. Routledge, London.

# Improving search engine retrieval using a compound splitter for Swedish


**Hercules Dalianis**
Department of Computer and System Sciences
KTH and Stockholm University
Forum 100, 164 40 Kista, Sweden
hercules@kth.se



## Abstract

In this paper we have investigated 128 high frequent Swedish compound queries (6.2 per thousand) with no search results among 1.6 million searches carried out at nine public web sites containing all together 100,000 web pages in Swedish. To these compound queries we added a compound splitter as a pre-processor and we found that after decompounding these queries they gave relevant results in 64 percent of the cases instead of zero percent hits. We give also examples on some rules for optimal compound splitting in a search situation.


## 1 Introduction

Today when searching on Internet it is very likely that you will find some answer, this is due to the immense amount of information that is present and the efficient global search engines. There is always some web pages that contains the answer of your question, but when searching on a web site the task is not so easy anymore, the reasons are manifold.

One obvious reason is that one website contains much fewer web pages than the whole Internet, but other not obvious reasons are that the search engine on the website is lousy, this means it is slow or does not work, the index does not cover the whole website, and the hits are not relevant. The user search and does not get any hits, but the information must be there! What is wrong? We will here concentrate on the processing of the query that the user has entered into the search engine.

## 2 Previous research

The first thing that can happen in a query situation is that the user enters a search query to the search engine and he does not get any hit. This can be one of the 10-12 percent of the queries that is misspelled and hence does not give any matching to the search engine index. (Dalianis 2002, Sarr 2003). This can be solved using a spelling support linked to the index of the search engine. When the user makes a spelling error the spelling correction module tries to match a word that has either similar spelling or pronunciation to one or more words in the index and consequently the user will get feedback in form of possible candidate word(s), (Dalianis 2002, Google 2002, Sarr 2003, Stolpe 2003).

Of course the search word can be correctly spelled and the error can be in the web site but never the less we want to help the user to find the answer and we will also propose misspelled words. According to Dalianis (2002) around 90 percent of the spelling errors are corrected using a spelling correction algorithm.

Other problems in searching is often that the user searches for a word and the word is written in an other inflected form, this is of course very common in cases when one uses languages that are morphologically complicated, (usually not English).

To solve the problem with word inflections one can use stemmers that will remove the inflections and make the words both in the search query and in the index stemmed and consequently able to match.

For Swedish, for example, precision and recall increased with 15 and 18 percent respectively using a stemmer, (Carlberger et al 2001). In Carlberger et al (2001) there is also an overview of different stemming experiments for European languages that show increase in precision and recall from 2-3 percent for English and up to 40 percent for Slovene, one can also read in Tomlinson (2003) that precision and recall increased immensely for European languages using stemming.

Two other methods to process queries are either compound splitting (decompounding) or compound joining. In Swedish for example we have a lot of compounds but we are heavily influenced by English written language and we tend to decompound Swedish words. This happens both in the situation when asking queries in search engines but also when writing text, therefore it is valuable to have a query analysis module that when obtaining sparse answers in a query situation tries to decompose the query word and consequently make a match possible. An other situation is when there are more than one search word and the user obtains no or sparse hits. Then the system should try different combinations in joining the words to compounds to obtain possible hits.

An example on the Swedish public medical website Vårdguiden, is when somebody is searching for *diabetespatient* and obtains no hits then the system tries to split the compound word to *diabetes patient* and the resulting hit become *patienter med diabetes* (patient with diabetes), notice that the stemmer will make it possible to automatically find the word *patienter* (plural form of patients). The other situation is that the user uses two search words *streptokock infektion* and does not obtain any hit then the system can propose the compound

*streptokockinfektioner (plural form)* that gives several relevant hits.

A compound splitter/decompounder was used in Tomlinson (2003) and this gave good results in increasing precision and recall for Finnish and German but decreased precision and recall for other languages, Spanish, Dutch, French, Italian, Swedish and English.

Stemming and compound splitting was used in Chen & Gey (2004) they obtained 14 percent higher precision for Dutch, 37 percent for German and 30 percent higher precision for Swedish and Finnish respectively. Rosell (2003) obtained 10 percent better clustering results using compound splitting for Swedish when clustering Swedish texts

## 3　Our study and method

We have studied nine Swedish public websites they encompass two municipalities, one university, one political party, a nature conservation site, a public authority site, a popular science site, and two insurance companies, these web sites ranges the size from 500 documents to 50 000 documents. They contain totally 100 000 documents and the search engines there obtained around 1.6 million queries of which 9.3 percent were misspelled.

The top 30 of the total 1.6 million queries with no answer at all, were 6 000 compounds, 128 different compounds. In total 3.7 per thousand of the number of total queries. On some specific web sites there were up to 2 percent of the total queries has no answers. (Another 600 were written decompounded and became compounds by putting them together).

We can also estimate from the findings of Dalianis (2002) that 40 percent of the misspelled words were compound related, this should give up to 4 percent of the total amount of the problematic queries are compound related. This gives something up to 60 000 queries of the total 1.6 million queries would benefit of a compound splitter. Karlgren (2005) writes that around 10 percent of all words in Swedish running text are compounds.

---

Dalianis: *Improving search engine retrieval*

We saw also that the two insurance company websites had a larger amount of compound queries in form of *studentförsäkring, skolförsäkring, garageförsäkring, villalarm, huslarm, hemlarm, bergvärme, luftvärmepump* (compounds with -insurance, -alarm, -heatpump) that does not give any hits without decomposition.

We connected the compound splitter described in (Sjöbergh & Kann 2004) to the search engine.

| Proper nouns | Ideal split (not carried out) |
|---|---|
| Östrasjukhuset | Östra sjukhuset |
| Gothiacup | Gothia cup |
| Gröntkort | Grönt kort |
| Idrottenshus | Idrottens hus |
| Välacentrum | Väla centrum |

| Nouns | Ideal split (not carried out) |
|---|---|
| fossilabränslen | fossila bränslen |
| fenomenografi | fenomeno grafi |
| läs-och skriv svårigheter | läs- och skriv svårigheter |

Table 2 and 3. The table shows five proper nouns and three nouns where the compound splitter failed.

| Compound | Oversplitting | Ideal split (not carried out) |
|---|---|---|
| Mullvad | mull vad | mullvad |
| Helsingborgsdagblad | Helsingborgs dag blad | Helsingborgs dagblad |
| bilbarnstol | bil barn stol | bil barnstol |
| uppsatsdatabas | Uppsats data bas | uppsats databas |
| missbruksbehandling | miss bruks behandling | missbruks behandling |
| missbruksvård | miss bruks vård | missbruks vård |
| arbetskraftinvandring | arbets kraft invandring | arbetskraft invandring |
| arbetskraftsinvandrare | arbets kraft s invandrare | arbetskraft s invandrare |
| ordningsvaktsutbildning | ordnings vakts utbildning | ordningsvakts utbildning |
| gruppliv | grupp liv | gruppliv |
| Nattliv | natt liv | nattliv |
| Visakort | Visa kort | Visakort |
| luftvärmepump | luft värme pump | luft värmepump |

Table 4. The table shows 13 compounds that became over split. All of the over split compounds have two parts shorter than 4 and 5 characters long respectively

We carried out compound splitting on each compound of the 128 compounds on each web site and it generated  in total 7 724 new hits. 64 percent of them relevant  to the query, 20 compounds were not splitted, over splitted  or incorrectly  splitted. That is 84 percent success rate of the compound splitter.

Of the 128 (100%) investigated compounds that none of the them obtained any hit at all first obtained hits after splitting them with a compound splitter and using the search engine on the split result again we found the following:

```
80  (64%)      relevant hits boosting the
                  search
                using compound splitting
29  (23%) gave us bad non relevant hits
+ 17  (13%)         gave us still no answers
Σ 128 (100%)
```

One method to obtain good hits when searching is to only allow a certain distance between the found decompounded parts of the original word. We would like to have some relations between the found words in the text. This can be carried out using the pseudo Boolean operator NEAR with say the parameter of 20 words distance.

How close to each other in the text should the splitted compound be to obtain relevant hits? We used the NEAR operator for counting number of words between the hits. The NEAR value could range from 1 to 70 words distance. Usually it was either around 1, 20 or 70 words distance. Average value 29 words distance.

## 4   Conclusions

Compound splitting as a post processing in a search engine works fine for Swedish, but one need a high quality compound splitter such that one does not get erroneous compound splitting that will deteriorate the precision of the search results. In other words bad compound splitting or over splitting will give us bad search results.

We have in our experiment seen that we obtained 64 percent more and relevant hits using the compound splitter described in (Sjöbergh & Kann 2004).

After our experiment we have also found that proper nouns need to be split in a smart and correct way. Nouns need to be split but not over split. We found also that a maximum of 29 words distance between the words in text in a compound splitting search gave relevant results. One clever strategy would then be that search hits using compound splitting should not stretch over sentence boundaries. 29 words can be considerd to be within one sentence distance.

Proper nouns need to be split in a smart and correct way. Nouns need to be split but not over split. One smart strategy is to split compounds at most two parts.

Hjelm and Schwarz (2005) that has been working with German compound splitting propose that The rightmost part of the compound part should be the longest. In Swedish we often use a genitive s in compounds. These "s" can be removed and the split boundary can be put there.

Some conclusions in rule form:

- Split compound in two parts
- Use genitive "s" as compound split marker and remove the "s"
- The rightmost should be the longest
- The compound split retrieval should be within one sentence, e.g. 29 words window.
- Treat Proper nouns specially.

## Acknowledgements

I would like to thank Jonas Sjöbergh and Viggo Kann at KOD KTH for letting me use their compound splitter. I would also like to thank Johan Carlberger at Euroling AB for letting me use the statistics from the SiteSeeker search engine.

## References

Carlberger, J., H. Dalianis, M. Hassel, O. Knutsson 2001. *Improving Precision in Information Retrieval for Swedish using Stemming*. In the Proceedings of NODALIDA 01 - 13th Nordic Conference on Computational Linguistics, May 21-22, Uppsala, Sweden.

Chen, A. and F. Gey. 2003. *Combining Query Translation and Document Translation in Cross Language Retrieval CLEF 2003*

http://clef.iei.pi.cnr.it/2003/WN_web/05.pdf

Cucerzan, S. and Eric Brill. 2004. *Spelling Correction as an Iterative Process that Exploits the Collective Knowledge of Web Users*. In the Proceedings of the 2004 Conference on Empirical Methods in Natural Language Processing, EMNLP 2004, pp. 293-300. http://acl.ldc.upenn.edu/acl2004/emnlp/pdf/Cucerzan.pdf

Dalianis, H. 2002. *Evaluating a Spelling Support in a Search Engine*, in Natural Language Processing and Information Systems, 6th International Conference on Applications of Natural Language to Information Systems, NLDB 2002 (Eds.) B. Andersson, M. Bergholtz, P. Johannesson, Stockholm, Sweden, June 27-28, 2002. Lecture Notes in Computer Science. Vol. 2553. pp. 183-190. Springer Verlag.

Google. 2002. Search Engine Showdown: Google press release http://www.searchengineshowdown.com/newsarchive/000611.shtml (Visited June 7, 2005).

Hjelm, H. and C. Schwarz: *LiSa - morphological analysis for information retrieval*. In the Proceedings of Nodalida 2005 - 15th Nordic Conference on Computational Linguistics, May 21-22, Joensuu, Finland

Karlgren, J 2005. *Occurrence of compound terms andtheir constituent elements in Swedish*, In the proceeding of Nodalida 2005 - 15th Nordic Conference on Computational Linguistics, May 21-22, Joensuu, Finland

Rosell, M, 2003. *Improving Clustering of Swedish Newspaper Articles using Stemming and Compound Splitting.* In the proceeding of Nodalida 2003, the 14th Nordic Conference of Computational Linguistics, Reykjavik, May 30-31, 2003.

Sarr, M. 2003. *Improving precision and recall using a spell checker in a search engine.* In the proceeding of Nodalida 2003, the 14th Nordic Conference of Computational Linguistics, Reykjavik, May 30-31, 2003.

Sjöbergh, J. and V. Kann 2004. *Finding the correct interpretation of Swedish compounds, a statistical approach*, Proc. LREC 2004 (4th Int. Conf. Language Resources and Evaluation), Lissabon, Portugal. http://www.nada.kth.se/theory/projects/xcheck/rapporter/sjoberghkann04.pdf

Stolpe, D. 2003. *Högre kvalitet med automatisk textbehandling? En utvärdering av SUNETs Webbkatalog*, Examensarbete i Datalogi på Kungliga Tekniska Högskolan 2003. (Master thesis in Swedish)

Tomlinson, S. 2003. *Experiments in 8 European Languages with Hummingbird SearchServer™ at CLEF 2002.* To appear in Carol Peters, Martin Braschler, Julio Gonzalo and Michael Kluck, editors, Evaluation of Cross-Language Information Retrieval Systems: Third Workshop of the Cross-Language Evaluation Forum, CLEF 2002, Rome, Italy, September 19-20, 2002. Revised Papers. To be published by Springer in their Lecture Notes for Computer Science (LNCS) series.

http://www.stephent.com/ir/papers/clef02.html

# Improbable morphological forms in a computational lexicon

**Kristin Hagen and Lars Nygaard**
The Text Laboratory, University of Oslo
http://www.hf.uio.no/tekstlab/
{kristin.hagen|lars.nygaard}@iln.uio.no

## Abstract

In the construction of a computational lexicon, one of the problems is how to handle cases where words have a partial morphological paradigm. In this paper we will describe this problem and sketch how we implemented a system for capturing the degree to which forms should be considered improbable. Also, we will describe how our results can be used in language applications.

## 1 Introduction

For semantic and morphological reasons some words are considered only to have a partial morphological paradigm. This can be abstracts like *kjærlighet* (love) or uncountable nouns like *melk* (milk) that only occur in singular. Or it can be adjectives like *entusiastisk* (enthusiastic) not inflected for degree because the adjective has five syllables.

For Norwegian, words with a partial morphological paradigm include:

- Nouns only used in singular. Most nouns have plural forms:

      stein → steiner
      (stone → stones)
      sang → sanger
      (song → songs)

  But not all:

      snø → *snøer
      (snow → *snows)
      musikk → *musikker
      (music → *musics)

- Adjectives not inflected for degree. Many adjectives have morphological comparative and superlative forms:

      pen → penere → penest
      (pretty → prettier → prettiest)
      god → bedre → best
      (good → better → best)

  But not all:

      abnorm → *abnormere → *abnormest
      (abnormal → *abnormaler → *abnormalest)
      spesiell → *spesiellere → *spesiellest)
      (special → *specialer → *specialest)

- Verbs not used attributively. Many verbs have attributive forms:

      en skrevet bok
      (a written book)
      et spist eple
      (an eaten apple)

  But not all:

      * en gått tur
      (* a walked walk)
      * et abonnert tidsskrift
      (* a subscribed magazine)

## 2 Partial paradigms in Norwegian dictionaries

In Norwegian dictionaries there is no information about whether an adjective can be inflected for degree or not. Grammars normally list some morphological criteria claiming that an adjective can not be inflected for degree if the adjective is too long, normally estimated as an adjective with three or more syllables. Adjectives with suffixes like *-ende, -et(e), -a,*
*-sk* and probably *-s* and *-en* also have a partial paradigm according to the rules.

For verbs, there is no systematic information about attributive use in the dictionaries, but *Bokmålsordboka* (Wangensteen, 2004) lists examples for some verbs in the definition part of the dictionary. For nouns, *Bokmålsordboka* has classified some nouns as singular nouns, but the classification is not complete.

For the computational lexicon the present authors use, *Norsk ordbank*, all words were originally given full paradigms.

## 3  Improbable, not impossible

The problem with many of these «extra» inflected forms is that they are not totally impossible, only *improbable* to a varying degree. When searching for an abstract like *musikk* on Google, *musikkene* is actually found more than twenty times. *Gåtte* is also frequently used according to Google, and *spesiellere* is used once:

> Men selv om de to *musikkene* har fellestrekk, er mye ulikt.
>
> (Though the two musics do have similarities, there are many differences.)
>
> Fikk dere vekttall per antall *gåtte* fotturer?
>
> (Were you awarded points per walked walk?)
>
> ... men det som er enda *spesiellere* i Gawadar er sjøen.
>
> (... but what is even specialer in Gawadar is the lake.)

## 4  Including improbable forms is problematic

To handle examples like *musikkene* and *gåtte*, improbable forms have to be present in a computational lexicon. Including the forms is, however, problematic as well:

- From a linguistic perspective because the representation does not reflect the typical usage

- From the perspective of computational linguistics and language technology because the extra forms introduce unnecessary ambiguity:

    - In analysis, the forms are homographs with other forms. Example: *gjelder* (improbable plural form for «debts»)

is homonymous with *gjelder* (verb, present tense of «be valid for» or «applies to»)

- In generation, the application will be presented with forms that are not idiomatic to use.

    > *Han er prinsipiellere enn jeg trodde
    >
    > (* He is fundamentalier than I thought)
    >
    > Han er mer prinsipiell enn jeg trodde
    >
    > (He is more fundamental than I thought)

When Norsk ordbank was going to be used in the LOGON machine translation project (Oepen et al., 2004), a project which uses deep linguistic knowledge for both analysis and generation, the need to identify the lemmas with partial morphological paradigms became more urgent.

## 5  A heuristic score

The main task was identifying lemmas with improbable forms. Additionally, we needed to store and use this information in a way that would give minimal ambiguity, while retaining full coverage.

We implemented a system for creating a heuristic score, attempting to capture the degree to which forms should be considered improbable. The score was based on frequencies in the Oslo Corpus of Tagged Norwegian texts (Johannessen et al., 2000). The Oslo Corpus is tagged with the Oslo-Bergen tagger (Hagen et al., 2000), a constraint grammar tagger where ambiguity is left if none of the constraints can disambiguate between two or more readings. In the Oslo Corpus this results in both ambiguous occurrences of word forms and unambiguous word forms. The formulas for nouns look like this:

For nouns with one or more occurrences in plural form:

$$\frac{P + Q}{Fk}$$

For nouns with zero occurrences in plural form:

$$(0 - F)m$$

$P$ is the total number of occurrences in plural form (both ambiguous and unambiguous), $Q$

is the number of unambiguous occurrences in plural form. $F$ is the total frequency, and $m$ and $k$ are weighting constants (we used $m = 2$ and $k = 100$).

A positive score indicates that a word has a full paradigm. A negative score indicates the opposite. The score also says something about the probability: A high negative score says that it is more unlikely that the noun can be used in plural than if the negative score is low.

Results are given in tables 1 and 2. The results are based on a medium-size corpus, where infrequent forms where penalized, since the score was likely to be less reliable: If there are two occurrences in singular and none in plural that is not necessarily an indication that the word only has a singular form.

We also found some problems with homonymy: *land* (a rare word for «urine from domestic animal») is clearly not a plural word, but since it is ambiguous with *land* (country), a frequent homonym in the corpus, it got a score indicating plural.

## 6   Improbable forms in Norsk ordbank

Instead of removing improbable forms from the lexical database Norsk ordbank, we will choose to flag them as improbable using the heuristic improbable-score. In this way, application developers can select what forms will be used. For example, a language generation application can choose not to include the improbable forms. For a tagger like the Oslo-Bergen-tagger, the forms can be included in the initial analysis, but removed later unless they are unambiguous.

In the Oslo-Bergen-tagger we mark the improbable words as <sjelden> (<rare>), and choose them as the correct reading only if the context is unambiguous.

In the following example *disse* in the meaning *huske* or *gynge* (swing) is marked as <rare>, but will still be disambiguated in a sentence like:

> Parken var en liten grønn plett med ei disse og ei sandkasse.

> (The park was a small green patch, with a swing and a sand pit.)

In some contexts it is hard for a tagger without semantic rules to disambiguate between the noun *disse* and the pronoun *disse*. When the noun *disse* is marked as <rare>, this reading can be deleted after the ordinary linguistic rules are applied:

> Ved behov kan disse allikevel kontaktes ved første anledning.

> (If need be, they can be contacted at the first opportunity.)

## 7   Further work

Although the initial results look promising, a full scale evaluation of the method remain. We plan to evaluate

- against a gold-standard set of hand annotated lemmas

- for application-specific tasks, including analysis and generation

## References

Kristin Hagen, Janne Bondi Johannessen, and Anders Nøklestad. 2000. A constraint-based tagger for norwegian. In *Proceedings of the 17th Scandinavian Conference of Linguistics*.

Janne Bondi Johannessen, Anders Nøklestad, and Kristin Hagen. 2000. A web-based advanced and user friendly system: The oslo corpus of tagged norwegian texts. In *Proceedings of the Second International Conference on Language Resources and Evaluation*.

Stephan Oepen, Helge Dyvik, Jan Tore Lønning, Erik Velldal, Dorothee Beermann, John Carroll, Dan Flickinger, Lars Hellan, Janne Bondi Johannessen, Paul Meurer, Torbjørn Nordgård, and Victoria Rosén. 2004. Som å kapp-ete med trollet? Towards MRS-based Norwegian-English Machine Translation. In *Proceedings of the 10th International Conference on Theoretical and Methodological Issues in Machine Translation*.

Boye Wangensteen. 2004. *Bokmålsordboka*. Universitetsforlaget.

| lemma | F | P | Q | score |
|---|---|---|---|---|
| norsk (norwegian) | 4598 | 0 | 0 | -9196 |
| død (death) | 3360 | 0 | 0 | -6720 |
| musikk (music) | 2934 | 0 | 0 | -5868 |
| politikk (politics) | 2825 | 0 | 0 | -5650 |
| forskning (research) | 2483 | 0 | 0 | -4966 |
| undervisning (teaching) | 1979 | 0 | 0 | -3958 |
| kaffe (coffee) | 1871 | 0 | 0 | -3742 |
| litteratur (literature) | 1418 | 0 | 0 | -2836 |
| folketrygd (social security) | 1316 | 0 | 0 | -2632 |
| bistand (aid) | 1234 | 0 | 0 | -2468 |
| snø (snow) | 1216 | 0 | 0 | -2432 |
| tillit (trust) | 1143 | 0 | 0 | -2286 |

Figure 1: Nouns least likely to have plural forms.

| lemma | F | P | Q | score |
|---|---|---|---|---|
| år (year) | 55928 | 44563 | 34462 | 3951179 |
| krone (crown) | 14396 | 13671 | 13671 | 1367005 |
| prosent (per cent) | 12801 | 12408 | 12025 | 1221554 |
| barn (children) | 20488 | 15114 | 7913 | 1151293 |
| folk (people) | 13445 | 11576 | 10342 | 1095818 |
| menneske (human being) | 14254 | 10322 | 10322 | 1032127 |
| forhold (relation) | 19407 | 14323 | 5014 | 966800 |
| million (million) | 10033 | 8981 | 8981 | 898010 |
| øye (eye) | 10509 | 8644 | 8644 | 864317 |
| kvinne (woman) | 14739 | 8283 | 8283 | 828243 |
| mann (man) | 20910 | 8462 | 6977 | 771913 |
| dag (day) | 37388 | 7100 | 7100 | 709981 |

Figure 2: Nouns most likely to have plural forms.

Hagen & Nygaard: *Improbable morphological forms in a computational lexicon*

# A generic architecture for data-driven dependency parsing

**Johan Hall and Joakim Nivre**

Växjö University
School of Mathematics and Systems Engineering
{jha,nivre}@msi.vxu.se

## Abstract

We present a software architecture for data-driven dependency parsing of unrestricted natural language text, which achieves a strict modularization of parsing algorithm, feature model and learning method such that these parameters can be varied independently. The design has been realized in MaltParser, which supports several parsing algorithms and learning methods, for which complex feature models can be defined in a special description language.

## 1 Introduction

One of the advantages of data-driven approaches to syntactic parsing is the relative ease with which they can be ported to new languages or domains, provided that the necessary linguistic data resources are available. Thus, the parser of Collins (1999), originally developed for English and trained on Wall Street Journal data, has been successfully applied to languages as different as Czech (Collins et al., 1999) and Chinese (Sun and Jurafsky, 2004). However, most available systems for data-driven syntactic parsing lack another kind of flexibility, namely the possibility to combine different parsing algorithms with different feature models and learning methods.

Data-driven dependency parsing has recently been explored as a robust and efficient method for syntactic parsing of unrestricted natural language text (Yamada and Matsumoto, 2003; Nivre et al., 2004). Dependency parsing means that the goal of the parsing process is to construct a dependency graph, of the kind depicted in Figure 1. The methodology is based on three essential components:

1. Deterministic parsing algorithms for building dependency graphs (Yamada and Matsumoto, 2003; Nivre, 2003)

2. History-based feature models for predicting the next parser action (Black et al., 1992)

3. Discriminative machine learning to map histories to parser actions (Yamada and Matsumoto, 2003; Nivre et al., 2004)

Given the restriction imposed by these components, we present a software design for data-driven dependency parsing of unrestricted natural language text. The most important feature of the design is a clean separation of parsing algorithms, feature models, and learning methods, so that these components can be varied independently of each other. Moreover, the design makes it possible to use the same basic components both for inducing a model from treebank data in the learning phase and for using the model to parse new data in the parsing phase. This architecture has been realized in the MaltParser system.[1]

This paper is structured as follows. Section 2 gives the necessary background and introduces the framework of *inductive dependency parsing* (Nivre, 2005). Section 3 presents the generic architecture for data-driven dependency parsing, and section 4 describes its realization in the MaltParser system. Finally, conclusions are presented in section 5.

## 2 Inductive dependency parsing

Given a set $R$ of dependency types, we define a *dependency graph* for a sentence $x = (w_1, \ldots, w_n)$ to be a labeled directed graph $G =$

---

[1]MaltParser is freely available for research and educational purposes and can be downloaded from http://www.vxu.se/msi/users/nivre/research/MaltParser.html.

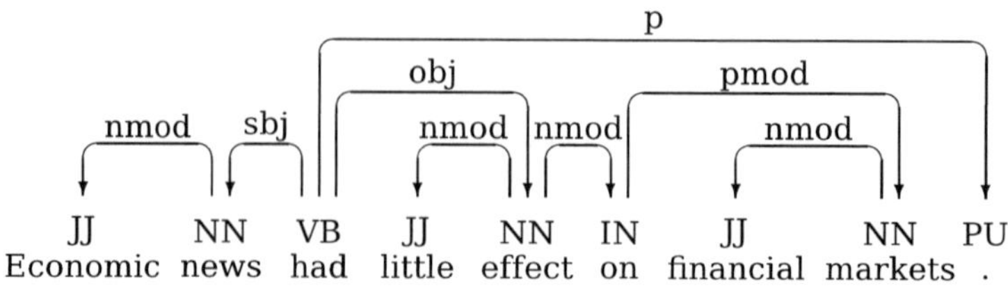

Figure 1: Dependency structure for English sentence

$(V, E, L)$, where $V$ is the set of input tokens $w_1, \ldots, w_n$, extended with a special root node $w_0$ and ordered by a linear precedence relation $<$; $E \subseteq V \times V$ is a set of directed arcs; and $L : E \to R$ is a function that labels arcs with dependency types. A dependency graph $G$ is *well-formed* iff (i) the node $w_0$ is a root of $G$, (ii) $G$ is connected, (iii) every node in $G$ has an indegree of at most 1, and (iv) $G$ is acyclic. Dependency parsing is the task of mapping sentences to well-formed dependency graphs.

Inductive approaches to natural language parsing can in general be defined in terms of three essential components:

1. A formal model $M$ defining permissible representations for sentences (such as the model of dependency graphs defined above).

2. A parameterized stochastic model $M_\Theta$, defining a score $S(x, y)$ for every sentence $x$ and well-formed representation $y$.

3. An inductive learning algorithm $L$ for estimating the parameters $\Theta$ from a representative sample $T_t = (x_1 : y_1, \ldots, x_n : y_n)$ of sentences with their correct representations (normally a treebank sample).

Inductive dependency parsing is compatible with a variety of different models, but we focus here on *history-based* models (Black et al., 1992; Magerman, 1995; Ratnaparkhi, 1997; Collins, 1999), which can be defined in three steps:

1. Define a one-to-one mapping between syntactic representations $y$ and decision sequences $D = (d_1, \ldots, d_m)$ such that $D$ uniquely determines $y$.

2. Define the score $S(x, y)$, for every sentence $x$ and representation $y$, in terms of

each decision $d_i$ in the decision sequence $D = (d_1, \ldots, d_m)$, conditioned on the history $H = (d_1, \ldots, d_{i-1})$.

3. Define a function $\Phi$ that groups histories into equivalence classes, thereby reducing the number of parameters in $\Theta$.

In a conditional history-based model, the score $S(x, y)$ defined by the model is the conditional probability $P(y \mid x)$ of the analysis $y$ given the sentence $x$, which means that the input sentence is a conditioning variable for each decision in the decision sequence:

$$P(y \mid x) = P(d_1, \ldots, d_m \mid x) =$$
$$\prod_{i=1}^{m} P(d_i \mid \Phi(d_1, \ldots, d_{i-1}, x))$$

The parameters of this model are the conditional probabilities $P(d \mid \Phi(H, x))$, for all possible decisions $d$ and non-equivalent conditions $\Phi(H, x)$.

Given a conditional history-based model, the conditional probability $P(y_j \mid x)$ of analysis $y_j$ given input $x$ can be used to rank a set of alternative analyses $\{y_1, \ldots, y_k\}$ of the input sentence $x$, derived by a nondeterministic parser. If the model allows a complete search of the analysis space, we can in this way be sure to find the analysis $y_j$ that maximizes the probability $P(y_j \mid x)$ according to the model:

$$\arg\max_{j} P(y_j \mid x) =$$
$$\arg\max_{j} \prod_{i=1}^{m} P(d_i \mid \Phi(d_1, \ldots, d_{i-1}, x))$$

With a deterministic parsing strategy, we instead try to find the most probable analysis $y_j$ without exploring more than one decision sequence, based on the following approximation:

$$\max_{j} P(y_j \mid x) \approx$$

---

Hall & Nivre: *A generic architecture for data-driven dependency parsing*

$$\prod_{i=1}^{m} \max_{i} P(d_i \mid \Phi(d_1, \ldots, d_{i-1}, x))$$

A deterministic parsing strategy is in this context a *greedy algorithm*, making a locally optimal choice in the hope that this choice will lead to a globally optimal solution (Cormen et al., 1990). The main problem with the greedy strategy is that it may not lead to a globally optimal solution. The main advantage of the greedy strategy is that it improves parsing efficiency by avoiding an exhaustive search of the analysis space, but an additional advantage is that it reduces the effective number of parameters of the stochastic model, since only the mode of the distribution $P(d_i \mid \Phi(H, x))$ needs to be estimated for each distinct condition $\Phi(H, x)$. This also means that a larger class of learning methods can be used, including purely discriminative methods.

With a discriminative learning method we can reduce the learning problem to a pure classification problem, where an *input instance* is a parameterized history $\Phi(H, x)$, which is represented by a feature vector, and an *output class* is a decision $d$. Using a supervised learning method, our task is then to induce a classifier $C$ given a set of training instances $T$, derived from a treebank sample, where $O$ is an oracle function that predicts the correct decision given the gold standard treebank:

$$T = \{(\Phi(H, x), d) \mid O(H, x) = d, x \in T_t\}$$

In order to construct a specific instance of the inductive dependency parser, we therefore need to specify three things:

1. A deterministic *parsing algorithm* used to derive dependency graphs, which defines the set $\mathcal{D}$ of permissible decisions, as well as the oracle function $O$ that determines the correct decision given a certain history $H$ and input sentence $x$.

2. A parameterization function $\Phi$ used to define equivalence classes of histories and sentences in terms of a feature vector $\Phi_{(1,p)} = (\phi_1, \ldots, \phi_p)$, where each feature $\phi_i$ is a function that maps a token to its part-of-speech, lexical form or dependency type (in the partially built dependency graph). We call $\Phi_{(1,p)}$ a *feature model*.

3. A discriminative *learning algorithm* used to approximate the mode function

$f(\Phi(H, x)) = \arg\max_d P(d \mid \Phi(H, x))$ given a set $T$ of training instances.

We will now turn to the description of an architecture that allows the user to construct such an instance in an efficient and flexible manner, given a suitable sample of a dependency treebank.

## 3  A generic architecture

We propose an architecture with a strict modularization of parsing algorithms, feature models and learning methods, thereby giving maximum flexibility in the way these components can be varied independently of each other. The architecture can be seen as a data-driven parser-generator framework, which constructs a parser without rebuilding the framework given a treebank and a specified parsing algorithm, feature model, learning method. The idea is to give the user the flexibility to experiment with the components in a more convenient way, although there are still dependencies between components, in the sense that not all combinations will perform well with respect to accuracy and efficiency.

The design of the architecture deals also with the fact that the parser can be executed in two different phases: *the learning phase* and *the parsing phase*. In the learning phase, the system uses a treebank to learn a model; in the parsing phase, it takes a previously learnt model and uses this to parse new and unseen data. Although these two tasks have a different structure, they often involve similar or even identical subproblems. For instance, learning normally requires the construction of a gold standard parse derivation in order to estimate the parameters of a model, which is exactly the same kind of derivation that is constructed during parsing.

The architecture consists of three main components:

1. Parser, which derives the dependency graph for a sentence (during both learning and parsing) using a deterministic parsing algorithm.

2. Guide, which extracts feature vectors from the current state of the system (according to the specified model) and passes data between the Parser and the Learner.

---

Hall & Nivre: *A generic architecture for data-driven dependency parsing*

3. Learner, which is responsible for inducing a model during learning time and for using this model to guide the Parser to make decisions at all nondeterministic choice points during the parsing phase.

In addition to the three main components the framework includes input/output components and an overall control structure. These components are responsible for reading a text $S = (x_1, \ldots, x_n)$ and invoking the Parser for each sentence $x_i \in S$. When the Parser has constructed the dependency graph $G_i$, the dependency graph should be outputted in a suitable format. The next three subsections describe the main components in more detail.

## 3.1  Parser

The Parser is responsible for the derivation of a well-formed dependency graph $G_i$ for a sentence $x = w_1, \ldots, w_n$, given a set $R = \{r_0, r_1, \ldots, r_m\}$ of dependency types ($r_0$ is a special symbol for dependents of the root). To perform this derivation we need a parsing algorithm that can map a dependency graph into a sequence of decisions $D = (d_1, \ldots, d_m)$ during learning time by using the gold standard. Each decision will be passed on to the Guide as an example of a correct decision. During parsing time the parsing algorithm constructs a dependency graph by asking the Guide for each nondeterministic decision $d_i$. During both learning and parsing time, the *parser configuration* will be updated according to the decision. We can define a *parser configuration* for $x$ as a sextuple $c = (\sigma, \tau, \upsilon, p, h, l)$, where:

1. $\sigma$ is a stack of partially processed tokens.

2. $\tau$ is a list of remaining input tokens.

3. $\upsilon$ is a stack of unattached tokens occurring between the token on top of the stack $\sigma$ and the next input token, called the context stack.

4. $p$ is the part-of-speech function, where $p(w_i)$ is the part-of-speech of the token $i$.

5. $h$ is the head function defining the partially built dependency structure, where $h(w_i)$ is the syntactic head of the token $i$ (with $h(w_i) = 0$ if $i$ is not yet attached to a head). $h_g$ is the gold standard head function, where $h_g(w_i)$ is the syntactic head of the token $i$, taken from a treebank.

6. $l$ is the dependency function labeling the partially built dependency structure, where $l(w_i)$ is the dependency type $r_i$ linking the token $i$ to its syntactic head (with $l(w_i) = r_0$ if $i$ is not yet attached to a head). $l_g$ is the gold standard dependency function, where $l_g(w_i)$ is the dependency type labeling the token $i$ to its syntactic head, taken from a treebank.

Moreover, one of the main ideas of the Parser component is that it should be capable of incorporating several parsing algorithms, which allow the user of the system to choose a suitable algorithm for a specific purpose. Not all parsing algorithms are of course applicable for this architecture and therefore we need to define the restrictions that the parsing algorithm must fulfil:

1. It must be able to operate the configuration $c = (\sigma, \tau, \upsilon, p, h, l)$ of the form defined above for each sentence $x$.

2. It must only assign a dependency relation between the token on top of the stack $\sigma$ and the next input token in the list $\tau$.

3. It must be deterministic, in the sense that it always derives a single analysis for each sentence $x$. However, the algorithm can be nondeterministic in its individual choice points such as adding a dependency arc between two tokens or shifting a new token onto its stack. This implies that the algorithm must be able to break down the parsing problem into a sequence of decisions $D$. However, not all decisions have to be nondeterministic, for example when the stack $\sigma$ is empty we can only shift the next token on to the stack.

4. It must be capable to make a gold standard parse given a training corpus $T_t = \{x_1, \ldots, x_n\}$ in the learning phase. In this way, the algorithm derives the correct decision in all nondeterministic choice points using an oracle function. This function defines the mapping between the dependency graph $G_i$ and the decision sequences $D = (d_1, \ldots, d_m)$ such that $D$ uniquely determines the dependency graph $G_i$.

5. It must define a set $\mathcal{D}_c$ of permissible decisions for each configuration $c$ and check

---

Hall & Nivre: *A generic architecture for data-driven dependency parsing*

that it does not perform an illegal decision. For example, if the stack $\sigma$ is empty then it is not possible to pop the stack. To comply with the requirement of robustness, it must therefore provide a default decision according to the current state of the system if an illegal decision is proposed by the guide.

## 3.2 Guide

The Guide is responsible for constructing a set of training instances $T$ for the Learner during the learning phase, and for passing the Learner's predictions to the Parser during the parsing phase.

At learning time, the Guide constructs one training instance $\Phi((H, x), d)$ for each decision $d_i$ passed from the Parser, where $\Phi(H, x)$ is the current vector of feature values (given the parameterization function $\Phi$ and the current state of the system), and passes this on to the Learner. At parsing time, the Guide constructs a feature vector $\Phi(H, x)$ for each request from the Parser, sends it to the Learner and passes on the predicted decision $d$ from the Learner to the Parser. In this way, the feature model is completely separated from the Parser, and the Learner only has to learn a mapping from feature vectors to decisions, without knowing either how the features are extracted or how the decisions are to be used. Moreover, the feature extraction is performed in exactly the same way during both learning and parsing.

The feature extraction uses the parameterization function $\Phi$, which is defined in terms of a feature vector $\Phi_{(1,p)}$, where each feature $\phi_i$ is a function, defined in terms of three simpler functions: an *address function* $a_{\phi_i}$, which identifies a specific token in a given parser configuration, an *attribute function* $f_{\phi_i}$, which picks out a specific attribute of the token, and a *mapping function* $m_{\phi_i}$, which defines equivalence classes of attribute values.

1. For every $i$, $i \geq 0$, $\sigma[i]$, $\tau[i]$ and $\upsilon[i]$ are address functions identifying the $i+1$th token from the top of the stack $\sigma$, the start of the input list $\tau$, and the top of the stack $\upsilon$, respectively. (Hence, $\sigma[0]$ is the top of the stack, $\tau[0]$ is the next input token and $\upsilon[0]$ is the top of the context stack.)

2. If $\alpha$ is an address function, then $h(\alpha)$, $lc(\alpha)$, $rc(\alpha)$, $ls(\alpha)$ and $rs(\alpha)$ are address func-

tions, identifying the head ($h$), the leftmost child ($lc$), the rightmost child ($rc$), the next left sibling ($ls$) and the next right sibling ($rs$), respectively, of the token identified by $\alpha$ (according to the partially built dependency graph $G_i$).

3. If $\alpha$ is an address function, then $p(\alpha)$, $w(\alpha)$ and $l(\alpha)$ are feature functions, identifying the part-of-speech ($p$), word form ($w$) and dependency type ($l$) of the token identified by $\alpha$ (where the dependency type, if any, is given by the partially built dependency graph $G_i$). We call $p$, $w$ and $l$ attribute functions.

Given a feature function $\beta$, we can also define a mapping function that maps each value of $\beta$ to a new value. For example, a mapping function can be used to restrict the value of a lexical feature ($w(\alpha)$) to the last $n$ characters of the word form.

Given this parameterization function $\Phi$, the Guide will extract a parser state $s_i = (v_1, \ldots, v_p)$ and passes this to the learner, where the $v_j$ is extracted value for the corresponding feature $\phi_j$. During learning it also provide the decision $d_i$ , or request the $d_i$ during parsing.

## 3.3 Learner

The Learner, finally, is responsible for inducing a classifier $g$ from the set of training instances $T$ by using a learning algorithm $L$. The *learned function* $g$ is an approximation of the true oracle $O$. The set of possible decisions is discrete and finite, and therefore we can view this as *classification* problem. The classifier $g$ is used to predict parser decisions given a parser state during the parsing phase. In practice, the Learner will normally be an interface to a standard machine learning package.

## 3.4 The learning and parsing phase

To conclude this section we will summarize the architecture by illustrating the data flow during the learning and parsing phase.

Figure 2 shows the architecture during the learning phase. The Parser takes as input a list of input tokens $\tau$ and the gold standard functions $(h_g, l_g)$. For each nondeterministic decision the Parser use the oracle function $O$ to derive the correct decision $d_{i+1}$ and updates the configuration according to $d_{i+1}$, which results in the next configuration $c_{i+1}$. The Guide takes

---

Hall & Nivre: *A generic architecture for data-driven dependency parsing*

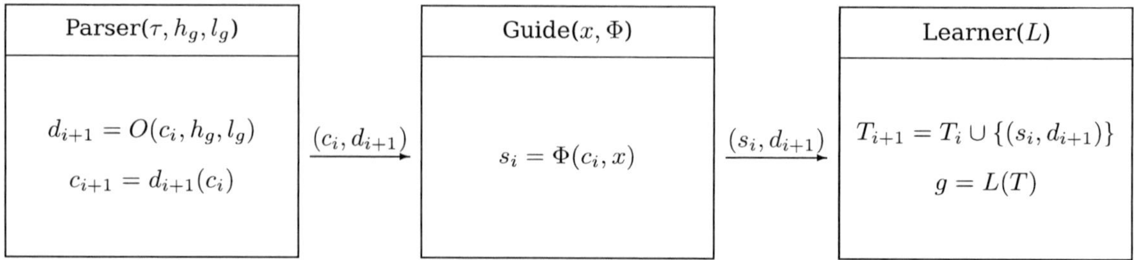

Figure 2: The data flow in the architecture during the learning phase.

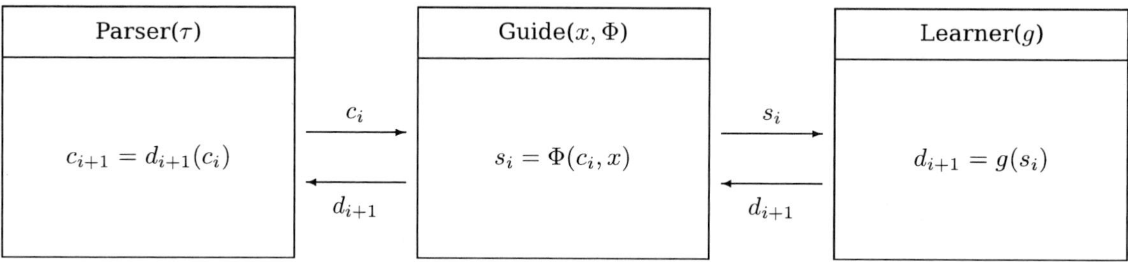

Figure 3: The data flow in the architecture during the parsing phase.

| Genom | pp | 3 | ADV |
| skattereformen | nn.utr.sin.def.nom | 1 | PR |
| införs | vb.prs.sfo | 0 | ROOT |
| individuell | jj.pos.utr.sin.ind.nom | 5 | ATT |
| beskattning | nn.utr.sin.ind.nom | 3 | SUB |
| ( | pad | 5 | IP |
| särbeskattning | nn.utr.sin.ind.nom | 5 | APP |
| ) | pad | 5 | IP |
| av | pp | 5 | ATT |
| arbetsinkomster | nn.utr.plu.ind.nom | 9 | PR |
| . | mad | 3 | IP |

Figure 4: An example sentence taken from the Swedish treebank Talbanken (Einarsson, 1976) in the Malt-TAB format. The first column is the word from, followed by the part-of-speech, the syntactic head and the dependency relation to the head (in that order).

as input a feature model $\Phi$, and a sentence $x_i$. For each nondeterministic decision, the Guide uses the feature model $\Phi$ to extract the parser state $s_i$. Finally, the Learner collects the instance $(s_i, d_{i+1})$ passed from the Guide in the training set $T$. When all training instances are collected the learning algorithm $L$ is applied to induce a classifier $g$.

The architecture during the parsing phase is shown in figure 3. The Parser takes as input a list of input tokens $\tau$. For each nondeterministic decision the Parser requests a prediction of the next decision from the Guide and updates the configuration according to $d_{i+1}$, which results in the next configuration $c_{i+1}$. The Guide acts as a middle layer between the Parser and the Learner by extracting the parser state $s_i = \Phi(c_i, x)$ in the same way as in the learning phase and passing $d_{i+1}$ from Learner to the Parser. The Learner uses the induced classifier $g$ to predict the decision $d_{i+1}$.

# 4  Implementation

The architecture described in section 3 has been realized in the MaltParser system, which can be applied to a labeled dependency treebank in order to induce a labeled dependency parser for the language represented by the treebank.

The system takes as input a file in the Malt-TAB format, there each token is represented on one line, with attribute values being separated by tabs and each sentence separated by a blank line. Figure 4 shows an example of the Malt-TAB format. During the learning phase the parser requires all four columns, but during parsing it only needs the first two columns, i.e. the word form and the part-of-speech. The output of the MaltParser system is a sequence of labeled dependency graphs in the Malt-TAB format or the Malt-XML format. The latter is an XML version of the Malt-TAB format.

In the sections below, we describe the main components in the architecture from the point of view of how they are implemented in the MaltParser system.

## 4.1  Parser

The user of MaltParser can choose between several deterministic parsing algorithms, including the algorithms described by Nivre (2003; 2004) and the incremental parsing algorithms described by Covington (2001).

Nivre's algorithm is a linear-time algorithm limited to projective dependency structures. It can be run in *arc-eager* or *arc-standard* mode (cf. (Nivre, 2004)).

Covington's algorithm is a quadratic-time algorithm for unrestricted dependency structures, which proceeds by trying to link each new token to each preceding token. It can be run in a *projective* mode, where the linking operation is restricted to projective dependency structures, or in a *non-projective* mode, allowing non-projective (but acyclic) dependency structures.

## 4.2  Guide

The MaltParser system comes with a formal specification language for feature functions, which enables the user to define arbitrarily complex feature models in terms of address functions, attribute functions and mapping functions (cf. section 3.2). Each feature model is defined in a *feature specification* file, which allows users to define feature models without rebuilding the system. The feature specification uses the syntax described in Figure 5. Each feature is specified on a single line, consisting of at least two tab-separated columns. Below follows a description of each column:

1. Defines the feature type to be part-of-speech (POS), dependency (DEP) or word form (LEX), corresponding to the attribute functions $p$, $l$ and $w$ in section 3.

2. Identifies one of the main data structures in the parser configuration: STACK (corresponding to $\sigma$), INPUT (corresponding to $\tau$ or CONTEXT (corresponds to $v$). The third alternative, CONTEXT, is relevant only together with Covington's algorithm in non-projective mode.

3. Defines a list offset $i$ which can only be positive and which identifies the $i+1$th token in the list/stack specified in the second column (i.e. $\sigma[i]$, $\tau[i]$ or $v[i]$).

4. Defines a linear offset $i$, which can be positive (forward/right) or negative (backward/left) and which refers to (relative) token positions in the original input string.

5. Defines an offset $i$ in terms of the function $h$ (head), which has to be non-negative and

```
<fspec>   ::= <feat>+
<feat>    ::= <lfeat>|<nlfeat>
<lfeat>   ::= LEX\t<dstruc>\t<off>\t<suff>\n
<nlfeat>  ::= (POS|DEP)\t<dstruc>\t<off>\n
<dstruc>  ::= (STACK|INPUT|CONTEXT)
<off>     ::= <nnint>\t<int>\t<nnint>\t<int>\t<int>
<suff>    ::= <nnint>
<int>     ::= (...|-2|-1|0|1|2|...)
<nnint>   ::= (0|1|2|...)
```

Figure 5: The syntax for defining a feature model in an external feature specification.

which specifies $i$ applications of the $h$ function to the token identified through preceding offsets.

6. Defines an offset $i$ in terms of the functions $lc$ (the leftmost child) or $rc$ (the rightmost child), which can be negative ($|i|$ applications of $lc$), positive ($i$ applications of $rc$), or zero (no applications).

7. Defines an offset $i$ in terms of the functions $ls$ (the next left sibling) or $rs$ (the next right sibling), which can be negative ($|i|$ applications of $ls$), positive ($i$ applications of $rs$), or zero (no applications).

8. If the first column specifies the attribute function $w$ (LEX), the eighth column, defines a mapping function which specifies a suffix of length $n$ of the word form $w$. By convention, if n = 0, the entire word form is included; otherwise only the n last characters are included in the feature value.

As syntactic sugar, any feature definition can be truncated if all remaining integer values are zero. Let us consider an example:

```
POS INPUT
DEP STACK 0 0 1
LEX INPUT 1
```

The first feature is the part-of-speech of the token located first in the list $\tau$ of remaining input tokens, i.e. $p(\tau[0])$. The feature defined on the second line is the dependency type of the head of the token located at the top of the stack $\sigma$ (zero steps down the stack, zero steps forward/backward in the input string, one step up to the head), i.e. $l(h(\sigma[0]))$. Finally, the third feature is the word form of the token immediately after the next input token, i.e. $w(\tau[1])$.

When the Guide extracts the features according to the specification, it stores the feature values in a dedicated data structure. The Learner later iterates through this data structure in a linear fashion and outputs each feature in the format by a specific machine learning package.

### 4.3  Learner

In the current implementation this component is actually a set of interfaces to machine learning packages. The interfaces prepare the set of training instances, provided by the Guide, for the specific package and invoke the appropriate functions to learn a model or predict a decision. MaltParser comes with two different learning algorithms: Memory-based learning and Support Vector Machines (SVMs), each with a wide variety of parameters.

Memory-based learning and classification is based on the assumption that a cognitive learning task to a high degree depends on direct experience and memory, rather than extraction of an abstract representation. Solving new problems is achieved by reusing solutions from similar previously solved problems (Daelemans et al., 1999). During learning time, all training instances are stored and at parsing time a variant of $k$-nearest neighbor classification is used to predict the next action. MaltParser uses the software package TiMBL (Tilburg Memory-Based Learner) (Daelemans and Van den Bosch, 2005) to implement this learning algorithm, and supports all the options provided by that package.

Support Vector Machines (SVMs) was formulated in the late seventies by Vapnik (1979), but the main development as a machine learning approach has taken place in the last decade. SVMs have been used for many pattern recognition problems. In the field of natural language

Hall & Nivre: *A generic architecture for data-driven dependency parsing*

processing, SVMs have been used for example for text categorization (Joachims, 1998) and syntactic dependency parsing (Kudo and Matsumoto, 2000). SVMs rely on kernel functions to induce a maximum-margin hyperplane classifier at learning time, which can be used to predict the next action at parsing time. MaltParser uses the library LIBSVM (Wu et al., 2004) to implement this algorithm with all the options provided by this library.

## 5  Conclusion

We have presented a generic architecture for data-driven dependency parsing that provides a strict modularization of parsing algorithm, feature model and learning method. The main advantage of this design is that these three dimensions can be varied independently of each other, but the design also enables the reuse of components between the learning and the parsing phase. The design has been implemented in the MaltParser system, which is freely available for research and educational purposes, and which supports several parsing algorithms and learning methods, as well as a specification language for feature models that lets the user specify complex combinations of different types of features.

## References

E. Black, F. Jelinek, J. Lafferty, D. Magerman, R. Mercer, and S Roukos. 1992. Towards history-based grammars: Using richer models for probabilistic parsing. In *Proceedings of the 5th DARPA Speech and Natural Language Workshop*, pages 31–37.

Michael Collins, Jan Hajič, Lance Ramshaw, and Christoph Tillmann. 1999. A statistical parser for Czech. In *Proceedings of the 37th Annual Meeting of the Association for Computational Linguistics*, pages 505–512.

Michael Collins. 1999. *Head-Driven Statistical Models for Natural Language Parsing*. Ph.D. thesis, University of Pennsylvania.

Thomas H. Cormen, Charles E. Leiserson, and Ronald L. Rivest. 1990. *Introduction to Algorithms*. MIT Press.

Michael A. Covington. 2001. A fundamental algorithm for dependency parsing. In *Proceedings of the 39th Annual ACM Southeast Conference*, pages 95–102.

Walter Daelemans and Antal Van den Bosch. 2005. *Memory-Based Language Processing*. Cambridge University Press.

Walter Daelemans, Antal van den Bosch, and Jakub Zavrel. 1999. Forgetting exceptions is harmful in language learning. *Machine Learning*, 34(1-3):11–41.

Jan Einarsson. 1976. *Talbankens skriftspråkskonkordans*. Lund University, Department of Scandinavian Languages.

T. Joachims. 1998. Text categorization with support vector machines. In *Proceedings of the 10th European Conference on Machine Learning (ECML'98)*, pages 137–142.

Taku Kudo and Yuji Matsumoto. 2000. Japanese Dependency Structure Analysis Based on Support Vector Machines. In *Empirical Methods in Natural Language Processing and Very Large Corpora*, pages 18–25.

D. M. Magerman. 1995. Statistical decision-tree models for parsing. In *Proceedings of the 33rd Annual Meeting of the Association for Computational Linguistics (ACL)*, pages 276–283.

Joakim Nivre, Johan Hall, and Jens Nilsson. 2004. Memory-based dependency parsing. In Hwee Tou Ng and Ellen Riloff, editors, *Proceedings of the 8th Conference on Computational Natural Language Learning (CoNLL)*, pages 49–56.

Joakim Nivre. 2003. An efficient algorithm for projective dependency parsing. In Gertjan van Noord, editor, *Proceedings of the 8th International Workshop on Parsing Technologies (IWPT)*, pages 149–160.

Joakim Nivre. 2004. Incrementality in deterministic dependency parsing. In Frank Keller, Stephen Clark, Matthew Crocker, and Mark Steedman, editors, *Proceedings of the Workshop in Incremental Parsing: Bringing Engineering and Cognition Together (ACL)*, pages 50–57.

Joakim Nivre. 2005. *Inductive Dependency Parsing of Natural Language Text*. Ph.D. thesis, Växjö University.

Adwait Ratnaparkhi. 1997. A linear observed time statistical parser based on maximum entropy models. In *Proceedings of the Second Conference on Empirical Methods in Natural Language Processing (EMNLP)*, pages 1–10.

Honglin Sun and Daniel Jurafsky. 2004. Shallow semantic parsing of Chinese. In *Proceedings of the Human Technology Conference of the North American Chapter of the Association for Computational Linguistics (HLT-NAACL)*, pages 249–256.

V. Vapnik. 1979. Estimation of dependences based on empirical data. Technical report, Nauka, Moscow.

T.-F. Wu, C.-J. Lin, and R. C. Weng. 2004. Probability estimates for multi-class classification by pairwise coupling. *Journal of Machine Learning Research*, 5:975–1005.

Hiroyasu Yamada and Yuji Matsumoto. 2003. Statistical dependency analysis with support vector machines. In Gertjan van Noord, editor, *Proceedings of the 8th International Workshop on Parsing Technologies (IWPT)*, pages 195–206.

# The 'Specifier' in an HPSG grammar implementation of Norwegian

**Lars Hellan** and **Dorothee Beermann**
NTNU,Trondheim, Norway
{lars.hellan,dorothee.beermann}@hf.ntnu.no

## Abstract

We present a principled background for the adoption of a category 'Specifier' in the analysis of noun phrases, and show how, under certain constraining assumptions, it can be successfully employed in the implementation of an HPSG grammar of noun phrases for Norwegian. How widely the assumptions can be applied on empirical grounds cross-linguistically, is still a matter for further investigation.

## 1  Introduction

Although the structure of NPs varies considerably across languages, the types of items encountered inside NPs seem on the whole to be the same. This could make the 'noun phrase' (among other construction types) a candidate for serving as a useful module in multilingual grammar development: as such, its specifications could potentially be reused in grammars from language to language, and semantic outputs could be harmonized, so as to simplify the construction of semantically-based applications cross-linguistically. In this paper we address an NP-module as suggested in computational HPSG-grammars using the LKB platform cf. (Copestake, 2002) and the 'HPSG Grammar Matrix' cf. (Bender et al., 2002). Here we focus on the notion 'Specifier' as proposed in the latter and in the HPSG tradition at large. Analyzing a central set of phenomena in Norwegian related to the notion 'Specifier', we conclude, that this construct is a useful one for a Norwegian grammar, but with some essential provisos.

Among the growing family of LKB based grammars related to the 'HPSG Grammar Ma-trix', is a grammar for Norwegian, NorSource,[1] which constitutes a background and test bed for proposals under discussion.

## 2  Formalism and assumptions

Central among the components delivered through the Matrix is the module Minimal Recursion Semantics ('MRS') for semantic composition cf. (Copestake et al., 2001) and (Copestake et al., submitted). MRS representations are 'flat' representations of the elementary predications that compositionally represent the meaning connected to individual constructions. The formalism seems a promising candidate for becoming a widely accepted exchange format within computational semantics. An example is given in figure 1 below, showing the MRS (as produced in a standard English grammar) for the sentence *The boy throws the ball*. The RELS list is a 'bag' of those elementary predications (EPs) that are expressed by the sentence; in this case there are six EPs, of which one reflects *throw*. The subject and object arguments of the verb are reflected by the coindexation of the ARG1/ARG2 of the verb with the ARG0 of the determiner and the noun, corresponding to the 'bound variable'. The remaining EP represents the 'message type'. Scope properties are expressed in the HCONS list, 'x QEQ y' meaning essentially that x scopes over y. HCONS thus records the scopal tree of the constituent

---

[1]See (http://www.ling.hf.ntnu.no/forskning/nor-source). This grammar was initiated in 2002, and had its first period of development inside the EU project DeepThought ((http://www.project-deepthought.net)). It takes part in the Delph-in initiative ((http://www.delph-in.net)), which is a cooperative effort within deep language processing, using LKB and many other types of software communicating with LKB, thereamongst the 'HPSG Grammar Matrix'.

in question, as outlined in (Copestake et al., submitted).

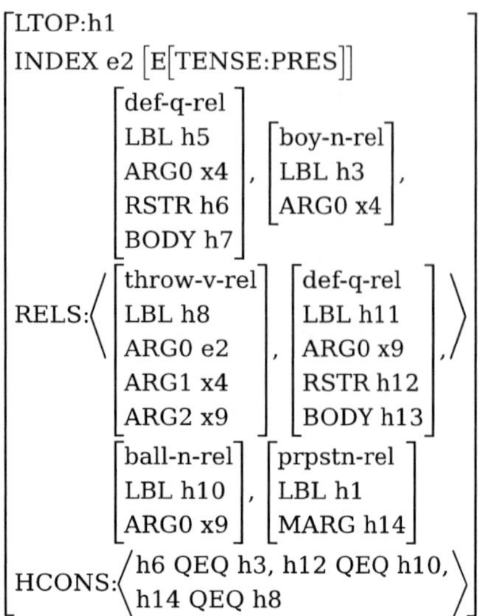

Figure 1: MRS-structure for the sentence *The boy throws the ball*

A standard MRS representation of an NP will include a quantifier and a restrictor predicate, as exemplified with *def-q-rel* and *boy-n-rel* in figure 1. EP-predicates used in MRSs can be either lexically induced, like *throw-v-rel* and the other predicates in figure 1, or constructionally induced, examples being provided below.

Background assumptions for the analysis of NPs in this framework come from many sources, including mainstream logical traditions arising with Frege and Russell, and generative syntax, here represented by HPSG, as, e.g. in (Pollard and Sag, 1994). Among important assumptions that are currently baked into the Matrix grammar design, we can mention:

From predicate logic:
- There can be only one variable per simple NP.
- There can be only one quantifier binding all instances of that variable in the representation of an NP.

From syntactic tradition
- In addition to complements and adjuncts, NPs also contain specifiers.

Specifiers enter the feature structure specifications in the following ways:
- A noun (N) signals the need for a specifier through a feature

　　SPR <[...] >

where properties of the specifier are stated inside '[...]'.
- An item whose typical function is to serve as a specifier, signals its need for something to specify through a feature

　　SPEC <[...]>

where properties of what is 'specified' are stated inside '[...]'.

A specifier item can be a word like *all, both, every; some, no, this, the, a* or a phrase like a prenominal genitive, as in *my best friend's money*, or a measure phrase, as in *tre gule krukker genever* ('three yellow jars (of) genever'). When a specifier item is encoded in a lexical entry, it is typically represented as introducing a quantifier relation in MRS, with a scope corresponding to the constituent 'specified'. When the specifier item is a phrase (e.g., a possessor or a measure NP), the quantifier relation in MRS has to be introduced as part of the operation combining that phrase with the constituent 'specified'. Either way, necessarily one, but only one, occasion is provided in the phrasal combinatorics for the introduction of a quantifier, and only one item is assigned the status as a specifier per NP.

Let us refer to these assumptions as *Spec-unique*. Theoretically, it represents a way of reconciling insights behind the 'DP-analysis' of NPs - cf. (Hellan, 1986), (Abney, 1997) - with the traditional notion of 'noun' being the head of NPs. Like a head relative to its complement, a specifier can determine certain properties of the noun (or attributes of the noun); still, the noun can be argued to be the overall head of the NP. Being thus counted as a type of 'attribute' of the noun, as are complements and adjuncts, the Specifier has a position intermediate between complements and adjuncts: complements are valence-bound and restricted in number, adjuncts are not valence-bound and unrestricted in number, whereas specifiers are not valence bound, but restricted in number. That this number is set to 'one' is partly conditioned by items like those mentioned above being mutually exclusive in English; but more importantly, it reflects the standard assumption of every NP being represented by just one (as 'type') variable, and hence just one quantifier binding that variable. This being hence a primarily theoretically motivated design, let us first briefly comment on its correctness as an empirical generalization across languages.

*Spec-unique* as 'There must be a Specifier':
The first part of *Spec-unique* says that there
*must* be a Specifier. English is in effect among
the very few languages in the world with a
requirement that there must be a word/phrase-
type Spec item in an NP: most languages
allow, e.g., a bare nominal form to constitute
an NP, also when the referent is countable.
That is, the 'only one' part of Spec-Unique is
typologically dubious.

*Spec-unique* as 'There can be at most one
Specifier':
The second part of *Spec-unique* says that there
can be at most one Specifier. An example
from Ga (spoken in Ghana) is suggestive of
the possibility of there being many potential
'specifier' items in an NP (from　(Dakubu,
2005):

(1)　nakai gbekɛ gbeei nɛ lɛ fɛɛ tɛɛ shi
　　　that child dog that DEF all go down
　　　Id N Poss N Dem Def Quant V N
　　　'all those FAM [dogs of the child]'

Possible Specifiers here include items
categorized as 'Identifier', 'Demonstrative',
'Definite (article)', 'Quantifier' and 'Possessor',
that is, altogether five items. To fully assess the
impact of the construction in the present setting would of course require an investigation
by itself, and we mention the example here only
as a pointer to a possibly significant counter
case to the 'at most one Spec' hypothesis.

In Norwegian, cases that *could* be construed
as multiple-Specifiers include:

(2)　alle mine tre gutter
　　　'all my three boys'

(3)　de tre energiske guttene
　　　'the three energetic boys'

If we want to maintain the 'at most one'-
part of *Spec-unique* for Norwegian, then
presumably numerals should not count as
Specifiers; then the definite article *de* will be
unique in having Spec status in (3), but in (2)

there is still a choice between the universal
quantifier and the possessor NP having Spec
status. In the following we consider a set of
phenomena in the Norwegian NP with a view
to the possible overall fruitfulness of the 'at
most-one' part of *Spec-unique* for its grammar,
and in conjunction with this, we return to the
question concerning (2). The phenomena to be
considered are:
　Definiteness
　Genericity
　the Referential/Attributive distinction
　Boundedness

## 3　Definiteness in Norwegian

'Definiteness' is standardly recognized as
having two morpho-syntactic instantiations in
Norwegian:

- the definite article suffix, as in *gutten*
- the weak adjective form, as in
*den snille gutten*
*min snille gutt*
Reference to definiteness in the grammar
is also made in constraining which NPs can
occur as (direct) objects in presentational
constructions (the so-called 'indefiniteness
requirement'). NP types *not* allowed in such
constructions include the forms above, but also
universally quantified NPs counting as indefinite relative to the above criteria, like *hver katt*
('each cat'), as exemplified in * *det sitter hver
katt i haven* ('there sits each cat in the garden').

Semantically, the two first instantiations of
definiteness seem to reside in an assumption
of shared familiarity with the item referred to
- that is, it signals that the referent is familiar
to the speaker, and it signals an assumption
on the part of the speaker that the referent
is familiar to the hearer as well. For the time
being, we include the 'familiarity' factor in
the standard MRS representation. One way
in which this inclusion could take place is as
a boolean attribute, for instance inside the
INDEX attribute; another is as a predicate
constituting its own EP, and we have chosen
the latter, with the relation type *familiar-rel*.

The third instantiation of definiteness (as in
*hver gutt* ('each boy')) does not carry the pre-

---

Hellan & Beermann: *The 'Specifier' in an HPSG grammar implementation of Norwegian*

supposition of familiarity. Typical of these NPs is that they express universal quantification, and they align with the Russellian notion of uniqueness in that their referent in a sense is unique, namely being the total set (in question) of instances of the restrictor predicate. Included in the 'Matrix package' of assumptions and specifications is a subtype of quantifier relations called *def-q-rel*, supposed to appear in the MRS of any NP counted as 'definite'; an instance was seen in Figure 1, and we adopt this convention. 'Indefinite' universally quantified NP like 'each cat' are characterized by the relation *univ-q-rel*, and their 'definiteness' has to be marked by features which we will not enter further into here.

Accordingly, there is no MRS relation common to all the types of definite NPs. As for those NPs represented through *familiar-rel*, the latter is not a quantifier relation, and given the formal requirement mentioned above to the effect that there be a quantifier in the representation of every NP, we implement this constraint by using also an EP with the relation type *def-q-rel* for the NPs instantiating the first two shapes of definiteness.

### 3.1 Constructing a grammar of definiteness in Norwegian

Since in the most standard case, *gutten*, definiteness is expressed through suffixation on the noun, it is reasonable to let the suffixed definite article consistently introduce the definite quantifier, represented in MRS as *def-q-rel*. The definite article suffix, as in *gutt-en*, is identified through the feature 'DEF-MORPH +'.
The second case, as in *min snille gutt*, will have a noun marked 'DEF-MORPH -', but the N projection as such still needs to marked as definite, and this 'guise' of definiteness will be marked 'DEFINITE +'. 'DEF-MORPH +' entails 'DEFINITE +', but not vice versa. Thus, the noun form *gutten* will be marked as

$$\left[\text{synsem | local | cat | head}\begin{bmatrix}\text{def-morph} & + \\ \text{definite} & + \end{bmatrix}\right]$$

The NP *min snille gutt* will be marked as

$$\left[\text{synsem | local | cat | head}\begin{bmatrix}\text{def-morph} & - \\ \text{definite} & + \end{bmatrix}\right]$$

and the lexical specification of *gutt* by itself will be ' DEF-MORPH -', leaving the value of

'DEFINITE' open for decision in the structure it enters.

In a lexically oriented framework, it is reasonable to let the assignment of the EP with *def-q-rel* to the form *gutten* be done at lexeme level, rather than as part of the phrasal composition of the NP. In the case of *min gutt*, however, which also receives *def-q-rel*, this will have to happen in the combinatorial rule combining the possessive *min* with *gutt*.

The weak adjective suffix *-e*, as in *den snille gutten* and *min snille gutt*, induces the following specification on the adjective it gets suffixed to:

$$\left[\text{...|head|mod}\,\langle[\text{local|cat|head|definite} \;+]\rangle\right]$$

Here, what comes after 'MOD' constrains the noun that the adjective can modify. This specification thus allows both *snille gutten* and *snille gutt*, but the latter only for a case where a definite article word or a possessive precedes the adjective, as in *den snille gutten* and *min snille gutt*, respectively. When this adjective combines with the noun, thus, the resulting phrase N' requires combination with one of these items at the next combinatorial stage. We encode this requirement through the specification

$$\left[\text{synsem|local|cat|val|spr}\,\langle[\text{l}]\rangle\right]$$

on the N', i.e., as a requirement that it combines with a specifier. Notably, this is a specification not inherent in the noun, but arising through a combinatorial rule. For nouns as lexical entities, in Norwegian, there is no reason to provide them with the requirement of a non-empty Specifier-list.

In cases like *den snille gutten*, the Specifier induced by the weak adjective is what we may call the *left-edge-def-word den*. It co-occurs with the suffixed article, and since the latter carries the definite quantifier and an NP can only have one quantifier, the left-edge word can only carry a non-quantificational relation, viz. *familiar-rel*, which in the MRS of *den snille gutten* thus occurs twice. (Thus, in the only case where Norwegian does have an obligatory Specifier, the lexical item filling this position lacks the quantifier-inducing capacity that is otherwise presupposed in the assumption-cluster of *Spec-unique*.) The 'left-edge' *den* thus has the specification

---

Hellan & Beermann: *The 'Specifier' in an HPSG grammar implementation of Norwegian*

$$\begin{bmatrix} \textit{local} \\ \text{cat|val|spec} \left\langle \begin{bmatrix} \textit{local} \\ \text{cat|head} \begin{bmatrix} \text{def-morph} & + \\ \text{definite} & + \end{bmatrix} \end{bmatrix} \right\rangle \end{bmatrix}$$

Figure 2: Partial feature-structure for left-edge *den*

whereby the occurrence of the def-suffixed noun is required, with its *def-q-rel*.

### 3.2 Generic and attributive readings

Another def-article word *den* should now be noted, which has a restricted use in Norwegian, but has a syntax corresponding to the normal *den* in Danish. It may be given the initial specification

$$\begin{bmatrix} \textit{local} \\ \text{cat|val|spec} \left\langle \begin{bmatrix} \textit{local} \\ \text{cat|head} \begin{bmatrix} \text{def-morph} & - \\ \text{definite} & + \end{bmatrix} \end{bmatrix} \right\rangle \end{bmatrix}$$

by which it induces *def-q-rel*. However, there is more to its semantics, pertaining to factors such as Genericity and Referentiality; consider the following examples:

(4) den bengalske tiger er utryddet
'the Bengal tiger is extinguished'

(5) ? den bengalske tigeren er utdÃÿdd

(6) den bengalske tigeren sitter bak deg
'the Bengal tiger sits behind you'

(7) ??* den bengalske tiger sitter bak deg

(8) ?* den sultne tiger sitter bak deg
'the hungry tiger sits behind you'

(9) den siste tiger du ser kan du springe fra
'the last tiger you see you may run away-from'

(10) den siste tigeren du ser kan du springe fra

In (4), the *den* under consideration induces a generic reading, a reading required by the adjective *utryddet*, and hence (4) is well-formed whereas in (5), the left-edge *den* is less felicitous in combination with such a generic verb. With the 'instantiated' status induced by *sitte bak* in (6), the left edge *den* goes fine, whereas the other *den* does not (cf. (7)). An 'instantiated' adjective like *sulten* enhances

this effect of incompatibility with the second *den* further, as seen in (8). Thus, we may call this second *den* a 'situationally detached' *den*, or, for short, we label it *den-aloof*. As (9) shows, this *den* also functions well with an attributive reading (in the sense of ( (Donnellan, 1966)); but unlike the genericity factor, an attributive reading can also obtain with the left-edge *den*, as seen in (10).

Our account so far yields identical MRSes for, and also does nothing to distinguish the grammaticality status between, (4) and (5). Suppose that we let *utryddet* require of its ARG1 that it have a feature 'GEN(ERIC) +', a feature entered under the path SYNSEM|LOCAL|CONT|HOOK|INDEX|SORT. A definite noun is unspecified for this feature, but the left-edge *den* would require of its SPEC item that it have the value '-' for this feature, i.e., it would have the following specification, rather than the one in figure 2:

Left-edge *den*:

$$\begin{bmatrix} \text{...spec} \left\langle \begin{bmatrix} \textit{local} \\ \text{cat|head} \begin{bmatrix} \text{def-morph} & - \\ \text{definite} & + \end{bmatrix} \\ \text{cont...gen} & - \end{bmatrix} \right\rangle \end{bmatrix}$$

The *den-aloof*, in contrast, would require 'GEN +', i.e:

$$\begin{bmatrix} \text{...spec} \left\langle \begin{bmatrix} \textit{local} \\ \text{cat|head} \begin{bmatrix} \text{def-morph} & - \\ \text{definite} & + \end{bmatrix} \\ \text{cont...gen} & + \end{bmatrix} \right\rangle \end{bmatrix}$$

Figure 3: Partial feature-structure for *den-aloof*

(5) is then ruled out by clashing INDEX values, since *utryddet* requires the path

$$\begin{bmatrix} \text{...| cont | hook | index | sort | gen} & + \end{bmatrix}$$

in the specification of its subject, while the NP in (5) actually has

$$\begin{bmatrix} \text{...| cont | hook | index | sort | gen} & - \end{bmatrix}$$

induced by the left-edge *den*. Notice that the following is accepted:

(11) tigeren er utryddet
'the tiger is extinguished'

---

since the noun form *tigeren* as such is neutral with regard to the GEN feature - only the two *dens* have particular concerns about this feature.

Conversely, in (7) and (8), the verb (helped by the adjective in (8)) requires of its subject that it be

$$\left[\, \ldots|\ \text{cont} \mid \text{hook} \mid \text{index} \mid \text{sort} \mid \text{gen} \;\text{-}\, \right]$$

but the *den-aloof* here induces

$$\left[\, \ldots|\ \text{cont} \mid \text{hook} \mid \text{index} \mid \text{sort} \mid \text{gen} \;\text{+}\, \right]$$

accounting for the ungrammaticality of (7) and (8).

As for the 'Attributive' reading possible in (9) and (10), what can be concluded from this is that even with non-generic verbs, *den-aloof* is acceptable if the reading can be construed as attributive. If we mark such a reading of an NP as 'ATTR +', and accept all generic readings as also attributive, then one full representation of *den-aloof* becomes:

*Den-aloof*-1:

$$\left[\, \ldots\text{spec} \left\langle \left[\, \text{loc} \begin{bmatrix} \text{cat}|\text{head} & \begin{bmatrix} \text{def-morph} & \text{-} \\ \text{definite} & \text{+} \end{bmatrix} \\ \text{cont}\ldots\text{sort} & \begin{bmatrix} \text{gen} & \text{+} \\ \text{attr} & \text{+} \end{bmatrix} \end{bmatrix} \,\right] \right\rangle \,\right]$$

and another becomes

*Den-aloof*-2:

$$\left[\, \ldots\text{spec} \left\langle \left[\, \text{loc} \begin{bmatrix} \text{cat}|\text{head} & \begin{bmatrix} \text{def-morph} & \text{-} \\ \text{definite} & \text{+} \end{bmatrix} \\ \text{cont}\ldots\text{sort} & \begin{bmatrix} \text{gen} & \text{-} \\ \text{attr} & \text{+} \end{bmatrix} \end{bmatrix} \,\right] \right\rangle \,\right]$$

to allow the non-generic status of (9). Conceivably, then, the 'general' *den-aloof* can be stated as follows, rather than as in figure 3:

*Den-aloof*-General:

$$\left[\, \ldots\text{spec} \left\langle \left[\, \text{loc} \begin{bmatrix} \text{cat}|\text{head} & \begin{bmatrix} \text{def-morph} & \text{-} \\ \text{definite} & \text{+} \end{bmatrix} \\ \text{cont}\ldots\text{sort} & \begin{bmatrix} \text{attr} & \text{+} \end{bmatrix} \end{bmatrix} \,\right] \right\rangle \,\right]$$

This will allow a generic reading when such a reading is induced by the verb, a possibility blocked for left-edge *den*. Such assignments will be possible, though, only if the grammar is able to make a decision for any NP whether it is attributive or referential; this may well be even harder to obtain than a computation of genericity, however.

## 4  Boundedness

As is well established in the literature (cf., e.g., (Smith, 1991)) an indefinite plural NP induces atelicity in the verbal construction; examples include, with NPs in object position:

(12)   Jon leste artikler i flere dager
'Jon read articles for many days'

(13)   ??Jon leste Goethes diktsamlinger i flere dager
Jon read Goethe's poem collections for many days

(14)   ?*Jon leste tre artikler i flere dag
Jon read three articles for many days'

According to an analysis implemented in this same grammar, as described in (Beermann and Hellan, 2000), in the verbal construction, unboundedness can be marked by a feature specification 'DELIMITED -' in the event-index of the verbal projection. An NP inducing this value can be marked 'BOUNDED -' in the ref-index of the nominal projection. Both annotations are exposed in MRS. Relative to the system we have so far outlined, the following algorithm can be used:

Adhering to the same lexicalist approach as above of representing semantically contentful inflection at lexeme level, non-boundedness is associated with a plural indefinite noun form as such. - The representation includes the feature 'BOUNDED -' already mentioned, and a quantificational relation *plurindef-q-rel*. - Doing this bottom-up, we need to ensure that the specifications mentioned are located in a constructional build-up leading to constructions of the pattern in (12), and not to patterns like (13) or (14). - Essential to ensure this is constraining the SPR list of a non-bounded noun form to be empty: combination with adjectives is possible, e.g., but not with quantifiers; only for nouns co-occurring with the latter will the combinatorics of a noun be checked via SPR-list cancellation. Thus, indefinite plurals will have the specification

$$\left[\, \ldots\text{spec} \left\langle \left[\, \text{loc} \begin{bmatrix} \text{cat}|\text{val}|\text{spr} & \langle\,\rangle \\ \text{cont}|\text{index}|\text{bounded} & \text{-} \end{bmatrix} \,\right] \right\rangle \,\right]$$

This analysis illustrates one more respect in which, by partial involvement of the construct 'Specifier', we are in a position to control the assignment of fairly subtle semantic values.

However, as will be recalled from the discussion in section 2 concerning the following examples,

(15)  alle mine tre gutter
'all my three boys'

(16)  de tre energiske guttene
'the three energetic boys'

to adhere to the *Spec-unique* assumption, it would be desirable to count numerals as not being Specifiers. On that assumption, (14) is still not accounted for. As it seems, there is no non-ad hoc way of both preserving *Spec-unique* and regulating the boundedness phenomenon *exclusively* through the use of the Specifier mechanism: what we need (and as is implemented) is an additional feature which will distinguish those indefinite plurals that do combine with a cardinality expression from those which don't. Hence, the Spec mechanism is not sufficient to encode all the boundedness distinctions needed.

We may also notice that for the case in (15), if we want to maintain the 'at most one'-part of *Spec-unique*, and we maintain the treatment of definiteness inducers as Specifier items, then we cannot also treat the quantifier *alle* as a Specifier. In the grammar in question, *alle* is consequently treated as a head and the following nominal projection as its complement; semantically, this configuration is treated analogously to a partitive construction, such that both the definite Specifier and the quantifier can introduce a variable, one each. This is then an analysis complying with the overall desiderata concerning NPs and quantifiers mentioned initially, and, what is crucial in the present connection, in such a way as not to be in conflict with the role designed for the Specifier category.

## 5  Conclusion

Although there are some clear limitations to how pervasively one can apply the Specifier category in the analysis of Norwegian, our discussion warrants a conclusion to the effect that the

Specifier, as conceived under the 'at most one' part of the *Spec-unique*, is a useful construct, motivated not only by the *à priori* concerns outlined in the beginning, but also in the analysis of rather subtle facts pertaining both to syntax, morphology and semantics of NPs. Having demonstrated this for the case of Norwegian, it of course remains to provide similar demonstrations for other languages. Motivation for trying this would reside in part in the theoretical background of the notion mentioned earlier, and in part in reusability advantages that such a potential cross-grammatically valid module might provide for multilingual grammar engineering. However, the linguistic facts must come first, and the 'Specifier' will have to earn its status through accommodation of the facts language by language.

## References

S. Abney. 1997. *The English Noun Phrase in its Sentential Aspect.* PhD dissertation, MIT.

D Beermann and L. Hellan. 2000. A treatment of directionals in two implemented hpsg grammars. In St Mueller, editor, *Proceedings of the HPSG04 Conference, Katholieke Universiteit Leuven*, pages –. CSLI Publications.

E. Bender, D. Flickinger, and S. Oepen. 2002. The grammar matrix: An open-source starterkit for the rapid development of cross-linguistically consistent broad-coverage precision grammars. In NN, editor, *Proceedings of the Workshop on Grammar Engineering and Evaluation, Coling 2002, Taipei*, pages 8–14. NN.

A. Copestake, A. Lascarides, and D. Flickinger. 2001. An algebra for semantic construction in constraint-based grammars. In *Proceedings of the 39th Annual Meeting of the ACL*, pages –.

A. Copestake, D. Flickinger, I. Sag, and C. Pollard. submitted. Minimal recursion semantics: an introduction. Submitted December 2003.

A. Copestake. 2002. *Implementing Typed Feature Structure Grammars.* CSLI Publications, Stanford.

M.E. Kropp Dakubu. 2005. Noun phrase structure in ga. Talk given at NTNU Spring 2005.

K. Donnellan. 1966. Reference and definite descriptions. *The Philosophical Review.*

L. Hellan. 1986. The headedness of noun phrases in norwegian. In P. Muysken and H. van Riemsdijk, editors, *Features and Projections*, pages –. Foris Publications.

C. Pollard and I. Sag. 1994. *Head-Driven Phrase Structure Grammar*. Chicago University Press.

C. Smith. 1991. *The Parameter of Aspect*. Kluwer Publishers.

# LiSa – morphological analysis for information retrieval

**Hans Hjelm**
CL Group, Department of Linguistics
Stockholm University
SE-106 91 Stockholm, Sweden
hans.hjelm@ling.su.se

**Christoph Schwarz**
Intrafind Software AG
Lortzingstraße 9
DE-81241 Munich, Germany
christoph.schwarz@intrafind.de

## Abstract

This paper presents LiSa, a system for morphological analysis, designed to meet the needs of the Information Retrieval (IR) community. LiSa is an acronym for *Linguistic and Statistical Analysis*. The system is lexicon- and rule based and developed in Java. It performs lemmatization, part of speech categorization, decompounding and compound disambiguation for German, Spanish, French and English, with the other major European languages under development. The lessons learned when developing the rules for disambiguation of German compounds are also applicable to other compounding languages, such as the Nordic languages. Since compounding is much more common and far more complex in German than in the other languages currently handled by LiSa, this paper will deal mainly with German.

A comparative evaluation of LiSa with the GERTWOL system[1], combined with a filter for disambiguation developed by Volk (Volk, 1999) has been performed. (The combination of GERTWOL and filter will from here on be referred to as *Filtered GERTWOL*.) The focus of the evaluation has been to measure how suitable the respective systems are for query processing and for building indices for IR-systems. Special attention has been paid to their abilities to select the correct analysis of compounds.

LiSa is developed by Intrafind Software AG, on whose homepage an online demo of LiSa can be found[2]. It is used in Intrafind's *iFinder* and also exists as an add-on to the open source free text indexing tool *Lucene*[3].

## 1 Introduction

(Sproat, 1992), p. 7, states that

*Lemmatization is normally not an end in itself, but is useful for other applications, such as document retrieval (...) or indexing.*

The cornerstone of almost any IR-system is the index; a table structure, showing which words appear in which documents, possibly also in which order and how often. The following sections describe how lemmatization, decompounding and compound disambiguation is helpful when constructing and searching the index. The usefulness of lemmatization has been questioned for English (Harman, 1991), but is asserted for other languages (Hull, 1996). (Note that these papers deal with *stemming* rather than lemmatization. Stemming is a more aggressive approach, reducing even words from different part of speech (POS) categories to common stems.) For compounding languages, research has shown that decompounding is a worthwhile effort (Braschler and Ripplinger, 2004). It should be noted that it is important to use the same methods of analysis for query processing as for constructing the index, e.g., if one uses lemmatization during query processing, one must use lemmatization also during indexing.

---

[1] http://www.lingsoft.fi/doc/gertwol/

[2] http://www.intrafind.org
[3] http://jakarta.apache.org/lucene

## 1.1  Lemmatization

Using a lemmatizer when constructing the index brings the main advantage of an increase in recall. Searching for "Bücher" (books), the system will also find documents containing "Buch" (book) or any of the other inflectional forms of that same word. Note that the usual trade-off between precision and recall does not necessarily apply here. In fact, Braschler and Ripplinger (2004) argue that precision might *increase* along with recall.

## 1.2  Decompounding

This is the process of splitting a compound word into its parts. E.g., the word "Bücherregale" (book shelves) would be split into the parts "Bücher" (books) and "Regale" (shelves). Usually this process is combined with lemmatization, to give the citation form[4] of the constituents: "Buch" (book) and "Regal" (shelf). These constituents are then added to the index, along with the citation form of the entire compound (here: "Bücherregal" (book shelf)). The purpose of decompounding is mainly to improve recall.

## 1.3  Compound disambiguation

Often more than one reading is possible for a complex word. The word "Kulturteilen" has (at least) four possible readings:

```
1.  "Kultur (noun) + teilen (verb)" (to
share culture)
2.  "Kultur (noun) + teilen (noun)"
(the culture section of a newspaper)
3.  "Kult (noun) + urteilen (verb)" (to
judge a cult)
4.  "Kult (noun) + urteilen (noun)"
(cult judgments)
```

Although all four readings are possible, the second reading is markedly more probable than the others. Compound disambiguation is the process of finding this most probable reading and is used within IR to increase precision in a system. This paper focuses mainly on this last task, since it is by far the most challenging one.

## 2  Related work

There exist a great number of systems for morphological analysis, both commercial and in the research community. It is not the purpose of this paper to give an exhaustive overview of the

---

[4]the word as it would appear in a dictionary entry

existing systems in the field of computational morphology. This section singles out relatively recently developed systems for the Nordic languages. Of course, GERTWOL (Haapalainen and Majorin, 1994), the system we use as a reference for our tests in this paper, is one of the more well-known for the German language. It is described in section 6.

**A statistically based system**   Sjöberg and Kann (2004) describe a system for morphological analysis, decompounding and compound disambiguation for the Swedish language. They use a variety of measures, including looking at the number of components in the analysis, analyzing the frequencies of words and POS-categories in the context and the POS-categories of the components. The best results, an accuracy of 94% for ambiguous compounds, are reached by using a hybrid system, where the most successful statistical measures are combined with some ad hoc rules.

**A rule-based system**   For Norwegian, Bondi Johannesen and Hauglin (1996) report of a system for decompounding and compound disambiguation to be used in a system for morphosyntactic tagging. Their approach resembles the one used in LiSa (see description in section 4), in that both systems have a hierarchy of rules that are used for the disambiguation. They report of an accuracy of 97.6%, where mistakes depending on missing lexicon entries were not counted as errors.

## 3  Aspects of analyzing for IR

Here we look at some further considerations that are important for IR, specifically, when performing morphological analysis.

## 3.1  Depth of analysis

Many systems use a strategy where a large list of inflected forms are kept in a dictionary, along with their citation forms. If the system finds the word the user is looking for, e.g., "Kulturteilen", the base form is returned to the user ("Kulturteil (noun)"). In such systems, decompounding is only used as a fallback option when the lexicon fails to deliver the base form. This will give the user the correct base form, but she or he will not be able to use the constituents for indexing. This is an example where the analysis is too shallow.

On the other hand, a very deep analysis is also of little use for indexing. E.g.,

---

*Hjelm & Schwarz: LiSa – morphological analysis for information retrieval*

it would be possible to identify the following morphemes in the word "Destabilisierungsvorgang" (procedure for destabilization): "De|stabilisier|ung|s|vor|gang". Including all these morphemes in the index would clutter it and decrease the precision and performance of the system. Here, then, the analysis is too deep - what we need is simply the main constituents of the compound: "Destabilisierungs|vorgang" (the respective lemmas being "Destabilisierung" and "Vorgang").

## 3.2 Category system

When building an index, the detailed POS-category of a word is of less importance. Since terms will be added to the index in citation form, and this form always has the same grammatical features for each POS-category, it would be enough to differentiate between the basic POS-categories, like nouns, verbs and adjectives. E.g., nouns will always be added to the index in the singular nominative form; therefore no case or number information appears in the index, only the basic POS-category is stated. However, when performing compound disambiguation, more detailed information can sometimes be useful (see 3.3). The category system used in LiSa is tailored towards this kind of analysis and disambiguation (two levels of detail are available during the analysis). The category system has also been developed with the detection of multi-word units in mind, but this paper will not explicitly deal with that topic.

## 3.3 Treatment of upper/lower case

Making use of information on capitalization can sometimes provide assistance in disambiguation. The obvious example for German is that nouns are capitalized in running text. If we therefore have more than one competing readings, all noun readings can be excluded if the word is not capitalized. E.g., upper case "Wein" can be both the noun (wine) and the verb (cry, second person imperative), since verbs and adjectives are also capitalized at the beginning of a sentence. Lower case "wein" though, can only be the verb reading. One also needs to take two other types of texts into consideration:

- **Orthographically non-standard texts**. This group includes, but is not limited to, e-mails (which are often all lower case) and

certain web pages (containing mainly lists or tables). Since these texts do not comply with standard capitalization rules, it is not possible to use capitalization information for disambiguation here.

- **Citation form**. Here the words appear as they would in a dictionary. This form actually allows for more precise disambiguation, since one also can exclude any upper case verb or adjective readings.

As can be seen in the previous example with "wein", capitalization can be used for disambiguating not only compounds, but simplex words as well. Similarly, for English, one can use the knowledge that verbs in second person never appear sentence initially, to rule out the verbal reading of, e.g., "Uses" (capitalized), leaving only the nominal reading.

## 3.4 Analysis of special characters (umlauts)

Some languages with so called special characters have a representation of these characters that is possible to write using an arbitrary keyboard for the Latin alphabet. This is the case for German, but also for Swedish and other Nordic languages. For German, the mapping looks like this:

```
ä -> ae
ö -> oe
ü -> ue
ß -> ss
```

Taking this possibility into consideration when indexing can increase the recall of a system, but also adds complexity, since these letter combinations also occur naturally in the language, especially at word boundaries in compounds. E.g., for "Bau|experte" (building expert), analysis will fail if it is first processed to "Baüxperte". Conversely, we will not be able to analyze "Drueck|experte" (printing expert), unless we first process it to "Drück|experte".

## 4 LiSa word analysis

This section describes the approaches taken in LiSa towards solving the issues discussed in this paper.

### 4.1 Lemmatization in LiSa

The backbone of the analysis in LiSa is the lexicon, stored in a letter tree format for fast

---

Hjelm & Schwarz: *LiSa – morphological analysis for information retrieval* and space efficient access (for running text, LiSa processes over 150.000 German words per second on a Pentium 4 machine with 512 MB RAM). The lexicon is a full form lexicon with mostly non-compound words, i.e., all possible inflectional forms of a word are stored, along with their respective lemmas and POS-categories. The LiSa lexicon distinguishes between simplex words, capable of appearing by themselves or as heads of compounds and words which can only appear inside compounds (and never as compound heads).

## 4.2　Decompounding in LiSa

If no complete match for a word is found in the lexicon, LiSa assumes we are dealing with a compound and produces all possible readings of the word, based on what the lexicon allows, using combinatorial rules. It is also possible to code compounds directly in the lexicon, which can be worthwhile for compounds which do not adhere to standard analysis patterns. LiSa gives the lemmas of the compound constituents, in addition to the lemma of the entire compound, also when the compound is coded in the lexicon.

## 4.3　Compound disambiguation in LiSa

During the decompounding step, it is frequently the case that a number of possible readings are produced. LiSa possesses a rule machinery with filtering rules for each language, some general and some language specific. The rules are chained together, each rule possibly reducing the number of possible readings and passing the rest along to the next rule in the chain, until, ideally, only one reading is left. The rules with the greatest coverage appear at the top of the rule hierarchy, for the sake of efficiency. Since each rule reduces the set of possible readings, the ordering of the rules is also important for producing the correct results. Some rules depend on other rules having been applied previously to function correctly.

In most cases, the goal of compound disambiguation is to be left with only one reading. In some rare cases, looking at a word in isolation, it is not possible to determine which reading is the more probable. E.g., the word "Nordpolen" has three almost equally probable readings:

```
"Norden + Pol" (North Pole)
"Norden + Pole" (Person from the north
```

of Poland)
```
"Norden + Polen" (Northern Poland)
```

The idea behind LiSa is to extract the most precise information possible on a word level. Once this has been done, tools working on a higher level (e.g. sentence level) can make use of this information and have a higher chance of succeeding. In the majority of cases, though, the information available on a word level is sufficient for performing the disambiguation.

The most basic filtering rule consists in choosing the reading with the smallest number of constituents. This rule would be effective in resolving the following ambiguity:

```
"Wohnungs|einrichtung" (Room
furnishing)
"Wohnungs|ein|richtung" (One direction
of a room)
```

Although the second reading is nonsensical, its constituents are all legitimate words and the reading has to be ruled out.

Another basic rule is to choose the reading with the longest right-most constituent. Here is an example for which this rule is applicable (the first alternative being the correct one):

```
"Erb|information" (inheritance
information)
"Erbin|formation" (heiress formation)
```

For ruling out particularly unlikely readings, some words get a marking in the dictionary, indicating that readings containing this word as a constituent should be disfavored when other readings are available. One example where this is put to use is the following (again, the first reading is the preferred one):

```
"Himmels|achse" (axis of heaven)
"Himmel|sachse" (heaven Saxonian)
```

Here, "sachse" has been marked as undesired in the dictionary, and hence the reading "Himmel|sachse" is filtered out, although it would be the preferred reading according to the rule concerning longest right-most constituent. A similar concept is described in (Volk, 1999). Words for which it is necessary to side-step this behavior, e.g., "Kursachse" (a kind of Saxonian), can be coded explicitly as "Kur|sachse" in the LiSa lexicon.

There are many other filtering rules implemented for German in LiSa. Some of them are specific to German, but most of them will carry over to other compounding languages, like Dutch and the Nordic languages.

---

# 5  Evaluation

To measure the quality of the analysis in general and the disambiguation in particular, a contrastive evaluation was carried out. The data for the evaluation comes from the articles appearing in the Swiss newspaper *Neue Zürcher Zeitung* in April 1994. From all articles in the data collection (near 3000 articles, totally about 1.8 million words), the longest words containing only alphanumerical characters were selected (306 word types). This collection is here referred to as `nzz_long` and is meant to present the most challenging task for compound disambiguation, the idea being that a longer word will contain more possibilities for ambiguity than a shorter word.

## 5.1  nzz_long  -

The results for the `nzz_long` test set have been processed for LiSa and Filtered GERTWOL. Although originally consisting of 306 types, four of these turned out to be typos or words written in a non-standard way, making the actual number of test words 302.

It should be noted that the errors reported are clear-cut errors - for less clear cases, we have adopted a more lenient approach. For example, one might argue whether "Infrastruktur" (infrastructure) should be analyzed as "Infra|struktur" or left as it is. Rather than deciding on a "correct" way in these murky cases, we have chosen to give both interpretations the benefit of the doubt. The results reflect the state of the systems as of April 2005.

In addition to the brief evaluation described here, it would be interesting to perform an application based evaluation. Using the test data from TREC[5] would provide valuable information, since one would be evaluating the effectiveness with regards to IR directly, which is what we are mainly interested in here.

# 6  Discussion - the systems contrasted

Here are some of the main issues that set LiSa apart from Filtered GERTWOL in terms of their aptness in an IR-environment.

## 6.1  Depth of analysis

The analysis produced by Filtered GERTWOL is more fine-grained than the one Lisa produces.

---

[5]http://trec.nist.gov

This might at first seem like a pleasant problem - the superfluous information can simply be ignored. However, this is not as simple as it might at first sound. E.g., this is the analysis given for the word "Destabilisierungsvorgang":
`"*de|stabil~is~ier~ung\s#vor|gang"`

Here, the strategy would be to split the word at the #-sign, get rid of the bounding morpheme after the \-character and use "destabilisierung" and "vorgang" for indexing. However, for the word "aufschreiben" (write down), we get the following analysis:
`"auf|schreib~en"`

There is no #-sign splitting the word in this case. Still, one would have liked to add at least "schreiben" (write) to the index. It is not a clear-cut case, which constituents to add to the index and which not. In LiSa, this problem does not arise, since the constituents delivered are always the base forms to be used for indexing.

## 6.2  Category system

The POS-category system used in Filtered GERTWOL is again more detailed than the one used in LiSa. Just as described in the previous section, this actually confuses rather than helps - a user of the system will have to post-process the output to get rid of unwanted duplicates. For the word "Bücherregale", Filtered GERTWOL produces the following readings, which are identical except for their POS-categories:
```
"*büch\er#regal" S NEUTR PL NOM
"*büch\er#regal" S NEUTR PL AKK
"*büch\er#regal" S NEUTR PL GEN
"*büch\er#regal" S NEUTR SELTEN SG DAT
```

Again, LiSa produces a single output for this case, giving exactly the information needed for indexing or query analysis.

## 6.3  Modularity

LiSa can easily be used as a module in a bigger software system, since it is equipped with a well defined API and since it is written in Java. GERTWOL, or especially Filtered GERTWOL, does not lend itself to system integration in the same way as LiSa does.

## 6.4  Further differences

The differences listed in the following section are not less substantial than the ones described in sections 6.1 to 6.3. However, they have all been discussed previously in section 3 and are

---

Hjelm & Schwarz: *LiSa – morphological analysis for information retrieval*

|          | No analysis | Incorrect analysis | Ambiguous analyses |
|----------|-------------|--------------------|--------------------|
| **LiSa**     | 1.0% (3)    | 0.3% (1)           | 0% (0)             |
| **GERTWOL**  | 2.0% (6)    | 0.7% (2)           | 4.0% (12)          |

Table 1: *Contrastive evaluation, LiSa and Filtered GERTWOL. The first column counts words for which no analysis was found. The second column counts words for which one or more analyses were found, but none of them were correct. The final column counts words for which more than one analysis was given (only one analysis is correct for each word).*

therefore given briefer descriptions in the following.

- **Lemmas of compound constituents**   Turning again to the example of "Bücherregale" from section 6.2, one sees that GERTWOL splits the noun, but the first constituent is still presented in its text form ("Bücher"). This seems counterproductive; we would like to get the base form of the entire compound ("Bücherregal") but also the base forms of the constituents ("Buch" and "Regal"), which is precisely the analysis given by LiSa.

- **Special characters treatment**   Another difference between the two systems, is their ability to deal with special characters (see section 3.4 for a description of the problem). This type of analysis is especially useful when analyzing queries, but certain types of texts (e.g. e-mails) also use this kind of conventions.

- **Filtering**   In addition to the issues raised previously, with regards to filtering, the Filtered GERTWOL system relies on capitalization complying with the citation form of words, which will produce filtering errors when analyzing running text.

- **Capitalization issues**   Filtered GERTWOL does not allow for treating texts differently, depending on their origin or the type of text, in the way LiSa does.

## 7   Conclusions

Perhaps more than the numbers presented in section 5, the differences described in the previous section point to the usefulness of LiSa in the IR setting. Considering also that LiSa is able to process the text efficiently, both in terms of time and resources, and its availability as a plug-in to the widely distributed Lucene engine, we believe LiSa will prove to be a valuable asset for many IR applications.

## References


Martin Braschler and Bärbel Ripplinger. 2004. How effective is stemming and decompounding for German text retrieval? *Information Retrieval*, 7(3–4):291–316.

Mariikka Haapalainen and Ari Majorin. 1994. Gertwol: ein System zur automatischen Wortformerkennung deutscher Wörter. Technical report, Lingsoft, Inc., September.

Donna Harman. 1991. How effective is suffixing? *Journal of the American Society for Information Science*, 42(1):7–15.

David A. Hull. 1996. Stemming algorithms - a case study for detailed evaluation. *Journal of the American Society for Information Science*, 47(1):70–84.

Janne Bondi Johannesen and Helge Hauglin. 1996. An automatic analysis of Norwegian compounds. In T. Haukioja, editor, *Papers from the 16th Scandinavian Conference of Linguistics*, pages 209–220, Turku/Åbo, Finland.

Jonas Sjöbergh and Viggo Kann. 2004. Finding the correct interpretation of Swedish compounds a statistical approach. In *Proceedings of LREC-2004*, pages 899–902, Lisbon, Portugal.

Richard Sproat. 1992. *Morphology and Computation*. The MIT Press, Cambridge, Mass, USA.

Martin Volk. 1999. Choosing the right lemma when analysing German nouns. In Jost Gippert and Peter Olivier, editors, *Multilinguale Corpora: Codierung, Strukturierung, Analyse*. Gesellschaft für Linguistische DatenVerarbeitung, Enigma Corporation.


---

# Creating bilingual lexica using reference wordlists for alignment of monolingual semantic vector spaces


**Jon Holmlund** and **Magnus Sahlgren** and **Jussi Karlgren**

Swedish Institute of Computer Science, SICS

Box 1263, SE-164 29 Kista, Sweden

{jon,mange,jussi}@sics.se



## Abstract

This paper proposes a novel method for automatically acquiring multi-lingual lexica from non-parallel data and reports some initial experiments to prove the viability of the approach. Using established techniques for building mono-lingual vector spaces two independent semantic vector spaces are built from textual data. These vector spaces are related to each other using a small *reference word list* of manually chosen reference points taken from available bi-lingual dictionaries. Other words can then be related to these reference points first in the one language and then in the other. In the present experiments, we apply the proposed method to comparable but non-parallel English-German data. The resulting bi-lingual lexicon is evaluated using an online English-German lexicon as gold standard. The results clearly demonstrate the viability of the proposed methodology.


## 1 Introduction

Using data to build multilingual lexical resources automatically or with minimum manual intervention is an important research goal. Lack of both general-case and domain-specific multi-lingual translation dictionaries hamper the usefulness and effectiveness of multi-lingual information access systems — most multilingual information retrieval systems use multilingual lexicon lookup coupled with standard search algorithms (for state of the art in multilingual information retrieval, see the proceedings of CLEF[1], TREC[2], and NTCIR[3]). Unfortunately, existing multilingual resources have limited coverage, limited accessibility, and are static in nature. Much of the research put into building lexical resources is vectored towards the needs of automatic translation rather than application to information access. The needs for a translation system are very different than those of a information access system: translation puts an emphasis on exact translation and works with fine-grained semantic distinctions, where information access systems typically can make good use of related terms even the match is less than exact. Our aim with the set of experiments presented here is to provide starting steps for the automatic distillation of multi-lingual correspondences from existing data with a minimal amount of processing.

Semantic vector space models are easy to use for experimentation in this vein — they are designed to be efficient, portable, and scalable. Vector space techniques that have been used for multi-lingual lexicon acquisition include Latent Semantic Indexing (Landauer and Dumais, 1997) and Random Indexing or Random Key Indexing (Sahlgren, 2004; Karlgren and Sahlgren, 2001). Both these techniques are originally designed to build semantic models for one language, and are later modified to handle bi-lingual data sets. Although the experiments published show surprisingly good results, given their rather limited scope, they typically require large amounts of aligned parallel data, which seriously limits the portability and coverage of the techniques.

In this paper, we propose a novel method for automatically acquiring multi-lingual lexica from non-parallel data. The idea is to make use

---

[1] http://clef.iei.pi.cnr.it/

[2] http://trec.nist.gov/

[3] http://research.nii.ac.jp/ntcir/index-en.html

of established techniques for building monolingual vector spaces, and to independently create two (or more) vector spaces, one for each language for which data are available. The basic assumption is that two vector spaces built on similar comparable data from two different languages should be isomorphic to some degree. We exploit this potential isomorphy by aligning the independent vector spaces using a set of reference points from a *reference wordlist* containing a smallish set of established lexical correspondences.

The reference wordlist consists of a set of $r$ bi-lingual pairs of one-word lexemes, which we call *reference words*, and that are thought to have similar semantic roles in the respective languages — e.g. "boat" in English and "boot" in German. The idea is that every word in the different languages could be profiled by measuring their correspondence in the monolingual vector spaces to each of the reference words. Thus, a word's *reference profile* would consist of one scalar measure for every reference word, resulting in a vector representation in an $r$-dimensional space, where each dimension is linked to the word's correspondence to a reference word. The resulting $r$-dimensional space effectively constitutes a multi-lingual lexicon, where words in different languages are related by their mutual correspondence to the reference words.

In the present experiments, we apply the proposed method to comparable but non-parallel English-German data. We have here used the Random Indexing technology to build the base vector spaces — conceivably other vector space models would work in a similar manner. The resulting bi-lingual lexicon is evaluated using an online English-German lexicon as gold standard.

## 2  Methodology

Figure 1 demonstrates a simplified schematic of the processing steps for the experiment methodology. The two text collections (1) are non-parallel, and consist of $n$ (some 50 000) unique words each. Co-occurrence statistics for the texts are then collected using the Random Indexing vector space technique, resulting in two $n \times k$ matrices (2). By measuring correspondences between words using some distance measure in the vector space, this space can be represented as a word-by-word matrix (3) of correspondences.

After $r$ words are manually chosen as reference words, a smaller matrix of word-by-word correspondences is produced. If the reference words are well chosen, the strength of the connections in step 4 are assumed to be enough for the matrices to be viewed as representing the same vector space, in a simple approximation of dimensional rotation. This estimate gives us (with $n_{en}$ and $n_{de}$ both $\approx$ 50 000) a 100 000 $\times$ 100 000 matrix (5) of English by German words. In this matrix, the best cross-language correspondences can be found for each row or column.

### 2.1  Choice of reference words

The reference word pairs need to be frequent in the texts to get reliable statistics. We therefore only consider words with a frequency above 75 occurrences. Finding one-to-one translations, however, has not been a priority. If the reference words for the most part have similar meanings in both languages their correspondence in occurrence will match even allowing for some usage difference and some occurrences of synonyms to blur the pictures somewhat. Above all, we have taken care to avoid obviously polysemous reference words. We have sought words as prototypically monosemous as possible. In practice, it has often been a struggle between the demands of rich coverage and occurrence on the one hand and monosemy on the other.

### 2.2  Random indexing

Random Indexing, or Random Key Indexing, first developed and published by Kanerva (Kanerva et al., 2000),äand later applied by Sahlgren and Karlgren (Karlgren and Sahlgren, 2001) to information access, is a technique for producing *context vectors* for words based on co-occurrence statistics. Random Indexing differs from other related reduced-dimension vector space methods, such as Latent Semantic Indexing/Analysis (LSI/LSA; (Deerwester et al., 1990; Landauer and Dumais, 1997)), by not requiring an explicit dimension reduction phase in order to construct the vector space. Instead of collecting the data in a word-by-word or word-by-document cooccurrence matrix that need to be reduced using computationally expensive matrix operations, Random Indexing

|   |                                              | English | German |
|---|----------------------------------------------|---------|--------|
| 1 | Text data                                    | $n_{en}$ | $n_{de}$ |
| Random Indexing | | | |
| 2 | Mono-lingual vector space                    | $n_{en} \times k$ | $n_{de} \times k$ |
| Vector space distance definition | | | |
| 3 | Mono-lingual correspondence thesaurus        | $n_{en} \times n_{en}$ | $n_{de} \times n_{de}$ |
| Establishing reference dimensions | | | |
| 4 | Mono-lingual reference list correspondence   | $n_{en} \times r$ | $n_{de} \times r$ |
| Aligning vector spaces | | | |
| 5 | Bi-lingual cross-language correspondence     | $(n_{en} + n_{de}) \times (n_{en} + n_{de})$ | |

Figure 1: Steps of the proposed method

incrementally collects the data in a *context* matrix with fixed dimensionality $k$, such that $k \ll D < V$, where $D$ is the size of the document collection, and $V$ is the size of the vocabulary. The fact that no dimension reduction of the resulting matrix is needed makes Random Indexing very efficient and scalable. Using document-based co-occurrences with Random Indexing, which we do in the present experiments, is a two-step operation:

1. A unique $k$-dimensional *index vector* consisting of a small number of randomly selected non-zero elements is assigned to each document in the data.

2. Context vectors for the words are produced by scanning through the text, and each time a word occurs in a document, the document's $k$-dimensional index vector is added to the row for the word in the context matrix. When the entire text has been scanned, words are represented in the context matrix by $k$-dimensional context vectors that are effectively the sum of the words' contexts.

In the present set of experiments, we set $k = 2\,000$, with 20 non-zero elements (10 negative and 10 positive unit values) randomly distributed in the $2\,000$-dimensional index vectors. Sahlgren has reported (Sahlgren, 2004) that in his original experiments on Random Indexing dimensionalities around $2\,000$ seem to be optimal, and our initial experiments have confirmed this to be a useful starting value.

### 2.3  Similarity measure

The vector space model offers a convenient way to statistically measure similarity between words, but exactly how this similarity is best represented is far from self-evident, especially in the case where semantic correspondences from one larger semantic space are mapped onto values in a smaller semantic space. The question what an ideal distribution of the semantic correspondence function would be is open. If there were a clear distinction where words tended to be either close or far away, a binary representation might very well be preferable; this property could be approximated by using some function with a non-linear increase at close proximities to better enhance the effect of thematic closeness.

The simplest way to define similarity in the vector space is to use the standard cosine measure between length-normalized vectors. Measured distributions of cosine-values appear to be close to linear, as seen in Figure 2 (which shows 1 000 sorted results from randomly selected word pairs in a document-coded model with 2 000 dimensions, trained on the texts used in our experiments). There is no non-arbitrary point in the value set where a threshold could be set, and in the present experiments we use the unmodified cosine function.

Only some values below 0 (angles above $90°$) and a few hits on 1 (where the angle is 0, and the words identical) can be found in the data. The distribution only slightly favors low and high values, but is comparable to a linear function. For our experiments, we settle with subtracting the median value, to get a good distribution of positive and negative values. Testing randomly selected words suggests a value of 0.33, and thus we will use the function $cos\theta - 0.33$ throughout, where $\theta$ is the angle between the vectors in the 2 000-dimensional space.

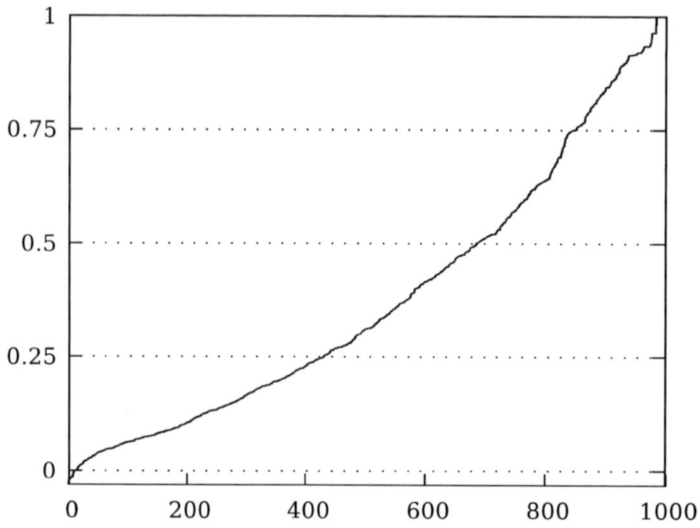

Figure 2: Distribution of correspondence (measured as $cos\theta$) between 1 000 random word pairs

## 2.4  Evaluation criteria

A possible gold standard in this type of experiment is comparison against a manually compiled English-German lexicon, something that we will be using in these experiments. The cross-references found in such a lexicon are however not typical of any results one could realistically expect. Experiments that sort out the closest matches in a vector space tend to find words that are similar in a very general sense. In going from a vector space of higher dimensionality to a smaller one, it is unavoidable to lose some information. This means that an absolute upper limit for the results would be the results our larger model delivers on one language, or possibly what could be reached by Random Indexing when document-trained on aligned bi-lingual texts. In experiments made on parallel texts Karlgren and Sahlgren (Karlgren and Sahlgren, 2001) report an approximate precision of 73%.

## 3  Experiment

### 3.1  Data

We have used a parallel and lemmatized English and German section of the translated proceedings from the European Parliament of Eu-

roparl[4]. 31 250 documents for each language have been chosen from the corpus — if a document has been chosen for the one language, the translation of it was not included. The English documents average 325 words per document and the German documents a bit over 300.

### 3.2  Reference wordlist

The reference wordlist is selected through judicious manual selection, by examining the topic matter and terminology of the training data and perusing independent published dictionaries. We have kept the domain of the reference words as close as possible to those discussed in the European Parliament. No independent assessment of reference term translation quality was made; it would be desirable to have a more principled approach to reference term selection, and it would seem to be possible to use term occurrence and distributional characteristics for this purpose.

---

[4]Europarl consists of parallel texts from the plenary debates of the European Parliament. The data is available at http://people.csail.mit.edu/people/koehn /publications/europarl/

---

Holmlund et al.: *Creating bilingual lexica using reference wordlists*

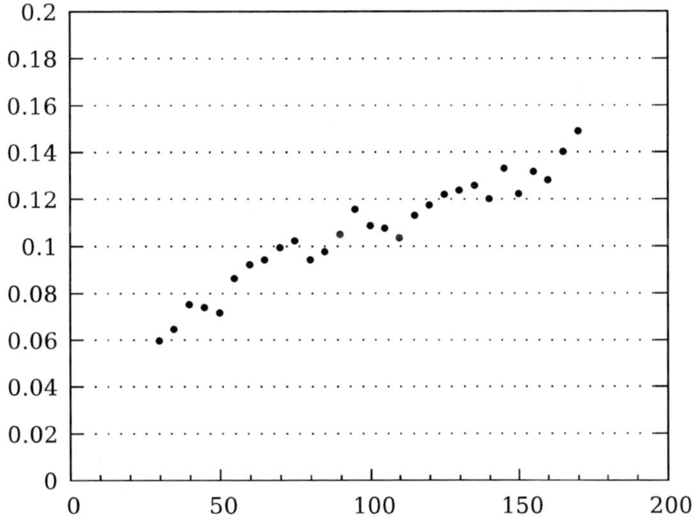

Figure 3: Precision by number of reference words, strict evaluation scheme.

### 3.3  Gold standard

We use the English-German dictionary of Technische Universität Chemnitz[5] to evaluate the closest word in the reduced vector space. Every German word given in the dictionary as a translation candidate to the English one is regarded as an equally valid hit in the conducted experiments.

### 3.4  Procedure

For each run, 50 different words were chosen from the English documents by randomly selecting them from the texts. Words already used in the run and reference words were discarded and new words drawn. We ran evaluation using two schemes: *strict* and *lenient*.

Strict evaluation was done by selecting the single closest German word in the combined cross-language correspondence vector space. If the German word was given as a candidate translation to the English word in the gold standard dictionary, it was counted as a hit. The precision of a run was calculated as the proportion of successful translations of the 50 words.

Lenient evaluation was done by selecting the *ten* closest German words in the combined

cross-language correspondence vector space. Also, if an English word did not appear in the gold standard dictionary at all it was discarded and a new word drawn. If any of the ten German words was given as a candidate translation to the English word in the gold standard dictionary, it was counted as a hit. The precision of a run was again calculated as the proportion of successful translations of the 50 words.

The size of the reference wordlist is varied: for each run, $r$ reference words were chosen randomly from the 170 word full reference word list. The test was performed with 50 runs of 50 random words with several different values for $r$ tested, and for each $r$ the average percentage of hits is recorded.

## 4  Results

Figure 3 shows the precision for the strict evaluation as the reference wordlist size varies from 30 to 170.

Figure 4 shows the precision for the lenient evaluation as the reference wordlist size varies from 5 to 170.

## 5  Discussion

The number of dictionary hits ranges from three to twelve out of fifty, depending on size of reference word list and on evaluation scheme.

---

[5]Technische Universität Chemnitz' German-English Dictionary contains a bit over 170 000 entries and can be found at: http://dict.tu-chemnitz.de

---

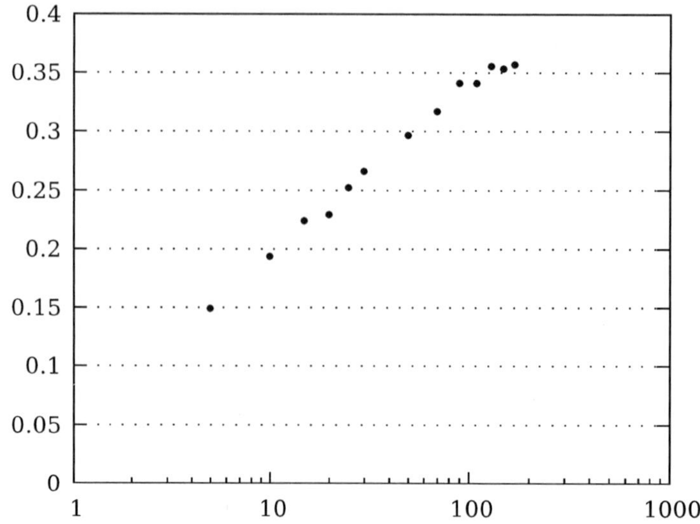

Figure 4: Precision by number of reference words, lenient evaluation scheme.

There are a number of observations that can be made from this seemingly low score.

Firstly, the results are amazingly high for reference word lists sizes of *five* and *ten*! With only a very small number of fix points several of the suggestions hit candidates from the lexicon. It is an impressive tribute to the underlying topical similarity of the data that the alignment can be done to that level with only a handful of reference points.

Secondly, the reference word lists were selected manually, and purposely kept small and of high quality. Some preliminary experiments with sloppier and larger word lists (not reported here) gave unsatisfactory results. The quality of the reference word list is — unsurprisingly — a major determining factor for the quality of the results. A principled method for selection and evaluation of the reference pairs would be desirable and the design of such an method is yet an open question. The coverage and scope of the set of words, the characteristics of the translations correspondences over the languages, the topical characteristics of the words themselves, and the domain orientedness of the set are all factors that have not been systematically studied by us.

Thirdly, the evaluation scheme is very straight-laced. As discussed above, translation dictionaries are designed for purposes different from those we envision for the resource we are developing. Related words of similar meaning but opposite polarity; variants along a semantic dimension; archaic turns of phrase; subsumption hierarchies are none counted as hits by the current scheme.

Fourthly, while this study makes first steps towards evaluating the effects of the reference list on the result quality, no examination of the effects of the quality of the original vector space on the result have been investigated.

In spite of these limitations and reservations, the results are surprisingly promising even given the narrow base of the data. Our belief is that these are the first steps towards a computationally tractable, cognitively plausible, and task- and application-wise reasonable solution for the problem of multi-lingual lexical resources.

## References

Scott Deerwester, Susan T. Dumais, George W. Furnas, Thomas K. Landauer, and Richard Harshman. 1990. Indexing by latent semantic analysis. *Journal of the Society for Information Science*, 41(6):391–407.

Pentti Kanerva, Jan Kristofersson, and Anders Holst. 2000. Random indexing of text samples for latent semantic analysis. In *Proceed-*

ings of the 22nd Annual Conference of the *Cognitive Science Society*, page 1036. Erlbaum.

Jussi Karlgren and Magnus Sahlgren. 2001. From words to understanding. In Yoshinori Uesaka, Pentti Kanerva, and Hideki Asoh, editors, *Foundations of Real-World Intelligence*, pages 294–308. CSLI Publications.

Thomas K. Landauer and Susan T. Dumais. 1997. A solution to plato's problem: The latent semantic analysis theory of acquisition, induction and representation of knowledge. *Psychological Review*, 104(2):211–240.

Magnus Sahlgren. 2004. Automatic bilingual lexicon acquisition using random indexing of aligned bilingual data. In *Proceedings of the fourth international conference on Language Resources and Evaluation, LREC 2004*.

# Naive Bayes spam filtering using word-position-based attributes and length-sensitive classification thresholds


**Johan Hovold**

Department of Computer Science
Lund University
Box 118, 221 00 Lund, Sweden
`johan.hovold.363@student.lu.se`



## Abstract

This paper explores the use of the naive Bayes classifier as the basis for personalised spam filters. Several machine learning algorithms, including variants of naive Bayes, have previously been used for this purpose, but the author's implementation using word-position-based attribute vectors gave very good results when tested on several publicly available corpora. The effects of various forms of attribute selection – removal of frequent and infrequent words, respectively, and by using mutual information – are investigated. It is also shown how n-grams, with $n > 1$, may be used to boost classification performance. Finally, an efficient weighting scheme for cost-sensitive classification is introduced.


## 1  Introduction

The problem of unsolicited bulk e-mail, or *spam*, gets worse with every year. The vast amount of spam being sent wastes resources on the Internet, wastes time for users, and may expose children to unsuitable contents (e.g. pornography). This development has stressed the need for automatic spam filters.

Early spam filters were instances of *knowledge engineering* and used hand-crafted rules (e.g. the presence of the string "buy now" indicates spam). The process of creating the rule base requires both knowledge and time, and the rules were thus often supplied by the developers of the filter. Having common and, more or less, publicly available rules made it easy for spammers to construct their e-mails to get through the filters.

Recently, a shift has occurred as more focus has been put on *machine learning* for the automatic creation of personalised spam filters. A supervised learning algorithm is presented with e-mails from the user's mailbox and outputs a filter. The e-mails have previously been classified manually as spam or non-spam. The resulting spam filter has the advantage of being optimised for the e-mail distribution of the individual user. Thus it is able to use also the characteristics of non-spam, or *legitimate*, e-mails (e.g. presence of the string "machine learning") during classification.

Perhaps the first attempt of using machine learning algorithms for the generation of spam filters was reported by Sahami et al. (1998). They trained a *naive Bayes classifier* and reported promising results. Other algorithms have been tested but there seems to be no clear winner (Androutsopoulos et al., 2004). The naive Bayes approach has been picked up by end-user applications such as the Mozilla e-mail client[1] and the free software project SpamAssassin[2], where the latter is using a combination of both rules and machine learning.

Spam filtering differs from other text categorisation tasks in at least two ways. First, one might expect a greater class heterogeneity – it is not the contents per se that defines spam, but rather the fact that it is unsolicited. Similarly, the class of legitimate messages may also span a number of diverse subjects. Secondly, since misclassifying a legitimate message is generally much worse than misclassifying a spam message, there is a qualitative difference between the classes that needs to be taken into account.

In this paper the results of using a variant of the naive Bayes classifier for spam filtering

---

[1] `http://www.mozilla.org/`
[2] `http://www.spamassassin.org/`

"

are presented. The effects of various forms of *attribute selection* are explored, as are the effects of considering not only single tokens, but rather sequences of tokens, as attributes. An efficient scheme for cost-sensitive classification is also introduced. All experiments have been conducted on several publicly available corpora, thereby making a comparison with previously published results possible.

The rest of this paper is organised as follows: Section 2 presents the naive Bayes classifier; Section 3 discusses the benchmark corpora used; in Section 4 the experimental results are presented; Section 5 gives a comparison with previously reported results, and in the last section some conclusions are drawn.

## 2   The naive Bayes classifier

In the general context, the instances to be classified are described by attribute vectors $\vec{a} = \langle a_1, a_2, \ldots, a_n \rangle$. Bayes' theorem says that the posterior probability of an instance $\vec{a}$ being of a certain class $c$ is

$$P(c|\vec{a}) = \frac{P(\vec{a}|c)P(c)}{P(\vec{a})}. \qquad (1)$$

The naive Bayes classifier assigns to an instance the most probable, or maximum a posteriori, classification from a finite set $C$ of classes

$$c_{MAP} \equiv \underset{c \in C}{\operatorname{argmax}} P(c|\vec{a}).$$

By noting that the prior probability $P(\vec{a})$ in Equation (1) is independent of $c$, we may rewrite the last equation as

$$c_{MAP} = \underset{c \in C}{\operatorname{argmax}} P(\vec{a}|c)P(c). \qquad (2)$$

The probabilities $P(\vec{a}|c) = P(a_1, a_2, \ldots, a_n|c)$ could be estimated directly from the training data, but are generally infeasible to estimate unless the available data is vast. Thus the *naive Bayes assumption* – that the individual attributes are conditionally independent of each other given the classification – is introduced:

$$P(a_1, a_2, \ldots, a_n|c) = \prod_i P(a_i|c).$$

With this strong assumption, Equation (2) becomes the naive Bayes classifier:

$$c_{NB} = \underset{c \in C}{\operatorname{argmax}} P(c) \prod_i P(a_i|c) \qquad (3)$$

(Mitchell, 1997).

In text classification applications, one may choose to define one attribute for each word position in a document. This means that we need to estimate the probability of a certain word $w_k$ occurring at position $i$ given the target classification $c_j$: $P(a_i = w_k|c_j)$. Due to training data sparseness, we introduce the additional assumption that the probability of a specific word $w_k$ occurring at position $i$ is identical to the probability of that same word occurring at position $m$, that is, $P(a_i = w_k|c_j) = P(a_m = w_k|c_j)$ for all $i, j, k, m$. Thus we estimate $P(a_i = w_k|c_j)$ with $P(w_k|c_j)$. The probabilities $P(w_k|c_j)$ may be estimated with maximum likelihood estimates, using Laplace smoothing to avoid zero probabilities:

$$P(w_k|c_j) = \frac{C_j(w_k) + 1}{n_j + |Vocabulary|},$$

where $C_j(w_k)$ is the number of occurrences of the word $w_k$ in all documents of class $c_j$, $n_j$ is the total number of word positions in documents of class $c_j$, and $|Vocabulary|$ is the number of distinct words in all documents. The class priors $P(c_j)$ are estimated with document ratios. (Mitchell, 1997)

Note that during classification, the index $i$ in Equation (3) ranges over all word positions containing words which are in the vocabulary, thus ignoring so called *out-of-vocabulary* words.

The resulting classifier is equivalent to a naive Bayes text classifier based on a *multinomial event model* (or *unigram language model*). For a more elaborate discussion of the text model used, see Joachims (1997) and McCallum and Nigam (1998).

## 3   Benchmark corpora

The experiments were conducted on the PU corpora[3] and the SpamAssassin corpus[4]. The four PU corpora, dubbed PU1, PU2, PU3 and PUA, respectively, have been made publicly available by Androutsopoulos et al. (2004) in order to promote standard benchmarks. The four corpora contain private mailboxes of four different users in encrypted form. The messages

---

[3]The PU corpora are available at `http://www.iit.demokritos.gr/skel/i-config/`.

[4]The SpamAssassin corpus is available at `http://spamassassin.org/publiccorpus/`.

---

**Table 1:** Sizes and spam ratios of the five corpora.

| corpus | messages | spam ratio |
|--------|----------|------------|
| PU1    | 1099     | 44%        |
| PU2    | 721      | 20%        |
| PU3    | 4139     | 44%        |
| PUA    | 1142     | 50%        |
| SA     | 6047     | 31%        |

have been preprocessed and stripped from attachments, HTML-tags and mail headers (except `Subject`). This may lead to overly pessimistic results since attachments, HTML-tags and mail headers may add useful information to the classification process. For more information on the compositions and characteristics of the PU corpora see Androutsopoulos et al. (2004).

The SpamAssassin corpus (SA) consists of private mail, donated by different users, in unencrypted form with headers and attachments retained[5]. The fact that the e-mails are collected from different distributions may lead to overly optimistic results, for example, if (some of) the spam messages have been sent to a particular address, but none of the legitimate messages have. On the other hand, the fact that the legitimate messages have been donated by different users may lead to underestimates since this should imply a greater diversity of the topics of legitimate e-mails.

The sizes and compositions of the five corpora are shown in Table 1.

# 4   Experimental results

As mentioned above, misclassifying a legitimate mail as spam ($L \to S$) is in general worse than misclassifying a spam message as legitimate ($S \to L$). In order to capture such asymmetries when measuring classification performance, two measures from the field of information retrieval, called precision and recall, are often used. Denote with $|S \to L|$ and $|S \to S|$ the number of spam messages classified as legitimate and spam, respectively, and similarly for $|L \to L|$ and $|L \to S|$. Then *spam recall* ($R$) and

*spam precision* ($P$) are defined by

$$R = \frac{|S \to S|}{|S \to S| + |S \to L|}$$

and

$$P = \frac{|S \to S|}{|S \to S| + |L \to S|}.$$

In the rest of this paper, spam recall and spam precision are referred to simply as recall and precision. Intuitively, recall measures effectiveness whereas precision gives a measure of safety. One is often willing to accept lower recall (more spam messages slipping through) in order to gain precision (fewer misclassified legitimate messages).

Sometimes *accuracy* ($Acc$) – the ratio of correctly classified messages – is used as a combined measure.

All experiments were conducted using 10-fold cross validation. That is, the messages have been divided into ten partitions[6] and at each iteration nine partitions were used for training and the remaining tenth for testing. The reported figures are the means of the values from the ten iterations.

## 4.1   Attribute selection

It is common to apply some form of attribute selection process, retaining only a subset of the words – or rather tokens, since punctuation signs and other symbols are often included – found in the training messages. This way the learning and classification process may be sped up and memory requirements are lowered. Attribute selection may also lead to increased classification performance since, for example, the risk of overfitting the training data is reduced.

Removing infrequent words and the most frequent words, respectively, are two possible approaches (Mitchell, 1997). The rationale behind removing infrequent words is that this is likely to have a significant effect on the size of the attribute set and that predictions should not be based on such rare observations anyway. Removing the most frequent words is motivated by the fact that common words, such as the English words "the" and "to", are as likely to occur in spam as in legitimate messages.

---

[5]Due to a primitive mbox parser, e-mails containing non-textual or encoded parts (i.e. most e-mails with attachments) were ignored in the experiments.

[6]The PU corpora come prepartitioned and the SA corpus has been partitioned according to the last digit of the messages' decimal ids.

---

*Hovld: Naive Bayes spam filtering*

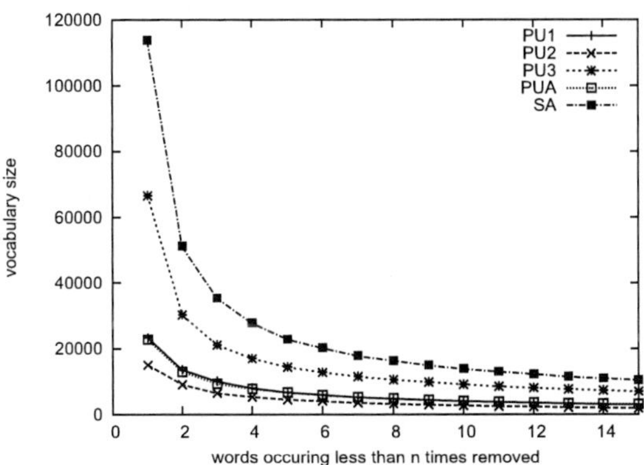

**Figure 1:** Impact on vocabulary size when removing infrequent words (from nine tenths of each corpora).

A very common method is to rank the attributes using *mutual information* ($MI$) and to keep only the highest scoring ones. $MI(X;C)$ gives a measure of how well an attribute $X$ discriminates between the various classes in $C$ and is defined as

$$\sum_{x\in\{0,1\}} \sum_{c\in C} P(x,c) \log \frac{P(x,c)}{P(x)P(c)}$$

(Cover and Thomas, 1991). The probability distributions were estimated as in Section 2. This corresponds to the multinomial variant of mutual information used by McCallum and Nigam (1998), but with the difference that the class priors were estimated using document ratios rather than word-position ratios. (Using word-position ratios gave almost exactly the same classification results.)

In the first experiment, tokens occurring less than $n = 1, \ldots, 15$ times were removed. The results indicated unaffected or slightly increased precision at the expense of slightly reduced recall as $n$ grew. The exception was the PU2 corpus where precision dropped significantly. The reason for this may be that PU2 is the smallest corpus and contains many infrequent tokens. On the other hand, removing infrequent tokens had a dramatic impact on the vocabulary size (see Figure 1). Removing tokens occurring less than three times seems to be a good trade-off between memory usage and classification performance, reducing the vocabulary size with 56–69%. This selection scheme was used throughout the remaining experiments.

Removing the most frequent words turned out to have a major effect on both precision

and recall (see Figure 2). This effect was most significant on the largest and non-preprocessed SA corpus where recall increased from 77% to over 95% by just removing the hundred most common tokens, but classification gained from removing the 100–200 most frequent tokens on all corpora. Removing too many tokens reduced classification performance – again most notably on the smaller PU2 corpus. We believe that this selection scheme increases performance because it makes sure that very frequent tokens do not dominate Equation (3) completely. The greater impact of removing frequent tokens on the SA corpus can thus be explained by the fact that it contains many more very frequent tokens (originating from mail headers and HTML) (see related discussion in Section 4.2).

In the last attribute-selection experiment, $MI$-ranking was used instead of removing the most frequent tokens. Although the gain in terms of reduced memory usage was high – the vocabulary size dropped from 7000–35000 to the number of attributes chosen to be kept (e.g. 500–3000) – classification performance was significantly reduced. When $MI$-ranking was performed after first removing the 200 most frequent tokens, the performance penalty was not as severe, and using $MI$-ranking to select 3000–4000 attributes then seems reasonable (see Figure 3). We are currently investigating further the relation between mutual information and frequent tokens.

Since learning and classification time is mostly unaffected – mutual information still has to be calculated for every attribute – we see no reason for using $MI$-ranking unless memory usage is crucial[7], and we decided not to use it further (with unigram attributes).

## 4.2 n-grams

Up to now each attribute has corresponded to a single word position, or unigram. Is it possible to obtain better results by considering also token sequences of length two and three (i.e. n-grams for $n = 2, 3$)? The question was raised and answered partially in Androutsopoulos et al. (2004). Although many bi- and trigrams were shown to have very high information contents, as measured by mutual information, no improvement was found.

---

[7]Androutsopoulos et al. (2004) reaches a different conclusion.

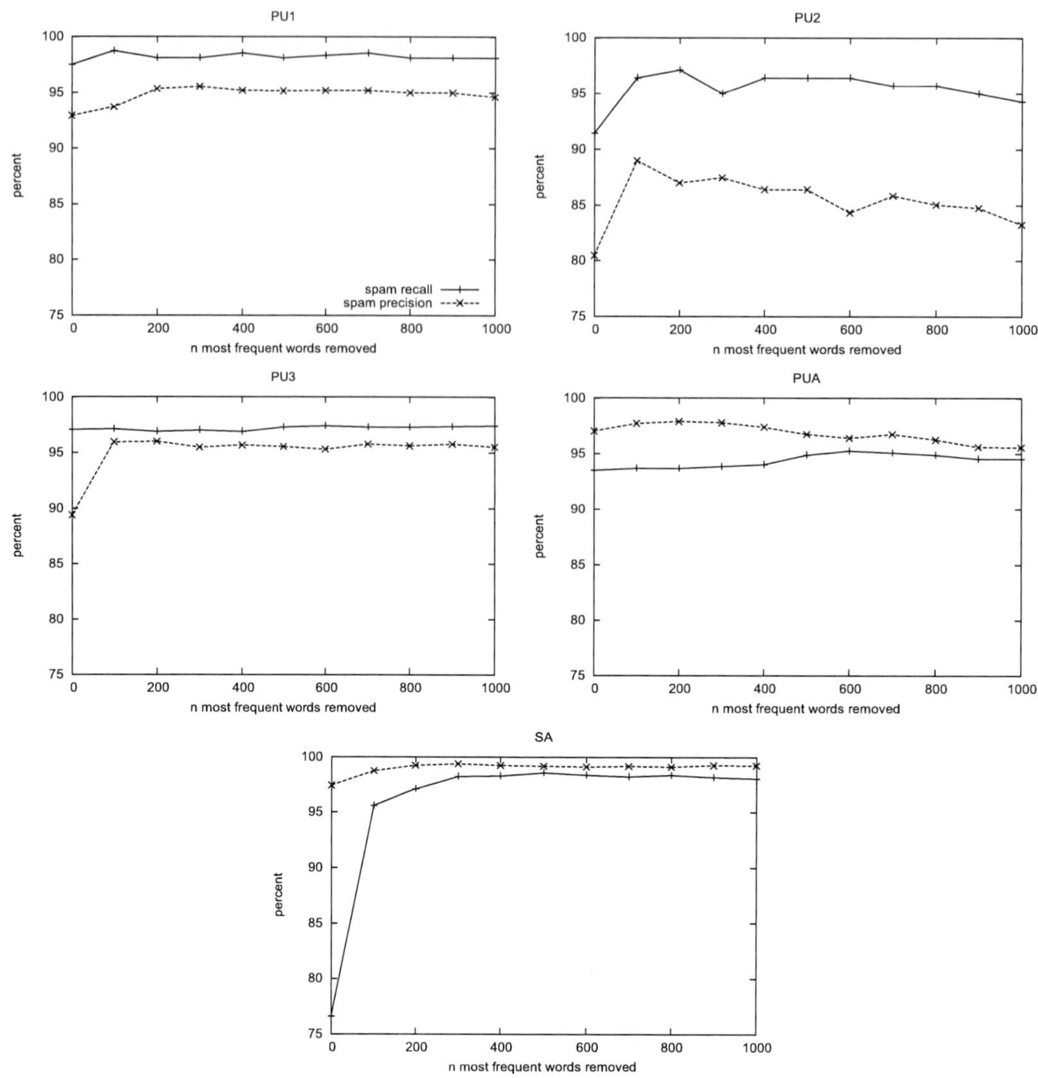

**Figure 2:** Impact on spam precision and recall when removing the most frequent words.

There are many possible ways of extending the attribute set with general n-grams, for instance, by using all available n-grams, by just using some of them, or by using some kind of back-off approach. The attribute probabilities $P(w_i, w_{i+1}, \ldots, w_{i+n}|c_j)$ are still estimated using maximum likelihood estimates with Laplace smoothing

$$\frac{C_j(w_i, w_{i+1}, \ldots, w_{i+n}) + 1}{n_j + |Vocabulary|}.$$

Note that extending the attribute set in this way can result in a total probability mass greater than one. Fortunately, this need not be a prob-

lem since we are not estimating the classification probabilities explicitly (see Equation (3)).

It turned out that adding bi- and trigrams to the attribute set increased classification performance on all of the PU corpora, but not (initially) on the SA corpus. The various methods for extending the attribute set all gave similar results, and we settled on the simple version which just considers each n-gram occurrence as an independent attribute[8]. The results are shown in Table 2.

---

[8]This is clearly not true. The three n-grams in the phrase "buy now" – "buy", "now" and "buy now" – are obviously not independent.

---

Hovld: *Naive Bayes spam filtering*

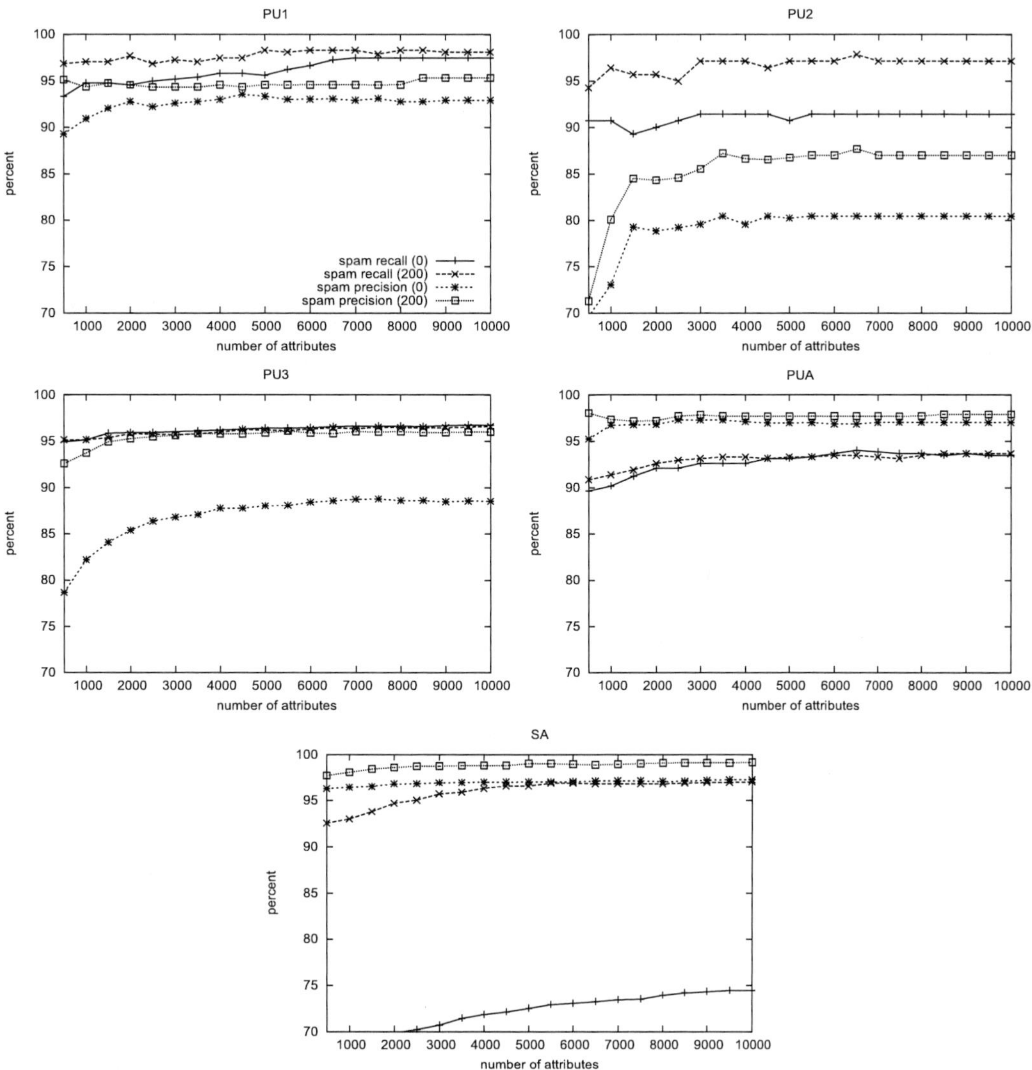

**Figure 3:** Attribute selection using mutual information – spam recall and precision versus the number of retained attributes after first removing no words and the 200 most frequent words, respectively.

The precision gain was highest for the corpus with lowest initial precision, namely PU2. For the other PU corpora the precision gain was relatively small or even non-existing. At first the significantly decreased classification performance on the SA corpus came as a bit of a surprise. The reason turned out to be that when considering also bi- and trigrams in the non-preprocessed SA corpus, a lot of very frequent attributes, originating from mail headers and HTML, were added to the attribute set. This had the effect of giving these attributes a too dominant role in Equation (3). By removing more of the most frequent n-grams, classifi-

cation performance was increased also for the SA corpus. The conclusion to be drawn is that mail headers and HTML, although containing useful information, should not be included by brute force. Perhaps some kind of weighting scheme or selective inclusion process would be appropriate.

Finally, we note that the gained classification performance came with a cost in terms of increased memory requirements. The vocabulary sizes became 17–23 times larger prior to attribute selection (i.e. during training) and 8–12 times larger afterwards (i.e. during operation) compared to when only using unigrams. The

**Table 2:** Comparison of classification results when using only unigram attributes and uni-, bi- and trigram attributes, respectively. In the experiment n-grams occurring less than three times and the 200 most frequent n-grams were removed. The second n-gram row for the SA corpus shows the result when the 5000 most frequent n-grams were removed.

| $n$-grams | $R$ | $P$ | $Acc$ |
|---|---|---|---|
| **PU1** | | | |
| $n = 1$ | 98.12 | 95.35 | 97.06 |
| $n = 1, 2, 3$ | 99.17 | 96.19 | 97.89 |
| **PU2** | | | |
| $n = 1$ | 97.14 | 87.00 | 96.20 |
| $n = 1, 2, 3$ | 95.00 | 93.12 | 96.90 |
| **PU3** | | | |
| $n = 1$ | 96.92 | 96.02 | 96.83 |
| $n = 1, 2, 3$ | 96.59 | 97.83 | 97.53 |
| **PUA** | | | |
| $n = 1$ | 93.68 | 97.91 | 95.79 |
| $n = 1, 2, 3$ | 94.74 | 97.75 | 96.23 |
| **SA** | | | |
| $n = 1$ | 97.12 | 99.25 | 98.95 |
| $n = 1, 2, 3$ | 92.26 | 98.70 | 97.42 |
| $n = 1, 2, 3$ | 98.46 | 99.66 | 99.46 |

latter figure may, however, be reduced to 0.7–4 (while retaining approximately the same performance gain) by using mutual information to select a vocabulary of 25000 n-grams.

### 4.3 Cost-sensitive classification

Generally it is much worse to misclassify legitimate mails than letting spam slip through the filter. Hence, it is desirable to be able to bias the filter towards classifying messages as legitimate, yielding higher precision at the expense of recall.

A common way of biasing the filter is to classify a message $d$ as spam if and only if the estimated probability $P(spam|d)$ exceeds some threshold $t > 0.5$, or equivalently, to classify as spam if and only if

$$\frac{P(spam|d)}{P(legit|d)} > \lambda,$$

for some real number $\lambda > 1$ (Sahami et al., 1998; Androutsopoulos et al., 2000; Androutsopoulos et al., 2004). This has the same effect as multiplying the prior probability of legitimate messages by $\lambda$ and then classifying according to Equation (3).

As noted in Androutsopoulos et al. (2004), the naive Bayes classifier is quite insensitive to (small) changes to $\lambda$ since the probability estimates tend to approach 0 and 1, respectively. As is shown below, this insensitivity increases with the length of the attribute vectors, and by exploiting this fact, a more efficient cost-sensitive classification scheme for word-position-based (and hence, variable-length) attribute vectors is made possible.

Instead of using the traditional scheme, we propose the following classification criterion:

$$\frac{P(spam|d)}{P(legit|d)} > w^{|d|},$$

where $w > 1$, which is equivalent to multiplying each posterior probability $P(w_i|c_{legit})$ in Equation (3) with the weight $w$. Intuitively, we require the spam posterior probability for each word occurrence to be on average $w$ times as high as the corresponding legitimate probability (given uniform priors).

When comparing the two schemes by plotting their recall-precision curves for the five benchmark corpora, we found that the length-sensitive scheme was more efficient than the traditional one – rendering higher recall at each given precision level (see Figure 4). This can be explained by the fact that the certainty quotient $q(d) = P(spam|d)/P(legit|d)$ actually grew (decreased) exponentially with $|d|$ for spam (legitimate) messages and thereby made it safe to use much larger thresholds for longer messages. With length-sensitive thresholds we were thus able to compensate for longer misclassified legitimate mails without misclassifying as many short spam messages in the process (as would a large $\lambda$ with the traditional scheme) (see Figure 5).

## 5 Evaluation

Many different machine learning algorithms besides naive Bayes, such as $k$-Nearest Neighbour, Support Vector Machines (SVM), and C4.5, have previously been used in spam-filtering experiments. There seems to have been no clear winner, but there is a difficulty in comparing the results of different experiments since the used corpora have rarely been made publicly available (Androutsopoulos et al., 2004). This section gives a brief comparison with the implementation and results of the authors of the PU corpora.

---

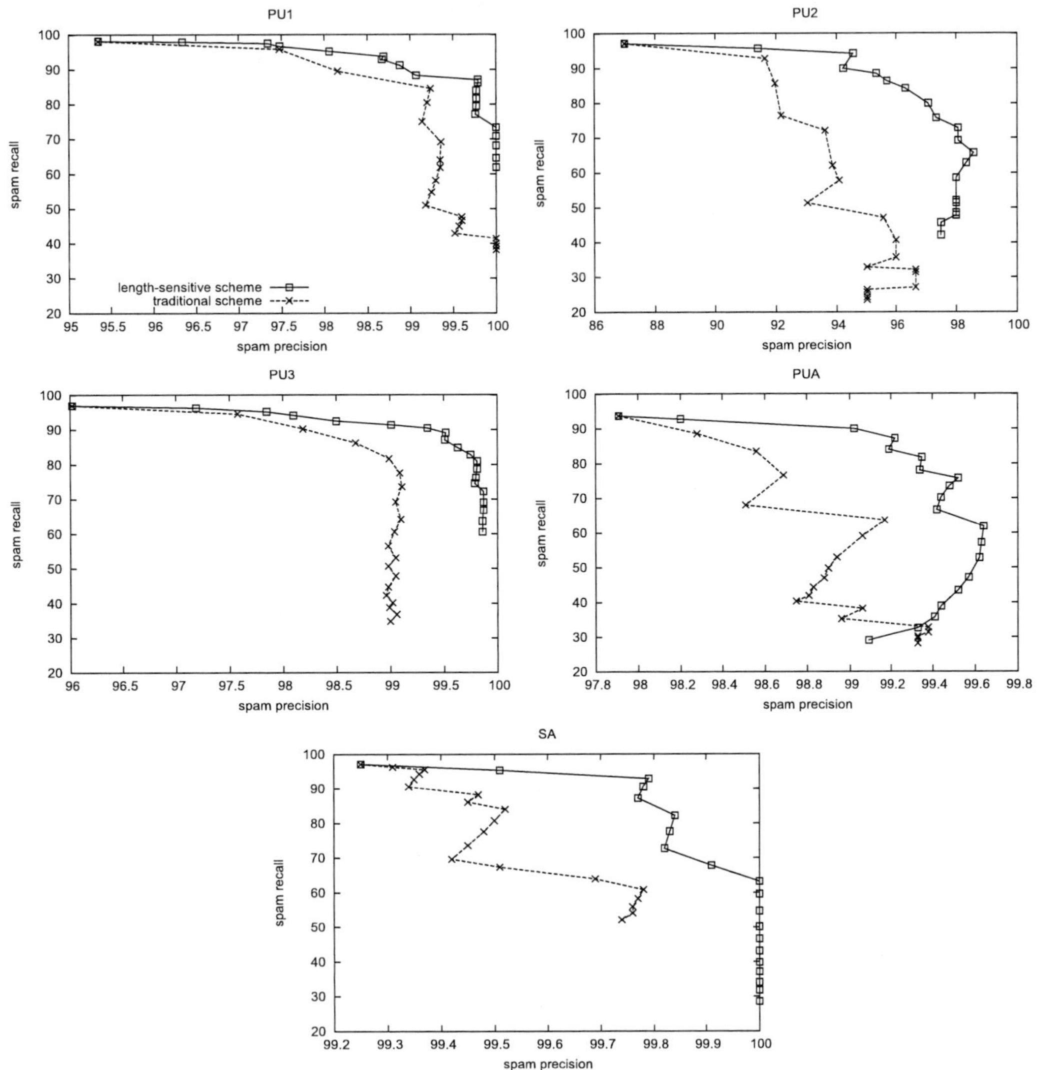

**Figure 4:** Recall-precision curves of the two weighting schemes from cost-sensitive classification on the five corpora using the weights $w = 1.0, 1.1, \ldots, 2.9$ and $\lambda = 10^0, 10^4, \ldots, 10^{76}$, respectively.

In Androutsopoulos et al. (2004), a variant of naive Bayes was compared with three other learning algorithms: Flexible Bayes, Logit-Boost, and Support Vector Machines. All of the algorithms used real-valued word-frequency attributes. The attributes were selected by removing words occurring less than four times and then keeping the 600 words with highest mutual information.[9] As can be seen in

Table 3, the word-position-based naive Bayes implementation of this paper achieved significantly higher precision and better or comparable recall than the word-frequency-based variant on all four PU corpora. The results were also better or comparable to those of the best-performing algorithm on each corpus.

In Androutsopoulos et al. (2000), the authors used a naive Bayes implementation based on Boolean attributes, representing the presence or absence of a fixed number of words selected using mutual information. In their experiments three different cost scenarios were explored, and the number of attributes used was opti-

---

[9]The authors only report results of their naive Bayes implementation on attribute sets with up to 600 words, but they seem to conclude that using larger attribute sets only have a marginal effect on accuracy.

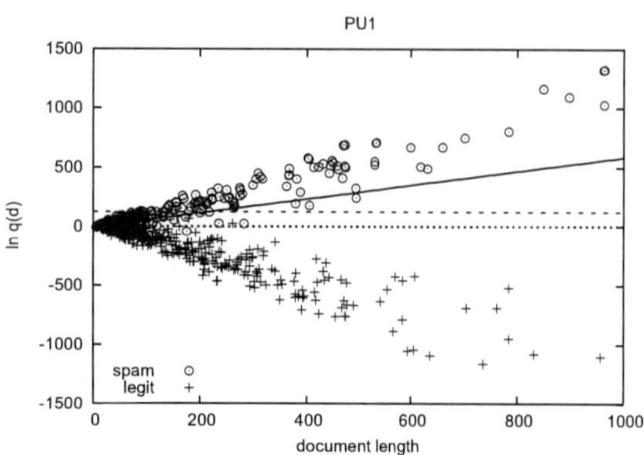


**Figure 5:** Certainty quotient $q(d) = \frac{P(spam|d)}{P(legit|d)}$ versus document length (after removing out-of-vocabulary words) for the PU1 corpus. The dashed lines corresponds to the constant thresholds $\lambda = 0$ (i.e. unweighted classification) and $\lambda = 10^{55}$, respectively, and the solid line correspond to the length-sensitive threshold $w^{|d|}$ with $w = 2.0$. A document $d$ is classified as spam if and only if $q(d)$ is greater than the threshold in use.

**Table 3:** Comparison of the results achieved by naive Bayes in Androutsopoulos et al. (2004) and by the author's implementation. In the latter, attributes were selected by removing the 200 most frequent words as well as words occurring less than three times. Included are also the results of the best-performing algorithm for each corpus as found in Androutsopoulos et al. (2004).

| learner | $R$ | $P$ | $Acc$ |
|---|---|---|---|
| PU1 | | | |
| Androutsopoulos | 99.38 | 89.58 | 94.59 |
| Hovold | 98.12 | 95.35 | 97.06 |
| Flexible Bayes | 97.08 | 96.92 | 97.34 |
| PU2 | | | |
| Androutsopoulos | 90.00 | 80.77 | 93.66 |
| Hovold | 97.14 | 87.00 | 96.20 |
| Flexible Bayes | 79.29 | 90.57 | 94.22 |
| PU3 | | | |
| Androutsopoulos | 94.84 | 93.59 | 94.79 |
| Hovold | 96.92 | 96.02 | 96.83 |
| SVM | 94.67 | 96.48 | 96.08 |
| PUA | | | |
| Androutsopoulos | 94.04 | 95.11 | 94.47 |
| Hovold | 93.68 | 97.91 | 95.79 |
| Flexible Bayes | 91.58 | 96.75 | 94.21 |

**Table 4:** Comparison of the results achieved by naive Bayes on the PU1 corpus in Androutsopoulos et al. (2000) and by the author's implementation. Results for the latter are shown for both unigram and n-gram ($n = 1, 2, 3$) attributes. In both cases, attributes were selected by removing the 200 most frequent n-grams as well as n-grams occurring less than three times. For each cost scenario, the weight $w$ has been selected in steps of 0.05 in order to get equal or higher precision.

| learner | $R$ | $P$ |
|---|---|---|
| Androutsopoulos ($\lambda = 1$) | 83.98 | 95.11 |
| Hovold, 1-gram ($w = 1$) | 98.12 | 95.35 |
| Hovold, n-gram ($w = 1$) | 99.17 | 96.19 |
| Androutsopoulos ($\lambda = 9$) | 78.77 | 96.65 |
| Hovold, 1-gram ($w = 1.20$) | 97.50 | 97.34 |
| Hovold, n-gram ($w = 1.05$) | 99.17 | 97.15 |
| Androutsopoulos ($\lambda = 999$) | 46.96 | 98.80 |
| Hovold, 1-gram ($w = 1.65$) | 91.67 | 98.88 |
| Hovold, n-gram ($w = 1.30$) | 96.04 | 98.92 |

mised for each scenario. Table 4 compares the best results achieved on the PU1 corpus[10] for each scenario with the results achieved by the naive Bayes implementation of this paper. Due to the difficulty of relating the two different weights, $\lambda$ and $w$, the weight $w$ has been selected in steps of 0.05 in order to get equal or higher precision. The authors deemed the $\lambda = 999$ scenario too difficult to be used in practise because of the low recall figures.

## 6 Conclusions

In this paper it has been shown that it is possible to achieve very good classification performance using a word-position-based variant of naive Bayes. The simplicity and low time complexity of the algorithm thus makes naive Bayes a good choice for end-user applications.

The importance of attribute selection has been stressed – memory requirements may be lowered and classification performance increased. In particular, removing the most frequent words was found to have a major impact on classification performance when using word-position-based attributes.

By extending the attribute set with bi- and tri-grams, even better classification performance may be achieved, although at the cost of significantly increased memory requirements.

---

[10]The results are for the *bare* PU1 corpus, that is, the stop list and lemmatiser have not been applied.

With the use of a simple weighting scheme based on length-sensitive classification thresholds, precision may be boosted further while still retaining a high enough recall level – a feature very important in real-life applications.

## Acknowledgements

The author would like to thank Jacek Malec and Pierre Nugues for their encouraging support. Many thanks also to Peter Alriksson, Pontus Melke, and Ayna Nejad for useful comments on an earlier draft of this paper.

## References

Ion Androutsopoulos, John Koutsias, Konstantinos V. Chandrinos, and Constantine D. Spyropoulos. 2000. An experimental comparison of naive bayesian and keyword-based anti-spam filtering with personal e-mail messages. In P. Ingwersen N.J. Belkin and M.-K. Leong, editors, *Proceedings of the 23rd Annual International ACM SIGIR Conference on Research and Development in Information Retrieval*, pages 160–167, Athens, Greece.

Ion Androutsopoulos, Georgios Paliouras, and Eirinaios Michelakis. 2004. Learning to filter unsolicited commercial e-mail. Technical Report 2004/2, NCSR "Demokritos". Revised version.

Thomas M. Cover and Joy A. Thomas. 1991. *Elements of Information Theory*. Wiley.

Thorsten Joachims. 1997. A probabilistic analysis of the Rocchio algorithm with TFIDF for text categorization. In Douglas H. Fisher, editor, *Proceedings of ICML-97, 14th International Conference on Machine Learning*, pages 143–151, Nashville, US.

Andrew McCallum and Kamal Nigam. 1998. A comparison of event models for naive bayes text classification. In *Learning for Text Categorization: Papers from the 1998 Workshop*, pages 41–48, Madison, Wisconsin. AAAI Technical Report WS-98-05.

Tom M. Mitchell. 1997. *Machine Learning*. McGraw-Hill.

Mehran Sahami, Susan Dumais, David Heckerman, and Eric Horvitz. 1998. A bayesian approach to filtering junk E-mail. In *Learning for Text Categorization: Papers from the 1998 Workshop*, pages 55–62, Madison, Wisconsin. AAAI Technical Report WS-98-05.

# An analytical relation between analogical modeling and memory based learning


**Christer Johansson & Lars G. Johnsen**
Dept. of Linguistics and Literature
University of Bergen
N-5007 Bergen, Norway
{christer.johansson, lars.johnsen}@lili.uib.no


## Abstract


Analogical modeling (AM) is a memory based model. Known algorithms implementing AM depend on investigating all combinations of matching features, which in the worst case is exponential ($O(2^n)$). We formulate a representation theorem on analogical modeling which is used for implementing a range of approximations to AM with a much lower complexity. We will demonstrate how our model can be modified to reach better performance than the original AM model a popular categorization task (chunk tagging).


## 1  Introduction

Analogical modeling (AM) is a method to evaluate the analogical support for a classification (Skousen, 1989; Skousen, 1992; Skousen et al., 2002), which is compatible with psycholinguistic data (Chandler, 2002; Eddington, 2002; Mudrow, 2002, inter al.). Chandler (1993) propose it as an alternative to rule based and connectionist models of language processing and acquisition.

AM has also been used within Optimality Theory (Myers, 2002) and similar exemplar-based studies have looked at the development of phonological regularities with the number of exemplars (Pierrehumbert, 2001). AM defines a natural statistic, which can be implemented by comparisons of subsets of linguistic variables, without numerical calculations (Skousen, 1992; Skousen, 2002).

The original AM model compares all subsets of investigated variables. This causes an exponential explosion in the number of comparisons. This has made it difficult to investigate large models with many variables ($> 10$) and large

databases. Johnsen & Johansson (2005) gives an accurate approximation of AM, which considers all analogical support from the database. The analytical upper and lower bounds of the approximation is also provided (ibid.).

The essential simplification (ibid.)  is that each exemplar in the database only contributes with its most specific match to the incoming pattern to be classified. This provides a basis for directly comparing Skousen's model to other models of memory based learning (MBL).

In MBL, an example E is classified as belonging to category C by computing the score of E by going through the whole database. Skousen's model require the computation of the full analogical set for E. We can show this computation to be approximated with resources that are close to a linear search through the database.

The Johnsen & Johansson approximation reduces the time complexity of the analogical algorithm. The results imply that AM and many MBL models are related by different evaluations of the nearest match set. MBL typically selects nearest neighbors, whereas AM attempt to look at all support from the entire database, thus not needing to specify how many neighbors to look for.

Full AM and the proposed approximation has both been tested on predicting chunk tags (Tjong Kim Sang and Buchholz, 2000), as well as some test sets provided by Skousen (1989; 1992), and the approximation agrees very well with full AM results. However, the initial results for the chunk tagging task where disappointing for both AM models. The performance of AM and MBL has previously been compared favourably (Daelemans, 2002; Eddington, 2002, inter al.), but for some reason the initial AM model does not do very well on the chunk tasks, presumably because this task involves many heterogeneous patterns, i.e. patterns with more than one outcome. MBL relates to AM through the Johnsen & Johansson(2005) approximation of AM with an alternative weighting of contexts; a weighting that favors homogeneous contexts for AM, whereas MBL look at a weighted majority of outcomes from nearest neighbors, without concern for which patterns are homogeneous or not.

## 2  Background on AM

We will not go into details of analogical modeling, beyond what is necessary for comparing it with memory based learning. Johnsen & Johansson (2005) showed that the outcome in AM can be determined by summing up scores for each match pattern, where we only have to match the input once with all the examples in the database.

Examples in the database and each new input are expressed by a vector of feature values, similar to standard MBL. The operation of AM depends on matches. Each feature value may either match, between an example and the new input, or not. This creates a match vector where matches are encoded with a 1 and non-matches with 0, for example $< 0, 1, 0, 1, 1 >$ for five features.

We may imagine these vectors as a pointer to a box where we collect all the corresponding outcomes in the database. After we have gone through the database, we can look in all the non-empty boxes (which typically is of a much lower number than the number of examples), and observe the distribution of the outcomes. We are interested in those boxes that contain only one outcome. We call these boxes *first stage homogeneous*. Boxes with more than one outcome are less important, and may be discarded if we find homogeneous boxes pointed to by a more specific context, i.e. a match vector with more matches. The remaining (non-empty) boxes need to be sorted according to how many matches the index pattern contains. A more general pattern (e.g. $< 0, 0, 1 >$ is either homogeneous for the same outcome as the more specific pattern that it dominates (e.g. $< 1, 0, 1 >$, $< 0, 1, 1 >$, or $< 1, 1, 1 >$), or it is indeed *heterogeneous* and should be discarded.

A $score(\theta(x))$ is summed up for the number of homogeneous elements it dominates. Each part in the summation corresponds to looking

in one of the above mentioned "boxes" (x). Each score for each box has an associated constant $c_x$, which would give us the exact value for full analogical modeling, if it was known.

The scoring of the analogical set expressed in mathematical notation is:

$$\sum_{x \in \mathcal{M}} c_x score(\theta(x)) \qquad (1)$$

where $\mathcal{M}$ is the match set, and $x$ is a context in the match set.

The implication of the work in (Johnsen and Johansson, 2005) is that the match set $\mathcal{M}$, which is simple to calculate, contains *all* the results necessary for computing the overall effect, without actually building the whole analogical structure. In order to accurately weigh each context we need to estimate how many extensions each homogeneous pattern has. Johnsen and Johansson (2005) develops a maximum and minimum bound for this, and also discusses the possibilities for using Monte Carlo methods for discovering a closer fit.

Let us start with a simple and hypothetical case where M has exactly

two members $x$ and $y$ with a different outcome. Any supracontextual label shared between $x$ and $y$ will be heterogeneous. The number of these heterogeneous labels are *exactly the cardinality of the power set of the intersection between $x$ and $y$*. To see this, consider an example

$$\tau = (c, a, t, e, g, o, r, y)$$

and let $x$ and $y$ be defined as (using supracontextual notation):

$$
\begin{aligned}
&x = (c, -, t, -, -, o, r, -) \\
&\text{with unique } score(\theta(x)) = (3, 0) \approx 3\,r \\
&y = (c, a, -, -, -, o, -, -) \\
&\text{with } score(\theta(y)) = (0, 8) \approx 8\,e
\end{aligned} \qquad (2)
$$

Their common and therefore heterogeneous supracontextual labels are

$$
\left.
\begin{aligned}
&(c, -, -, -, -, o, -, -) \\
&(c, -, -, -, -, -, -, -) \\
&(-, -, -, -, -, o, -, -) \\
&(-, -, -, -, -, -, -, -)
\end{aligned}
\right\} \qquad (3)
$$

The total number of elements that dominate $x$ is sixteen; the homogeneous labels out of these sixteen are those that dominate $x$ and no other

---

element with a different outcome; in this case $y$. The labels $x$ shares with $y$ are the four labels in (3), and $x$ has 16-4=12 homogeneous labels above it. How is that number reached using sets?

Viewed as sets, the elements $x$ and $y$ are represented as:

$$x = \{c_1, t_3, o_6, r_7\} \text{ and } y = \{c_1, a_2, o_6\}.$$

Their shared supracontexts are given by the power set of their common variables.

$$x \cap y = \{c_1, t_3, o_6, r_7\} \cap \{c_1, a_2, o_6\} = \{c_1, o_6\}$$
$$\mathcal{P}(x \cap y) =$$
$$\mathcal{P}(\{c_1, o_6\}) = \{\emptyset, \{c_1, o_6\}, \{o_6\}, \{c_1\}\} \tag{4}$$

This set has four elements all in all, which all are equivalent to the labels in (3). The sets in (4) represent the heterogeneous supracontextual labels more general than either $x$ or $y$ and these are the only heterogeneous supracontexts in the lattice $\Lambda$ of supracontextual labels, given the assumptions made above.

The power sets for $x$ and $y$ have 16 and 8 elements respectively, so the total number of homogeneous supracontextual labels more general than either $x$ or $y$ is the value for the coefficients $c_x$ and $c_y$ from (1) calculated as:

$$\left. \begin{array}{l} c_x = \|\mathcal{P}(x) - \mathcal{P}(x \cap y)\| = 16 - 4 = 12 \\ c_y = \|\mathcal{P}(y) - \mathcal{P}(x \cap y)\| = 8 - 4 = 4 \end{array} \right\} \tag{5}$$

Plugging these numbers into the formula (1) gives the score of the analogical set for this case:

$$\sum_{x \in M} c_x score(\theta(x)) =$$
$$= 12 score(\theta(x)) + 4 score(\theta(y))$$
$$= 12(3,0) + 4(0,8) \tag{6}$$
$$= (36,0) + (0,32)$$
$$= (36,32)$$

In the general case however, the set $M$ consists of more elements, complicating the computation somewhat. Each $x \in M$ may share a number of supracontextual elements with other elements of $M$ that have a different outcome. The situation may be as depicted in the following table, where columns are labelled by elements of $M$ (in boldface) with their associated hypothetical outcomes (in italics).

Each cell in table 1 is associated with the power set $\mathcal{P}(x \cap y)$. This power set is only computed if the outcome of x is not equal to the outcome of y, and both outcomes are unique. The

| $\mathcal{M}$ | $\mathbf{a}_r$ | $\mathbf{g}_e$ | $\mathbf{h}_r$ | $\mathbf{d}_f$ |
|---|---|---|---|---|
| $\mathbf{a}_r$ | | $\mathcal{P}_{(a \cap g)}$ | | $\mathcal{P}_{(a \cap d)}$ |
| $\mathbf{g}_e$ | $\mathcal{P}_{(g \cap a)}$ | | $\mathcal{P}_{(g \cap h)}$ | |
| $\mathbf{h}_r$ | | $\mathcal{P}_{(h \cap g)}$ | | $\mathcal{P}_{(h \cap d)}$ |
| $\mathbf{d}_f$ | $\mathcal{P}_{(d \cap a)}$ | $\mathcal{P}_{(d \cap g)}$ | $\mathcal{P}_{(d \cap h)}$ | |

Table 1: Accessing disagreement in $\mathcal{M} \times \mathcal{M}$

intersection is computed for all labels with a non-unique outcome, even for those with identical outcomes. If two elements are non-unique, any label that is a subset of both will match up with their respective and disjoint data sets (see propositions 1 and 2 in (Johnsen and Johansson, 2005)), thereby *increasing* the number of disagreements, and consequently turning any such label into a heterogeneous label. Note that $a$ and $h$ have the same outcome in this table making their intersective cells empty.

Each non-empty cell corresponds to the simple case above. The complication stems from the fact that different cells may have non-empty intersections, i.e., it is possible that

$$\mathcal{P}(a \cap g) \cap \mathcal{P}(a \cap d) \neq \emptyset$$

Arithmetic difference of the cardinality of the cells may be way off the mark, due to the possibility that supracontexts may be subtracted more than once. Something more sophisticated is needed to compute the desired coefficients $c_x$. A couple of approximations are given in the following.

The approximations are gotten at by first collecting all subcontexts different from $a$ in a set $\delta(a)$:

$$\delta(a) = \{x \in \mathcal{M} | o(a) \neq o(x)\}$$

This equation represents the column labels for the row for $a$. The total number of homogeneous supracontexts $(=c_a)$ more general than $a$ is the cardinality of the set difference

$$\mathcal{P}(a) - \bigcup_{x \in \delta(a)} \mathcal{P}(a \cap x) \tag{7}$$

The second term in (7) corresponds to the value of the function H in JJ, and is the union of the power sets in the row for $a$. It represents the collection of supracontextual labels

---

more general than $a$, which also are shared with another subcontext, thus making all of them heterogeneous. The first term, $\Pi(a)$, is the set of all supracontextual labels more general than $a$. Therefore, the difference between these two sets is equal to the collection of homogeneous supracontextual labels more general than $a$. However, it is not the content of these sets that concerns us here; the goal is to find the cardinality of this difference.

The cardinality of $\mathcal{P}(a)$ is given the normal way as

$$\|\mathcal{P}(a)\| = 2^{\|a\|}$$

but how are the behemoth union to be computed? This raises the question of computing the union of power sets:

$$\bigcup_{x \in \delta(a)} \mathcal{P}(a \cap x) \qquad (8)$$

The exponential order of the analogical algorithm lies in trying to compute this set. The union is bounded both from below and above. A lower bound is:

$$\mathcal{P}(max(\{a \cap x | x \in \delta(a)\}))$$

and a higher bound is:

$$\mathcal{P}(\bigcup_{x \in \delta(a)} a \cap x)$$

Both these bounds are fairly simple to calculate. In the implementation (written in C), we have chosen a weighted average between the lower bound and the higher bound as a good approximation. We found that values that are weighted in favor of the higher bound gave better performance. This is not equivalent to say that the true AM values are closer to the higher bound.

## 3 Results from the implementation

We have evaluated the performance of our implementation using the chunk identification task from CoNLL–2000 (Tjong Kim Sang and Buchholz, 2000). The best performance was obtained by a Support Vector Machine (Kudoh and Matsumoto, 2000, F=93.48). This implementation has the disadvantage that it is computationally very intensive, and it might not be applicable to much larger data sets. Their results have later improved even more for the same

task. The standard for memory based learning on this task is an $F$ value of 91.54 (Veenstra and Bosch, 2000), a value which can be improved upon slightly, as is shown by using a system combining several different memory-based learners (Tjong Kim Sang, 2000, F=92.5). Johansson (2000) submitted an NGRAM model which used only 5 parts-of-speech tags , centered around the item to be classified. That model (ibid.) used a backdown strategy to select the largest context attested in the training data, and gave the most frequent class of that context. It used a maximum of 4 lookups from a table, and is most likely the fastest submitted model. The table could be created by sorting the database. The advantage being that it could handle very large databases (as long as they could be sorted in reasonable time). The model gives a minimum baseline for what a modest $NGRAM$-model could achieve (F=87.23) on the chunking task.

The implementation deviates slightly from the discussed, theoretical model. First, it implements a "sloppy" version of homogeneity check, which does not account for non-deterministic homogeneity (Skousen, 1989; Skousen, 1992; Skousen et al., 2002). We tried to implement this in an earlier version, but the results actually deteriorated, so we decided to go for the "sloppy" version. Second, it allows feedback of the last classification, and thirdly it allows centering on some central feature positions. The positions containing a) the parts-of-speech tags and b) the words that are to be given a chunk tag are given a high weight (100), and their immediate left and right context are given weight as well (3 and 2 respectively). The weights are multiplied together for every matching feature position. The highest weight is thus $3*100*2*3*100*2 = 600*600 = 360000$. A method for automatically setting the focus weights is under development. From table 2 we can see that using only lexical features (i.e. 5 lex and 6 lex), performs below baseline (F=87.23). The implementation without anything extra, performs as the base line for five parts-of-speech features (F=87.13), and centering improves that to 88.87. Feedback on its own does not improve results (87.02; 6 pos), while feedback + centering (F=89.36) improves results more than just centering. Feedback on its own rather seems to deteriorate results. The model approaches MBL–results with only centering using both lexical and parts-of-speech features, and performs slightly better with feedback and centering (F=92.05), although not as good as the SVM-implementation (Kudoh and Matsumoto, 2000), and not as good as the system combining several memory based learners (Tjong Kim Sang, 2000). A system that used 11 word features, and 11 parts-of-speech features, as well as a feedback feature was also trained, but did not perform better. The testing time for that 23-feature model was about 30 hours, making systematic testing difficult.

| # | F+C | C | F | 0 |
|---|---|---|---|---|
| 5 lex | | 82.91 | | 80.40 |
| 5 pos | | 88.87 | | 87.13 |
| 6 lex | 86.33 | | 83.17 | |
| 6 pos | 89.36 | | 87.02 | |
| 10 | | 91.16 | | 89.48 |
| 11 | 92.05 | | 89.41 | |

Table 2: Results: F–scores. Number of features, Feedback + Centering, Centering only, Feedback only, nothing extra.

### 3.1 Computational complexity

The test were made using a 867MHz PowerPC G4, with 1 MB L3 cache and 256 MB SDRAM memory using Mac OS X version 10.3.9. When the number of features changed, the number of unique patterns varied. The time to process all test patterns were therefor divided by the number of unique database items and reported as how many milliseconds per database item the processing took. The results are shown in table 3. This shows an almost linear increase with the number of features, which has to do with a) that more comparisons are made because there are more features to compare, and b) that the match set $\mathcal{M}$ grows faster when there are more features. When the size of the database is accounted for, the main contribution to complexity is proportional to the square of the size of the match set times the number of features. That complexity does not grow faster is an indication that the match set does not grow very fast for this task. However, when using 23 features, computing demanded more time than accounted for by the trend shown for less features. We speculate that this is mainly because of the limited RAM memory available. The values in table 3 are approximated by the formula:

$time = 0.05 * f^2 + f + 11.5$, with $R^2 > 0.98$; f = number of feature positions (variables), and time is in ms per database item, for processing all 49393 instances in the test set.

| # | $D$ | ms |
|---|---|---|
| 5 lex | 213532 | 17.44 |
| 5 pos | 92392 | 17.84 |
| 6 lex | 213562 | 19.14 |
| 6 pos | 92392 | 19.80 |
| 10 | 213562 | 26.07 |
| 11 | 213591 | 28.68 |

Table 3: Results: Processing time needed to solve the full task, per item in the database.

## 4 Future research

We are trying to invent a method for automatically focussing on the relevant variables (feature positions), set optimal weights for these variables. The goal is to get even better results from this method, than from using the rather ad hoc weights used in this presentation. The focus on central variables reminds of the backdown strategy used in (Johansson, 2000), the results are very similar to that NGRAM–method for using only parts-of-speech information. The lexical information might be integrated in an NGRAM–model, weighted in an efficient way to produce results similar to the best results in this presentation (F=92.05), but without the computational overhead of the analogical model. The advantage of such a model is that it could use larger databases, and therefore be much more practical, even if it does not deliver optimal results for smaller sets of data. Computation in the NGRAM–model (Johansson, 2000) consists of a fixed number of fast look-up operations, and training is feasible if the data can be sorted in reasonable time. Admittedly, non-naive implementations of a nearest neighbor model, such as TiMBL (Daelemans et al., 2004), are already doing well for large data sets, which make it hard to compete on combined accuracy and processing time.

## 5 Conclusion

We have shown an outline of a theoretical reconstruction of Skousen's Analogical Modeling of Language (Skousen, 1989; Skousen, 1992; Skousen et al., 2002), this is described in more detail elsewhere (Johnsen and Johansson, 2005; Johnsen, 2005). This reconstruction led to a more efficient approximation of full analogy modeling, and the results were implemented in a computer program, and tested on the $CoNLL - 2000$ chunk tagging task. Our implementation showed to be competitive with other memory based learners. An empirical confirmation of the computational complexity showed a very slow increase with an increased number of features, although processing times increased with more demands on memory, an effect which is likely due to limits on internal memory.

We are presently not using feature weighting, such as information gain, which typically works on the level of individual feature values. Future research involves working on a method for automatically finding the relevant variables, and finding optimal weights for these variables.

**Acknowledgement** Support by a grant from the Norwegian Research Council under the KUNSTI programme (project BREDT) is kindly acknowledged. The computer program will be made available for download from http://bredt.uib.no with some example data.

# References

S. Chandler. 1993. Are rules and modules really necessary for explaining language? *Journal of Psycholinguistic Research*, 22:593–606.

S. Chandler. 2002. Skousen's analogical approach as an exemplar-based model of categorization. In *Skousen et al.*, pages 51–105.

W. Daelemans, J. Zavrel, K. van der Sloot, and A. van den Bosch. 2004. *TiMBL: Tilburg Memory Based Learner, version 5.1. Reference guide.* ILK Technical report Series 04–02., Tilburg, the Netherlands.

W. Daelemans. 2002. A comparison of analogical modeling to memory-based language processing. In *Skousen et al.*, pages 157–179.

D. Eddington. 2002. A comparison of two analogical models: Tilburg memory-based learner versus analogical modeling. In *Skousen et al.*, pages 141–155.

C. Johansson. 2000. A context sensitive maximum likelihood approach to chunking. In *Proceedings of CoNLL-2000 and LLL-2000*, pages 136–138, Lisbon, Portugal.

L. Johnsen and C. Johansson. 2005. Efficient modeling of analogy. In A. Gelbukh, editor, *Proceedings of the 6th Conference on Intelligent Text Processing and Computational Linguistics*, volume 3406 of *Lecture Notes in Computer Science*, pages 682–691. Springer Verlag, Berlin, Germany.

L. Johnsen. 2005. *Commentary on exegesis of Johnsen and Johansson, 2005.* (ms.).

T. Kudoh and Y. Matsumoto. 2000. Use of support vector learning for chunk identification. In *Proceedings of CoNLL-2000 and LLL-2000*, pages 142–144, Lisbon, Portugal.

M. Mudrow. 2002. Version spaces, neural networks, and analogical modeling. In *Skousen et al.*, pages 225–264.

J. Myers. 2002. Exemplar-driven analogy in optimality theory. In *Skousen et al.*, pages 265–300.

J. Pierrehumbert. 2001. Exemplar dynamics: Word frequency, lenition, and contrast. In *Frequency effects and the emergence of linguistic structure*, pages 137–157, Amsterdam, the Netherlands. John Benjamins.

R. Skousen, D. Lonsdale, and D.B. Parkinson. 2002. *Analogical Modeling: An exemplar-based approach to language*, volume 10 of *Human Cognitive Processing*. John Benjamins, Amsterdam, the Netherlands.

R. Skousen. 1989. *Analogical Modeling of Language.* Kluwer Academic, Dordrecht, the Netherlands.

R. Skousen. 1992. *Analogy and Structure.* Kluwer Academic, Dordrecht, the Netherlands.

R. Skousen. 2002. Issues in analogical modeling. In *Skousen et al.*, pages 27–48.

E.F. Tjong Kim Sang and S. Buchholz. 2000. Introduction to the CoNLL-2000 shared task: Chunking. In *Proceedings of CoNLL-2000 and LLL-2000*, pages 127–132, Lisbon, Portugal.

E.F. Tjong Kim Sang. 2000. Text chunking by system combination. In *Proceedings of CoNLL-2000 and LLL-2000*, pages 151–153, Lisbon, Portugal.

J. Veenstra and A. van den Bosch. 2000. Single-classifier memory-based phrase chunking. In *Proceedings of CoNLL-2000 and LLL-2000*, pages 157–159, Lisbon, Portugal.

# Dependency treebanks: methods, annotation schemes and tools

**Tuomo Kakkonen**
Department of Computer Science
University of Joensuu
P.O. Box 111
FI-80101 Joensuu
`tuomo.kakkonen@cs.joensuu.fi`

## Abstract

In this paper, current dependency-based treebanks are introduced and analyzed. The methods used for building the resources, the annotation schemes applied, and the tools used (such as POS taggers, parsers and annotation software) are discussed.

## 1 Introduction

Annotated data is a crucial resource for developments in computational linguistics and natural language processing. Syntactically annotated corpora, *treebanks*, are needed for developing and evaluating natural language processing applications, as well as for research in empirical linguistics. The choice of annotation type in a treebank usually boils down to two options: the linguistic resource is annotated either according to some constituent or functional structure scheme. As the name treebank suggests, these linguistic resources were first developed in the phrase-structure framework, usually represented as tree-shaped constructions. The first efforts to create such resources started around 30 years ago. The most well-known of such a treebank is the *Penn Treebank* for English (Marcus et al., 1993).

In recent years, there has been a wide interest towards functional annotation of treebanks. In particular, many dependency-based treebanks have been constructed. In addition, grammatical function annotation has been added to some constituent-type treebanks. *Dependency Grammar* formalisms stem from the work of Tesnieére (1959). In dependency grammars, only the lexical nodes are recognized, and the phrasal ones are omitted. The lexical nodes are linked with directed binary relations. The most commonly used argument

for selecting the dependency format for building a treebank is that the treebank is being created for a language with a relatively free word order. Such treebanks exist *e.g.* for Basque, Czech, German and Turkish. On the other hand, dependency treebanks have been developed for languages such as English, which have been usually seen as languages that can be better represented with constituent formalism. The motivations for using dependency annotation vary from the fact that the type of structure is the one needed by many, if not most, applications to the fact that it offers a proper interface between syntactic and semantic representation. Furthermore, dependency structures can be automatically converted into phrase structures if needed (Lin, 1995; Xia and Palmer, 2000), although not always with 100% accuracy. The *TIGER Treebank* of German, a free word order language, with 50,000 sentences is an example of a treebank with both phrase structure and dependency annotations (Brants et al., 2002).

The aim of this paper is to answer the following questions about the current state-of-art in dependency treebanking:

- What kinds of texts do the treebanks consist of?

- What types of annotation schemes and formats are applied?

- What kinds of annotation methods and tools are used for creating the treebanks?

- What kinds of functions do the annotation tools for creating the treebanks have?

We start by introducing the existing dependency-based treebanks (Section 2). In Section 3, the status and state-of-art in dependency treebanking is summarized and analyzed. Finally in Section 4, we conclude the findings.

## 2   Existing dependency treebanks

### 2.1   Introduction

Several kinds of resources and tools are needed for constructing a treebank: *annotation guidelines* state the conventions that guide the annotators throughout their work, a software tool is needed to aid the annotation work, and in the case of semi-automated treebank construction, a *part-of-speech (POS) tagger, morphological analyzer* and/or a *syntactic parser* are also needed. Building trees manually is a very slow and error-prone process. The most commonly used method for developing a treebank is a combination of automatic and manual processing, but the practical method of implementation varies considerably. There are some treebanks that have been annotated completely manually, but with taggers and parsers available to automate some of the work such a method is rarely employed in state-of-the-art treebanking.

### 2.2   The treebanks

#### 2.2.1   Prague Dependency Treebank

The largest of the existing dependency treebanks (around 90,000 sentences), the *Prague Dependency Treebank* for Czech, is annotated in layered structure annotation, consisting of three levels: morphological, analytical (syntax), and tectogrammatical (semantics) (Böhmová et al., 2003). The data consist of newspaper articles on diverse topics (*e.g.* politics, sports, culture) and texts from popular science magazines, selected from the *Czech National Corpus*. There are 3,030 morphological tags in the morphological tagset (Hajič, 1998). The syntactic annotation comprises of 23 dependency types.

The annotation for the levels was done separately, by different groups of annotators. The morphological tagging was performed by two human annotators selecting the appropriate tag from a list proposed by a tagging system. Third annotator then resolved any differences between the two annotations. The syntactic annotation was at first done completely manually, only by the aid of ambiguous morphological tags and a graphical user interface. Later, some functions for automatically assigning part of the tags were implemented. After

some 19,000 sentences were annotated, *Collins lexicalized stochastic parser* (Nelleke et al., 1999) was trained with the data, and was capable of assigning 80% of the dependencies correct. At that stage, the work of the annotator changed from building the trees from scratch to checking and correcting the parses assigned by the parser, except for the analytical functions, which still had to be assigned manually. The details related to the tectogrammatical level are omitted here. Figure 1 illustrates an example of morphological and analytical levels of annotation.

There are other treebank projects using the framework developed for the Prague Dependency Treebank. *Prague Arabic Dependency Treebank* (Hajič et al., 2004), consisting of around 49,000 tokens of newswire texts from *Arabic Gigaword* and *Penn Arabic Treebank*, is a treebank of Modern Standard Arabic. The *Slovene Dependency Treebank* consists of around 500 annotated sentences obtained from the *MULTEXT-East Corpus* (Erjavec, 2005b; Erjavec, 2005a).

#### 2.2.2   TIGER Treebank

The *TIGER Treebank* of German (Brants et al., 2002) was developed based on the *NEGRA Corpus* (Skut et al., 1998) and consists of complete articles covering diverse topics collected from a German newspaper. The treebank has around 50,000 sentences. The syntactic annotation combining both phrase-structure and dependency representations is organized as follows: phrase categories are marked in nonterminals, POS information in terminals and syntactic functions in the edges. The syntactic annotation is rather simple and flat in order to reduce the amount of attachment ambiguities. An interesting feature in the treebank is that a MySQL database is used for storing the annotations, from where they can be exported into *NEGRA Export* and *TIGER-XML* file formats, which makes it usable and exchangeable with a range of tools.

The annotation tool *Annotate* with two methods, interactive and *Lexical-Functional Grammar* (LFG) parsing, was employed in creating the treebank. *LFG parsing* is a typical semi-automated annotation method, comprising of processing the input texts by a parser and a human annotator disambiguating and correcting the output. In the case of TIGER Treebank, a

---

Kakkonen: *Dependency treebanks: methods, annotation schemes and tools*

*Proceedings of the 15th NODALIDA conference, Joensuu 2005*　　　Ling@JoY 1, 2006

```
<f cap>Do<l>do<t>RR-2————-<A>AuxP<r>1<g>7
<f num>15<l>15<t>C=————-<A>Atr <r>2<g>4
<d>.<l>.<t>Z:————-<A>AuxG<r>3<g>2
<f>května<l>květen<t>NNIS2——A—-<A>Adv<r>4<g>1
<f>budou<l>být<t>VB-P—3F-AA—<A>AuxV<r>5<g>7
<f>cestující<l>cestující<t>NNMP1——A—-<A>Sb <r>6<g>7
<f>platit<l>platit<t>Vf————A—-<A>Pred<r>7<g>0
<f>dosud<l>dosud<t>Db————-<A>Adv<r>8<g>9
<f>platným<l>platný<t>AAIS7—-1A—-<A>Atr<r>9<g>10
<f>zpøusobem<l>způsob<t>NNIS7——A—-<A>Adv<r>10<g>7
<d>.<l>.<t>Z:————-<A>AuxK<r>11<g>0
```

Figure 1: A morphologically and analytically annotated sentence from the Prague Dependency Treebank (Böhmová et al., 2003).

broad coverage LFG parser is used, producing the constituent and functional structures for the sentences. As almost every sentence is left with unresolved ambiguities, a human annotator is needed to select the correct ones from the set of possible parses. As each sentence of the corpus has several thousands of possible LFG representations, a mechanism for automatically reducing the number of parses is applied, dropping the number of parses represented to the human annotator to 17 on average. *Interactive annotation* is also a type of semi-automated annotation, but in contrast to human post-editing, the method makes the parser and the annotator to interact. First, the parser annotates a small part of the sentence and the annotator either accepts or rejects it based on visual inspection. The process is repeated until the sentence is annotated completely.

### 2.2.3 Arboretum, L'Arboratoire, Arborest and Floresta Sintá(c)tica

*Arboretum* of Danish (Bick, 2003), *L'Arboratoire* of French and *Floresta Sintá(c)tica* of Portuguese (Afonso et al., 2002), and *Arborest* of Estonian (Bick et al., 2005) are "sibling" treebanks, Arboretum being the "oldest sister". The treebanks are hybrids with both constituent and dependency annotation organized into two separate levels. The levels share the same morphological tagset. The dependency annotation is based on the *Constraint Grammar* (CG) (Karlsson, 1990) and consists of 28 dependency types. For creating each of the four treebanks, a CG-based morphological analyzer and parser was applied. The annotation process consisted of CG parsing of the texts followed by conversion

to constituent format, and manual checking of the structures.

Arboretum has around 21,600 sentences annotated with dependency tags, and of those, 12,000 sentences have also been marked with constituent structures (Bick, 2003; Bick, 2005). The annotation is in both TIGER-XML and PENN export formats. Floresta Sintá(c)tica consists of around 9,500 manually checked (version 6.8, October 15th, 2005) and around 41,000 fully automatically annotated sentences obtained from a corpus of newspaper Portuguese (Afonso et al., 2002). *Arborest* of Estonian consists of 149 sentences from newspaper articles (Bick et al., 2005). The morphosyntactic and CG-based surface syntactic annotation are obtained from an existing corpus, which is converted semi-automatically to Arboretum-style format.

### 2.2.4 The Dependency Treebank for Russian

The *Dependency Treebank for Russian* is based on the *Uppsala University Corpus* (Lönngren, 1993). The texts are collected from contemporary Russian prose, newspapers, and magazines (Boguslavsky et al., 2000; Boguslavsky et al., 2002). The treebank has about 12,000 annotated sentences. The annotation scheme is XML-based and compatible with *Text Encoding for Interchange* (TEI), except for some added elements. It consists of 78 syntactic relations, divided into six subgroups, such as attributive, quantitative, and coordinative. The annotation is layered, in the sense that the levels of annotation are independent and can be extracted or processed independently.

The creation of the treebank started by processing the texts with a morphological analyzer

*Proceedings of the 15th NODALIDA conference, Joensuu 2005*  Ling@JoY 1, 2006

and a syntactic parser, *ETAP* (Apresjan et al., 1992), and was followed by post-editing by human annotators. Two tools are available for the annotator: a *sentence boundary markup tool* and *post-editor*. The post-editor offers the annotator functions for building, editing, and managing the annotations. The editor has a special split-and-run mode, used when the parsers fails to produce a parse or creates a parse with a high number of errors. In the mode the user can pre-chunk the sentence into smaller pieces to be input to the parser. The parsed chucks can be linked by the annotator, thus producing a full parse for the sentence. The tool also provides the annotator with the possibility to mark the annotation of any word or sentence as doubtful, in order to remind at the need for a later revision.

### 2.2.5  Alpino

The *Alpino Treebank* of Dutch, consisting of 6,000 sentences, is targeted mainly at parser evaluation and comprises of newspaper articles (van der Beek et al., 2002). The annotation scheme is taken from the *CGN Corpus* of spoken Dutch (Oostdijk, 2000) and the annotation guidelines are based on the TIGER Treebank's guidelines.

The annotation process in the Alpino Treebank starts with applying a parser based on *Head-Driven Phrase Structure Grammar* (HPSG) (Pollard and Sag, 1994) and is followed by a manual selection of the correct parse trees. An interactive lexical analyzer and a constituent marker tools are employed to restrict the number of possible parses. The *interactive lexical analyzer* tool lets the user to mark each word in a sentence belonging to correct, good, or bad categories. 'Correct' denotes that the parse includes the lexical entry in question, 'good' that the parse may include the entry, and 'bad' that the entry is incorrect. The parser uses this manually reduced set of entries, thus generating a smaller set of possible parses. With the constituent marker tool, the annotator can mark constituents and their types to sentences, thus aiding the parser.

The selection of the correct parse is done by the help of a *parse selection tool*, which calculates *maximal discriminants* to help the annotator. There are three types of discriminants. Maximal discriminants are sets of shortest dependency paths encoding differences between parses, lexical discriminants represent ambiguities resulting from lexical analysis, and constituent discriminants group words to constituents without specifying the type of the constituent. The annotator marks each of the maximal discriminants as good or bad, and the tool narrows down the number of possible parses based on the information. If the parse resulting from the selection is not correct, it can be edited by a parse editor tool.

### 2.2.6  The Danish Dependency Treebank

The annotation of the *Danish Dependency Treebank* is based on *Discountinuous Grammar*, which is a formalism closely related to *Word Grammar* (Kromann, 2003). The treebank consists of 5,540 sentences covering a wide range of topics. The morphosyntactic annotation is obtained from the *PAROLE Corpus* (Keson and Norling-Christensen, 2005), thus no morphological analyzer or POS tagger is applied. The dependency links are marked manually by using a command-line interface with a graphical parse view. A parser for automatically assigning the dependency links is under development.

### 2.2.7  METU-Sabanci Turkish Treebank

Morphologically and syntactically annotated *Turkish Treebank* consists of 5,000 sentences obtained from the *METU Turkish Corpus* (Atalay et al., 2003) covering 16 main genres of present-day written Turkish (Oflazer et al., 2003). The annotation is presented in a format that is in conformance with the *XML-based Corpus Encoding Standard* (XCES) format (Anne and Romary, 2003). Due to morphological complexity of Turkish, morphological information is not encoded with a fixed set of tags, but as sequences of *inflectional groups* (IGs). An IG is a sequence of inflectional morphemes, divided by derivation boundaries. The dependencies between IGs are annotated with the following 10 link types: subject, object, modifier, possessor, classifier, determiner, dative adjunct, locative adjunct, ablative adjunct, and instrumental adjunct. Figure 2 illustrates a sample annotated sentence from the treebank.

The annotation, directed by the guidelines, is done in a semi-automated fashion, although relatively lot of manual work remains. First, a morphological analyzer based on the two-level morphology model (Oflazer, 1994) is ap-

---

Kakkonen: *Dependency treebanks: methods, annotation schemes and tools*

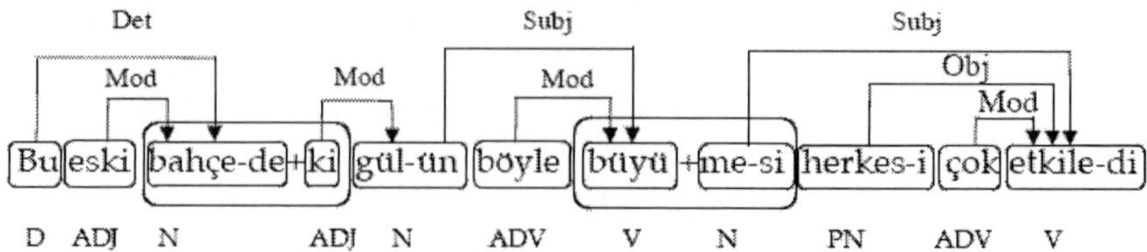

Figure 2: A sample sentence from the METU-Sabanci Treebank (Oflazer et al., 2003).

plied to the texts. The morphologically analyzed and preprocessed text is input to an annotation tool. The tagging process requires two steps: morphological disambiguation and dependency tagging. The annotator selects the correct tag from the list of tags proposed by the morphological analyzer. After the whole sentence has been disambiguated, dependency links are specified manually. The annotators can also add notes and modify the list of dependency link types.

### 2.2.8  The Basque Dependency Treebank

The *Basque Dependency Treebank* (Aduriz and al., 2003) consists of 3,000 manually annotated sentences from newspaper articles. The syntactic tags are organized as a hierarchy. The annotation is done by aid of an annotation tool, with tree visualization and automatic tag syntax checking capabilities.

### 2.2.9  The Turin University Treebank

The *Turin University Treebank* for Italian consisting of 1,500 sentences is divided into four sub-corpora (Lesmo et al., 2002; Bosco, 2000; Bosco and Lombardo, 2003). The majority of texts is from civil law code and newspaper articles. The annotation format is based on the *Augmented Relational Structure* (ARS). The POS tagset consists of 16 categories and 51 subcategories. There are around 200 dependency types, organized as a taxonomy of five levels. The scheme provides the annotator with the possibility of marking a relation as *underspecified* if a correct relation type cannot be determined.

The annotation process consists of automatic tokenization, morphological analysis and POS disambiguation, followed by syntactic parsing (Lesmo et al., 2002). The annotator can interact with the parser through a graphical interface, in a similar way to the interactive method in the TIGER Treebank. The annotator can either accept or reject the suggested

tags for each word in the sentence after which the parser proceeds to the next word (Bosco, 2000).

### 2.2.10  The Dependency Treebank of English

The *Dependency Treebank of English* consists of dialogues between a travel agent and customers (Rambow et al., 2002), and is the only dependency treebank with spoken language annotation. The treebank has about 13,000 words. The annotation is a direct representation of lexical predicate-argument structure, thus arguments and adjuncts are dependents of their predicates and all function words are attached to their lexical heads. The annotation is done at a single, syntactic level, without surface representation for surface syntax, the aim being to keep the annotation process as simple as possible. Figure 3 shows an example of an annotated sentence.

The trained annotators have access to an on-line manual and work off the transcribed speech without access to the speech files. The dialogs are parsed with a dependency parser, the *Supertagger and Lightweight Dependency Analyzer* (Bangalore and Joshi, 1999). The annotators correct the output of the parser using a graphical tool, the one developed by Prague Dependency Treebank project. In addition to the standard tag editing options, annotators can add comments. After the editing is done, the sentence is automatically checked for inconsistencies, such as the difference in surface and deep roles or prepositions missing objects *etc.*

### 2.2.11  DEPBANK

As the name suggests, the *PARC 700 Dependency Bank* (DEPBANK) (King et al., 2003) consists of 700 annotated sentences from the *Penn Wall Street Journal Treebank* (Marcus et al., 1994). There are 19 grammatical relation types (*e.g.* subject, object, modifier) and 37

**This page intentionally left blank.**

Table 1: Comparison of dependency treebanks. (*Due to limited number of pages not all the treebanks in the Arboretum "family" are included in the table. **Information of number of utterances was not available. M=manual, SA=semi-automatic, TB=treebank)

| Name | Language | Genre | Size (sent.) | Annotation methods | Autom. tools | Supported formats |
|---|---|---|---|---|---|---|
| *Prague Dep. TB* | Czech | Newsp., science mag. | 90,000 | M/SA | Lexicalized stochastic parser (Collins) | FS, CSTS SGML, Annotation Graphs XML |
| *TIGER TB* | German | Newsp. | 50,000 | Post-editing & interactive | Probabilistic/ LFG parser | TIGER-XML & NEGRA export |
| *Arboretum & co.** | 4 lang. | Mostly newsp. | 21,600 (Ar) 9,500 (Flo) | Dep. to const. conversion, M checking | CG-based parser for each language | TIGER-XML & PENN export (Ar.) |
| *Dep. TB for Russian* | Russian | Fiction, newsp., scientific | 12,000 | SA | Morph. analyzer & a parser | XML-based TEI-compatibe |
| *Alpino* | Dutch | Newsp. | 6,000 | M disambig. aided by parse selection tool | HPSG-based Alpino parser | Own XML-based |
| *Danish Dep. TB* | Danish | Range of topics & genres | 5,540 | Morphosyn. annotation obtained from a corpus, M dep. marking | - | PAROLE-DK with additions, TIGER-XML |
| *METU-Sabanci TB* | Turkish | 16 genres | 5,000 | M disambiguation & M dependency marking | Morph. analyzer based on XEROX FST | XML-based XCES compatible |
| *Basque TB* | Basque | Newsp. | 3,000 | M, automatic checking | - | XML-based TEI-compatible |
| *TUT* | Italian | Mainly newsp. & civil law | 1,500 | M checking of parser & morph. analyzer output | Morph. analyzer, rule-based tagger and a parser | Own ASCII-based |
| *Dep. TB of English* | English | Spoken, travel agent dial. | 13,000 words ** | M correction of parser output & autom. checking of inconsistencies | Supertagger & Lightweight Dep. Analyzer | FS |
| *DEP-BANK* | English | Financial newsp. | 700 | M checking & correction, autom. consistency checking | LFG parser, checking tool | Own ASCII-based |

Kakkonen: *Dependency treebanks: methods, annotation schemes and tools*

*Proceedings of the 15th NODALIDA conference, Joensuu 2005*　　Ling@JoY 1, 2006

example, in the METU-Sabanci Treebank a special type of morphological annotation scheme was introduced due to the complexity of Turkish morphology.

Semi-automated creation combining parsing and human checker is the state-of-art annotation method. None of the dependency treebanks are created completely manually; at least an annotation tool capable of visualizing the structures is used by each of the projects. Obviously, the reason that there aren't any fully automatically created dependency treebanks is the fact there are no parsers of free text capable of producing error-free parses.

The most common way of combining the human and machine labor is to let the human work as a post-checker of the parser's output. Albeit most straight-forward to implement, the method has some pitfalls. First, starting annotation with parsing can lead to high number of unresolved ambiguities, making the selection of the correct parse a time-consuming task. Thus, a parser applied for treebank building should perform at least some disambiguation to ease the burden of annotators. Second, the work of post-checker is mechanic and there is a risk that the checker just accept the parser's suggestions, without a rigorous inspection. A solution followed *e.g.* by the both treebanks for English and the Basque treebank is to apply a post-checking tool to the created structures before accepting them. Some variants of semi-automated annotation exist: the TIGER, TUT, Alpino, and the Russian Treebanks apply a method where the parser and the annotator can interact. The advantage of the method is that when the errors by the parser are corrected by the human at the lower levels, they do not multiply into the higher levels, thus making it more probable that the parser produces a correct parse. In some annotation tools, such as the tools of the Russian, the English Dependency treebanks, the annotator is provided with the possibility of adding comments to annotation, easing the further inspection of doubtful structures. In the annotation tool of the TUT Treebank, a special type relation can be assigned to mark doubtful annotations.

Although more collaboration has emerged between treebank projects in recent years, the main problem with current treebanks in regards to their use and distribution is the fact that instead of reusing existing formats, new

ones have been developed. Furthermore, the schemes have often been designed from theory and even application-specific viewpoints, and consequently, undermine the possibility for reuse. Considering the high costs of treebank development (for example in the case of the Prague Dependency Treebank estimated USD600,000 (Böhmová et al., 2003)), reusability of tools and formats should have a high priority. In addition to the difficulties for reuse, creating a treebank-specific representation format requires developing a new set of tools for creating, maintaining and searching the treebank. Yet, the existence of exchange formats such as XCES (Anne and Romary, 2003) and TIGER-XML (Mengel and Lezius, 2000) would allow multipurpose tools to be created and used.

## 4　Conclusion

We have introduced the state-of-art in dependency treebanking and discussed the main characteristics of current treebanks. The findings reported in the paper will be used in designing and constructing an annotation tool for dependency treebanks and constructing a treebank for Finnish for syntactic parser evaluation purposes. The choice of dependency format for a treebank for evaluating syntactic parser of Finnish is self-evident, Finnish being a language with relatively free word order and all parsers for the language working in the dependency-framework. The annotation format will be some of the existing XML-based formats, allowing existing tools to be applied for searching and editing the treebank.

The findings reported in this paper indicate that the following key properties must be implemented into the annotation tool for creating the treebank for Finnish:

- An interface to a morphological analyzer and parser for constructing the initial trees. Several parsers can be applied in parallel to offer the annotator a possibility to compare the outputs.

- Support for an existing XML annotation format. Using an existing format will make the system more reusable. XML-based formats offer good syntax-checking capabilities.

- An inconsistency checker. The annotated

sentences to be saved will be checked against errors in tags and annotation format. In addition to XML-based validation of the syntax of the annotation, the inconsistency checker will inform the annotator about several other types of mistakes. The POS and morphological tags will be checked to find any mismatching combinations. A missing main verb, a fragmented, incomplete parse etc. will be indicated to the user.

- A comment tool. The annotator will be able to add comments to the annotations to aid later revision.

- Menu-based tagging. In order to minimize errors, instead of typing the tags, the annotator will only be able to set tags by selecting them from predefined lists.

## 5  Acknowledgments

The research reported in this work has been supported by the European Union under a Marie Curie Host Fellowship for Early Stage Researchers Training at MULTILINGUA, Bergen, Norway and MirrorWolf project funded by the National Technology Agency of Finland (TEKES).

## References

Anne Abeillé. 2003. Introduction. In Anne Abeillé, editor, *Treebanks: Building and Using Syntactically Annotated Corpora.* Kluwer Academic Publishers, Dordrecht, The Netherlands.

Itziar Aduriz and al. 2003. Construction of a Basque dependency treebank. In *Proceedings of the 2nd Workshop on Treebanks and Linguistic Theories*, Växjö, Sweden.

Susana Afonso, Eckhard Bick, Renato Haber, and Diana Santos. 2002. "Floresta Sintá(c)tica": a treebank for Portuguese. In *Proceedings of the 3rd International Conference on Language Resources and Evaluation*, Las Palmas, Gran Canaria, Spain.

Nancy Anne and Laurent Romary. 2003. Encoding syntactic annotation. In Anne Abeillé, editor, *Treebanks: Building and Using Syntactically Annotated Corpora.* Kluwer Academic Publishers, Dordrecht, The Netherlands.

Jurij Apresjan, Igor Boguslavsky, Leonid Iomdin, Alexandre Lazursku, Vladimir Sannikov, and Leonid Tsinman. 1992. ETAP-2: the linguistics of a machine translation system. *META*, 37(1):97–112.

Nart B. Atalay, Kermal Oflazer, and Bilge Say. 2003. The annotation process in the Turkish treebank. In *Proceedings of the EACL Workshop on Linguistically Interpreted Corpora*, Budapest, Hungary.

Srinivas Bangalore and Aravind K. Joshi. 1999. Supertagging: An approach to almost parsing. *Computational Linguistics*, 25(2):237–265.

Eckhard Bick, Heli Uibo, and Kaili Müürisep. 2005. Arborest - a growing treebank of Estonian. In Henrik Holmboe, editor, *Nordisk Sprogteknologi 2005. Nordic Language Technology 2005.* Museum Tusculanums Forlag, Copenhagen, Denmark.

Eckhard Bick. 2003. Arboretum, a hybrid treebank for Danish. In *Proceedings of the 2nd Workshop on Treebanks and Linguistic Theories*, Växjö, Sweden.

Eckhard Bick. 2005. Current status of Arboretum treebank. Electronic mail communication, October 12th, 2005.

Igor Boguslavsky, Svetlana Grigorieva, Nikolai Grigoriev, Leonid Kreidlin, and Nadezhda Frid. 2000. Dependency treebank for Russian: Concept, tools, types of information. In *Proceedings of the 18th International Conference on Computational Linguistics*, Saarbrücken, Germany.

Igor Boguslavsky, Ivan Chardin, Svetlana Grigorieva, Nikolai Grigoriev, Leonid Iomdin, Leonid Kreidlin, and Nadezhda Frid. 2002. Development of a dependency treebank for Russian and its possible applications in NLP. In *Proceedings of the 3rd International Conference on Language Resources and Evaluation*, Las Palmas, Gran Canaria, Spain.

Alena Böhmová, Jan Hajič, Eva Hajičová, and Barbora Hladká. 2003. The Prague dependency treebank: Three-level annotation scenario. In Anne Abeillé, editor, *Treebanks: Building and Using Syntactically Annotated Corpora.* Kluwer Academic Publishers, Dordrecht, The Netherlands.

Cristina Bosco and Vincenzo Lombardo. 2003. A relation-based schema for treebank annotation. In *Proceedings of the Advances in Artificial Intelligence, 8th Congress of the Italian Association for Artificial Intelligence*, Pisa, Italy.

Cristina Bosco. 2000. An annotation schema for an Italian treebank. In *Proceedings of the Student Session, 12th European Summer School in Logic, Language and Information*, Birmingham, UK.

Sabine Brants, Stefanie Dipper, Silvia Hansen, Wolfgang Lezius, and George Smith. 2002. The Tiger Treebank. In *Proceedings of the Workshop on Treebanks and Linguistic Theories*, Sozopol, Bulgaria.

Tomaž Erjavec. 2005a. Current status of the Slovene dependency treebank. Electronic mail communication, September 29th, 2005.

Tomaž Erjavec. 2005b. Slovene dependency treebank. http://nl.ijs.si/sdt/. (Accessed November 9th, 2005).

Jan Hajič, Otakar Smrž, Petr Zemáánek, Jan Šnaidauf, and Emanuel Beška. 2004. Prague Arabic dependency treebank: Development in data and tools. In *Proceedings of the NEMLAR International Conference on Arabic Language Resources and Tools*, Cairo, Egypt.

Jan Hajič. 1998. Building a syntactically annotated corpus: The Prague dependency treebank. In Eva Hajičová, editor, *Issues of Valency and Meaning. Studies in Honor of Jarmila Panevová*, pages 12–19. Charles University Press, Prague, Czech Republic.

Fred Karlsson. 1990. Constraint grammar as a framework for parsing running text. In *Proceedings of the 13th Conference on Computational Linguistics - Volume 3*, Helsinki, Finland.

Britt-Katrin Keson and Ole Norling-Christensen. 2005. PAROLE-DK. Det Danske Sprog- litteraturselskab. http://korpus.dsl.dk/e-resurser/parole-korpus.php. (Accessed October 7th, 2005).

Tracy H. King, Richard Crouch, Stefan Riezler, Mary Dalrymple, and Ronald M. Kaplan. 2003. The PARC 700 dependency bank. In *Proceedings of the 4th International Workshop on Linguistically Interpreted Corpora, the 10th Conference of the EACL*, Budapest, Hungary.

Matthias T. Kromann. 2003. The Danish dependency treebank and the DTAG treebank tool. In *Proceedings of the 2nd Workshop on Treebanks and Linguistic Theories*, Växjö, Sweden.

Leonardo Lesmo, Vincenzo Lombardo, and Cristina Bosco. 2002. Treebank development: the TUT approach. In *Proceedings of the International Conference on Natural Language Processing*, Mumbai, India.

Dekang Lin. 1995. A dependency-based method for evaluating broad-coverage parsers. In *The 1995 International Joint Conference on AI*, Montreal, Canada.

Lennart Lönngren. 1993. Chastotnyj slovar' sovremennogo russkogo jazyka. (A frequency dictionary of modern Russian). In *Acta Universitatis Upsaliensis, Studia Slavica Upsaliensia 32*, Uppsala, Sweden.

Mitchell Marcus, Beatrice Santorini, and Mary Ann Marcinkiewicz. 1993. Building a large annotated corpus of English: The Penn Treebank. *Computational Linguistics*, 19(2):313–330.

Mitchell Marcus, Grace Kim, Mary Ann Marcinkiewicz, Robert MacIntyre, Ann Bies, Mark Ferguson, Karen Katz, and Britta Schasberger. 1994. The Penn treebank: Annotating predicate argument structure. In *Proceedings of the ARPA Human Language Technology Workshop*, Princeton, New Jersey, USA.

Andreas Mengel and Wolfgang Lezius. 2000. An XML-based representation format for syntactically annotated corpora. In *Proceedings of the International Conference on Language Resources and Evaluation*, Athens, Greece.

Michael Nelleke, Jan Hajič, Eric Brill, Lance Ramshaw, and Christoph Tillmann. 1999. A statistical parser of Czech. In *Proceedings of 37th Annual Meeting of the Association for Computational Linguistics*, College Park, Maryland, USA.

Kermal Oflazer, Bilge Say, Dilek Zeynep Hakkani-Tür, and Gökhan Tür. 2003. Building a Turkish treebank. In Anne Abeillé, editor, *Treebanks: Building and Using Syntactically Annotated Corpora*. Kluwer Academic Publishers.

Kemal Oflazer. 1994. Two-level description of Turkish morphology. *Literary and Linguistic Computing*, 9(2):472–472.

Nelleke Oostdijk. 2000. The Spoken Dutch Corpus: Overview and first evaluation. In *Proceedings of the 2nd International Conference on Language Resources and Evaluation*, Athens, Greece.

Carl Pollard and Ivan A. Sag. 1994. *Head-Driven Phrase Structure Grammar*. University of Chicago Press and CSLI Publications, Chicago, Illinois, USA.

Owen Rambow, Cassandre Creswell, Rachel Szekely, Harriet Taber, and Marilyn Walker.

2002. A dependency treebank for English. In *Proceedings of the 3rd International Conference on Language Resources and Evaluation,* Las Palmas, Gran Canaria, Spain.

Wojciech Skut, Thorsten Brants, Birgitte Krenn, and Hans Uszkoreit. 1998. A linguistically interpreted corpus of German newspaper text. In *Proceedings of the 10th European Summer School in Logic, Language and Information,* Saarbrücken, Germany.

Lucien Tesnieére. 1959. *Éléments de syntaxe structurale.* Klincksiek, Paris, France.

Leonoor van der Beek, Gosse Bouma, Robert Malouf, and Gertjan van Noord. 2002. The Alpino dependency treebank. In Mariet Theune, Anton Nijholt, and Hendri Hondorp, editors, *Computational Linguistics in the Netherlands 2001. Selected Papers from the Twelfth CLIN Meeting.* Rodopi, Amsterdam, The Netherlands.

Fei Xia and Martha Palmer. 2000. Converting dependency structures to phrase structures. In *Proceedings of the First International Conference on Human Language Technology Research,* San Diego, California, USA.

# Free construction of a free Swedish dictionary of synonyms

**Viggo Kann** and **Magnus Rosell**
KTH Nada
SE-100 44 Stockholm
Sweden
{viggo, rosell}@nada.kth.se

## Abstract

Building a large dictionary of synonyms for a language is a very tedious task. Hence there exist very few synonym dictionaries for most languages, and those that exist are generally not freely available due to the amount of work that have been put into them.

The Lexin on-line dictionary[1] is a very popular web-site for translations of Swedish words to about ten different languages. By letting users on this site grade automatically generated possible synonym pairs a free dictionary of Swedish synonyms has been created. The lexicon reflects the users intuitive definition of synonymity and the amount of work put into the project is only as much as the participants want to.

**Keywords:** Synonyms, dictionary construction, multi-user collaboration, random indexing.

## 1 Introduction

The Internet has made it possible to create huge resources through voluntary co-operation of many people. The size of, or effort put into, each contribution does not matter – with many participators the sum may be great and useful. The most well-known example is the free-content encyclopedia Wikipedia[2] that anyone can edit. It has more than a thousand articles in 75 different languages. The English version has about 700,000 articles.

Wiktionary[3] is the lexical companion of Wikipedia. It is, as Wikipedia, a collaborative project, with the aim to produce a free dictionary in every language. The English Wiktionary has about 90,000 articles, and the Swedish about 3,750.

Both Wikipedia and Wiktionary use the copyleft[4] license GNU FDL[5], which means that the content is free to use. This often motivates people to contribute as they know that their work will be available to everyone.

To start a new similar project requires a lot of users that are interested in the matter and want to help. A suitable and very popular Swedish web site is the Lexin on-line dictionary[6]. Our plan was to let the Lexin users cooperate to build a free Swedish dictionary of synonyms.

To construct the dictionary of synonyms we followed these steps:

1. Construct lots of possible synonyms.
2. Sort out bad synonyms automatically.
3. Let the Lexin users grade the synonyms.

---

[1]http://lexin.nada.kth.se

[2]Wikipedia (http://www.wikipedia.org/) was founded in January 2001 by Jimmy Wales and Larry Sanger.

[3]http://www.wiktionary.org/

[4]http://www.gnu.org/copyleft/copyleft.html

[5]http://www.gnu.org/copyleft/fdl.html

[6]http://lexin.nada.kth.se

4. Analyze gradings and decide which pairs to keep.

The rest of the paper deals with these steps and presents the results so far of the efforts of the Lexin users. The project started in March 2005, and five months later a free Swedish dictionary of synonyms consisting of 60,000 graded pairs of synonyms was completed.

## 2  Possible synonym pairs

The first step is to create a list of possible pairs of Swedish synonyms. If you have access to a dictionary $D_1$ from Swedish to another language $X$ and a dictionary $D_2$ from $X$ to Swedish you can collect possible synonym pairs by translating each Swedish word to $X$ and back again to Swedish, i.e.,

$$\{(w, v) : \exists y : y \in D_1(w) \land v \in D_2(y)\}$$

We may also consider only the dictionary $D_1$ from Swedish to $X$:

$$\{(w, v) : \exists y : y \in D_1(w) \land y \in D_1(v)\}$$

Similarly we may also consider only $D_2$. The pairs obtained in this way will sometimes be synonyms, but due to ambiguous word senses there will also be lots of rubbish.

If there are dictionaries available between Swedish and other languages one can get lists of word pairs from them using the same method. Such lists can then be used either to complement or to refine the original list. If $(w, v)$ is a pair included in many lists it becomes more probable that $w$ and $v$ are real synonyms.

By using this technique we have constructed a list of 616,000 pairs of possible synonyms.

## 3  Automatic refinement

A possible way to improve the quality of the list would be to part-of-speech tag the words and only keep pairs containing words that may have the same word class. We chose not to do this, because words of different word classes could be (seldomly) synonyms, for example words of the word classes participles and adjectives. In retrospect it was a mistake not to remove words of different word classes, because it is annoying for many users to be asked whether for example a noun and a verb are synonymous.

We also refined the list of synonyms using a method called Random Indexing or RI (Kanerva et al., 2000). In RI each word is assigned a random label vector of a few thousand elements. Using these vectors one constructs a co-occurrence representative vector for each word by adding the random vectors for all words appearing in the context of each occurrence of the word in a large training corpus. For each word pair $(w, v)$ the cosine distance between the co-occurrence vectors of $w$ and $v$ is a measure of relatedness between the two words; words that appear in similar contexts get a high value. Synonyms often appear in similar contexts. So this is a suitable method for deciding on whether a pair of possible synonyms are likely to be actual synonyms.

To find as many related words as possible we have used several different corpora. Table 1 gives some statistics for them. The three top sets are extracted from the KTH News Corpus (Hassel, 2001). Aftonbladet and DN are two Swedish newspapers and DI is a daily economic paper. Med is a set of medical papers from Läkartidningen[7] and Parole is a part of the Swedish Parole Corpus[8].

Before building the Random Index we removed stopwords and lemmatized all words. We chose random vectors with 1800 dimensions and eight randomly selected non-zero elements (four ones and four minus ones). When building the context vectors we used four words before and four

----

[7] http://www.lakartidningen.se/
[8] http://spraakbanken.gu.se/lb/parole/

| Text set | Texts | Words | Lemmas |
|---|---|---|---|
| Aftonbladet | 29,602 | 751,804 | 34,262 |
| DN | 6,954 | 593,055 | 63,164 |
| DI | 19,488 | 1,606,743 | 70,539 |
| Med | 2,422 | 2,146,788 | 150,627 |
| Parole | – | 1,694,556 | 135,205 |

Table 1: Text set statistics (stopwords not included)

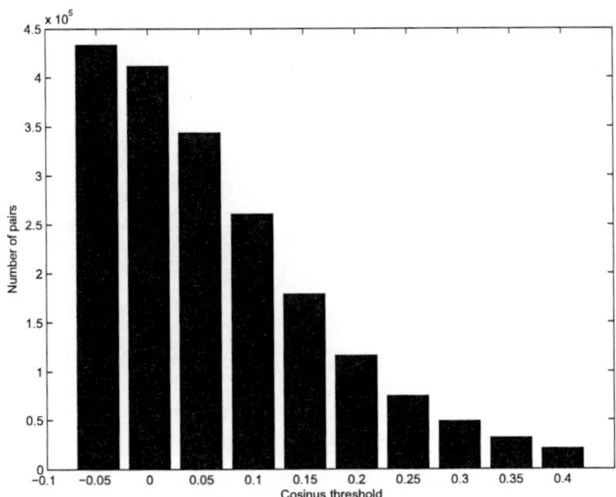

Figure 1: Number of pairs with cosine threshold

words after as the context for each word and added the random labels for these context words to the context vector of the center word weighted by $2^{1-d}$, where $d$ is the distance between the context word and the center word.

For each text set we then calculated the cosine of all word pairs in the list of possible synonyms and chose the maximum of these as their similarity. Of the 616,000 possible synonym pairs 435,000 appeared in any of the texts sets. Figure 1 shows the number of pairs (the vertical axis) with higher similarity than certain values (horizontal axis).

We chose to remove all pairs with a similarity value lower than 0.1 after studying this figure and some examples. This left 226,000 pairs.

## 4　Manual refinement

The Lexin on-line dictionary is a very popular web-site for translations of Swedish words to about ten different languages. During the year 2004 the number of lookups in Lexin was 101 millions. This means more than three lookups each second of the year. During 2005 this has increased to five lookups each second.

As the users of Lexin ask language (translation) questions they obviously like the idea of an on-line dictionary. Therefore they are probably motivated to put a small effort in producing a free Swedish dictionary of synonyms.

Many users are of course not native Swedes and are using Lexin to learn Swedish. In order to not bother them with questions about Swedish synonyms we chose to only include the synonym question in the Swedish-English dictionary with Swedish user interface. This will still cover two thirds of the total number of lookups of Lexin.

The Swedish Agency for School Improvement has allowed us to use the Lexin lookup answer web page. As a user gets an answer to a translation question she is also presented with the possibility to answer a question in order to help with the dictionary of synonyms. A question could for example be: *Are 'spread' and 'lengthen' synonyms? Answer using a scale from 0 to 5 where 0 means 'I do not agree' and 5 means 'I fully agree', or answer 'I do not know'.*

---

Kann & Rosell: *Free construction of a free Swedish dictionary of synonyms*

When a user have answered this question a web page of the growing synonym dictionary opens and the user may choose to grade more pairs, suggest new synonym pairs, lookup in the synonym dictionary or download the synonym dictionary. Prototypes of the programs taking care of the answers and the synonym dictionary were developed by a student project group at KTH.

## 5  Synonymity

It is interesting to note that the exact meaning of "synonym" does not need to be defined. The users will grade the synonymity using their intuitive understanding of the concept and the words in the question. The produced dictionary of synonyms will therefore use the People's definition of synonymity, and hopefully this is exactly what the people wants when looking up in the same dictionary.

Of this reason we called the dictionary *The People's Dictionary of Synonyms.*

## 6  Abuse

Every web page that invites the public to participate will be subjected to attempts of abuse. Thus the synonym dictionary must have ways to prevent this. Our solution is threefold. First, many gradings of a pair are needed before it is considered to be a good synonym pair and become possible to lookup in the synonym dictionary.

Second, the pair that a user is asked to grade has been randomly picked from the list of about quarter of a million pairs. The same user will almost never be asked to grade the same pair more than once. If most of the users answer honestly and have an acceptable idea of the synonymity when they think they have, the quality of the synonym dictionary should be good.

Third, the word pairs that users suggest themselves are first checked using a spelling checker and are then added to the long list of pairs, and will eventually be graded by other users. The probability that a user will be asked to grade his own suggested pair is extremely small.

## 7  Results and discussion

In five months 2.1 million gradings were made (1.2 million gradings during the first two months). They were distributed over the different grades as shown in Figure 2. The distribution between grades 1–5 is remarkably even. Only the 0 grade is a lot more common than the other grades.

Table 2 gives a few examples of user graded synonyms. Pairs given grade 5 or 4 are very good synonyms. Pairs of grade 3 are synonyms to a less degree, for example *cistern* and *pot*, and pairs of grade 2 are often of different word classes (for example one adjective and one verb). Words of grade 1 are relatad but not synonymous, and grade 0 words are not even (obviously) related.

As the pairs are picked at random from the list some pairs are graded more times than others. Figure 3 shows the distribution of how many times the pairs were graded. Note that when a word has received three 0 gradings it will be removed from the list. Therefore there is a maximum point at 3.

In Figure 4 the number of pairs with different mean gradings are presented. Pairs with very small and very large mean gradings have several times during the period been removed from the list of words to be graded.

Figure 5 confirms that Random Indexing is useful for automatic refinement. The cosine similarity between pairs that are graded 0 by users is considerably lower than between all pairs on average.

The users could propose new synonym pairs. During the first five months 55,000 pairs (23,000 unique pairs) were proposed. After spelling correction end removal of non-serious words 15,000 pairs remained.

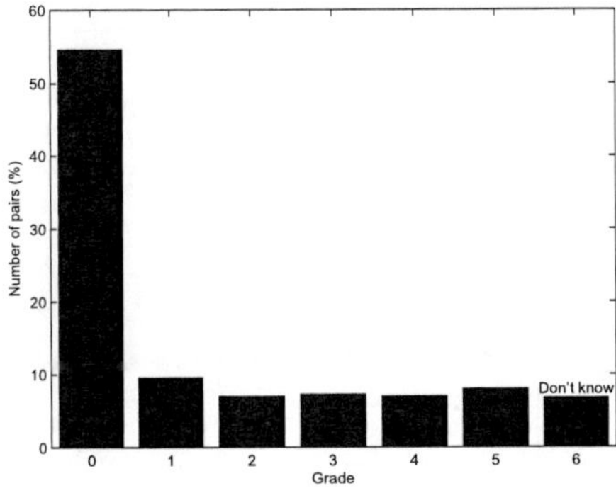

Figure 2: Gradings made by the users

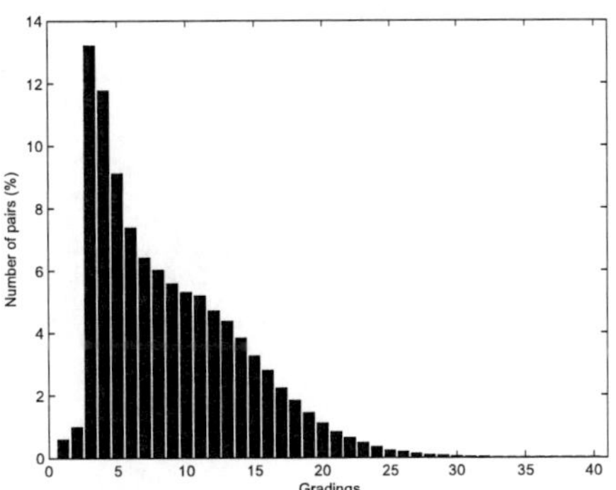

Figure 3: Number of gradings

These were regularly added to the list of pairs to be graded.

After five months we have 60,000 pairs in the dictionary of synonyms. All these pairs have been given a grade larger than 0 at least three times with a mean value of at least 2.0. When a user makes a lookup in the dictionary the synonyms are presented with their mean grades. This means that this dictionary of synonyms is much more useful than a standard one that only gives a bunch of words that may be more or less synonymous.

The 25,000 best synonym pairs have been publically available for downloading in a simple XML format for about a month. More than 50 downloadings each day are currently being performed, which shows that there is indeed a large need for a free dictionary of synonyms in Swedish.

Many users have commented that there were too many bad pairs. Lots of pairs were graded 0 (not at all synonyms) by all users. After some weeks 25,000 such pairs were removed. Later 60,000 more pairs were removed, improving the quality of the remaining pairs considerably.

## 8  Lessons learned

The list of suggested synonyms should be huge, as we want to find as many synonyms as possible. But bad pairs irritate the users.

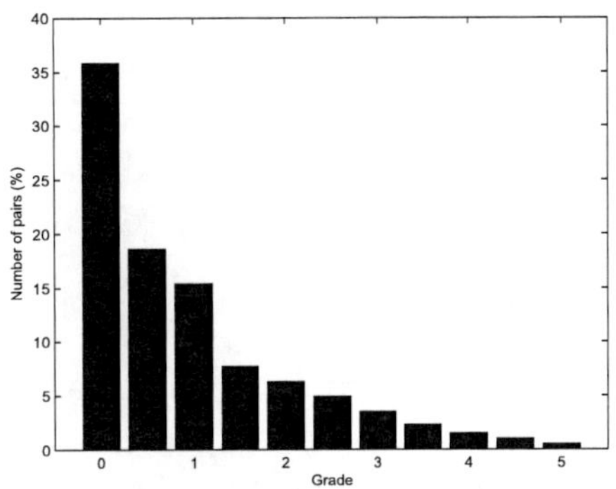

Figure 4: Mean gradings

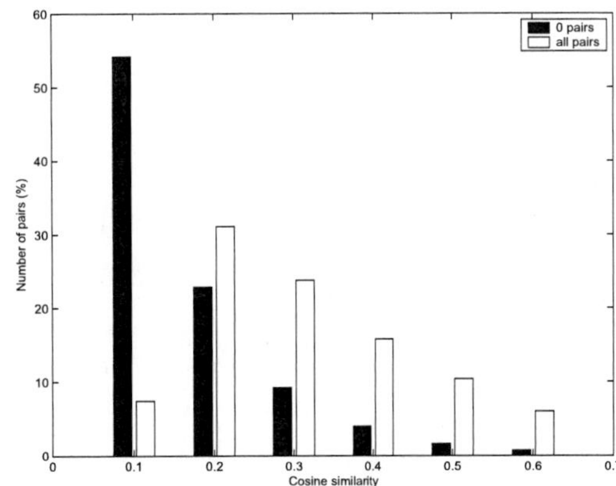

Figure 5: Cosine similarity for pairs graded 0 and for all pairs

| 5 | | 4 | | 3 | |
|---|---|---|---|---|---|
| hipp | häftig | bisarr | konstig | cistern | burk |
| betraktare | iakttagare | dåraktig | idiotisk | folkskola | grundskola |
| gäng | grupp | hall | foajé | kamrat | väninna |

| 2 | | 1 | | 0 | |
|---|---|---|---|---|---|
| ansenlig | åtskilligt | bestiga | stiga | hake | kröka |
| fackförening | union | fatta | följa | ynklig | deltagande |
| glida | slinka | feja | ren | | |
| hölja | omfatta | hård | tätt | | |

Table 2: Examples of user graded pairs

Therefore it is important to improve the quality of the list as much as possible. This could be done automatically, using for instance Random Indexing, word class tagging, and other dictionaries, for example for different languages. As the number of answers grows it is also a good idea to remove pairs that often get a zero grading.

## 9  Conclusions

We have found that it is possible to create a free dictionary of synonyms almost for free. The constructed dictionary is even more useful than a standard one, since the synonyms are presented with gradings.

There is no reason to believe that the method presented in this paper may not be used to create lists of other word relations, such as hypernymy, hyponymy, holonymy and meronymy.

The growing and improving dictionary of synonyms can be found at http://lexin.nada.kth.se/cgi-bin/synlex.

## Acknowledgements

We would like to thank the Swedish Agency for School Improvement, and especially Kiros Fre Woldu, for letting us use the Lexin on-line web page to ask users for gradings of synonym pairs.

Thanks to the KTH students Sara Björklund, Sofie Eriksson, Patrik Glas, Erik Haglund, Anna Hilding, Nicholas Montgomerie-Neilson, Helena Nützman, and Carl Svärd for building the dictionary system prototype.

## References

M. Hassel. 2001. Automatic construction of a Swedish news corpus. In *Proc. 13th Nordic Conf. on Comp. Ling. – NODALIDA '01*.

P. Kanerva, J. Kristofersson, and A. Holst. 2000. Random indexing of text samples for latent semantic analysis. In *Proc. of the 22nd Annual Conference of the Cognitive Science Society*.

---

Kann & Rosell: *Free construction of a free Swedish dictionary of synonyms*

# Compound terms and their constituent elements in information retrieval

**Jussi Karlgren**

Swedish Institute of Computer Science

Box 1263, SE-164 29 Kista, Sweden

jussi@sics.se

## Abstract

Compounds, especially in languages where compounds are formed by concatenation without intervening whitespace between elements, pose challenges to simple text retrieval algorithms. Search queries that include compounds may not retrieve texts where elements of those compounds occur in uncompounded form; search queries that lack compounds will not retrieve texts where the salient elements are buried inside compounds. This study explores the distributional characteristics of compounds and their constituent elements using Swedish, a compounding language, as a test case. The compounds studied are taken from experimental search topics given for CLEF, the Cross-Language Evaluation Forum and their distributions are related to relevance assessments made on the collection under study and evaluated in terms of divergence from expected random distribution over documents. The observations made have direct ramifications on e.g. query analysis and term weighting approaches in information retrieval system design.

## 1 What is a compound?

Compounding is one of the basic methods of word-formation in human language. Two or more base word elements which typically occur independently as single words are juxtaposed to form a more complex entity. The compound elements can be concatenated without space, joined with a hyphen, or form an open compound with white space in between: "classroom", "cross-lingual", "high school". Compounding is a productive process: new compounds can be formed on the fly for ad-hoc purposes to treat topical elements in the discourse at hand. The semantics of a compound is typically related to the constituent elements, and most often the former constituent modifies the latter. Compounding has been studied in detail although not always in terms of function by linguists, terminologists, grammarians, and lexicologists over the past years; there are excellent overviews available for most any language one might be interested in. Compounding processes may show great surface differences between languages. Some languages use script systems that make no discernible difference between compounds and happenstance or syntactically motivated juxtaposition – ideogram-based Asian scripts, such as Japanese or Chinese, e.g. Some languages show a preponderance of open compounds and are restrictive in forming new closed compounds, such as the English language (see Quirk et al. (1985) for a comprehensive treatment of English compounding). Other languages again, such as Swedish, a near relation of English both in terms of cultural and linguistic history, tend towards closed compounds – with no white space between elements (see Noréen (1906) for a comprehensive treatment of Swedish compounding).

Compounds that originally are formed on the fly are eventually lexicalized and gain status as terms in their own right in a language. Terms such as "staircase", "blackbird" or "doorjamb" are not dynamically constructed for the purpose of a single discourse session or a single text – they are single simple words from the perspective of the language user. Compounds can also be borrowed from and loaned to other

S. Werner (ed.), *Proceedings of the 15th NODALIDA conference, Joensuu 2005*, Ling@JoY 1, 2006, pp. 111–115
ISBN 952-458-771-8, ISSN 1796-1114. http://ling.joensuu.fi/lingjoy/

languages and then often lose their character as a composite term: "homicide" is only in some sense an English compound. Other types of derivation such as affixation also resembles compounding to the extent that it may be difficult to draw a line. Is "eatable" a compound of "eat" and "able"? These types of process make compound analysis a demanding task for language engineering applications. When is it motivated to segment a compound to make it understandable and when should it be understood to be a lexical item in its own right?

## 2   Compounds in information retrieval

In information retrieval the problem of matching compounds to its separate elements has sparked some recent interest.   Since compounds are typically formed topically, the constituent elements are quite likely to have topical focus in the text at hand.   In languages where compounding often results in closed compounds (a "compounding" language) this will pose a problem for typical string search based retrieval systems: the query terms may contain a crucial element buried inside a compound, or alternatively, the index entries for some document may lack crucial constituent elements if they occur only or mainly inside compounds. In the last few years of growing interest in cross-lingual and multi-lingual information retrieval, several recent research efforts have addressed aspects of compounding and decompounding for the purposes of information retrieval.

A retrieval system tailored to the requirements of a compounding language would thus ideally split compounds both when indexing and when processing query terms.   This has been tested by Braschler and Ripplinger (2004), who performed a set of information retrieval experiments on German text collections using various approaches to morphological analysis including decompounding, and found, much as expected, that decompounding efforts improved retrieval results considerably.

For indexing Swedish material splitting compounds at indexing time could be expected to improve recall by allowing queries to find elements that otherwise would be hid inside compounds.   In experiments, Ahlgren (2004) has found that splitting compounds and indexing

documents for both the entire compound and each constituent element separately yielded no significant effects, but in his experiments he did not attempt to decompound the query terms. In other experiments, Cöster et al. (2004) found that judicious splitting and expansion of query terms provided promising, if not entirely convincing results. Both index and query are likely to need decompounding to deliver practically useful results.

In a cross-lingual context, languages may have different compounding strategies. Translating from Swedish – tending towards closed compounds – to English – tending towards open compounds allows the strategy of splitting compound query terms and then translated element by element to formulate an English query to retrieve documents from an English index. Since most compounds in English are open, this strategy does not require any separate treatment of the index: the separate constituent elements are mostly reasonably elements of the query in terms of what the index contains. Hedlund (2003) has tested this strategy with productive and successful application to structured query construction, where the structure of the compounds can be translated into a structure of disjunctions and conjunctions of single term elements. It is evident that the structure of the compound itself carries information — which should not be discarded out of hand but instead be utilized in the analysis.

## 3   Experiment methodology

This present study is not an information retrieval experiment in the traditional sense. Most of the cited research efforts above have performed large-scale experiments using a retrieval system of their choice or of their own construction, and report aggregated results from several retrieval runs. However, most also seem to feel the need to supplement their results with a more detailed performance analysis, analyzing term and constituent element occurrences using an implicitly set theoretic approach: "the term XY occurred only rarely in the relevant documents whereas the constituent element X was fairly frequent". For the purposes of this study, no retrieval system was employed at all and only the primary data, term (and constituent element, as the case may be) occurrences are reported.

Terms may occur in texts for various reasons. Some occurrences are incidental and thus spurious for the purposes of topical retrieval; other occurrences are focussed, topical, and salient for topical retrieval systems. In this present study an arguably drastic simplified approximation to topicality is employed: if a term occurs in a document *more than once* it is considered topical; if the term occurs only once it is considered incidental. This is based on a three-parameter model of term distributions defined by Katz (1996): it postulates among others the parameter $\gamma$ – the probability a term is topical or not. Katz' $\gamma$ is estimated by the observed relative frequency of it appearing at least twice:

$$\gamma = \frac{N - n_0 - n_1}{N - n_0}$$

where $n_0$ is the number of documents without the term, $n_1$ is the number of documents with the term exactly once, and $N$ is the total number of documents under consideration.

Katz' $\gamma$ estimate here constitutes an estimate of the bound of usefulness of terms for information access analysis. The assumption, following Katz, is that if a term tends to reoccur in a document, it will tend towards topical use. Topical use can then presumably be utilized by a search algorithm, if well crafted.

## 4   Data

The annual Cross-language Evaluation Forum (CLEF) conferences provide a stable test bench of document collections, queries ("topics"), and manually obtained relevance judgements which relate sets of documents to topics. Each topic thus has a set of relevance judgments to select which documents are judged topically relevant to it. Typically the number of topically relevant documents for a topic is on the order of a few dozen and the number of assessed documents around two hundred.

The document databases consisted of the CLEF collection of Swedish newsprint for the years 1994 and 1995, the sixty Swedish-language topics for the 2003 evaluation cycle (numbers 141-200; only the title and description fields were used for this study, as in most experiments performed on the data), and the relevance judgements given for those topics. The document collection consists of some 140 000 documents of news articles in Swedish, most rather brief.

## 5   Occurrence statistics for compounds

In Swedish running text between a tenth and a fifth of tokens are compounds: the material in the CLEF collection seems to tend towards the higher figure. Search queries can be assumed to be more topical than other types of textual material, and compounds can accordingly be expected to be more frequent in information need specifications. Statistics on CLEF topics bear out this assumption. Taking the sixty Swedish CLEF topics from 2003 we find about one thousand term token occurrences. Once morphological variants are conflated and stop words are taken out (including query specific terms such as "find" and "document"), we find that out of the somewhat less than four hundred individual terms used in the topics more than ninety are compounds, and that if duplicates are removed the numbers are even more striking: almost every second unique noun is a compound. (Compound analysis is always a question of judgments: some analyses are debatable, other compounds are missed. Hand checking by several assessors indicates these errors cancel each other out for the purposes of this study.) As a comparison, the English versions of these topics contain only two or three closed or hyphenated compounds. The statistics as shown in table 3 establishes beyond any doubt that for compounding languages such as Swedish queries should be understood to be compound dense. Any query analysis for a compounding language procedure should reflect this fact.

## 6   Goal task

The following statistical observations are meant to guide the task of query generalization. Given that a query contains a set of terms, some of which are compounds $A+B$, would the query be enhanced by adding further terms to it, e.g. constituent elements such as $A$ or $B$?

## 7   Topical relevance and compounds

If compound query terms are frequent, they should be expected to be frequent in the target document set as well. Documents that are assessed as relevant with regard to the query topic in question contain compound terms in

---

Table 1: Occurrences of compounds in one year of Swedish CLEF topics.

|  | Tokens | Two-place compounds | Three-place compounds |
|---|---|---|---|
| All | 392 | 78 | 14 |
| Unique | 333 | 77 | 14 |

general with about the same frequency that other documents in the collection, and the occurrence of single terms and compounds is not dramatically different between relevant retrieved and non-retrieved documents.

The constituent elements do not behave symmetrically, however. As can be seen in table 7 former elements taken from a compound query term more often to be topically used in relevant documents than latter elements or new compounds based on either former or latter elements. This is consistent with arguments in the philological literature (Quirk et al., 1985; Noréen, 1906) where the former element of a compound is observed to be a focal component in an implicit predication.

These statistics show that on average it would seem to be advisable to add the former element of the compound to the query: if the query contains term "diamantindustri" (*diamond+industry*) "diamant" is likely to be a useful query expansion, far more than other "industri" would, and more than new compound terms such as "diamantring" (*diamond ring*), "oljeindustri" (*oil industry*), or "bilindustri" (*automobile industry*).

## 8 Remaining questions to study

### 8.1 Distributional overlap

While the preceding set of statistics indicate that compounds can profitably be analyzed and elements treated individually, the overlap between compounds and their elements remains a factor in determining the informational value of constituent elements vs entire compound: if the overlap is large, the marginal gain from introducing new terms can be assumed to be of low utility.

## 9 Principled prediction of topical overlap

The above argument is based on the assumption that compounds follow a general pattern. The generalization may be useful and practical but is likely to obscure underlying system-

atic differences between different types of compounding processes and different types of constituent element. The question is whether it is possible to predict the likely utility of adding constituent elements to a compound query term by observing the relative distributional statistics of the constituent elements and the compound in the collection without involving relevance assessments or human intervention.

The statistical treatment of compound elements is a special case of the general question of terminological topical interdependence.

Questions that are being investigated in continuing research efforts aim at the prediction of topical characteristics based on observed distributional characteristics. They include questions such as: Can we make a principled choice of elements to generalize from? Are elements in certain positions more valuable than others? Can we use characteristics of the bare elements to make that choice? Can we use total overlap to predict usefulness of constituent elements?

## 10 Discussion

The results of the present study are unequivocal on one level of analysis. As previous studies have shown, compounding languages should be treated as such. This study confirms that observation.

Additionally, this study observes that compounds are not simple and happenstance juxtapositions of equally salient elements. Compounding is a mechanism used by authors and speakers for a reason, and this can be usefully utilized in the analysis of e.g. information retrieval queries. It would appear to be worth the trouble to select constituent elements by their distributional characteristics and by the structure of the compound term rather than by their appearance as an unanalyzed compound in a query.

Thirdly, on a methodological level, this study claims that the set theoretical and distributional methodology used, while yielding less immediate results in terms of ranked retrieved document sets, gives better purchase for imple-

Table 2: Katz' $\gamma$ for compound term (AB) elements in the target collection.

|  | all documents | relevant documents | $N$ |
|---|---|---|---|
| Single query terms | 0.253 | 0.368 | 295 |
| Compound query terms (A+B) | 0.215 | 0.273 | 92 |
| Former element alone (A) | 0.276 | 0.383 | 94 |
| Latter element alone (B) | 0.270 | 0.338 | 99 |
| Former element recombined (A*) | 0.235 | 0.335 | 232 |
| Latter element recombined (*B) | 0.267 | 0.362 | 117 |

mentation in various systems rather than evaluation based on the quirks and characteristics of large scale information retrieval systems, however competent and useful the systems are for the task they are built for.

# References


Per Ahlgren. 2004. *The Effects of Indexing Strategy-Query Term Combination on Retrieval Effectiveness in a Swedish Full Text Database.* Ph.D. thesis, Department of Library and Information Science, University College of Borås.

Martin Braschler and Bärbel Ripplinger. 2004. How effective is stemming and decompounding for German text retrieval? *Information Retrieval*, 7:291–306.

Rickard Cöster, Magnus Sahlgren, and Jussi Karlgren. 2004. Selective compound splitting of Swedish queries for boolean combinations of truncated terms. In Carol Peters, Martin Braschler, Julio Gonzalo, and Martin Kluck, editors, *Fourth Workshop of the Cross–Language Evaluation Forum (CLEF 2003)*. Lecture Notes in Computer Science (LNCS), Springer, Heidelberg, Germany.

Turid Hedlund. 2003. *Dictionary-Based Cross-Language Information Retrieval: Principles, System Design and Evaluation*. Ph.D. thesis, Department of Information Science, University of Tampere.

Slava Katz. 1996. Distribution of content words and phrases in text and language modelling. *Natural Language Engineering*, 2:15–60.

Adolf Noréen. 1906. *Vårt språk*, volume 7. CWK Gleerup, Lund, Sweden.

Randolph Quirk, Sidney Greenbaum, Geoffrey Leech, and Jan Svartvik. 1985. *A comprehensive grammar of the English language.* Longman, London, England.

# Synthetic regional Danish

**Bodil Kyst and Peter Juel Henrichsen**
Center for Computational Modelling of Language
Copenhagen Business School
bodilkyst@yahoo.com pjuel@id.cbs.dk

## Abstract

The speech technological scene in Denmark is slowly gaining public and commercial attention, and today there is a call for more diverse products than just recognition and synthesis of standard Danish (i.e. the Copenhagen regiolect). In this working paper, we demonstrate how an existing synthesis engine may be tuned to provide a regiolect speaking voice, involving - in its simplest form - prosodic alterations only. We present the first publicly accessible Danish synthetic voice for a non-standard regiolect - in casu Århusian.

## 1  Introduction

So far synthetic speech in Denmark has been based on the standard variety of Danish spoken in the area around Copenhagen, normally referred to as standard Danish. The purpose of our current project "Synthetic regional Danish" is to develop a Danish artificial voice for the variety of Danish spoken in Århus (the second biggest city).

Many of the local dialects in Denmark have died out. Danish spoken in Århus today (hereafter "Århusian") cannot be described as a genuine dialect, since it hardly differs from Copenhagen standard Danish in terms of vocabulary and grammar, or the sound of the individual phones. Århusian is rather a regional variety Ű a regiolect. A major difference between Århusian regiolect and Copenhagen standard Danish concerns the tone pattern of the stress group. Hence synthetic Århusian must at least diverge from existing applications in the prosodic assignment function (i.e. the function assigning fundamental frequency values to the phonetic segments). In addition, lexical, phonetic, and further prosodic alterations must be considered (e.g. vowel prolongation, schwa-reduction).

Our project has two main objectives: Firstly we want to establish the fact that existing Danish synthesis applications can be modified with relatively little effort to cover Danish regional variants. This fact may be of linguistic as well as commercial interest concerning the localization of speech technology. Secondly, we want to create an experimental environment for testing our theoretical understanding of the distinctive features of the regional variants of spoken Denmark.

In addition to this, there are further perspectives in creating a regiolect-speaking synthetic voice: Firstly it might bring the synthetic voice closer to the user by leading the voice to be associated with local proximity. Secondly it might add to a greater tolerance towards non-standard varieties of Danish.

A version of our Århusian synthetic voice can be tested at: **http://www.id.cbs.dk/~pjuel/ TtT_region**

## 2  Phonetic basics

### 2.1  The Copenhagen stress group tone pattern

The tone pattern of the Copenhagen stress group is described by Nina Grønnum (Grønnum, 1992). The first syllable of the stress group (the tonic syllable) is pronounced in a low tone. The following unstressed syllable (the post-tonic syllable) is pronounced in a high tone and the following unstressed syllables within the stress group are also pronounced in high tones, yet gradually losing altitude according to the overall downdrift of the tones in the stress group. This tone-pattern of the stress group can be described as low-high since the tone relation between the first two syllables is low-high. See fig. 1

Fig.1

The big dot is the stressed syllable and the small ones are the unstressed syllables within the stress group.

## 2.2 The Århusian stress group tone pattern

The tone pattern of the first two syllables of the Århusian stress group is, roughly speaking, the opposite of the Copenhagen tone pattern: In most stress groups the relationship between the tonic syllable and the post-tonic syllable can be described as high-low. Still a considerable part of the stress groups have a low-high tone pattern. As described in Kyst (Kyst, 2004) the tone pattern depends on the segmental composition of the tonic and the post-tonic syllables. Two factors play a determining role: A: Stød and B: The occurrence of non-sonorant elements between the tonic and posttonic vowels:

### 2.2.1 A. Stød

Stød is a phonation type articulated by a glottal constriction resulting in a sound resembling creaky voice. It is a distinctive feature and its presence/non-presence results in minimal pairs like finner [*f2en!C*] (noun) (the / is the stød) with stød meaning Finns from Finland vs. finner [*f2enC*] (noun) without stød meaning finns on a fish (for an introduction to our phone alphabet, see footnote 2).

In the Århusian stress group stød in the tonic syllable affects the F0 (fundamental frequency = tone height) of the following syllable in a consistent manner.

**Group 1:**
Stress groups with stød (on the tonic syllable) always have a high-low tone pattern:

Tonic syllable: high
Posttonic syllable: low
The following unstressed syllables: low, gradu-

ally getting lower

Examples of stress groups of this kind could be:
*finner* [*f2en!C*] (noun) meaning Finns from Finland
*bruser* [*br2u :!sC*] (verb) meaning rushes.

See fig. 2:

Fig.2

### 2.2.2 B. The occurrence of non-sonorant elements between the tonic and posttonic vowels

Stress groups without stød (on the tonic syllable) sometimes have a high-low tone pattern and sometimes a low-high tone pattern. This depends on the second factor determining the tone pattern of the stress group in Århus, namely the occurrence of non-sonorant elements between the tonic and posttonic vowels:

**Group 2a:**
If only sonorant elements occur between the vowel of the tonic syllable and the vowel of the posttonic syllable, the resulting tone pattern is low-high:

Tonic syllable: low
Posttonic syllable: high
The following unstressed syllables: low, gradually getting lower

An example of this is
*finner* [*f2enC*] (noun) meaning finns on a fish

See fig. 3:

Fig.3

**Group 2b:**
If at least one non-sonorant element occurs, the resulting tone pattern is high-low:

Tonic syllable: high
Posttonic syllable: low
The following unstressed syllables: low, gradually getting lower (The drop in tone between the tonic and posttonic syllable is not as steep as in the case of syllables with stød (group 1 above). We did incorporate this in our synthetic voice).

An example of this kind of stress group is
$[br2u : sC]$ (noun) meaning shower

See fig. 4:

Fig.4

## 2.3 Differences between natural and synthetic speech

It should be kept in mind that the model of tone patterns outlined above is simplified compared to natural speech in at least two respects:
Firstly in natural speech, the tones of the syllables are not constant in height like steps on a staircase, rather like curves moving up and down. Secondly the low tone in syllables without stød and only sonorant elements between the two vowels (group 2a) is not as low as the low tones of the other types of stress groups. Fig. 5 and 6 below show the tone patterns from recordings of natural speech.[1] These are the patterns that are imitated by the synthetic voice in a simplified way with level tones (fig. 1-4 above).

## 3 Danish speech synthesis

For reference synthesis application, we selected the so-called TtT Workbench (Tekst-til-Tale, Text-to-Speech), an experimental speech synthesizer for Danish which has been devel-

oped at the Center for Computational Modelling (among other places). The TtT system is a largely traditional design based on a pipeline of modules:

### 3.1 The synthesis application for standard-Danish

1. Text Preparation (expanding abbreviations, converting digits to their written equivalent, etc.) not shown in fig.70

2. Text Analysis (PSG-style grammar rules enriched with prosodic markers for main stress reduction, stød elimination, etc.)

3. Prosody Assignment (phone-based annotation rules: F0, timing, vowel prolongation, schwa reduction, onset of stød depression, etc.)

4. Signal Processing (converting the quantified phone string into sound files using diphone re-synthesis).

Figure 7 below shows the functional parts of the speech engine.
The web-based interface allows the user to control the speech engine using a standard browser (e.g. Netscape, Mozilla, or MS-Explorer). The advanced user can insert and upload a distribution of lexical and grammatical resources, thus defining his own language model.[2] The workbench, however, also allows the user to simply enter ready-made strings of phones (cf. note 1) such as:

User input: ,ensdit2ud,fC,d2z:taleNvisdig, ("Institut for Datalingvistik", Dept. of Computational Linguistics)

User input: ,f2en!Cn0,f2en!C,f2enCn0,mE,f2eNCn0, ("finnerne finder finnerne med fingrene", the Finns find the finns with their fingers)

Words may be comma separated. The commas have no influence on the acoustic rendering,

---

[1] Recordings from Kyst (Kyst, 2004) Ű stress groups cut out of longer sentences read loud by native speakers.

[2] The TtT Workbench phonetic inventory is based on the Danish SAMPA (**www.phon.ucl.ac.uk/home/sampa**), a many-to-one mapping of the IPA (International Phonetic Alphabet) on the Danish sound inventory. Since certain SAMPA symbols are inconvenient for use with regular expressions (as in the TtT server scripts) and for transfer over the Internet (used by the TtT web-interface), we use an alphanumeric SAMPA mapping. Our phone table may be consulted at **www.id.cbs.dk/~pjuel/TtT**

---

Kyst & Henrichsen: *Synthetic regional Danish*

but they tend to make phonetic strings more readable.

> TtT phone table summary (cf. Henrichsen 2001b)
>
> 2 is "tryk" (main stress)
>
> ! is "stød" (a quick glottal contraction)
>
> : is vowel prolongation
>
> z is the full vowel in e.g. "tabe" (lose)
>
> C is the vowel occurring twice in "kopper" (cups)
>
> 0 is schwa as in e.g. "tabe" (lose)
>
> TtT phonetics does not include secondary stress

By pressing the button phon2wav, the client transmits his input to the server, which in turn returns the sound file (in .wav format) produced from the phone string. Most browsers will then allow the user to just click on the link on the answer page in order to listen to the sound file. For pedagogic reasons, the TtT server application adopts a rather conservative style of feedback rejecting, (with a comment), any irregular phone string. Examples of phone strings which are rejected:

- Strings beginning with a semivowel (e.g. R, J, or w) in conflict with the Danish phonotactics.

- Strings with zero instances of symbol 2 (main stress); any utterance must contain a stressed syllable in order to be pronounceable.

- Strings with illegal stød. Only two stød loci are permitted, viz. immediately after a long vowel (as in "ben", [b2e:!n]), and immediately after a short vowel + voiced consonant (as in "bind" [b2en!]).

The TtT workbench is found at **www.id.cbs.dk/~pjuel/TtT**. Access is free of charge, but advanced users need a password issued by the author. Further details on the access and options of the publicly available Danish synthesis engine are found in Henrichsen (Henrichsen, 2005). (Henrichsen, 2005) contains reprints of a number of early research papers on Danish synthesis.

## 3.2 The Århusian voice

The current project has involved modifications in especially module 3 and - to a lesser extent - module 2 cf. fig. 7. The single most significant research task has been the quantification of the phonological patterns discussed in sect. II.

For the standard-Danish voice, F0 steps (i.e. fundamental frequency variation for the main vowels in two adjacent syllables) come in two flavors - an "up-step" and a "down-step" - computed as:

$$\text{upstep} = \text{currentF0} + (\text{maxF0} - \text{currentF0})*\text{deltaF0}$$
$$\text{downstep} = \text{currentF0} - (\text{currentF0} - \text{minF0})*\text{deltaF0}$$

where maxF0 (minF0) is the global F0 maximum (minimum) and deltaF0 is the relative step size (set to 0.3 for standard-Danish).

For the Århusian voice, a slightly more elaborate model is engaged, defining "up-step", "small-down-step" and "large_down_step", in accordance with our description of Århusian prosody (see 3.2.b).

$$\text{upstep} = \text{currentF0} + (\text{maxF0} - \text{currentF0})*\text{deltaF0}*0.8$$
$$\text{smalldownstep} = \text{currentF0} - (\text{currentF0} - \text{minF0})*\text{deltaF0}*0.5$$
$$\text{largedownstep} = \text{currentF0} - (\text{currentF0} - \text{minF0})*\text{deltaF0}*1.0$$

As seen, large-down-step for Århusian is equal to the general F0-step for standard-Danish, while small-down-step is only half that size, and up-step is somewhere in between, in order to provide a balanced prosodic curve, assuming that small and large downsteps are fairly evenly distributed.

The various F0-steps are assigned using an array of boolean flags, marking each syllable as 'un-voiced', 'with-stød', etc.

## 4 Project Status

We have concluded a pilot test involving six people with knowledge of Danish dialectology. The subjects were asked to determine the local origin of the voice and whether it was natural or synthetic.[3] Based on these and other results we are currently preparing a test environment

---

[3] Each test person heard four sound clips, some heard one of each kind and others heard the same clip twice. Each of the four sound clips were played six times in total.

---

for larger-scale listening tests.

The sentence played to the test persons was:

*Den store viser er den der viser minuttallet*
$[dEn, sd2o \ : \ C, v2i \ : \ sC, a, d2En!, dA, v2i \ : \ !sC, min2udtal!0D]$
- meaning: the big hand is the one that indicates the minutes

The result of the pilot test can be read from the confusion matrix displayed in fig. 8 below.

All test persons were able to distinguish the natural voices from the synthetic voice, and all natural voices were identified correctly according to their geographic location. The geographic origin of the synthetic Århusian voice was determined correctly in four out of six cases, and the geographic origin of the Copenhagen voice was determined correctly in five out of six cases.

## 5  Conclusions

Although our experiments are still only in a preliminary stage, we have reasons to believe that synthetic Århusian (or perhaps any Danish regiolect) in within easy reach, given the existing sophisticated Danish applications for speech synthesis proper, and the long record of dialectological research in Denmark. We also note that our experiments - including the small user test presented in section IV - have stirred a considerable public interest, especially among non-Copenhageners. In the next phase of our project we therefore intend to apply for research grants arguing that (i) synthetic regiolects can be developed as minor extensions to existing applications, (ii) west-Danes will certainly give a non-standard Danish synthetic voice a warm welcome.

## References

Nina Grønnum.  1992.  *The Groundworks of Danish Intonation. An Introduction.*, volume 1. Museum Tusculanum Press, Copenhagen, Denmark.

Peter Juel Henrichsen.  2004.  *The Twisted Tongue, Tools for Teaching Danish Pronunciation Using a Synthetic Voice; in Copenhagen Studies in Language 30/2004 (ed. PJH)*, volume 1.  Samfundslitteratur, Copenhagen, Denmark.

Peter Juel Henrichsen. 2005. *Tekster til Taleteknologi - med saerlig vaegt paa syntese af dansk talesprog (antology of texts on Danish linguistic research in speech synthesis; several texts are in Danish)*, volume 1.  Copenhagen Business School Press, ISBN 87-6340-549-0, Copenhagen, Denmark.

Bodil Kyst.  2004.  *Trykgruppens toner i Århusiansk regionalsprog.* Unpublished masterthesis, see www.bodilkyst.dk, Århus University, Denmark.

Fig.5 Group 2a vs. group 1, Århus vs Copenhagen

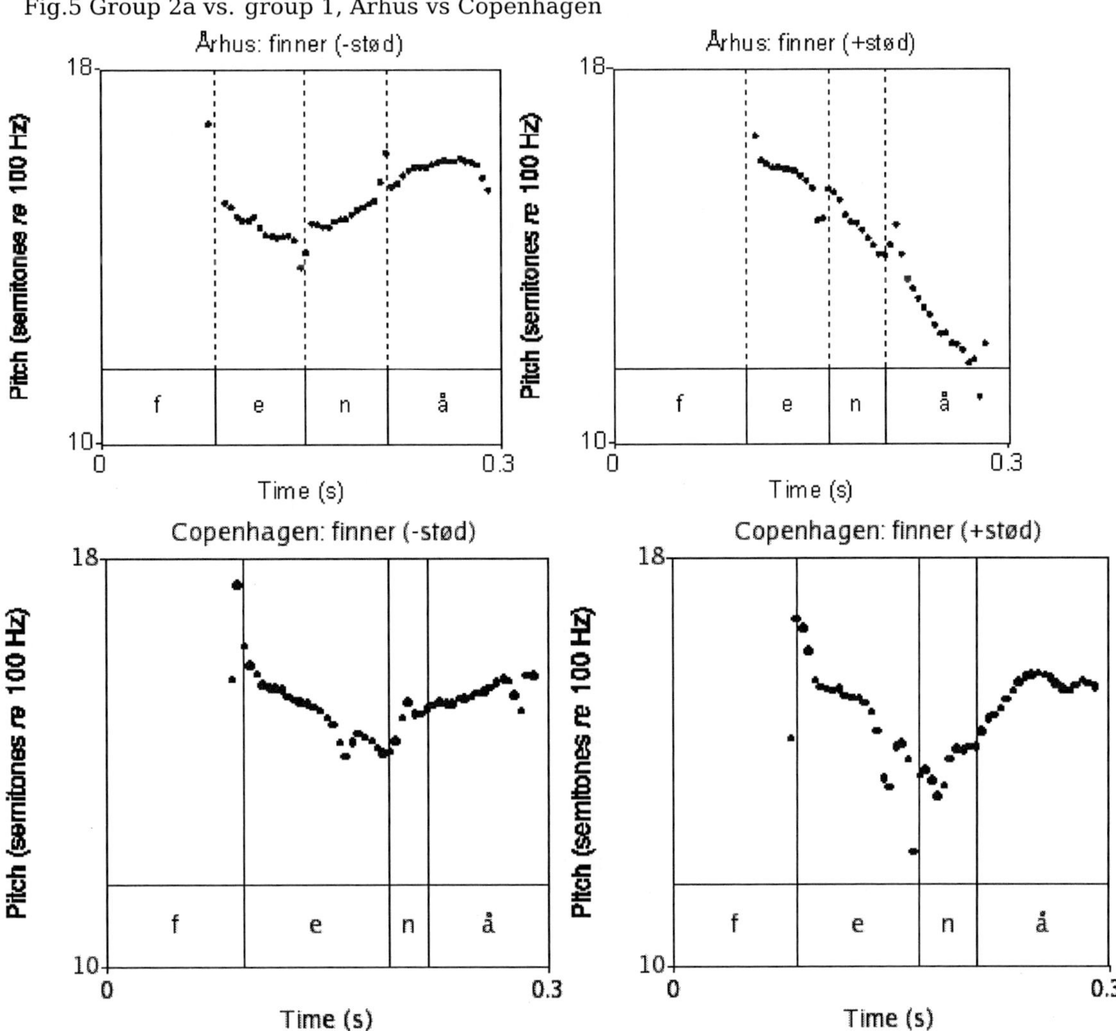

Fig.6 Group 2b vs. group 1, Århus[4] vs. Copenhagen

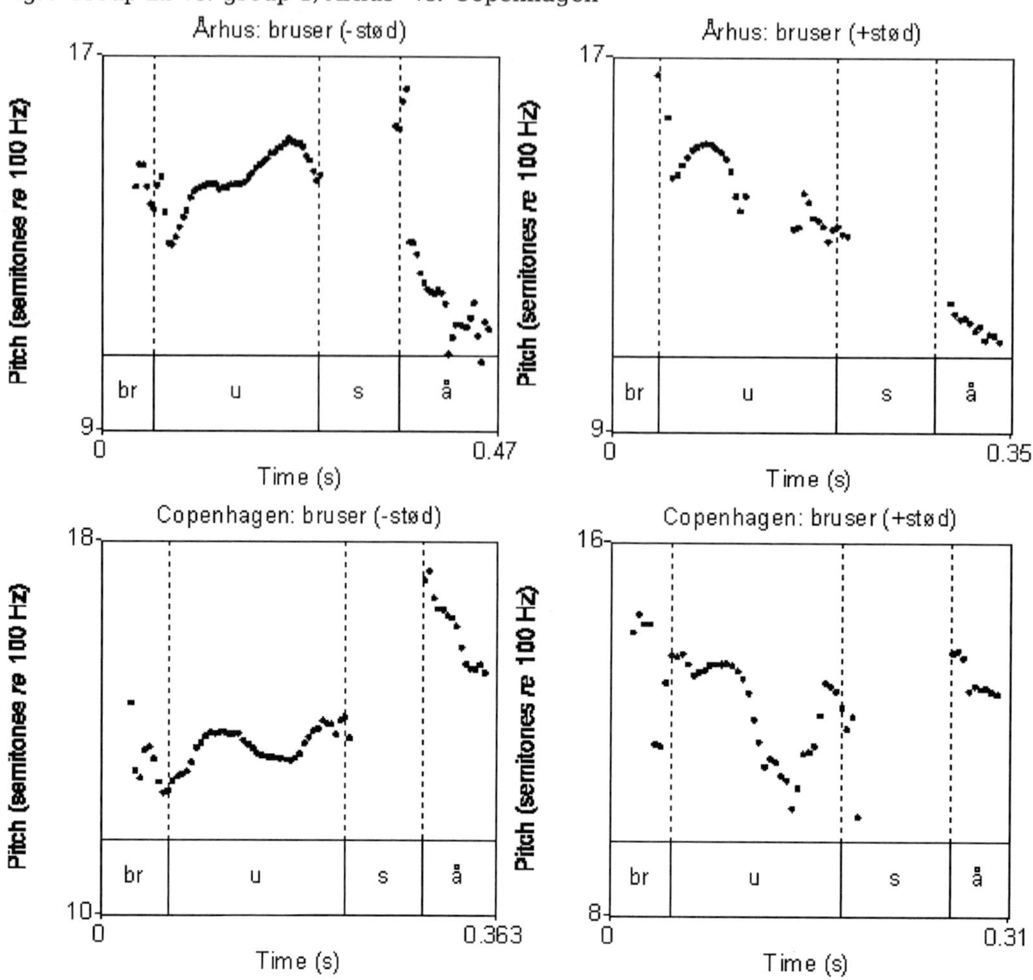


---

[4]Stress groups with short tonic vowels (and at least one non-sonorant element between the two vowels) also have this high-low tone pattern Ű see (Kyst, 2004)

Kyst & Henrichsen: *Synthetic regional Danish*

Fig.7

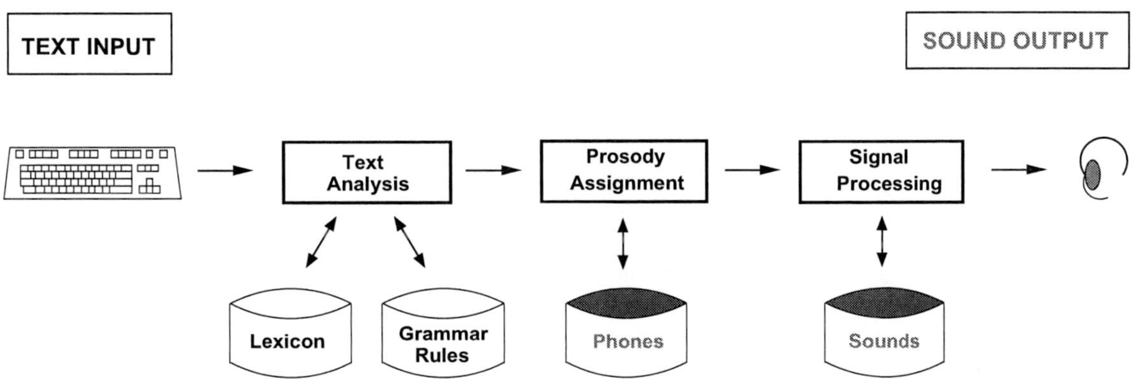


Fig.8

| Played / Heard | Natural Århus | Natural Copenhagen | Synthetic Århus | Synthetic Copenhagen |
|---|---|---|---|---|
| Natural Århus | 6/6 | | | |
| Natural Copenhagen | | 6/6 | | |
| Synthetic Århus | | | 4/6 | 1/6 |
| Synthetic Copenhagen | | | 2/6 | 5/6 |

Kyst & Henrichsen: *Synthetic regional Danish*

# Compounds and other oddities in machine translation

**Hanne Moa**

Department of Language and Communication Studies

Norwegian University of Science and Technology

7491 Trondheim, Norway

hannemo@stud.ntnu.no

## Abstract

ReCompounder is a working proto-type for automatic translation of compounds by using the web as language model and a comprehensive bilingual dictionary as translation model. Evaluation shows this strategy is viable also with current search engine technologies.

In addition to a detailed overview of the system, there is a discussion of the current capabilities of the search engines used (Google and Yahoo! Search) and some tendencies relevant to lexicography. As the system currently translates from Norwegian to English, a brief introduction to compounding in Norwegian is included.

## 1   Introduction

A major problem in machine translation is what to do with words that are not found in the machine-readable lexicon.

A possible solution is to somehow connect a regular bilingual dictionary to the system, all the time keeping in mind that definitions are made in the lexicographical tradition and not finely tuned to the particular framework and methods used in the MT-system in question.

ReCompounder extends on the connected-dictionary idea. It is a proof-of-concept proto-type which tries to translate previously unseen compounds. It is part of the LOGON machine translation project (Lønning et al., 2004) which aims to translate tourism[1]-relevant texts from

---

[1] More specifically hiking trip information

Norwegian to English, using an approach based on semantic transfer.

The underlying idea is similar to what is done in Rackow et al.(1992) and Tanaka and Baldwin (2003), but using the world wide web as corpus. Grefenstette (1999) used a similar technique for example-based machine translation with the then popular search-engines.

Using a web search engine directly greatly limits what sort of translation is possible, but since the web and the indexes of the search engines continuously grow by the addition of new and newly written pages, the data one *can* analyze more closely resembles language as it used *just now*.

As for the rest of this paper, section 2 gives a brief overview of compounds in Norwegian and what they might translate to in English, section 3 presents ReCompounder in some detail, section 4 summarizes the first round of evaluation of the system, section 5 gives an overview of the results so far, and thereafter follows the conclusion.

## 2   The problem

Compounding as a word-formation process is *very* productive in Norwegian (Johannesen and Hauglin, 1996). Thus any MT-system translating to or from Norwegian needs a way to handle newly minted compounds that was not found in the system's lexicon.

The LOGON-project has access to several dictionaries and wordlists. Those which were used for this system and are referred to in this paper includes the Engelsk Stor Ordbok (Eek and others, 2001), Bokmålsordboka (Wangensteen, 2005) and the NorKompLeks-lists (Nordgård, 1996).

The Engelsk Stor Ordbok is a paper dictionary containing over 42000 Norwegian nouns translated to English. Bokmålsordboka is a dictionary of Norwegian while the NorKompLeks-lists are lists of Norwegian words in both inflected and uninflected forms and with pronunciations. The NorKompLeks lists were designed from the beginning to be machine-readable while the two others originally only existed on paper.

## 2.1 Compounding in Norwegian

The list of examples marked 1a) to e) below starts with a compound that were not found in any of the available dictionaries and wordlists, both text-versions and machine-readable, and derives other compounds from it:

(1)　a.　gårdshus
　　　　gård+hus
　　　　farmhouse

　　　b.　gårdshustak
　　　　gård+hus+tak
　　　　farmhouse roof

　　　c.　gårdshustakstein
　　　　gård+hus+tak+stein
　　　　farmhouse roof tile

　　　d.　gårdshustaksteinsproblem
　　　　gård+hus+tak+stein+problem
　　　　problem with the roof tiles of farmhouses

　　　e.　storgårdshus
　　　　stor+gård+hus
　　　　house of a large farm

This paper will not debate the definition of compounds, especially when or if a word form ceases to be a compound and instead turns into a proper lexical item. Instead a very pragmatic stance is taken: when it is *useful* to treat something as if it was a compound, it is treated as if it *is* a compound.

Most Norwegian compounds consists of noun-stems, as in example 1a) to d) above. Some nouns have compound-only suppletive stems, as in example 5 below.

The stems are in general *not* to be written with spaces, but occasionally they are separated by an epenthetic *s* or *e*. Compounds containing abbreviations are written with a hyphen, and newer compounds often are as well. See Johannesen and Hauglin (1996) for details.

(2)　Direct juxtaposition
　　realfag
　　real+fag
　　natural science + mathematics

(3)　Epenthesis
　　a.　gårdshund
　　　　gård+hund
　　　　farm dog

　　b.　sauebonde
　　　　sau+bonde
　　　　sheep farmer

(4)　Hyphen
　　ABC-våpen
　　ABC+våpen
　　ABC weapon

(5)　Suppletive stem
　　klesklype
　　klær+klype
　　clothes pin

(6)　Spelling changes
　　busstasjon
　　buss+stasjon
　　bus station

When three or more identical letters are adjacent, only two are written, as shown in example 6 above. Furthermore, many Norwegian words can be spelled in more than one way, for instance the compound *andregradsligning* (second-degree equation) can also be spelled *andregradslikning*, *annengradsligning* and *annengradslikning*.

Finally, when more than two stems are involved, the compound can technically be split more than one way. Example 1e), *storgårdshus*, can be split as

(7)　a.　(stor+gård)+hus
　　　　house of a large farm

　　b.　* stor+(gård+hus)
　　　　large farmhouse

The split in example 7b) is not reasonable because the epenthetic *s* tends to force a split when ambiguity arises.

An example like 1d) splits to ((gård+hus)+(tak+stein))+problem since both *gårdshus* and *takstein* functions as stems of their own.

---

## 2.2 Compounding in English

Compounding in English is not so clear cut. It is more fruitful to look at what Norwegian compounds translate to in English[2]:

(8)　noun + noun

　　a.　gårdshus - farmhouse

　　b.　bygård - apartment building

(9)　adjective + noun

　　a.　statsvitenskap - political science

　　b.　forretningsstrøk - commercial area

(10)　noun + *of*-phrase

　　a.　produksjonsmidler - means of production

　　b.　streikevarsel - notice of a/the strike

　　c.　allemannsrett - public right of access

(11)　single words

　　a.　arbeidsgiver - employer

　　b.　hovedstad - capitol

(12)　other

　　a.　arbeidsro - opportunity to work undisturbed

　　b.　skoleplikt - compulsory school attendance

　　c.　skolevei - way to and from school

　　d.　streikerett - right to strike

　　e.　kjøpelyst - desire to buy

Of the examples 8 to 12, only example 8a) wasn't found in any dictionary, while the examples 10c), 12a) and 12e) were found in the bilingual dictionary but not in Bokmålsordboka.

# 3　The prototype

The entire recompounding process is shown in figure 1.

At point a), after having been handed an already lemmatized word, ReCompounder first tries to look up the word in its bilingual dictionary. If the word is not found it tries to treat the source-language term as a compound by attempting to split the potential compound into stems. If this is possible, each stem is translated into the target language at point b). The translated stems are then recombined first with each other in point c), then with the templates

---

<sup></sup>[2]Most of the examples were found in Hasselgård et. al. (1998).

of point d) into possible compounds of the target language at point e). Finally, ReCompounder checks whether these potential compounds are in use on the web at point f), and from the result of that test, in point g), the most frequent candidate is chosen as the best translation.

The assumptions are as follows:

- The stems in a compound each carry their most frequent meanings

- The translations/meanings in the bilingual dictionary are sorted by frequency, most frequent first

- It is sufficient to split a compound only once, into just two stems, because if a compound stem is used in a larger compound, it carries only its most frequent meaning

- If a compound exists in Norwegian there is a construction in English with approximately the same meaning that already exists on the indexed part of the web

## 3.1　Use of the dictionaries

The prototype searches through a digitized version of the Engelsk Stor Ordbok, treating it as a treebank. Furthermore, the number of known Norwegian stems have been increased by the stems in the NorKompLeks-lists, and checked against Bokmålsordboka.

## 3.2　The compound splitter/recognizer

The compound splitter[3] at point a), figure 1 works by attempting to split the word in two. Each piece, hereafter called the *original stems*, is then looked up in a list of known stems, so as to filter out misspelled stems.

## 3.3　The stem-translator

After having been split, each each original stem is looked up in the bilingual dictionary at point b). The translations of each are then stored in a single ordered, duplicate-free list per original stem, as in example 13.

(13)　gård: $\{farm, estate, \ldots\}$
　　　　hus: $\{house, building, \ldots\}$

These lists of *stem candidates* are then stored in the order they were made into another ordered list, thereby maintaining the order of the original stems, as in example 14.

---

<sup></sup>[3]The compound splitter can also be used as a compound recognizer

---

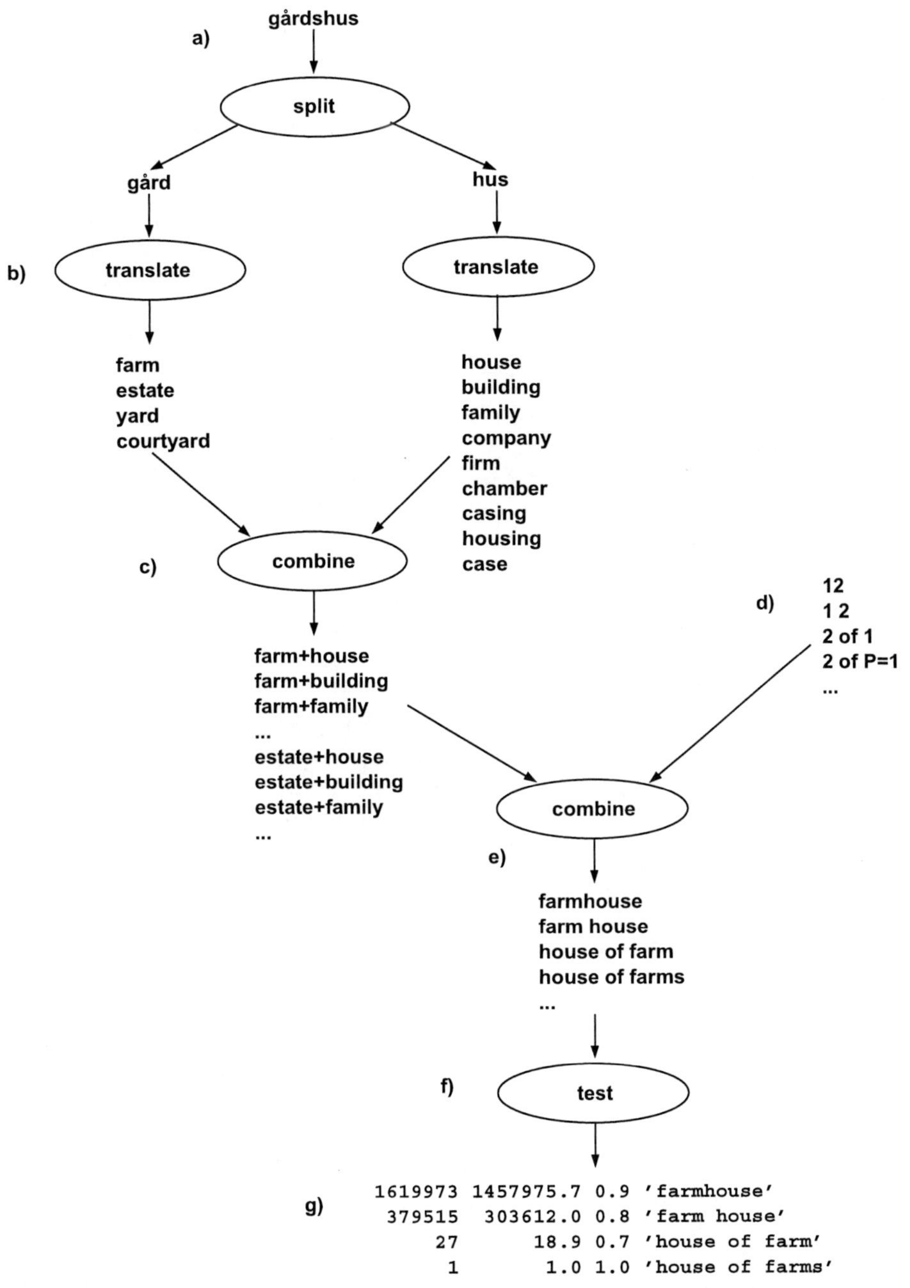


Figure 1: The recompounding process from a), the splitting of the compound, to g), the result from the web search.

(14)  $\{\{farm, estate, \ldots\}, \{house, building, \ldots\}\}$

### 3.4  Potential translation candidates

The *translation candidates* are the strings to be tested with an Internet search engine. They are derived by first combining each stem candidate for each position in the original compound while maintaining the order of the original stems, as shown in point c) of figure 1, then combining these with the *templates* from point d), resulting in the translation candidates at point e).

In table 1, the examples 8 to 10 have been used to show how the templates bridge the translation between the Norwegian and English words.

| Norwegian | Template | English |
|---|---|---|
| $gård_1$+$hus_2$ | 1 2 | $farm_1$ $house_2$ |
| $by_1$+$gård_2$ | 1 2 | $apartment_1$ $building_2$ |
| $forretning_1$+$strøk_2$ | A=1 2 | $commercial_1$ $area_2$ |
| $produksjon_1$+$middel_2$ | P=2 of 1 | $means_2$ of $production_1$ |
| $streik_1$+$rett_2$ | 2 to 1 | $right_2$ to $strike_1$ |

Table 1: Each digit in the template is replaced by the correspondingly indexed stem candidate. A= means the following stem is an adjective derived from the indexed noun, P= means the following noun-stem must be in the plural.

### 3.5  Testing the candidates

Each translation candidate is then tested by doing a web search on Google or Yahoo!, at point f), yielding a list like the one at point g). The first column is the raw frequency as extracted from the search, the second is the frequency adjusted for quality, the third is the quality and the fourth is the translation candidate.

Adjusting for quality is needed due to the limits mentioned in section 3.7. The first ten results of each run are checked to see if they actually contain the search terms in the required order and without intruding punctuation. The number of results that *do* contain the search terms in the returned context is then divided by ten, yielding the *quality* of the search, a number between 0.0 and 1.0, inclusive. Assuming that following pages of results have the same ratio of good hits to bad[4]. The total frequency is

---

[4]The number of bad hits generally increases, but does so depending both on filtering done by the particular search engine as well as the number of hits.

then multiplied with the quality, yielding the *adjusted frequency*. To date, this has not changed the order of the two highest scoring candidates.

### 3.6  Other oddities

The prototype has been used to experiment with *snowclones* (Pullum, 2004), a variety of cliched fixed expressions where one or more specific words can be replaced by words that look almost the same written, sound almost the same spoken, or belong to the same part of speech. One example is "All your base are belong to us.", a catchphrase that still has over 500000 hits on Google. Variations include "All your base are belong to U.S", "All your bias are belong to us" and "All your office are belong to me".

If the target language has a construction with similar meaning and same number and types of replaceable parts, these can be translated in the same vein as ReCompounder translates compounds. However, since there are few if any snowclones in the texts in the domain of the LOGON project, further experiments have been put on hold.

### 3.7  Search engine capabilities

Due to consolidation and mergers in the search engine industry, as of today the two leading search engines, both in terms of users and index-size, are Google at `http://www.google.com/` and Yahoo!'s search engine at `http://search.yahoo.com/`. *Alta Vista*, which was previously used for a similar purpose (Grefenstette, 1999), is now a front-end to Yahoo!, as is *Alltheweb* (personal communication with Yahoo!). Not only are the indexes much larger[5], but the query syntax and ranking algorithms are also different from 1999. In addition, instead of parsing a web page of results the search engines can now be accessed and used through stable APIs (Application Program Interface).

#### 3.7.1  Number of queries

When this paper was written, the Google-API had a limit of 1000 queries per developer id per undefined day. The limits for Yahoo! were 5000 queries per application id per ip address per 24 hour period. An exhaustive search for a translation of *gårdshus* costs 200 queries,

---

[5]As of September 27, 2005, index-size is no longer given on the search-pages (Sullivan, 2005).

meaning there's a very limited amount of exhaustive searches possible per "day". Using a page scraper[6] would get around the limits but the search engine providers provided the APIs so that various web-robots do not count as people for statistical purposes.

### 3.7.2　Possible queries

Currently, it is not possible to use web search to discover whether an English compound is written with or without a hyphen due to how "hyphen" is interpreted by the search-engines. When this paper was written, a search for `"stem1-stem2"` now yields approximately the same result as a search for `"stem1 stem2"` `stem1stem2` (Liberman, 2005) if using Google.

### 3.7.3　Possible results

Punctuation is completely ignored, so a search for rare phrases like `"repair truck"` might return only results containing the two words separated by punctuation. The hits might not even contain the exact search terms at all, so it is always necessary to check if the returned pages actually contains the query, especially if the number of returned pages is in the low hundreds.

### 3.7.4　Precision and recall

Web search excels at recall. If there is a document in the index that contains one of the words of the search query, or a link to a document that is not indexed but was found to contain one of the words of the search query, or it fulfills other criteria only known to the designers of the search engine in question, a link to the document will be returned. As can be seen from the previous paragraph, these criteria doesn't necessarily lead to the same results as what a language researcher would call a relevant hit.

Furthermore, the algorithms for how the hits are ranked are not known and are subject to change, as does the actual number of total documents indexed, the number of documents containing information relevant to the query, how the query is interpreted, how the relevancy is computed, how the frequency given is estimated from the actual frequency and how the data is presented to the consumer. Ergo, the traditional formulas for precision and recall cannot be used.

---

[6]Page scraping: parsing a page directly, synonyms: web scraping, site scraping, screen scraping

The web search presents you to a snapshot of the document index and query syntax and ranking algorithm at the moment of search. A later search might not return the same results, the same ranking or the same frequency, but the relative frequency of the query as compared to another query changes only when the index is updated, thus slowly. This means that the differences between the frequencies of the results of many searches done in a short and limited period of time will be approximately the same, and that is the measure used here.

### 3.7.5　Linguistic limits

There is no guarantee that the most frequent candidate translation is the *best* translation. The system as it stands does no domain checking what so ever, using the entire index for its searches. The readers and writers of documents on the web are the subset of people that can afford to and have the time to access it, there is thus a systematic bias. A document might have been written by someone with only a basic grasp of the language.

## 4　Evaluation

|  | Count | %of nouns |
|---|---|---|
| Nouns, total | 228 | 100.0% |
| Known | 151 | 66.2% |
| Unknown, not recompoundable | 20 | 8.8% |
| Unknown, recompoundable | 57 | 25.0% |

Table 2: Overview of the nouns in the corpus.

The prototype was tested on a small corpus built by Ola Huseth in January 2004. It is a collection of tourist information built from web pages that had both a Norwegian and an English version. Stylistically they resemble advertisements, having a high frequency of adjectives per sentence.

The evaluation corpus consisted of 112 sentences including fragments. A locally made postagger was used to extract the common nouns, finding 263 potential, inflected, nouns. While the tagger is capable of returning uninflected forms of known words, compounds are generally unknown, so a basic lemmatizer based on the same principle as the compound splitter was made to derive the base forms of the nouns.

The lemmatizer rejected 21 of the tagged nouns as they did not end with an in-

---

flected noun or noun stem[7], another 14 words mistagged as nouns was found by manual inspection. Of the remaining, 151 already had translations in the dictionary and was discarded. At this point, duplicates were removed, leaving 77 potential compounds to be translated by ReCompounder.

ReCompounder had translation suggestions for 57 of the remaining words.

While most of the failures was due to misspellings and mistaggings that had not been caught earlier or the original stems not being in the bilingual dictionary, there were two very interesting instances of a related, non-software problem. The word *bautastein* could not be translated because the original stem *bauta* translates to "menhir", a menhir is a standing stone, and there were no instances of menhir stone or with other synonyms for stone on the web. This is a good indication that the word bautastein itself needs to be added to the bilingual dictionary. A similar case was *fiskevær*, meaning "fishing village". One of the meanings of the stem *vær* is also "fishing village", ergo one wound up with a reduplicated stem in the candidate.

|  | Random | Ranked |
| --- | --- | --- |
| Highest ranked is good | 7.0% | 36.9% |
| At least one good | 21.1% | 31.6% |
| At least one possible | 33.3% | 17.5% |
| No good candidates | 38.6% | 14.0% |

Table 3: Evaluation-results: random sample of size 5 from all possible combinations and five best existing collocations sorted by score

Evaluation was done by having a human bilingual in Norwegian and English rate the suggestions. For each list of translation candidates, the evaluator was presented with a context for the original compound and with up to five of the best candidates[8], as seen in figure 2. The evaluator was then asked to quickly mark each candidate as to whether it was an acceptable translation, completely unacceptable or potentially acceptable. This is summarized in the column *Ranked* in table 3.

In addition to the sets of ranked candidates the evaluator was also given sets of candidates that were random samples of all generated,

___
[7]and thus not translatable in the current system

[8]Sorted by score, but the evaluator was not made aware of this.

unchecked candidates, to serve as a basis for comparison. This is the column *Random* in table 3.

The most desirable outcome is that the candidate of the highest frequency is suitable as a translation, as shown in the second row of table 3. More interestingly, there was at least one good translation out of five about two thirds of the time, as shown by the second and third rows.

## 5   Results so far

Already while testing the system during the development stage, certain tendencies emerged. All the compounds so far tested can be categorized as follows:

**Good to excellent translations**

(15)   gårdshus → gård + hus
       ⟹ farm house → farmhouse

The top five of the complete results for farmhouse are in table 4.

| 1427890 | 1285101.0 | 0.9 | farmhouse |
| --- | --- | --- | --- |
| 332322 | 265857.6 | 0.8 | farm house |
| 72417 | 50691.9 | 0.7 | farm family |
| 35695 | 24986.5 | 0.7 | estate family |
| 34652 | 31186.8 | 0.9 | farm building |

Table 4: Top five results for "farmhouse". Notice how "farm building" beats "estate family" when ranking by adjusted frequency.

**Unsplittable compound**   No stems to search, no result. Often this is due to a compound-only suppletive stem missing from the dictionary or wordlists, as discussed in section 2.1, example 5.

**Bilingual dictionary lacks usable English stem**   Sometimes, this is due to the stem missing from the dictionary, but there are also cases where there are no single word translations of the stem.

(16)   seterbu → seter + bu
       ⟹ no useful translations + ...

In the above case, there are no suitable one-word translations of *seter*. This is different from the last category in that here the target language lacks an adequate term, while the last category is when the source language term lacks an entry for the adequate meaning.

___

Moa: *Compounds and other oddities in machine translation*

```
46. 604 meter over Lysefjorden henger denne markante fjellformasjonen.

fjellformasjon

[ ] mountain formation
[ ] formation of mountains
[ ] formation of mountain
[ ] formation of mount
[ ] mount formation
```

Figure 2: Evaluation

**One of the stems of the compound means the same as the compound** This was the case with *bautastein* and *fiskevær* as discussed in section 4.

**The meaning of the Norwegian compound stem systematically differs from stand-alone stem**

(17)  ulvestamme → ulv + stamme
      ⟹ wolf + no useful translations

This is so far the most interesting result, showing that the meaning of the stem when part of a compound is missing from the dictionary. <mammal> + *stamme* means approximately "total population of <mammal> in a certain area" and is this synonymous with *bestand*. A similar problem is *bil*, when in a compound it generally translates to "truck", not "car". While ReCompounder can be used some of the way to discover such holes in the dictionary, making the definition of the missing stem or meaning still takes a lexicographer.

## 6  Conclusion

Using current web search engines instead of traditional static corpora is a workable strategy for automatic translation of compounds.

Compared to a baseline where all combinations are equally likely, the results are pretty good. As a bonus, the system as-is detects errors and gaps in the bilingual dictionary and is therefore useful as a tool for lexicography.

The strategy itself will be used in the machine-translation project LOGON to improve coverage there.

## References

Øystein Eek et al., editors. 2001. *Engelsk stor ordbok: engelsk-norsk/norsk-engelsk.* Kunnskapsforlaget, Norway.

Gregory Grefenstette. 1999. The WWW as a resource for example-based machine translation tasks. In *Proceedings of the ASLIB Conference on Translating and the Computer*, London, October.

Hilde Hasselgård, Stig Johansson, and Per Lysvåg. 1998. *English Grammar: Theory and Use.* Universitetsforlaget, Oslo, Norway.

Janne Bondi Johannesen and Helge Hauglin. 1996. An Automatic analysis of compounds. In T. Haukioja, editor, *Papers from the 16th Scandinavian Conference of Linguistics*, pages 209–220, Turku/Åbo, Finland.

Mark Liberman. 2005. Google usage. Language Log, `http://itre.cis.upenn.edu/~myl/languagelog/archives/001956.html`, 6 March.

Jan Tore Lønning, Stephan Oepen, Dorothee Beermann, Lars Hellan, John Carroll, Helge Dyvik, Dan Flickinger, Janne Bondi Johannsen, Paul Meurer, Torbjørn Nordgård, Victoria Rosén, and Erik Velldal. 2004. LOGON. A Norwegian MT effort. In *Proceedings of the Workshop in Recent Advances in Scandinavian Machine Translation*, Uppsala, Sweden.

Torbjørn Nordgård. 1996. NorKompLeks: Some Linguistic Specifications and Applications. In Lindebjerg, Ore, and Reigem, editors, *ALLC-ACH '96. Abstracts*, Bergen. Universitetet i Bergen, Humanistisk Datasenter.

Geoffrey K. Pullum. 2004. Snowclones: lexicographical dating to the second. Language Log, `http://itre.cis.upenn.edu/~myl/languagelog/archives/000350.html`, 6 January.

Ulrike Rackow, Ido Dagan, and Ulrike Schwall. 1992. Automatic translation of noun compounds. In *Proceedings of COLING 92*, pages 1249–1253, Nantes, France, August.

Danny Sullivan. 2005. End Of Size Wars? Google Says Most Comprehensive But

Drops Home Page Count. Search Engine Watch, `http://searchenginewatch.com/searchday/article.php/3551586`, 27 September.

Takaaki Tanaka and Timothy Baldwin. 2003. Translation selection for Japanese-English Noun-Noun Compounds. In *Proc. of Machine Translation Summit IX*, pages 378–385, New Orleans, USA.

Boye Wangensteen, editor. 2005. *Bokmålsordboka*. Kunnskapsforlaget, Norway.

# Towards modeling the semantics of calendar expressions as extended regular expressions

**Jyrki Niemi** and **Lauri Carlson**
Department of General Linguistics
University of Helsinki
P.O. Box 9, FI-00014 University of Helsinki, Finland
{jyrki.niemi,lauri.carlson}@helsinki.fi

## Abstract

This paper proposes modeling the semantics of natural-language calendar expressions as extended regular expressions (XREs). The approach covers expressions ranging from plain dates to such ones as *the second Tuesday following Easter*. The paper presents basic calendar XRE constructs, sample calendar expressions with their representations as XREs, and possible applications in reasoning and natural-language generation.

## 1 Introduction

Temporal information and calendar expressions are essential in various applications, for example, in event calendars, appointment scheduling and timetables. The information should often be both processed by software and presented in a human-readable form.

Calendar expressions denote periods of time that do not depend on the time of use of the expression. They can be plain dates, times of the day, days of the week or combinations of them, or they can be more complex, such as *the second Tuesday following Easter*. The denotation may be underspecified or ambiguous without context.

In this paper, we propose modeling the semantics of natural-language calendar expressions as extended regular expressions (XREs). The well-known semantics of XREs can be used in reasoning with the temporal information so represented. We also believe that XREs are structurally so close to the corresponding natural-language expressions that the latter can be generated from the former fairly straightforwardly.

The rest of the paper is organized as follows. Section 2 outlines a string-based model of time. Section 3 presents a number of calendar expression constructs and the corresponding XREs. Section 4 briefly describes experiments on reasoning with calendar XREs and natural-language generation from them. Section 5 mentions some related work in temporal expression research. Section 6 concludes with discussion and some directions for further research.

## 2 A string-based model of time

To be able to represent calendar expressions as XREs, we represent periods of time as strings of symbols. The model outlined here is only one possible one.

Time can be modelled as an infinite timeline. We choose a finite subset of the infinite timeline and partition it into a finite number of consecutive basic periods, for example minutes or seconds. For each basic period $t_i$, there is a unique corresponding symbol $a_i$ in the alphabet $\Sigma$ of calendar XREs, as illustrated in Figure 1. The string $a_1 \ldots a_n$ corresponds to the finite subset of the timeline; we denote it as T.

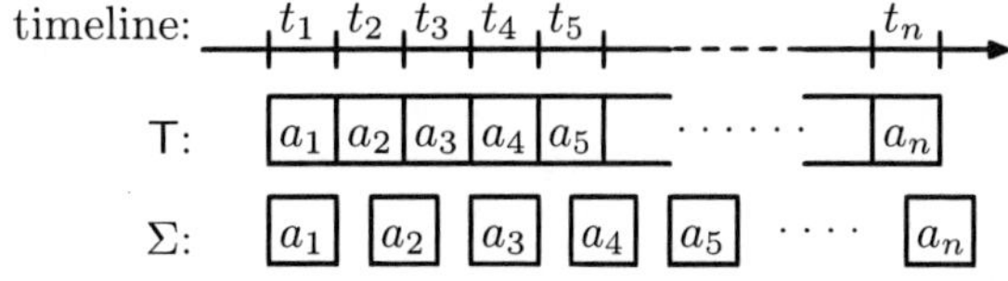

Figure 1: The relationship of the timeline, the timeline string T and the XRE alphabet $\Sigma$.

A single calendar XRE defines a regular language (a set of symbol strings) corresponding to a set of possibly disconnected periods of time. An XRE representing an inconsistent temporal expression, such as *30 February*, denotes the empty set.

The language of an XRE may contain strings that are not substrings of the timeline string T. They typically result from a concatenation or a complement operation. Such a string contains a symbol $a_i$ followed by $a_j$, where $i \geq j$. It is not meaningful as a representation of time, as a period of time may not be followed by the same or a preceding period. We can limit the languages of XREs to meaningful periods by intersecting them with the set of (possibly disconnected) substrings of T. However, we leave the intersection implicit in the examples in this paper.

## 3 Calendar expressions and their XREs

### 3.1 General features

The calendar expression constructs presented in this section demonstrate key features of calendar XREs. The constructs were found in a corpus of Web pages. Table 1 lists examples of the calendar expression constructs that we have treated. A description of the constructs omitted from this paper and more details of the described ones can be found in Niemi (2004).

---

*12.00; September; year; Easter*
*4 to 10 hours; 3 weeks short of 2 years*
*Mondays and Wednesdays*
*Mon and Wed or Tue and Thu*
*on Friday; in September*
*Christmas Eve falling on a Friday*
*22 May; in 2005 by April*
*a weekend containing Christmas Day*
*Monday to Friday; before 15 May*
*from 10 am on Sunday to 6 pm on Friday*
*8 am, except Mondays 9 am*
*every day except Monday*
*the second Tuesday following Easter*
*four weeks before Christmas*
*the weekend preceding a mid-week Christmas*
*on three consecutive Sundays*
*six consecutive months from May 2002*
*the third and fourth Wednesday of the month*
*every second Wednesday of the year*
*even Tuesdays of the month*
*four weeks a year*
*two Saturdays a month during the school year*

---

Table 1: Examples of calendar expressions.

We are mainly interested in the semantics of calendar expressions, abstracted from different syntactic variants. We assume the semantics to be mostly language-independent.

We generally present the expressions in a simple form, without considering special cases that might complicate the required XRE.

We have tried to make the calendar XRE constructs compositional, so that they would combine with each other analogously to the corresponding natural language calendar expressions. However, a number of constructs are compositional only to a limited extent or not at all.

### 3.2 Regular expression operations

To construct more complex calendar XREs from basic ones, we use a number of regular expression operations. They include concatenation (.), union (∪) and Kleene star (*); intersection (∩), complement (¬) and difference (−); and substring, quotient and affix operations. (Notations are explained where they are used.) The last three types of operations extract parts of their operand strings, so they are defined by means of regular relations (finite transducers).

Exponentiation is a notational shorthand denoting generalized concatenation power: $A^N$ denotes the expression $A$ concatenated $N$ times, where $N$ may be either a single natural number or a set of natural numbers.

We also use simple parametrized macros to simplify XREs containing repeating subexpressions and to make temporal XREs structurally closer to the corresponding natural-language expressions. The macros have no recursion or other means of control.

### 3.3 Basic calendar expressions

The basic expressions of calendar XREs denote sets of calendar periods, such as a day, month or year. An unqualified natural-language calendar expression, such as *Monday* or *January*, typically refers to the nearest past or future period relevant in the context. In this work, however, we interpret such expressions as underspecified, for example, referring to any Monday. The calendar XRE corresponding to *Monday* is Mon, which denotes the set of all Mondays.

The basic expressions correspond to the basic periods of the Gregorian calendar. They are represented as predefined constant sets of substrings of the timeline string. These include both generic periods, such as day, month and year (min to year), and specific ones, such as

---

each hour (h00 to h23), day of week (Mon to Sun), day of month (1st to 31st), month (Jan to Dec) and year (y*nnnn*). Hours and shorter units of time are also treated as periods; for example, hour 10 is the hour beginning at 10 am. We also assume appropriately predefined sets for seasons and holidays, such as Easter and Christmas_Day.

The generic calendar periods are unions of the corresponding specific calendar periods; for example, a week is any connected seven-day period from a Monday to the following Sunday. However, a week may also be a duration or a measurement unit of any seven days or 168 hours, possibly disconnected. A variable-length duration, such as a month, is represented as the union of the possible lengths.

Figure 2 illustrates the relationship of basic calendar periods to the timeline string T.

T: ...
Februarys: ... 
Wednesdays: ...
Calendar weeks: ...

Figure 2: Basic calendar periods related to a timeline string T, assuming a year that begins with a Monday.

### 3.4 Basic combining constructs

Four basic constructs combining basic calendar expressions are lists, concatenation, refinement and intervals.

Lists of calendar expressions are in general represented using union. For example, *Mondays and Wednesdays* is represented as the XRE Mon ∪ Wed, meaning "any single Monday or Wednesday".

Concatenation juxtaposes periods of time. Concatenating non-adjacent periods results in a disconnected period; for example, *two Sundays* is represented as Sun . Sun.

If a calendar expression contains both *and*s and *or*s, we use concatenation for *and* and union for *or*: for example, *Mon and Wed or Tue and Thu* is represented as (Mon . Wed) ∪ (Tue . Thu).

Refinement combines periods of different lengths to more specified expressions using intersection and the substring operation **in**$_+$. Figure 3 illustrates refinement with an XRE representing the expression *20 May*. First, any periods of time of any May are represented using

the substring operation: **in**$_+$ May. The resulting set is then intersected with the set 20th representing any 20th days of a month, yielding exactly those periods of any May that correspond to a 20th day of the month: 20th ∩ **in**$_+$ May.

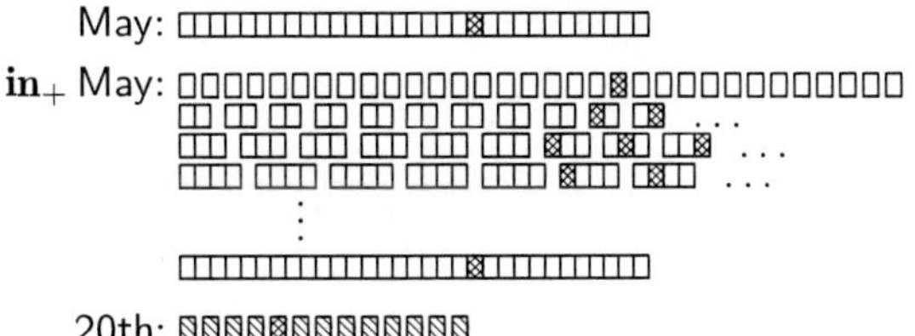

Figure 3: Constructing the XRE for the calendar expression *20 May*.

An interval *Monday to Friday* begins from a Monday and almost always ends to the closest following Friday. This interval can be expressed as the calendar XRE Mon . ¬ (Σ*.Mon.Σ*) . Fri, or, using the right closure shorthand operation ▷, as Mon▷ . Fri. Both XREs read as "a Monday followed by anything not containing a Monday, followed by a Friday".

### 3.5 More complex calendar expressions

In this subsection, we present exception expressions, anchored expressions and ordinal expressions as examples of more complex types of calendar expressions.

The expression *8 am, except Mondays 9 am* is an exception expression, where *8 am* is a default time, *Mondays* an exception scope and *9 am* an exception time (cf. Carlson (2003)). This can be expressed in XREs using union, difference and intersection: (h08 − **in**$_+$ Mon) ∪ (h09 ∩ **in**$_+$ Mon). If the exception time is omitted, the difference alone suffices.

An anchored expression, such as *the second Tuesday following Easter*, denotes a time relative to an anchor time. The expression denotes the last day in a string of days beginning from Easter, containing exactly two Tuesdays and ending in a Tuesday. Using the closure operation, it can be expressed as the XRE (Easter.(Tue▷)$^2$)\\Tue. The suffix operation $A$\\$B$ denotes the $B$ at the end of $A$. We have defined for this construct a macro, with which the XRE would be nth_following(2,Tue,Easter). Similar *preceding*-expressions can be represented by changing the order of the elements and the direction of the closure and affix operations.

---

The expression *every second Wednesday of the year* is an ordinal expression. We interpret it as denoting the first, third, fifth and so on, Wednesday of the year. We represent it as the XRE $((((\lhd \mathrm{Wed})^2)^*.\lhd \mathrm{Wed}) \cap \mathrm{pref}_+ \mathrm{year}) \setminus\setminus \mathrm{Wed}$. The left closure $\lhd A$ is a shorthand for $\neg(\Sigma^*.A.\Sigma^*).A$, and the untyped prefix operation $\mathrm{pref}_+ A$ denotes all non-empty prefixes of $A$. Since this XRE construct contains a concatenation power inside a Kleene star, it counts multiples of a natural number larger than one, and thus it is not star-free (McNaughton and Papert, 1971). The only other non-star-free type of calendar expressions that we have encountered are parity expressions, such as *even Tuesdays of the month*. They can be represented similarly.

## 4  Application experiments

We have briefly experimented on temporal reasoning with calendar XREs, and on generating corresponding natural-language expressions from them.

### 4.1  Temporal reasoning with calendar XREs

We have mainly considered a form of temporal reasoning that finds common periods of time denoted by two calendar XREs, which can be used in querying temporal data. For example, a query to an event database could be used to find out which museums are open on Mondays in December, or at what time a certain museum is open on Mondays in December. For the former query, we should find the set of periods of time common to the query XRE and each target XRE, and for the latter, whether they have common periods or not. Both require basically computing the intersection of the query and target XREs.

In principle, such reasoning could be implemented straightforwardly as model checking, by constructing finite-state automata from the XREs and intersecting them, and by either enumerating their languages or checking if the intersection is empty. In practice, however, constructing the automata would often require too much space or time or both to be tractable. Moreover, the resulting language as such is usually not desirable as the result, as it may be very large and incomprehensible to a human.

We have used the Xerox Finite-State Tool (XFST) (Karttunen et al., 1997) to experiment with XREs and with reasoning based on model-checking.

### 4.2  Natural-language generation from calendar XREs

Calendar XREs could be used as a language-independent input formalism for calendar expressions in a possibly multilingual natural-language generation system. Our hypothesis was that calendar XREs should be structurally close enough to the corresponding natural-language expressions to make simple generation feasible. We thus experimented with a simple XSLT-based natural-language generation component for calendar XREs.

We encountered more complexities in our experiments than we had expected, but they were at the surface-syntactic and morphological level, not in higher-level structures. The use of XRE macros was essential; without them, the natural-language expressions generated from complex XREs would have been cumbersome and their intended meaning probably impossible to understand.

We simplified the generation component proper by assuming it to be preceded by a separate transformation phase. This phase could, for example, reorder or regroup the subexpressions of an XRE while preserving the meaning of the whole. For instance, it could transform *on Mondays in December* to *in December on Mondays*, or *1 May to 25 May* to *1–25 May*.

## 5  Related work

Temporal expressions in general have been much studied, including modeling and reasoning with the semantics of calendar expressions. Our main inspiration has been Carlson's (2003) event calculus, a part of which is modeling calendar expressions as XREs.

The Verbmobil project (Wahlster, 2000) had a formalism of its own to represent and reason with temporal expressions occurring in appointment negotiation dialogues (Endriss, 1998). Its coverage of natural-language calendar expressions was similar to that of calendar XREs, but it did not cover disconnected periods of time.

The calendar logic of Ohlbach and Gabbay (1998) can represent calendar expressions of various kinds. However, calendar logic expressions are not structurally as close to natural-language expressions as calendar XREs.

---

Han and Lavie (2004) use their own formalism in conjunction with reasoning using temporal constraint propagation. They explicitly cover more types of expressions than we do, including underspecified and quantified expressions, such as *every week in May*.

Regular expressions are used in conjunction with temporal expressions by Karttunen et al. (1996) who express the syntax of dates as regular expressions to check their validity. They limit themselves to rather simple dates, however.

Fernando (2002; 2004) uses regular expressions to represent events with optional temporal information. Focusing on events, his examples feature only simple temporal expressions, such as *(for) an hour*.

## 6    Discussion and further work

In our view, extended regular expressions would in general seem to be fairly well suited to modeling the semantics of calendar expressions. Calendar XREs are structurally relatively close to natural-language calendar expressions, and the semantics of regular expressions is well known. The former property can be of use in natural-language generation, the latter in reasoning. The approach can also be extended to cover a number of deictic and anaphoric temporal expressions.

We have applied XREs only to calendar expressions of the Gregorian calendar system, but we expect the representation to work with any calendar system based on similar principles of hierarchical periods, provided that appropriate basic calendar expressions have been defined.

Our main future research goal is to find a tractable and practical reasoning method, possibly processing XREs syntactically using term rewriting. A major drawback of term rewriting is that each different XRE operation should be separately taken into account in the rewriting rules. We could also try combining several different approaches, using each one where it is best.

While calendar XREs cover a large number of different types of calendar expressions, they cannot naturally represent certain kinds of expressions: fuzzy or inexact calendar expressions, such as *about 8 o'clock*; internally anaphoric expressions, such as *9.00 to 17.00, an hour later in winter*; or fractional expressions, such as *the second quarter of the year*. Extending the formalism to cover these expression types would be another major goal. The representation of fuzzy temporal expressions has been researched by for example Ohlbach (2004).

There are also a number of limitations in the compositionality of the calendar XRE constructs, and the XREs required for some types of calendar expressions are rather complex. In particular, an expression allowing disconnected periods of time can be significantly more complex than a similar one only working with connected periods. We would also like to try to treat these issues.

Lastly, we also intend to explore options to combine calendar XREs with event information, or at least to consider calendar expressions in their context. Such an approach might in some cases help resolve the meaning of a single fuzzy or underspecified calendar expression.

## References

Lauri Carlson. 2003. Tense, mood, aspect, diathesis: Their logic and typology. Unpublished manuscript, February.

Ulrich Endriss. 1998. Semantik zeitlicher Ausdrücke in Terminvereinbarungsdialogen. Verbmobil Report 227, Technische Universität Berlin, Fachbereich Informatik, Berlin, August.

Tim Fernando. 2002. A finite-state approach to event semantics. In *Proceedings of the 9th International Symposium on Temporal Representation and Reasoning (TIME-02), Manchester*, pages 124–131. IEEE Computer Society Press, July.

Tim Fernando. 2004. A finite-state approach to events in natural language semantics. *Journal of Logic and Computation*, 14(1):79–92.

Benjamin Han and Alon Lavie. 2004. A framework for resolution of time in natural language. *ACM Transactions on Asian Language Information Processing (TALIP)*, 3(1):11–32, March.

L[auri] Karttunen, J[ean]-P[ierre] Chanod, G[regory] Grefenstette, and A[nne] Schiller. 1996. Regular expressions for language engineering. *Natural Language Engineering*, 2(4):305–328, December.

Lauri Karttunen, Tamás Gaál, and André Kempe. 1997. Xerox finite-state tool. Technical report, Xerox Research Centre Europe, Grenoble, France, June. http://www.xrce.xerox.com/competencies/content-analysis/fssoft/docs/fst-97/xfst97.html.

Robert McNaughton and Seymour Papert. 1971. *Counter-Free Automata*. Number 65 in Research Monographs. M.I.T. Press, Cambridge, Massachusetts.

Jyrki Niemi. 2004. Kalenteriajanilmausten semantiikka ja generointi: semantiikan mallintaminen laajennettuina säännöllisinä lausekkeina ja lausekkeiden luonnolliskielisten vastineiden XSLT-pohjainen generointi [The semantics and generation of calendar expressions: Modelling the semantics as extended regular expressions and generating the corresponding natural-language expressions using XSLT]. Master's thesis, University of Helsinki, Department of General Linguistics, Helsinki, November.

Hans Jürgen Ohlbach and Dov Gabbay. 1998. Calendar logic. *Journal of Applied Non-classical Logics*, 8(4):291–324.

Hans Jürgen Ohlbach. 2004. Relations between fuzzy time intervals. In *Proc. 11th International Symposium on Temporal Representation and Reasoning (TIME 2004)*, pages 44–50.

Wolfgang Wahlster, editor. 2000. *Verbmobil: Foundations of Speech-to-Speech Translation*. Artificial Intelligence. Springer, Berlin.

# SUiS – cross-language ontology-driven information retrieval in a restricted domain

**Kristina Nilsson**[*†], **Hans Hjelm**[*†], **Henrik Oxhammar**[*]
[*]CL Group, Department of Linguistics
Stockholm University, SE-106 91 Stockholm, Sweden
[†]Graduate School of Language Technology (GSLT)
{kristina.nilsson,hans.hjelm,henrik.oxhammar}@ling.su.se

## Abstract

In this paper we present SUiS - Stockholm University Information System. SUiS tries to find answers to a predefined set of question types: who, what, when and where. A domain-specific ontology is used for query expansion and translation, for answer generation, and for document analysis together with Named Entity Recognition modules for recognizing people, locations, organizations, and date expressions. Qualitative user evaluations show satisfactory results as well as indications of areas where the system could be improved.

## 1 Introduction

SUiS, Stockholm University Information System, functions as an automatic answering service, which tries to find answers to a restricted set of question types: who, what, when and where. The question set is predefined in order to increase the precision of the results: by restricting the questions we can predict what kind of analysis is needed to find the answer, e.g., what type of named entities must be recognized in the retrieved documents in order to find the answer to the posed question. The answers are presented as text excerpts, where the relevant entities are marked up. SUiS is not a prototypical question answering system as described in e.g., (Harabagiu and Moldovan, 2003) in that it is restricted to a specific domain, and does not allow for free-form questions.

SUiS uses the Stockholm University Ontology[1], a domain-specific ontology covering the university domain, for query expansion and translation. Concepts in the ontology are referred to by words and expressions in both English and Swedish. Thus, SUiS can be used for cross-language information retrieval of Swedish and English documents. SUiS is currently restricted to the Stockholm University web domain[2].

Research on using semantic information stored in e.g., thesauri or ontologies for query expansion shows that general-purpose resources such as WordNet (Fellbaum, 1998) seem to have very little, or even negative, impact on the results. If queries are expanded with synonyms, hyponyms, and hypernyms to increase recall, this can lead to a too broad interpretation with a resulting decrease in precision (Tzoukermann et al., 2003; Vossen, 2003). Domain-specific ontologies however usually work well for the domain they were created (ibid.), and by using a conservative form of query expansion where only synonyms and/or more specific terms (i.e., hyponyms) are added, this problem can be avoided.

### 1.1 Related work

Within the MOSES project, a cross-language QA system for free-form querying of knowledge bases is used. The facts in the knowledge bases are extracted from two separate web sites in the university domain. NLP techniques such as part-of-speech tagging, lemmatization, and query analysis are used to produce a semantic representation of each query, which is then matched against the knowledge bases (Atzeni et al., 2004). The ontologies are each created specifically for the web sites of the two universities, and thus there are differences between the ontologies: they are in different languages (Italian with concepts labels in English, and Dan-

---

[1] Henceforth referred to as the SU Ontology.

[2] Stockholm University, URL: http://www.su.se

**This page intentionally left blank.**

*Proceedings of the 15th NODALIDA conference, Joensuu 2005*                                    Ling@JoY 1, 2006

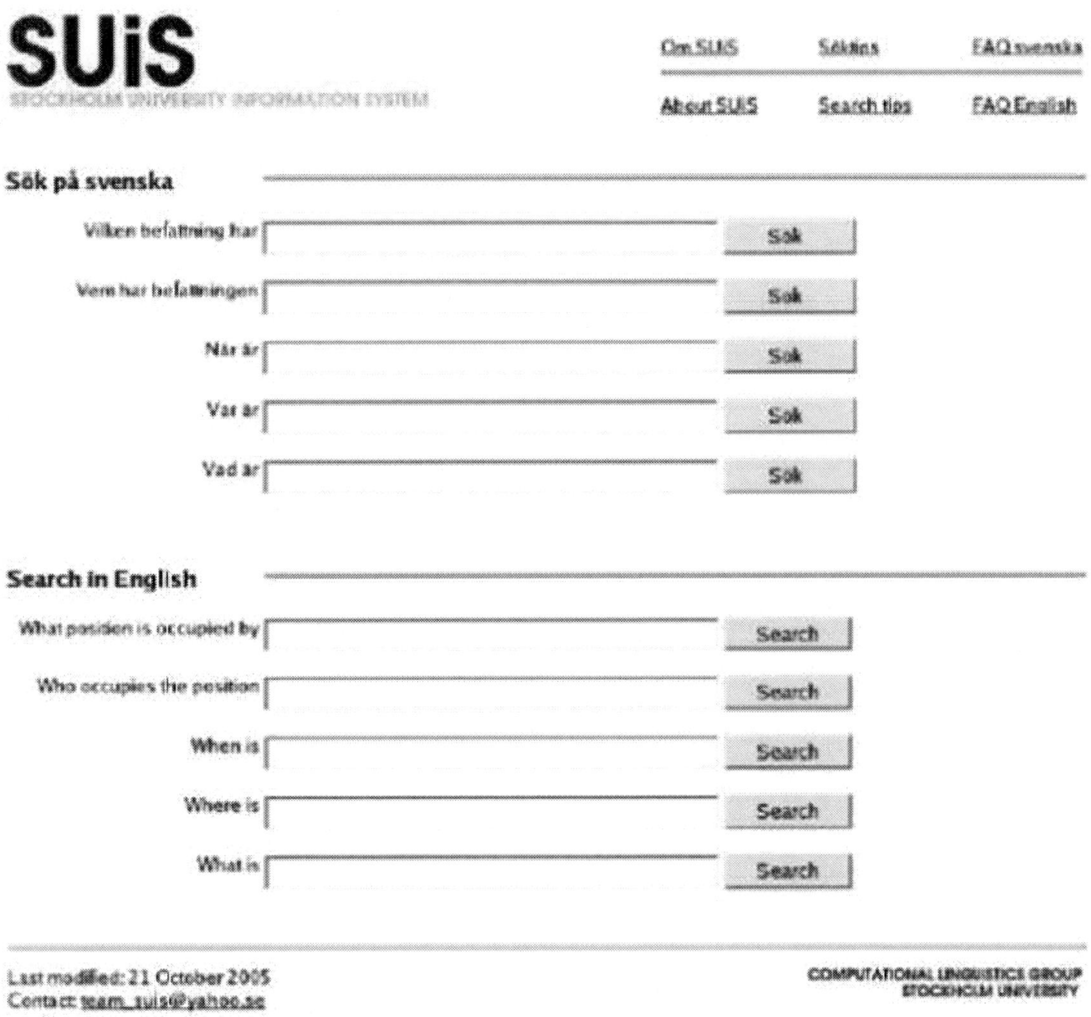

Figure 2: SUiS Interface.

**Interface**   The interface is an HTML-page, communicating with the rest of the system over a CGI-connection (see figure 2). The interface constricts the user to a specific question format. SUiS can handle the following types of factual questions:

- What position is occupied by `person`?

- Who occupies the position `position`?

- When is `event`?

- Where is `location/organization`?

- What is `entity`?

Information on what type of question has been posed is passed along to the system. This information determines which modules are applied (e.g., the what-question, as opposed to other question types, bypasses the IR-part and the answer is generated directly from the ontology).

**Query Parser**   The query parser removes stop words and extracts query parts relevant for expansion. E.g., from the query string 'Who occupies the position of Vice Chancellor of Stockholm University?', the title 'Vice Chancellor' is extracted for expansion in the Query Expansion Module. The preposition 'of' is removed and the remainder of the string ('Stockholm University') is kept as it is.

---

Nilsson et al.: *SUiS – cross-language ontology-driven information retrieval*

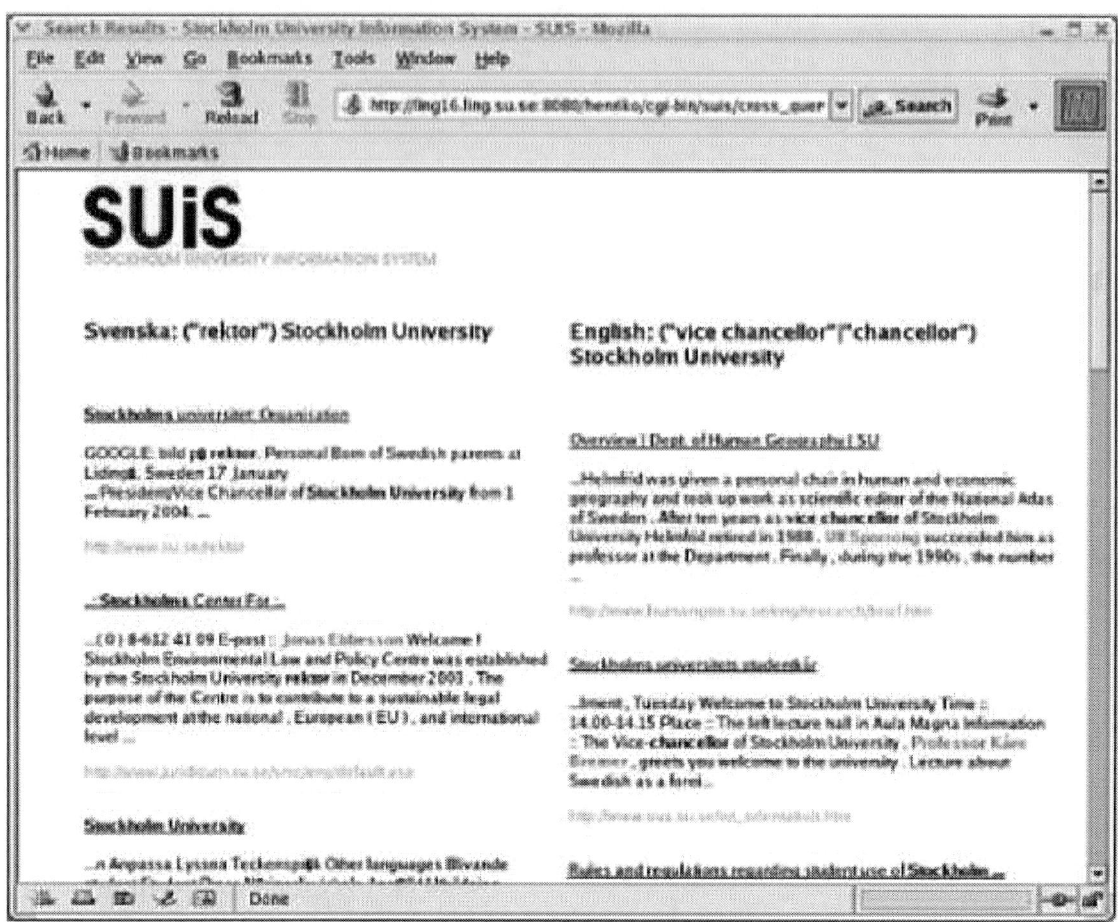

Figure 3: SUiS output for the query 'Who is Vice Chancellor of Stockholm University?'.

**Query Expansion and Translation Module** Continuing with our previous example, this module looks up 'vice chancellor' in the ontology and, having found the corresponding concept 'ViceChancellor', looks for hyponyms (sub concepts) and synonyms to expand the query. Query translation for cross-language querying is performed by looking up translation equivalents for that concept. The translation equivalents are in turn expanded with hyponyms and synonyms, if possible. We end up with one expanded English query, 'vice chancellor OR chancellor' and its Swedish translation 'rektor' (see figure 3).

**Google Web API** For searching the web pages in the Stockholm University domain (presently about 495.000 pages) the Google Web API is used. Google's language restrict option enables SUiS to search a predefined subset of the in-dex, and thus to retrieve pages in English and in Swedish separately.

**Document Retrieval** For each query, we receive a ranked list of URLs from Google. The corresponding documents are retrieved and stripped from HTML.

**Named Entity Recognition** For questions of the type 'Who occupies the position *position*?', each retrieved document is processed by a named entity recognition module. This module marks up the person names in the text. The named entity recognition module for locations is used for questions of the type 'Where is *location/organization*?'. The named entity recognition modules are not used for the other question types.

**Date Recognizer** When answering questions of the type 'When is *event*?', the date recognizer marks up any date and time expressions found in the text.

**Ontology** The purpose of the ontology is threefold:

1. It is used during *query expansion and translation*, as described above. The added concepts and synonyms are connected by the Boolean OR operator.

2. When answering the question type 'What position is occupied by *person*?', the part of the ontology describing the sub-domain *occupations* is used for marking up occupations in the text.

3. When answering the question type 'What is *entity*?', e.g., 'What is a teaching assistant?', 'teaching assistant' is looked up in the ontology and the answer is generated from its super concept and siblings.

**Output Generator** The results are presented to the user as a ranked list of URLs and a brief excerpt of the document, following the ranking from Google. In this excerpt, the query term(s) are highlighted in bold and named entities and dates are highlighted in color codes, using different colors for different types of names (see figure 3).

## 4 Future work

A qualitative user evaluation has been performed, indicating a number of areas where SUiS can be improved. Firstly, the ontology needs to be expanded and enhanced. Currently the SU Ontology covers around 140 occupations, 70 educational programs and degrees, 80 locations and 80 types of events. But many important concepts are not yet modeled in the ontology, and must be added. Further, inconsistencies, incorrect relationships and incomplete translation information need to be corrected or added to improve on the quality of the ontology.

The question is how one can tackle the problem of expanding the ontology. There exist several methods within the area of Ontology Learning for automating the process of populating and enriching ontologies with new concepts as well as maintaining ontologies (see e.g., (Aguirre et al., 2000; Faatz and Steinmetz, 2002; Hahn and Schnattinger, 1998)).

However, the university domain is believed to be rather static, in comparison to other domains (e.g., IT, medicine), and does not undergo frequent changes. Organizations (e.g., departments), locations (e.g., seminar rooms), occupations (e.g., dean, research assistant), and degrees (e.g., master/bachelor degree) are unlikely to change names or even less so to disappear. There are of course exceptions, for instance concepts denoting educational programs and courses. Having said that, a manual approach, provided a good editing- and visualization tool such as Protégé (Noy et al., 2001), should be sufficient for keeping the ontology current and of good quality.

Aside from enhancement of the ontology, future efforts will be focused on two areas in particular:

**1. Query translation** A query such as 'Who is the assistant professor in Computational Linguistics?' is translated through lookup of the concepts in the ontology (see section 3), but as there is no concept 'ComputationalLinguistics' in the ontology, this phrase cannot be translated by the current system. The present solution is to translate as much of the query as possible, and add any remaining query terms untranslated. Thus, the example query is translated into a string consisting of the Swedish translation 'Vem är lektor i'(*Who is the assistant professor in*) and the original English query string 'Computational Linguistics'. A possible solution would be to add a lexicon, with both general and domain specific terminology, or to add a machine translation system.

**2. Re-ranking and grouping of search results** The current version presents the analysis of the retrieved documents in the same order as the documents are returned from Google. However, after the system has analyzed the documents, it has more information about the relevancy of the documents at its disposal than was present during Google's ranking. E.g., a document returned for the search 'Who is NN?', where the system finds no matching occupation or title, should be given a low ranking, no matter how relevant Google's ranking algorithm judged the document to be. Conversely, a document where an occupation appears in close proximity to the name entered in the query, should be given a high ranking. Another way to re-rank the results would be

---

to try to find groups of documents which all give the same answers. These documents could be grouped together in the presentation of the results, to give the user a better overview of which possible answers the system has found. Within these groups, the results could be ordered according to relevancy as described previously. The groups themselves could also be ordered, with the most relevant group presented first.

## 5  Concluding remarks

In this article, we have described a prototype for ontology-driven cross-language information retrieval in a restricted domain. The system uses a domain-specific ontology for query expansion and translation, together with modules for recognizing named entities and temporal expressions.

The ontology contains concepts from the university domain in general as well as concepts specific to Stockholm University. It contains concepts from four sub-domains: *occupations, educational programs and degrees, places* and *events*. Synonyms and hyponyms are used for query expansion and the corresponding terms in the target language are used for the cross-language search. The named entity recognition modules also contain knowledge resources, but these have a flat structure (i.e., they are kept as lists) as opposed to the ontology resources.

The SUiS system consists of six major components: the web interface, the query parser, the query expansion and translation module, the named entity recognition module, the ontology and the output generator.

A user evaluation was carried out, partly confirming our theories of the effectiveness of the system but also pointing towards a number of areas where the system could be improved or extended. The areas where improvements or extensions would have the greatest impact are the ontology (correcting and extending it), query translation (increasing the robustness) and re-ranking and grouping the search results.

Although covering the university domain in the present version, we believe that the system is highly portable to other domains (e.g., the financial domain) and languages. When porting the system to another language, it would be necessary to update the knowledge sources used in the named entity recognition modules.

The content of the ontology would also have to be adapted to the new domain. However, updating the knowledge resources represents a comparatively minor effort, considering that the rest of the system can be reused as it is.

## Acknowledgments

We would like to thank professor Martin Volk of Stockholm University, who initiated this project, and the students who participated in the work of compiling the SU Ontology, as well as in the first evaluation of the system.

## References

Eneko Aguirre, Olatz Ansa, Edward Hovy, and David Martinez. 2000. Enriching very large ontologies using the WWW. In *Proceedings of the Ontology Learning Workshop, organized by ECAI*, Berlin, Germany.

Paolo Atzeni, Roberto Basili, Dorte H. Hansen, Paolo Missier, Patricia Paggio, Maria Teresa Pazienza, and Fabio Massimo Zanzotto. 2004. Ontology-based question answering in a federation of university sites: the MOSES case study. In *Proceedings of the 9th International Conference on Applications of Natural Language to Information Systems (NLDB'04)*, Manchester, United Kingdom.

Andreas Faatz and Ralf Steinmetz. 2002. Ontology Enrichment with Texts from the WWW. In *Proceedings of ECML-Semantic Web Mining 2002*, Helsinki, Finland, August.

Christiane D. Fellbaum, editor. 1998. *WordNet: An Electronic Lexical Database*. MIT Press.

Udo Hahn and Klemens Schnattinger. 1998. Towards text knowledge engineering. In *AAAI'98/IAAI'98 Proceedings of the 15th National Conference on Artificial Intelligence and the 10th Conference on Innovative Applications of Artificial Intelligence*, pages 524–531, Madison, Wisconsin, July. MIT Press.

Sanda Harabagiu and Dan Moldovan. 2003. Question Answering. In Ruslan Mitkov, editor, *The Oxford Handbook of Computational Linguistics*, chapter 31, pages 560–582. Oxford University Press.

Ruslan Mitkov, editor. 2003. *The Oxford Handbook of Computational Linguistics*. Oxford University Press.

Natalya F. Noy, Michael Sintek, Stefan Decker, Monica Crubézy, Ray W. Fergerson, and Mark A. Musen. 2001. Creating semantic

---

web contents with protege-2000. *IEEE Intelligent Systems*, 16(2):60–71.

Maria Teresa Pazienza, Armando Stellato, Lina Henriksen, Patrizia Paggio, and Fabio Massimo Zanzotto. 2005. Ontology mapping to support ontology-based question answering. In *Proceedings of the second MEANING workshop*, Trento, Italy, February.

Evelyne Tzoukermann, Judith L. Klavans, and Tomek Strzalkowski. 2003. Information Retrieval. In Ruslan Mitkov, editor, *The Oxford Handbook of Computational Linguistics*, chapter 29, pages 529–544. Oxford University Press.

Martin Volk and Simon Clematide. 2001. Learn-Filter-Apply-Forget. Mixed Approaches to Named Entity Recognition. In *Proc. of 6th International Workshop on Applications of Natural Language for Information Systems*, Madrid, Spain.

Martin Volk, Spela Vintar, and Paul Buitelaar. 2003. Ontologies in Cross-Language Information Retrieval. In *Proceedings of the 2nd Conference on Professional Knowledge Management*, Lucerne.

Piek Vossen. 2003. Ontologies. In Ruslan Mitkov, editor, *The Oxford Handbook of Computational Linguistics*, chapter 25, pages 464–482. Oxford University Press.

# Towards automatic recognition of product names: an exploratory study of brand names in economic texts

**Kristina Nilsson**[†*] **and Aisha Malmgren**[*]
[†]Computational Linguistics Group
[*]Department of Linguistics
Stockholm University
SE-106 91 Stockholm, Sweden
`kristina.nilsson@ling.su.se, aishart@yahoo.com`

## Abstract

This paper describes the first stage of research towards automatic recognition of *brand names* (trademarks, product names and service names) in Swedish economic texts. The findings of an exploratory study of brand names in economic texts by Malmgren (2004) are summarized, and the work of compiling a corpus annotated with named entities based on these findings is described. A Named Entity Recognition experiment using transformation-based learning on this data shows that what is problematic to the annotator is difficult also to the recognizer; company names and brand names are closely connected and thus hard to disambiguate.

## 1 Introduction

In economic news texts, names denoting companies, trademarks, products and services are frequent. The production, sales and purchase of goods and services are often the topics of these texts, and such names must therefore be recognized by e.g., Information Extraction systems in this domain. However, existing guidelines for named entity annotation either include brand names in a wide category of artefacts (Sekine and Isahara, 1999) or completely ignore this name type (Chinchor, 1998), and methods for automatic recognition of names do not always make a distinction between e.g., company names and product names (Dalianis and Åström, 2001), or between product names and names of other types of objects in the domain (Kokkinakis, 2003).

Named Entity Recognition (NER) entails identifying and classifying named entities into predefined categories (Grishman, 2003). It is common for successful NER methods to use name lists in combination with context patterns (see e.g., (Volk and Clematide, 2001)) although there are several drawbacks of using such static knowledge sources; they are often domain- and language-specific, and their compilation and maintenance are time-consuming tasks. By using machine learning methods the need for static resources can be reduced. However, these methods require training and test data. Corpora annotated with named entities can thus be used to train and evaluate machine learning or statistical algorithms, and also for linguistic research and for evaluation of knowledge-based NER systems.

In this paper, we describe the work of compiling such data: a corpus of Swedish economic texts tagged with part of speech and named entities. In this corpus the following types of named entities have been found: **person, location, organization, financial index, miscellaneous**, and what can collectively be called *brand names*: **trademark, product**, and **service**.[1] The brand names found in the corpus have subsequently been analyzed within the framework of lexical cohesion (Halliday and Hasan, 1976). The analysis shows that 40 percent of the brand names can be classified through lexical cohesion within and across sentences, whereas the classification of the remaining 60 percent require analysis of collocations and background knowledge.

The focus of this paper is on the first stage of research in automatic recognition of brand names, building on an exploratory study of brand names in economic texts by Malmgren (2004). Below, an initial experiment –

---

[1]When the term *brand names* is used is this paper, we are referring to these three name types collectively.

where a transformation-based learner is applied to Swedish NER using this corpus as training and testing data – is described; some problems of automatic classification of brand names are also discussed.

## 2  The corpus

Stockholm Ekonomikorpus (SEK) consists of about 2.800 documents collected from the on-line economy section of a Swedish daily newspaper. The documents in the corpus exist in two formats: in the original HTML format, and as raw text. A subset of 365 documents (about 122.000 tokens) has been chosen for further processing, which entails annotation of part of speech and named entities.

The part of speech annotation has been done automatically using TreeTagger, a probabilistic dependency-tree based tagger by Schmid (1994), trained on SUC, the Stockholm-Umeå Corpus (Ejerhed et al., 1992).[2]

Words and phrases that function as proper names in a wide sense have been annotated as named entities. This annotation has been done in two stages:

- Automatically, using the Learn-Filter-Apply-Forget method described in (Volk and Clematide, 2001) for the name types **person**, **location** and **organization**.

- Manually. The result of the automatic annotation was corrected, and the name types **trademark**, **product name** and **service name** were added (based on the study by Malmgren (2004)), as well as the additional name types **financial index**, and **miscellaneous**.

In total, there are 6725 names (tokens) in the corpus each annotated with one of these eight name types (see table 1, above).

The largest category is organization; there are 995 different names occurring 3486 times which denote companies and other types of organizations. This category includes a wide range of organizations, with the common denominator that they are organizations of people with a common goal, such as financial gain (companies), academic research and education

---

[2]The TreeTagger has been trained for Swedish on SUC by David Hagstrand of the CL Group of the Linguistics Department, Stockholm University.

| Name type | Tokens | Types |
|---|---|---|
| Person | 1408 | 618 |
| Organization | 3486 | 995 |
| Location | 1153 | 243 |
| Trademark | 28 | 20 |
| Product | 131 | 104 |
| Service | 212 | 76 |
| Financial Index | 241 | 39 |
| Miscellaneous | 67 | 47 |
| Total | 6725 | 2142 |

Table 1: Named Entities in SEK: tokens and types per name type, and total no of NEs.

(universities and institutes), or handling of public sector funds (governmental organizations), etc. The second largest category is person with 1408 occurrences of 618 person names.

The location category, the third largest with 1152 occurrences of 243 different names, is one of the most problematic, in that location names such as *Sverige* ('Sweden') can denote both the geographical and the geopolitical area (although the difference between these categories are not always clear), for example:

**Geographical**  ... *och huvudkontoret kommer att ligga i Sverige.* ('... and the head quarters will be located in Sweden.')

**Geopolitical**  ... *Det har upprört många fattiga länder och även Sverige har tryckt på för att deras makt ska öka.* ('Many poor countries are upset and Sweden too has argued for an increase in influence for them.')

For Information Extraction purposes, the second instance should be classified as an organization name, but in the current version of the corpus all geographical and geopolitical names are annotated as location.

In the SEK corpus, 371 occurrences of brand names have been found; among these occurrences, 28 denote 20 different trademarks, 131 denote 104 different product names, and 212 denote 76 different service names.

The category service includes names of e.g., news papers, television stations, and news agencies when these names refer to the service of providing information. Often there is also a company with the same name, and contextual clues are needed for disambiguation (see

---

section 3.2, below). Names of financial services are also included in this category; this is a modification of the classification described in (Malmgren, 2004).

A large number of texts in the corpus give a fairly standardized account of the situation at stock markets around the world. In these texts, names of stock market indices such as *Dow Jones* and *CAC 40-index* are common. There are 241 occurrences of names denoting financial indices, but only 39 different types.[3] Finally, there are 67 names marked as miscellaneous, e.g., *Vita huset*, 'The White House', and *Internet*.

To our knowledge, there exist two other Swedish corpora annotated with named entities: the Stockholm-Umeå Corpus (SUC) of about a million words, manually annotated with 9 classes of named entities (Wennstedt, 1995), and the KTH news corpus which consists of about 108.000 Swedish news articles. In this corpus, 100 documents (about 18.000 tokens) have been manually annotated with four types of named entities: person names, locations, organizations, and time and date expressions (Hassel, 2001; Dalianis and Åström, 2001).

## 3   Brand names in Swedish economic texts

Brand names, and especially product names, differ from other name types such as person names and organization names in that they do not necessarily refer to a unique individual. Rather, brand names refer to a unique group of individuals that share the same name and that can be distinguished from other groups of individuals of the same kind, e.g., the group of individuals named *Volvo* can be distinguished from the group of individuals named *Saab*.

### 3.1   A note on terminology

As mentioned above, *brand names* is used as an umbrella term for trademarks, product names and service names. However, there is wide variation in the use of these terms both within linguistics and other fields such as marketing and law. The categorization here described is an attempt to capture the different functions that

these names have in the corpus drawing on terminology described by linguists such as Piller (1996) and Clankie (2002) and by organizations like the International Trademark Association[4] and the World Intellectual Property Organization.[5]

Trademarks are viewed as having a broader scope than product and service names: while trademarks refer to diverse groups of tradable goods or services (e.g., the trademark *Volvo* identifies a range of vehicles), product and service names identify a class of (identical) objects within the group (e.g., *Volvo C 70* is one model of the trademark *Volvo*). Regarding the distinction between product and service names, it is mainly their identification of tangible and intangible concepts respectively (e.g., a car versus a TV show) that is the basis for our categorization.

### 3.2   Brand names and company names

Names denoting companies and brand names are closely connected. This close relation is especially noticeable when a part of a company name is found in a brand name[6]. An example from our corpus is the trademark *Volvo*, which has inherited the dominant part *Volvo* of the company name *Volvo Car Company*.

The fact that company names and brand names share the dominant causes difficulties in categorizing these names, particularly as the company name seldom occurs in its complete form in the corpus. A word like *Volvo* can refer either to the trademark or to the company itself, and can only be correctly interpreted through an analysis of the collocational context. The different name types described here are thus not discrete categories and pose a challenge to the annotators.

While trademarks usually consist of a dominant and therefore are especially difficult to disambiguate from company names, product and service names tend to be a combination of a dominant and a specific reference, e.g., *Volvo V/C 70*. However, not all brand names are created this way, but rather given a specific

---

[3]It could be argued that this category of names is superfluous, but as it is easier to merge categories than to subcategorize we decided to add this name type.

[4]International Trademark Association. http://www.inta.org
[5]World Intellectual Property Organization. http://www.wipo.int
[6]This part of a name, which can be used to denote both a company and its brands, is hereafter called the *dominant*.

---

**This page intentionally left blank.**

tions or specially created words that lack meaning, e.g., *Losec.*

Due to this internal heterogeneity, name-external evidence has been analyzed by Malmgren (2004) according to the theoretical framework of textual cohesion (Halliday and Hasan, 1976). The focus has been on lexical cohesion, i.e., on the occurrences of co-referential noun phrases that allow the identification and interpretation of brand names. Through this analysis, it has been observed that about 40 percent of the occurrences of brand names found in the corpus are co-referred by common nouns located in different parts of the text, while the remaining 60 percent require analysis of collocations and background knowledge for interpretation.

### 4.1  Lexical cohesion within sentences

Co-references found within sentences have been analyzed as syntactic relations between the brand names and their identifications as "relations within the sentence are fairly adequately expressed already in structural terms, so that there is no need to involve the additional notion of cohesion" (Halliday and Hasan, 1976, p. 146). These relations consist mainly of appositive phrases, where the brand name is added to a common noun phrase that identifies/describes the product or service, for example:

- ... *pansarvärnsroboten AT4 CS* ...('the anti-tank weapon AT4 CS')

- ... *den enarmade banditen Jack Vegas* ... ('the slot machine Jack Vegas')

- ... *tidskriften Der Spiegel* ... ('the magazine Der Spiegel')

- ... *den nya marknadsplatsen för privatannonser Koll.se* ... ('the new portal for private ads Koll.se')

Of all brand names in the corpus, 34.8 percent can be classified on the basis of this type of lexical cohesion within sentences.

### 4.2  Lexical cohesion across sentences

The anaphoric co-references found across sentences can be described as reiterations, e.g., the product name *Saab 9-2* is reiterated as the definite noun phrase *bilen* ('the car'), or the generic product name *den kinesiska colan*

('the Chinese coke') is reiterated as the product name *Future Cola.* In the documents where reiterations have been found, the average number of reiterations is 4.5, which indicates that a NER system for this domain could benefit from handling this type of lexical cohesion, even though only 4.5 percent of all brand names in the corpus can be classified based on lexical cohesion across sentences.[8]

### 4.3  Background knowledge and collocations

Of the analyzed brand names, 60 percent lack a direct lexical identification. As a third of these names can be identified and interpreted through the collocational environment, it is possible to pattern specific constructions in which certain trademarks, product names, and service names tend to occur. However, the identification of the remaining two thirds requires background knowledge about e.g., how these types of entities typically behave, or what properties they possess. But by combining analysis of the lexical environment and assumptions about the reader's background knowledge we might be able to handle some such instances. The types of phenomenon found in the corpus include:

- Pre and post modifiers
  ... *nya Mazda 6* ... ('the new Mazda 6')
  ... *Delix mot högt blodtryck* ... ('Delix for high blood pressure')

- Meronymic relations
  ... *XC 90 med dieselmotor* ... ('XC 90 with diesel engine')

- Coordination with other brand names
  ... *Vauxhall Corsa, Peugeot 206, Ford Fiesta* ...

It can be concluded from our corpus study that brand names that tend to occur without lexical cohesion can be assumed to be well-known to most readers, and further that these names often share the dominant with the company that produces them, e.g., *Volvo XC 90* shares the dominant *Volvo* with the producer, and that the name of the producer

---

[8]Unfortunately, this is a hen and egg problem: for co-reference resolution we need the named entities, and for named entity recognition we need the co-references.

---

Nilsson & Malmgren: *Towards automatic recognition of product names*

can be found in the lexical environment (see section 3). In addition, the following variation in the collocational environment has been found:

**Trademark** is the smallest category of names with only 28 occurrences in the corpus, and the most difficult category for the human annotators. However, about a third of the instances occur with the appositive phrase *varumärket* ('the trademark').

**Product names** tend to co-occur with verbs like *producera* ('produce'), *sälja* ('sell'), *bygga* ('build'), *introducera* ('introduce'), *presentera* ('present'), *registrera* ('register'), *utveckla* ('develop'), and *använda* ('use'), and also with company names. Product names (P) can also be found as the complement of prepositional phrases modifying verbal nouns that are related to certain commerce domains, for example:

- *utveckling av* ('development of') + P

- *tillverkning av* ('production of') + P

- *introduktion av* ('introduction of') + P

- *försäljning av* ('sales of') + P

**Service names** tend to co-occur with verbs like *skriva* ('write'), *informera* ('inform'), *avslöja* ('reveal'), *rapportera* ('report'), *tillkännage* ('announce')[9], and also with company names and person names. Common constructions where service names (S) can be found are for example:

- *enligt* ('according to') + S

- *rapporterar* ('reports') + S

- *säger* ('says') + PERS + *till* ('to') + S

- *säger* + PERS + *i en intervju med* ('in an interview with') + S

A combination of background knowledge and knowledge about brand names is needed in order to classify the unknown names *XC 90*, *S 40*, and *V 40* in the example below. The background knowledge includes, e.g., that

---

[9]The majority of the occurrences of service names found in the corpus denote services within communication.

Volvo Personvagnar makes cars, and that some cars have diesel engines. The knowledge about brand names includes both knowledge about how brand names typically behave, e.g., that partial names are allowed when the dominant is shared with the company name, and that name can be found in the lexical environment, and about collocational distribution, e.g., that words such as *efterfrågan* ('demand'), *sålt* ('have sold'), *modellerna* ('the models'), and company names typically co-occur with product names.

**Example**　*Vår ökning beror främst på stor efterfrågan på XC 90 med dieselmotor, men vi har också sålt bra av modellerna S 40 och V 40, säger Volvo Personvagnars presschef ...* ('Our increase is mostly due to great demand for XC 90 with a diesel engine, but the S 40 and V 40 models have also sold well, says the press officer of Volvo Personvagnar ...')

# 5　Named Entity Recognition: an initial experiment

A first experiment on supervised learning of Named Entity Recognition rules was performed using $\mu$-TBL (Lager, 1999), a Prolog-implementation of Brill's algorithm for transformation-based learning (Brill, 1995). Named Entity Recognition entails both identification of named entities, and classification of these entities into predefined name types.

## 5.1　Transformation-based learning

In transformation-based learning, templates are used to learn candidate transformation rules consisting of a rewrite rule and a triggering environment from annotated training data. Learning is an iterative process, during which the output of each iteration is compared to a gold standard, and the best transformation is found. The learning continues until no transformations that will improve the annotation of the training data can be found (Brill, 1995).

Based on the analysis described in (Malmgren, 2004), 34 templates were constructed. These templates draw on three kinds of internal and external information: part of speech templates, lexical templates, and name type templates. Internal information is defined as the word itself, and any available information about part of speech. External information is found in

---

the context; the words (as well as information about their part of speech) in a context window of 5 words around each word in a name. The name types of the adjacent words are also included in the definition of external information.

The part of speech templates look at the part of speech of the current word, and/or the part of speech of words in the context window; thus finding e.g., name types such as product that is often preceded by a verb and a preposition ('development of *product*').

```
Change name type tag A to B if:

  - The current word has part of speech
    tag P.
  - The preceding (following) word has
    part of speech tag P.
  - The preceding (following) two words
    have part of speech tag P and Q.
  - The word two before (after) has part
    of speech tag P.

where P and Q are variables over all
parts of speech defined in the part of
speech tag set for the corpus.
```

The lexical templates make reference to the current word and/or the adjacent words. By applying these templates to the training data, rules handling both lexical cohesion within sentences (mainly appositive phrases) and collocations can be derived.

```
Change name type tag A to B if:

  - The current word is C.
  - The preceding (following) word is C.
  - The word two before (after) is C.
  - One of the tree preceding
    (following) words is C.
  - The preceding word is C and the
    foll- owing word is D.
  - The current word or one of the two
    words before is C and one of the
    three following words are D.
  - One word in the left context window
    is C and one word in the right
    context window is D.

where C and D are variables over all
words in the training corpus.
```

The name type templates look at the name type attribute values of the adjacent words. These templates are based on the ideas that two neighboring words are likely to belong to the same type (i.e., that names are often coordinated with names of the same type) and

that some name types are more likely to occur together (e.g., company names and brand names).

```
Change name type tag A to B if:

  - The preceding (following) word has
    name type attribute value T.
  - One word in the left (right) context
    window has name type attribute value
    T.

where T is a variable over all name type
attribute values.
```

Although the templates were based on the analysis described in section 3, we cannot fully exploit the findings of the study. Due to the learning method chosen for this experiment and the lack of coreference annotation in the training and test data, we are not able to explicitly model cohesion across sentences. But most re-iterations should be handled by the lexical rule that says that a certain name should be marked as a specific name type, given that there is reliable evidence of the correct name type for another occurrence of this name. Further, we do not attempt to model background knowledge in this experiment, but rely on appositive phrases and collocations as modeled by the lexical templates.

| Name type | Precision | Recall |
|---|---|---|
| Person | 98.1 % | 92.7 % |
| Organization | 80.9 % | 94.2 % |
| Location | 83.3 % | 82.4 % |
| Trademark | 84.6 % | 57.9 % |
| Product | 89.3 % | 76.3 % |
| Service | 92.2 % | 71.2 % |
| Financial Index | 96.7 % | 93.5 % |
| Miscellaneous | 69.2 % | 33.3 % |
| Overall | 86.9 % | 88.5 % |

Table 2: NER results: precision and recall for each name type, and overall precision and recall.

## 5.2  Results

Training on about 100.000 words resulted in 130 rules, which in testing on about 20.000 words gave a result of overall precision of 86.9 percent, and overall recall of 88.5 percent (see table 2). Precision and recall were calculated on partial recognition, that is, when measuring the recognition of named entities consisting of

*Proceedings of the 15th NODALIDA conference, Joensuu 2005*　　　　　Ling@JoY 1, 2006

| **Error type** | | Error analysis | | | |
|---|---|---|---|---|---|
| (Incorrect classification > | Total no. | No. of | No. of | No. of | No. of |
| Correct name type) | of errors | Apposit. | Reiterat. | Colloc. | Backgr. |
| Organization > Trademark | 8 | 0 | 1 | 6 | 1 |
| Organization > Product | 30 | 16 | 7 | 5 | 2 |
| Location > Product | 3 | 2 | 0 | 1 | 0 |
| Organization > Service | 17 | 4 | 7 | 2 | 4 |
| **Total** | 58 | 22 | 15 | 14 | 7 |

Table 3: NER analysis: total number of errors per error type, and grouped per type of classification clue (appositive phrase, reiteration, collocation and background knowledge).

more than one orthographic unit each recognized unit was counted individually.

The system performs well on the name types person and financial index regarding the precision, 98.1 present and 96.7 present respectively, while the best recall value 94.2 percent for organization.

Both precision and recall of the relatively closed class financial index (all in all 39 names, such as *Dow Jones* and *CAC 40*) is rather high, 96.7 and 93.5 percent respectively, to be compared to the category with the lowest scores: the heterogeneous category miscellaneous with 69.2 percent precision and 33.3 percent recall.

The lower precision values for organization names can be explained by the properties of organizations; on the one hand they are objects that can be bought or sold just like products, and on the other they can act much like humans – they can buy or sell products or other organizations, or even have opinions. The consequences of this can be seen in our results: the majority of all unrecognized brand names are classified as organization names (55 out of 58), and the majority of all unrecognized organization names are misclassified as brand names, location names, or person names.

The effects of the ambiguous use of geographical and geopolitical names (in the present version of the corpus annotated as location names, see section 2) can also be observed: within the group of location names that have been misclassified as organizations, a large group (19 out of 51) are names of geopolitical entities that behave like organizations.

The most interesting aspect of this experiment is the systems ability to correctly recognize brand names (i.e., the precision and recall of these name types). The results are encouraging with 89.3 percent precision and 76.3

percent recall for product, and 92.2 percent precision and 71.2 percent recall for service. The most difficult name type for the annotators, trademark, proved difficult also for the system to recognize with the lowest precision score of all brand names, 84.6 percent, and 57.9 percent recall, the second lowest recall score overall after miscellaneous.

### 5.3 Brand name error analysis

Error analysis shows that the vast majority of unrecognized brand names (55 out of 58) are misclassified as organization names, again confirming that what is difficult to the annotators is difficult to the recognizer, i.e., the distinction between organization names and brand names (see table 3).

Named entity classification can be viewed as a word sense disambiguation problem as the classifier chooses between a predefined set of name types (i.e., senses). Yarowsky (1995) has shown that, in most cases, when an ambiguous word occurs more than once in a discourse, the word sense is consistent within the discourse. This is not applicable to our classification problem due to the close relationship between company names and brand names.

The misclassified trademarks were homonyms with organization names (e.g, Nokia, Daewoo, Renault). These trademarks were also difficult to classify for the human annotators, even though typical (but in this small corpus however, infrequent) collocations could be found in 6 out of 8 cases, and all trademarks appeared in typical trademark contexts.

More than half of the identified but wrongly classified product names were marked by appositive phrases describing the product, and 7 out of the 17 erroneously classified service names were reiterations of service names that

---

Nilsson & Malmgren: *Towards automatic recognition of product names*

had been misclassified as organization names due to unrecognized appositive phrases. This indicates that the results of this system might be improved by adding methods for handling appositive phrases; although the individual appositive phrases might not be frequent enough for the machine learning system, there are resources such as product ontologies which could be used for recognition of appositive phrases describing goods and services, e.g., the EU standard document for classification of products and services in common procurement, the Common Procurement Vocabulary (CPV),[10] which is available in 11 European languages (Union and Parliament, 2002).

## 6 Conclusion

In this paper, we have described the first stage of research towards automatic recognition of *brand names* (trademarks, product names and service names) in Swedish economic texts.

The task of Named Entity Recognition is twofold: the identification of a name, and the classification into different categories. The study on brand names in Swedish economic texts presented in this paper shows that while the brand names in the corpus can be identified as names by their orthography, classification requires analysis of the context. 40 percent of the brand names found in the corpus are co-referred by common nouns, but the remaining names cannot be classified through the study of lexical cohesion but through collocations and background knowledge (Malmgren, 2004).

A NER experiment using transformation-based learning on this data shows that what was problematic to the annotator was difficult also to the recognizer; company names and brand names are closely connected and thus hard to disambiguate, and the most problematic name type for the annotators, trademark, was also the most problematic for the recognizer. Identifying appositive phrases describing e.g., products also proved difficult to the recognizer, whereas humans have no difficulty in identifying such phrases. However, the results of the experiment are encouraging.

---

[10]The Common Procurement Vocabulary can be downloaded at http://simap.eu.int (last checked Sept. 6, 2005)

## References

Eric Brill. 1995. Transformation-Based Error-Driven Learning and Natural Language Processing: A Case Study in Part of Speech Tagging. *Computational Linguistics*, December.

Nancy Chinchor. 1998. MUC-7 Named Entity Task Definition (version 3.5). In *Proceedings of the Seventh Message Understanding Conference (MUC-7)*. Available from http://www.itl.nist.gov/ (Last checked Oct. 14, 2005.).

Shawn M. Clankie. 2002. *A Theory of Genericization on Brand Name Change*. The Edwin Mellen Press.

Hercules Dalianis and Erik Åström. 2001. Swenam - A Swedish Named Entity recognizer. Its construction, training, and evaluation. Technical Report TRITA-NA-P0113, NADA-KTH, July.

Eva Ejerhed, Gunnel Källgren, Ola Wennstedt, and Magnus Åström. 1992. The Linguistic Annotation System of the Stockholm-Umeå Corpus Project. Technical Report 33, Department of General Linguistics, University of Umeå.

Ralph Grishman. 2003. Information extraction. In Ruslan Mitkov, editor, *The Oxford Handbook of Computational Linguistics*, chapter 30, pages 545–559. Oxford University Press.

M. A. K. Halliday and Ruqaiya Hasan. 1976. *Cohesion in English*. Longman.

Martin Hassel. 2001. Internet as Corpus. Automatic Construction of a Swedish News Corpus. In *NoDaLiDa'01*. NoDaLi.

Dimitrios Kokkinakis. 2003. Swedish NER in the Nomen Nescio Project. In *Nordisk Sprogteknologi - Nordic Language Technology. Årbog for Nordisk Sprogteknologisk Forskningsprogram 2000-2004*. Nordisk Sprogteknologisk Forskningsprogram.

Torbjörn Lager. 1999. The $\mu$-TBL System: Logic Programming Tools for Transformation-Based Learning. In *Proceedings of the Third International Workshop on Computational Natural Language Learning (CoNLL'99)*, Bergen.

Aisha Malmgren. 2004. Brand names in text: An exploratory study of the identification and interpretation of brand names. Unpublished B.A. Thesis, Department of Linguistics, Stockholm University.

---

*Proceedings of the 15th NODALIDA conference, Joensuu 2005*     Ling@JoY 1, 2006

David D. McDonald. 1996. Internal and external evidence in the identification and semantic categorization of proper names. In B. Boguraev and J. Pustejovsky, editors, *Corpus processing for lexical acquisition*, pages 21–39. MIT.

Ingrid Piller. 1996. *American Automobile Names*. Die Blaue Eule.

Helmut Schmid. 1994. Probabilistic part-of-speech tagging using decision trees. In *Proceedings of International Conference on New Methods in Language Processing*.

Satoshi Sekine and Hitoshi Isahara. 1999. IREX project overview. In *Proceedings of the IREX workshop*, Tokyo, Japan.

European Union and European Parliament. 2002. Regulation (EC) No 2195/2002 of the European Parliament and of the Council of 5 November 2002 on the Common Procurement Vocabulary (CPV). *Official Journal L 340 , 16/12/2002 P. 0001 - 0562*.

Martin Volk and Simon Clematide. 2001. Learn-Filter-Apply-Forget. Mixed Approaches to Named Entity Recognition. In *Proc. of 6th International Workshop on Applications of Natural Language for Information Systems*, Madrid, Spain.

Ola Wennstedt. 1995. Annotering av namn i SUC-korpusen. In Kjartan G. Ottósson, Ruth V. Fjeld, and Arne Torp, editors, *The Nordic Languages and Modern Linguistics 9. Proceedings of the Ninth International Conference of Nordic and General Linguistics*, pages 315–324. University of Oslo, Novis forlag, January.

David Yarowsky. 1995. Unsupervised Word Sense Disambiguation Rivaling Supervised Methods. In *Proceedings of the 33rd Annual Meeting of the Association for Computational Linguistics*, pages 189–196.

# Detecting reference chains in Norwegian


**Anders Nøklestad**
Dept. of Linguistics
Univ. of Oslo
P.O. Box 1102 Blindern
NO-0317 Oslo
Norway
Anders.Noklestad@ilf.uio.no

**Christer Johansson**
Dept. of Linguistics
Univ. of Bergen
Sydnesplassen 7
NO-5007 Bergen
Norway
Christer.Johansson@lili.uib.no



## Abstract

This article describes a memory-based mechanism for anaphora resolution and coreference. A program labels the words in the text with part-of-speech tags, functional roles, and lemma forms. This information is used for generating a representation of each anaphor and antecedent candidate. Each potential anaphor-antecedent pair has a match vector calculated, which is used to select similar cases from a database of labeled cases. We are currently testing many feature combinations to find an optimal set for the task. The most recent results show an overall F-measure (combined precision and recall) of 62, with an F-measure of 40 for those cases where anaphor and antecedent are non-identical, and 81 for identical ones. The coreference chains are restricted so that an anaphor is only allowed to link to the last item in a chain.


## 1 Introduction

This article discusses a method for deciding whether an anaphor is coreferential with a potential antecedent. An early algorithm (Hobbs, 1978) performs searches for antecedents in parsed syntactic trees. Preferences in the model are present in the order of the tree search. Another approach is to model the salience of possible antecedents (Lappin and Leass, 1994). Salience factors are weighted somewhat ad hoc, but with a rank-order inspired by observed ratings of salience in psycho-linguistic experiments. A third influential theory is Centering Theory (Grosz et al.,

1995). Centering too, assumes a salience rating, but has an added constraint that there is a single item which is in focus at any given time and therefore most likely to be pronominalized. None of these models can be regarded as robust models, as they rely on fixed methods, which are not changed by experience. Hobbs' method relies heavily on parsing, and depends on having the correct parse trees available. Lappin and Leass' approach relies on a saliency rating, as well as parsing and finding functional roles. Their algorithm also has a heuristics that takes distance into account. Centering depends on maintaining forward and backward looking centers, and selecting the most likely candidate to be in focus.

Recently, anaphora resolution has been performed by machine learning techniques, using resources that are less demanding. For example, Lappin and Leass' algorithm has been modified so that it can operate on the result of a statistical part-of-speech tagger (Kennedy and Boguraev, 1996). Cardie and Wagstaff (1999) introduced an unsupervised clustering technique that performs better than many hand-crafted systems on the related task of noun phrase coreference. Because the algorithm is unsupervised, finding coreference does not rely on pre-classified exemplars. Other benefits of using a clustering technique is that it can more easily be adapted to different domains. Coreference can also be viewed as a classification task. A comparison between decision tree learning (classification) and the clustering algorithm, shows, not surprisingly, that training on pre-classified examples can provide better results (Soon et al., 2001). An F-ratio of 62.6 was obtained for decision tree learning, whereas the clustering algorithm produced a measure of 53.6 on the same dataset (MUC-6). There is, however, a slight gap to the best system, which produced a measure of 65, according to Cardie and Wagstaff (1999, p.82).

This article will discuss the use of memory-based learning (using the Tilburg Memory Based Learner application, known as TiMBL) in anaphora resolution. Exemplar based models have been tried before, as noted above in the works on clustering (Cardie and Wagstaff, 1999), and decision tree learning (Soon et al., 2001). TiMBL internally uses decision tree techniques to make faster nearest neighbor decisions. The main advantage of, and theoretical point of, memory-based learning is that all information is regarded as useful. All examples may contribute to a correct classification, even rare examples, exceptions and sometimes even examples of misclassifications (Bosch and Daelemans, 1998). A further motivation is to let the exemplars decide the classification as far as possible, and not the prejudices of a biased linguist, who enters the task with (too) much background knowledge about how the phenomenon should work, and (too) little coverage of all the cases that are exceptions, restricted to the situation, or limited by performance demands for efficient communication. We still claim that a linguistic analysis is necessary, as we have no other means of judging which factors might contribute to the solution. The decision is however let to the examples, when it comes to judging how the factors we have pre-selected interact towards a classification decision. We should also acknowledge that there are certainly many relevant factors that have not been selected for representation, either because they did not contribute to the solution with the current set of features, or because we have not thought of them.

In what follows, we will first explain the memory-based machine learning approach, and then we will describe our database and the features we have used in order to train our classifier on the task of anaphora resolution. Finally, we report on the results of running 10-fold cross-validation experiments, which are done as a test of classification ability of this method. In 10-fold cross-validation, a tenth of the training data is left out and classified by the rest of the instances. This is repeated until all items have been classified this way. This validation is different from using entirely new test data, since it is guaranteed to be within the types of texts we have selected for training. (In our web demonstrator[1], we have chosen a test text based on a children's story, which is definitely in a different genre than the training examples.)

## 2  Memory-based learning

We decided to work with memory-based learning, as implemented in the TiMBL software package (Daelemans et al., 2004). This decision was inspired by anaphora resolution results from decision tree learning (Soon et al., 2001), which is a type of exemplar based machine learning mechanism. We have chosen a slightly different approach, using a nearest neighbor mechanism, within the field of memory-based learning. TiMBL is an efficient implementation of this algorithm, and recent results using this software package has shown good results, often better than decision tree learning, for example on chunking (Tjong Kim Sang and Buchholz, 2000). Decision tree learning does not use all the examples. It is what is sometimes classified as a greedy learner (i.e. trying to make generalizations as soon as possible), whereas TiMBL is a lazy learner (i.e. postponing the classification decision until it is needed).

Memory-based learning is a kind of k-nearest neighbor approach, which operates on exemplars, or *instances*, in the form of feature vectors. It is a supervised machine learning method that requires an annotated training corpus. During the training phase, training instances are stored in a database, or *instance base*, along with their annotated categories.

Classifying a new instance amounts to comparing it to the instances in the instance base, finding the ones that are most similar to the new instance (i.e., its *nearest neighbors*), and selecting the category that is shared by the majority of those neighbors. The notion of similarity is taken in a geometrical sense, as examples are represented as points, with an associated category, in an n-dimensional space. The degree of similarity between instances is influenced by the choice of similarity metric and feature weighting scheme. The size of the neighborhood is also influenced by the value of $k$ used for the $k$-nearest neighbor classifier. If k=1, only the most similar instances are used, with k=2, the next best matches are also included, and so on.

------

[1]see demo at http://bredt.uib.no

------



157

The classification process is illustrated in general terms in table 1, which shows three training instances and a test instance. The features can take the values plus or minus. The reader is encouraged to look for feature values that are the same for the test instance and the training instance.

The test instance matches Train1 on Feature1 and Feature2, and it matches Train2 on Feature2 and Feature4, while Train3 only matches on Feature2. Thus, Train1 and Train2 constitute the set of nearest neighbors for Test. Since the majority (in this case all) of the nearest neighbors share the C1 category, this category is also selected for the Test instance.

|          | Train1 | Train2 | Train3 | Test |
|----------|--------|--------|--------|------|
| Feature1 | +      | –      | –      | +    |
| Feature2 | –      | –      | –      | –    |
| Feature3 | –      | –      | –      | +    |
| Feature4 | +      | –      | +      | –    |
| Category | C1     | C1     | C2     | *C1* |

Table 1: Classification based on nearest neighbors.

## 3 Anaphora resolution

We use a corpus which has been automatically annotated for part-of-speech tags and syntactic categories, and hand annotated for coreference. The algorithm was trained on a subset of 41970 tokens, of which 35780 were words and the rest typographical annotations. From these 35780 words, we have 11831 markables (potential members of reference chains).

In order to experiment with a more limited material, we selected a set of pronouns which had all been marked either with or without an antecedent. Pronouns without antecedents refer to something not present in the (preceding) text. The chosen pronouns were *han* "he", *hun*, "she", *seg* "himself/herself/itself/themselves", *den* "it" masc./fem., and *de* "they". The set of pronouns consisted of 2199 anaphor candidates, of which 2129 were marked with a coreferential antecedent in the text. Cataphors were excluded from the training set.

### 3.1 Salience

The classification of an anaphor–antecedent pair is affected by a number of features, such as whether they agree in number, person, case

and gender. All these features create subdivisions of the representational space. Since the model is not probabilistic, it is not correct to associate probabilities to this selection. The method selects from the nearest neighbors, regardless of their likelihood of occurrence, or likelihood of predicting the correct class. Additional constraints may stem from syntactic restrictions (for example, whether a reflexive interpretation is possible), and selectional restrictions (e.g., which are the typical objects of specific verbs). Real knowledge of what is possible, may help. Recency, repeated mention and parallelism are other important factors in deciding coreference (Jurafsky and Martin, 2000, pp.678–684).

The factors we use are taken from a machine annotated corpus, so not all of these factors necessarily have correct values.

The factors are as follows (see also table 3):

- Do the lemmas of the anaphor candidate and the antecedent candidate match?

- Do the anaphor candidate and the antecedent candidate have the same

  - syntactic function?
  - grammatical gender? (We also want to add natural gender in the future.)
  - number?

- Is the anaphor candidate a distinctly human pronoun (*han* "he" or *hun* "she") and the antecedent candidate a proper name?

  - If so, do they have the same (natural) gender?

- Is the anaphor candidate a reflexive and the antecedent candidate its closest subject?

- Is the antecedent candidate a subject?

- Is the number of sentence boundaries, as detected by the tagger (e.g. some conjunctions, and punctuation), between anaphor and antecedent candidates

  - less than 2?
  - less than 3?

- The lemmas of the anaphor and the antecedent candidates concatenated

Note that we have no information about natural gender for lexical noun phrases, which is information we would want to have, in addition to grammatical gender. Various ways of finding the natural gender (Hale and Charniak, 1998, inter al., for English) will be tried out later in our project.

Since we are using memory-based learning for this task, the full impact of each feature is determined after the nearest neighbors have been found. A feature that is highly valuable in some contexts may simply not add anything in other contexts, for example if all the selected nearest neighbors contain the same feature. This is an advantage of memory-based learning, since it does not rely heavily on global statistics. TiMBL may also weigh features by their informativeness, by calculating the information gain of each feature (i.e. how much we gain in classification accuracy by knowing the value of the feature). Still, TiMBL is essentially a selection mechanism and not a probabilistic mechanism.

### 3.2  Percolation

A strategy to percolate most of the matching features to the next referring expression in a chain was adapted. This means that the most recent antecedent candidate matches the union of its own matching features and those of the preceding antecedent candidates of the same chain. Sometimes information is not available immediately, but will be known after we have established coreference (see table 2) .

| 3 | | 3.1 | | 3.2 |
|---|---|---|---|---|
| Calvin | $\rightarrow$ | who | $\rightarrow$ | he |
| — | | Calvin | | — |
| — | | .... | | — |

Table 2: Percolation of *Calvin* to *who*

Take for example the following discourse, adapted and translated from a folk tale: *"[Three brothers lived in a forest.]  The oldest was called Adam₁, the second Bert₂, and the youngest Calvin₃, who₃.₁ used to tend to the ashes₄.  The Sunday₅ when the notice₆ from the King₇ about the ship₈ was posted, he₃.₂ happened to be there. When he₃.₃ came home and told about it₆.₁, Adam₁.₁ wanted to set out immediately, and prepared some food₉ for the journey₁₀. For he? wanted to find out ..."*

The second time that *he* refers to Calvin at point 3.2, the information from the first mention of Calvin at point 3 has been percolated to the *who* at 3.1. After linking up, the information in 3.2 contains the (lemma)/name "Calvin", the functional roles of position 3 (predicate filler), 3.1 (subject), and 3.2 (subject), as well as the number (singular), and the gender (masculine). If we presume that the name Calvin was not found in the lexical resources, then the gender of Calvin may be established by a co-occurrence relation.

| feature | 3 | 3.1 | $3 \cup 3.1$ |
|---|---|---|---|
| match on | | | |
|   lemma | – | – | – |
|   syn.func. | – | + | + |
|   gender | – | – | – |
|   number | + | + | + |
|   human pro. | | | |
|     and prop. | + | – | + |
|     and gen | – | – | – |
| refl+subject | – | – | – |
| subject-ant | – | + | + |
| *dist.* $< 2$ | + | + | + |
| *dist.* $< 3$ | + | + | + |

Table 3: Match between *he* at 3.2.  and antecedents *Calvin*(3), or *who* (3.1), or 3∪3.1) with percolation

This strategy is thought to be important for full anaphora resolution. From table 3, we see that we get a match vector with six matching features with percolation, instead of four features for match with Calvin, and five features matching *who*. It is an open question whether there should be a lemma match between a pronoun and the same pronoun only, or if a pronoun should be able to unify with all kinds of strings for surface match. We have decided to allow a lemma match between the same form of pronouns only, but we will try using an unknown value for this type of match. Notice that it would be a good idea to have three values for gender matches: +, –, and *unknown*. If *Calvin* was found to be a male name, for example from a list of male names, we would be able to access a masculine gender for both *Calvin* and *who*. (This is not to say that "who" is a word with inherent gender.)  An unknown value would be good to have when we cannot disprove a match. In addition, we would create and search for the concatenated lemmas *he/Calvin*, and *he/who* respectively. These items are not percolated, but contain the value of the candidate antecedent and the anaphor.

Table 4 shows the match vectors, after percolation, for *he?* matching with either *Adam* or *Calvin*. As can be seen, *Calvin* matches on more features than *Adam*. Still, Adam might be selected as antecedent because it is closer to the anaphor. This is due to the fact that the search for an antecedent moves backwards in the text, starting at the anaphor and stopping as soon as there is a positive classification. Hence, if the match vector for Adam has more positive than negative nearest neighbors in the instance base, *Adam* will be selected as antecedent, and *Calvin* will never be considered.

| feature | 1.1 | 3.3 |
|---|---|---|
| match on | | |
|   lemma | – | + |
|   syn.func. | + | + |
|   gender | – | + |
|   number | + | + |
|   human pro. | | |
|     and prop. | + | + |
|     and gen | – | – |
| refl+subject | – | – |
| subject-ant | + | + |
| *dist.* $< 2$ | – | – |
| *dist.* $< 3$ | + | – |

Table 4: Match vectors for *he?*, with *Adam*1.1, and *he*$_{3.3}$/*Calvin*

Two important points are illustrated. First, that a closer antecedent will have an advantage, because it will be selected before its competitors if TiMBL decides for it, since the search for an antecedent is stopped when there is a positive classification. Second, that the final categorization does not depend on how many matches are recorded, but on how the full vector and its neighbors have been classified previously. A last point is that proper names are assumed to be in the singular; however, for some types of proper names (e.g. organizations) the *number* featuremay have a different default than singular, or may come from a knowledge base. This is crucially an issue of what our lexical resources will deliver.

## 3.3 Future extensions

All the features we are using are language independent, and can be found with commonly available tools for part-of-speech tagging and functional role assignment. We will therefore be able to extend our work fairly easily to handle other similar languages, where appropriate taggers are available, such as Dutch, English and Swedish. Databases of correctly annotated examples will have to be built up incrementally, but it might help to have a system that can suggest correct anaphor–antecedent relations in a majority of the cases automatically. This procedure is enhanced if a tool is provided that makes it easy to correct mistakes made by the automatic procedure. We have work in progress that will provide such a tool on the internet. If people use it we will also benefit from their work, since we will have access to the annotated data after editing, and because we will get useful feedback on the mechanism. A very interesting research question is whether it is possible to use a common database for many different languages. Will the examples from different languages support or interfere with each other? Factors such as matching functional roles, parallelism, semantic similarity and function, may very well vary in a similar way across many (related) languages. We are further helped by the fact that only factors that are important in the *target* language (the language of the text to be processed) will be important. For example, if a language does not have grammatical gender it can not discriminate on that feature for any of the languages in the database, it will be as if the feature did not exist. When it comes to functional roles, they are designed to be annotated similarly across languages.

## 4 Training and testing

Several different combinations of the available features were tried, and the previously presented 9 features were those that gave the highest scores. They are most likely not the optimal features, but they are the features that are available in our machine tagged example collection. We have only scored hits on the closest antecedent in a chain, whereas it could be argued that a hit on any antecedent in a chain would suffice.

| Selection | Proportion | Recall | Precision | F-measure |
|---|---|---|---|---|
| Identical anaphor-antecedent | 67% | 83.95 | 78.88 | 81.31 |
| Non-identical anaphor-antecedent | 33% | 40.75 | 40.32 | 40.51 |
| All cases | 100% | 62.12 | 62.18 | 62.14 |

Table 5: Results from 10-fold cross-validation experiments.

Feature percolation allows previously found antecedents of a chain to influence the decision on anaphoric status. Features percolate and accumulate towards the most recent member of a chain.

Training consists of providing postive and negative examples to the memory-based learner. Positive examples are pairs of anaphor and antecedent candidates, described by how they match on the features we have decided to include. Negative examples are pairs consisting of an anaphor and any markable that is closer to the anaphor than the actual antecedent. Typically, there are many more negative examples than positive examples.

In testing, we start searching from the pronoun (or potential anaphor, in the more general case of coreference detection) backwards in the text until the algorithm finds a markable that is classified as an antecedent for the pronoun. The classification decision is binary, so we assign the first found candidate marked by the mechanism as an antecedent. We have experimented with using the strength of the classification decision (recalculated into z-scores, for general comparison), but this did not improve the results and was abandoned.

The classification decision is therefore simplistic: The memory-based learner is consulted for each markable that is encountered. If the positive nearest neighbor examples in the database outvote the negative examples, the classification is a yes, otherwise a no. When the mechanism says yes, there is no need to search further.

The results of our cross-validation experiments are shown in Table 5. The overall F-measure is 62.14. It should be noted, however, that the system performs much better in those cases where the anaphor and the antecedent are identical than in cases where they are not identical. Closely related to this observation is the fact that in 78% of the test cases, the classifier selects an antecedent that is identical to the anaphor. This strong tendency to select identi-

cal pairs is likely due to the fact that 67% of all manually annotated anaphor–antecedent pairs in the training data fit this characteristic. This is particularly noticeable for *han* "he" and *hun* "she", which also account for 78% of the relevant pronouns. The problem with this pattern is that we often miss many of the more interesting pairs, where there is a non-pronoun as antecedent. We simply do not have enough recall to find these more interesting cases. The examples favor a negative classification, simply because this is correct most of the time. A simple bias towards positive answers will hurt our precision, but this could be worth it if we could quantify how much more such a pair is worth. This is a highly task dependent decision. In many tasks, chains containing only pronouns would not make much difference, whereas a correct chain that links with keywords would be highly valuable (for example in estimating the topic of a paragraph).

We performed our 10-fold cross-validation experiments on a corpus of novels, which is a complex type of text with typically elaborate and long reference chains. Newspaper texts, in contrast, select for shorter, coherent paragraphs since space is a more limited resource in this domain.

## 5 Conclusion

We have presented a system for automatic resolution of pronominal anaphora in Norwegian that is based on memory-based learning. The system reaches a performance level, which is comparable to that of earlier systems developed for English in the context of the Message Understanding Conferences.

The performance of the system is considerably better on identical anaphor-antecedent pairs than on non-identical pairs, reflecting the higher proportion of identical pairs in the training data. We are currently testing new feature combinations, and the addition of more lexical resources, some of which are found by statistical association, in order to improve results.

We plan to apply our system to related languages, in order to see how language independent our selected features are. We would like to investigate whether patterns learned from the Norwegian data could actually be applied directly in order to perform anaphora resolution in these other languages without having to re-train the system for each language.

**Acknowledgements** The BREDT project is supported by a grant from the Norwegian Research Council under the KUNSTI programme. The first author is supported by a Ph.D. grant from the University of Oslo. We thank Dr Kaja Borthen for many valuable comments. A demonstrator of early results for anaphora resolution is available from http://bredt.uib.no

# References

A. van den Bosch and W. Daelemans. 1998. Do not forget: Full memory in memory-based learning of word pronunciation. In D.M.W. Powers, editor, *proceedings of NeMLap3/CoNLL98*, pages 195–204, Sydney, Australia.

C. Cardie and K. Wagstaff. 1999. Noun phrase coreference as clustering. In *Proc. of the joint SIGDAT Conf. on Empirical Methods in NLP and Very Large Corpora*, pages 82–89.

W. Daelemans, J. Zavrel, K. van der Sloot, and A. van der Bosch. 2004. TiMBL: Tilburg Memory-Based Learner, Version 5.1, Reference Guide. Technical Report ILK 04–02, the ILK Group, Tilburg, the Netherlands.

B.J. Grosz, A. Joshi, and S. Weinstein. 1995. Centering: A framework for modeling the local coherence of discourse. *Computational Linguistics*, 21(2):203–225.

J. Hale and E. Charniak. 1998. Getting Useful Gender Statistics from English Text. Technical Report CS-98-06, Comp. Sci. Dept. at Brown University, Providence, Rhode Island.

J.R. Hobbs. 1978. Resolving pronoun references. *Lingua*, 44:311–338.

D. Jurafsky and J.H. Martin. 2000. *Speech and Language Processing*. Prentice Hall, New Jersey.

C. Kennedy and B. Boguraev. 1996. Anaphora for everyone: Pronominal anaphora resolution without a parser. In *Proceedings of the 16th International Conference on Computational Linguistics.*, Copenhagen, Denmark.

S. Lappin and H. J. Leass. 1994. An algorithm for pronominal anaphora resolution. *Computational Linguistics*, 20(4):535–561.

Wee Meng Soon, Hwee Tou Ng, and D. Chung Yong Lim. 2001. A machine learning approach to coreference resolution of noun phrases. *Computational Linguistics*, 27(4):521–544.

E. F. Tjong Kim Sang and S. Buchholz. 2000. Introduction to the CoNLL-2000 Shared Task: Chunking. In *Proceedings of CoNLL-2000 and LLL-2000*, pages 127–132. Lisbon, Portugal.

# Mapping product descriptions to a large ontology

**Henrik Oxhammar**
Department of Linguistics
Stockholm University
116 63 Stockholm
Sweden
`henrik.oxhammar@ling.su.se`

## Abstract

In this paper we describe an information retrieval approach for mapping online business information texts to concepts in a large ontology. We adopt the traditional vector space model by representing the texts as queries and the concept labels in the ontology as documents.

Because of the size of the ontology and the fact that concept labels are very sparse and generic, we conducted additional experiments for *reducing* the set of concepts, as well as the *enrichment* and *enlargement* of concept labels.

The documents in our collection were of too poor quality for this task, and although we show that our enrichment technique did provide us with an ontology with good overall similarity to our query collection, individual concepts did not include enough terms for our method to achieve good results.

## 1 Introduction

In this paper we describe our first attempts in building a system that assigns product and service concept labels in a large ontology, to online business information texts. Our method can be viewed as an information retrieval approach to standard text categorization.

The task of mapping such business information is a difficult one because of the number of concepts (over 8300) and the fact that the *labels* that describe these concepts are very sparse. Further, only a small percentage of the terms that these labels include, are also present in the vocabulary used on corporate websites. We therefore also describe a number of techniques for improving the performance of a baseline system, including a technique for reducing the number of candidate concept labels for a document and two techniques for *enlarging* and *enriching* sparse concept labels.

## 2 The Common Procurement Vocabulary

The Common Procurement Vocabulary (CPV) (European Union and European Parliament, 2002) is a standardized vocabulary developed by the European Union. It is a classification scheme for public procurement and its purpose is to help procurement personnel and contracting authorities describe and classify their procurement contracts.

The CPV ontology defines products and services as concepts in a strict taxonomic relationship structure. Each concept consists of a unique eight-digit code and a *concept label* that describes the concept in natural language. E.g.,

```
18000000 "Clothing and accessories"
 18500000 "Leather clothes"
  18510000 "Leather clothing accessories"
   18512000 "Leather belts and bandoliers"
    18512100 "Belts"
    18512200 "Bandoliers"
```

The ontology defines 8323 unique concepts of this kind. By a concept's code, it is possible to derive a number of useful facts. First, we can determine at what level the concept is defined. E.g., `18512000 "Leather belts and bandoliers"` resides on level five. Leaf concepts, i.e., concepts that have the finest granularity, make up almost 68% (5644) of the total number of concepts.(Warin et al., 2005)

The ontology is a strict taxonomy, i.e., concepts are related by the hyponomy/hyperonomy (sub/super) relationships. Therefore, it is possible to also derive a concept's *parent*(s), *descendant*(s) and *sibling*(s). E.g., the direct parent of 18512100 "Belts" is 18512000 "Leather belts and bandoliers", and 18512200 "Bandoliers" is its sibling since 18512200 shares the same parent as 18512100. 18512100 "Belts" has no descendants since it is a leaf concept.

## 3   The vector space model

Our method of mapping product descriptions to concepts in the CPV is based on the classical information retrieval approach for querying documents.

The *vector space model* (VSM) (Salton et al., 1975) assigns weights to document- and query terms and the model represents each document and query as multi-dimensional feature vectors. By computing the cosine angle between the vectors the similarity of a document and a query can be established. The smaller this angle is the more similar the query and the document are said to be. The model then usually returns a ranked list that includes the most similar documents to the query given.

The vector model has several advantages, including its partial matching ability, its simplicity, its quick retrieval times and the fact that it can allow queries to be of any size. The vector space model has proved to be superior or as good as other retrieval models.(Baeza-Yates and Ribeiro-Neto, 1999)

The task for the system we present in this paper was to suggest a number of concepts in the ontology that the model regarded being most similar, given a business information text as query. We further regard the *concept labels* that describe the concepts in the ontology as documents. The model returns the suggested concepts in ranked list according to relevance, with the most relevant concept first.

Our implementation of the vector model included stemming, term weighting by document frequency and vector normalization by unit length.

## 4   Resources

### 4.1   Query collection

A collection of 739 documents crawled from various corporate web sites was at our disposal. We briefly inspected the texts for them to at least include *some* information of the company's activities. The size of the documents varied from about 20 Bytes to about 400 Kbytes. Below is an example of a text in our query collection:

```
"Electronic Assembly Wire and Cable
The variety of electrical cable applications,
provided by EDEC Kabel bv , is widely spread.
Edec Kabel bv is a Sales Office specialised
in electrical cable. We represent and or
cooperate with several cable manufactures
like : E&E GmbH Germany, GmbH Germany
and others. In addition to this, EDEC
Kabel bv, also supplies a comprehensive
line of standard wire and cable to
offer a total cable product range"
```

Far from all texts were of this quality. Because of the limited number of documents, we however decided to keep documents with less information in our query collection.

### 4.2   Gold standard

To evaluate our method, we had manually made mappings, between each of the 739 documents in the query collection and a number of concepts in our ontology. For example, the document in the previous section had been associated with:

```
28400000 "Cable, wire and related products"
31300000 "Insulated wire and cable"
31330000 "Coaxial cable"
```

The number of associated concepts ranged from one to 60 in one case. The and the total number of relevant concepts for our query collection was 3348, giving an average number of 4.5 associated concepts in our gold standard.

Unfortunately, many of the associated concept labels did not describe their respective document as well as the example above indicate.

## 5   Evaluation measures

The most commonly used measures for evaluating information retrieval systems are *precision* and *recall*. Precision gives the percentage of the number of correctly retrieved documents among all documents retrieved, while recall reflects the percentage of relevant documents retrieved by a query among all relevant documents for this query.

However, recall and precision are not appropriate measures when a system returns answers to a query in a ranked list according to their relevance, simply because precision and recall (by default) do not take the ranking in to account. A proper evaluation measure for such systems is instead a measure known as *interpolated precision averages at 11 standard recall levels*. This measure shows the overall quality and effectiveness of the system, by taking the ranking into account. (Baeza-Yates and Ribeiro-Neto, 1999)

Since it still can be difficult to compare two systems' precision averages at various recall levels, another *single* measure can be used that provides a *summary* of a system's performance over all relevant documents. *Average precision* is a single-valued measure that calculates the average of precision values after each relevant document has been retrieved, that enables two systems to be compared by a single value.(Baeza-Yates and Ribeiro-Neto, 1999)

When we evaluated the experiments described in section 6, we only did so according to *exact* matches. As mentioned in section 2, there are several relationships that the ontology describe, including the parent-child and sibling relations. Since these concepts are closely related, we could regard the mapping of a document to its correct concept's sibling, parent or child concept, not as *incorrect* but, instead, as partially *correct*. E.g., suppose a document is associated with 29521321 "Drilling machinery". This tells us that, the company described in the document does not manufacture drills for, say, *home use*, but drills used for things such as *mining*, since the parent of 29521321 is 29521320 "Oil drilling equipment". So if the system suggests 29521320 "Oil drilling equipment", then we can regard the system to be correct to some extent.

We can further induce from an associated concept that a document can also belong to the associated concept's children. E.g., a document originally associated with e.g., 15500000 "Dairy products" can therefore also belong to any of 15500000's children concepts, including 15510000 "Milk and cream, 15550000 "Assorted dairy products" and 15551310 "Unflavored yoghurt".

Two approaches, for adopting standard performance measures to hierarchically ordered categories, has been proposed by e.g., Sun and Lim (2001). They show that these extended precision and recall measurements, by including

| Recall level | Precision Average |
|---|---|
| 0.00 | 0.1485 |
| 0.10 | 0.1303 |
| 0.20 | 0.1051 |
| 0.30 | 0.0865 |
| 0.40 | 0.0661 |
| 0.50 | 0.0596 |
| 0.60 | 0.0412 |
| 0.70 | 0.0372 |
| 0.80 | 0.0365 |
| 0.90 | 0.0356 |
| 1.00 | 0.0356 |
| **Average precision:** | **0.0662** |

Table 1: Interpolated precision-recall values and average precision for baseline experiment

*category similarity* and *category distance*, do contribute positively compared to the standard precision and recall measurements.

## 6   Experiments

In the experiments we describe here, we provided each of the 739 documents described in section 4.1 to the model as queries. We used stop word removal, stemming and weighting by document frequency. We evaluated each experiment using interpolated precision-recall and average precision as we described in section 5.

### 6.1   Baseline

We set up a baseline for mapping each of the documents in the query collection to *any* of the concept labels in our ontology. This meant that for any given query, the system needed to find the correct concept(s) for this query among all 8323 sparsely described concepts in the ontology.

### 6.1.1   Results

Table 1 displays the interpolated precision-recall values and average precision for the baseline. As we had expected, the performance of the baseline was poor, only achieving an average precision of 6.62% over all queries.

We believed that the reason for the poor performance had to do with the large number of concepts in the ontology as well as the obvious fact that the concept labels in our ontology were so sparse and too selective, meaning that very few of them included the same terms as our queries.

---

Oxhammar: *Mapping product descriptions to a large ontology*

Therefore, we set up three additional experiments that would 1) reduce the set of concepts, 2) enlarge parent concept labels with related terms from the ontology itself and 3) enrich the leaf concept labels with semantically similar terms from WordNet. We describe the outcomes of these three experiments in the following sections.

## 6.2 Varying levels

The baseline tried to find the correct concept(s) for a given query among all the 8323 concepts, the ontology defines. Since the ontology is taxonomically structured, an alternative approach was to map our queries only according to concepts on a certain level or with certain *granularity*. In this case, we could measure how good the model was at finding the correct *branch* of the ontology and not necessarily the correct concept.

### 6.2.1 Experiment setup

We set up this experiment as follows. First we needed to collect a subset of concepts against which the documents in the query collection should be mapped. Let us call this subset the *concept collection*. Since the idea was to cut the original ontology at eight different levels, the technique omitted all concepts below the selected level and only included concepts *on*, and *above* this level. As we select deeper levels to map against, the number of concepts in the concept collection increases, each time with number concepts on previous levels plus the number of concepts on the selected level. E.g., if we are mapping our documents according to level three we have 487 (12+97+378) concepts in the concept collection. The model then returns the most relevant *branches* to which that document belongs.

Table 2 shows the number of concepts on each level as well as the number of concepts in each concept collection.

It is clear that as we choose to map documents according to deeper levels, the task becomes more difficult since we get more and more possible concepts for each document. Mapping according to level 8 is therefore the same as the baseline task in section 6.1.

Since a document can be associated with a concept that is located on a lower level than we are mapping to, and since the technique omitted all these concepts from the concept

| Level | No. of Concepts | Concept Collection |
|---|---|---|
| 1 | 12 | 12 |
| 2 | 97 | 109 |
| 3 | 378 | 487 |
| 4 | 1022 | 1509 |
| 5 | 2048 | 3557 |
| 6 | 2420 | 5977 |
| 7 | 1636 | 7613 |
| 8 | 710 | 8323 |

Table 2: Number of concepts at various levels and above

collection, the system would not suggest these concepts. Therefore, we replaced all concepts in the gold standard that were below the selected level with their ancestor concept on the level selected. E.g., if a document had originally been associated with 29131000 and the level was set to two, this document would now instead be associated to 29000000 which is 29131000's ancestor on level two. If several of the associated concepts had the same ancestor (i.e., associated concepts were located in the same branch) then the document would only be associated with this parent once. Associated concepts that resided on higher levels than the selected level we left unchanged.

These preliminary steps resulted in eight modified gold standards and eight different concept collections that we mapped each of the 739 documents in the query collection against. No propagation of children label terms to parent labels was used in this experiment. We describe that experiment in section 6.4.

### 6.2.2 Results

Figures displayed in table 3 show the results we obtained for these experiments.

We thought that, by reducing the number of concepts in this fashion, it would be easier for our model to do the correct mappings. This was not the case. We were surprised about the numbers the model returned. Although we could see some small improvements, still, the performance was poor.

Early on when we started implementing this system, we realized that the labels describing the concepts in our ontology were too uninformative for our method to correctly map the business information texts to.

---

| Level | Average Precision |
|-------|-------------------|
| 1 | 0.1874 |
| 2 | 0.1048 |
| 3 | 0.0950 |
| 4 | 0.0838 |
| 5 | 0.0748 |
| 6 | 0.0716 |
| 7 | 0.0692 |
| 8 | 0.0662 |

Table 3: Interpolated Precision-recall values and Average Precision for various levels

In the following subsection we describe two techniques we hoped would bridge the gap between the terms in our queries and the terms in concept labels.

### 6.3　WordNet-enriched leaf concepts

We had previously developed a method (Warin et al., 2005), for enriching the *leaf concepts* in our ontology using WordNet (Fellbaum, 1998). This technique adds synonyms and introduce a broader terminology to these concepts. The method uses semantic similarity measures as disambiguation techniques for adding synset descriptions (glosses) to leaf concepts, including synonyms and other, less selective terms. E.g., the method enriched concept 15811200 `"Rolls"` with: `"small rounded bread either plain or sweet bun, roll"`.

In this method, terms from leaf concepts and their parents are looked up in WordNet that returns their senses. The semantic similarity is then computed for the pair of word senses. The leaf sense with the highest (total) score is assumed to be a good candidate for enriching the leaf concept label. The outcome of this process provided us with a new ontology with 5366 out of the 5644 leaf concepts enriched.

### 6.3.1　Results

Neither in this experiment could we see any improvements compared to the baseline. The average precision only increased to about 6.74%. A possible explanation we found to this, as we also discuss in section 8, was that for the documents we looked at, few of the associated concepts in gold standard tended to be leaf concepts.

### 6.4　Term propagation

The next thing we tried was to enlarge parent concept labels with related terms from their children. By propagating children concept label terms upward in the ontology, parent concepts will become larger, and include all of their children concept labels. Thus, the parent concept labels will include a cluster of highly related terms and in effect, describe a complete branch in one single concept. Again, we envisioned that this would increase the probability that individual concepts would include terms also present in our queries.

### 6.4.1　Experiment setup

The technique we used for adding children's concept label terms to parent concept labels was straightforward. In a bottom-up fashion, starting at the finest granularity of the ontology, each concept label was added to each of that concept's parent label. The procedure then added these propagated parent labels to each of their parent labels and so on. This meant that each child's label was added to all of its ancestor labels. The idea was that this would constitute a sort of weighting for terms occurring on lower levels by the fact that on upper levels, these terms would become frequent.

E.g., the branch 29566000 originally look like this:

```
29566000 "Machinery for the treatment of
         sewage"
  29566100 "Comminutors"
    29566110 "Macerators for the
               treatment of sewage"
  29566200 "Sewage presses"
  29566300 "Scrapers"
  29566400 "Mixer units"
  29566500 "Sewage screens"
  ...
  29566900 "Sludge-processing
             equipment"
```

After these concepts had been propagated, 29566000 and 29566100 now included all children label terms as well:

```
29566000 "Machinery for the treatment
  of sewage Macerators for the
  treatment of sewage Sedimentation
  beds Scrapers Sewage presses
  Precipitators Sewage screens
  Sludge-processing equipment
```

---

```
Comminutors Macerators for the
treatment of sewage Oxygenation
equipment Mixer units"

29566100 "Comminutors Macerators
   for the treatment of sewage"
```

The other concepts in the example were unaffected by the propagation since these are leaf concepts.

Again, we queried each of the documents in the query collection according to the 8323 concept labels, many of which we now had enlarged with related terms from their children concept labels.

### 6.4.2  Results

Again the results were poor, and the propagation technique was unable to improve the results significantly. Although this model achieved the highest average compared all previous experiments (6.93%) it was still very low. We explain this further in section 8.

## 7  Related work

The work most similar to ours in the literature is the work done by Ding et al. (2002). They introduce 'GoldenBullet', a system that classifies product descriptions according to the UN-SPSC classification scheme, which is similar to our ontology. They also view this as an information retrieval problem, treating product descriptions as queries and category labels in UN-SPSC as documents. Although they also use more sophisticated methods that are able to achieve fairly good results, they report of a classification accuracy of less than 1% for the method most comparable to ours.(Ding et al., 2002)

Although our method can be regarded as an information retrieval approach to automatic text categorization (cf. (Sebastiani, 2002)), the task we are facing is also related to work conducted within *hierarchical* text categorization. Most effort in this area has been put in to classifying text according to *web directories* (Labrou and Finin, 1999; Choi and Peng, 2004; Pulijala and Gauch, 2004), the *Reuters collection* (Sun and Lim, 2001; Weigend et al., 1999), as well as the automatic assignment of Gene Ontology (GO) terms to medical articles (Seki and Mostafa, 2005; Raychaudhuri et al., 2002; Kir-

| Ontology | Relevance to Query Collection |
|---|---|
| Original | 0.47 |
| Propagated | 0.45 |
| WordNet Enriched | 0.54 |

Table 4: Ontology and query collection similarity scores

itchenko et al., 2004; Ruiz and Srinivasan, 1999).

## 8  Qualitative study

The results that we obtained for the baseline were, although not satisfactory, not surprising. However, the results we obtained using the propagated and WordNet enriched ontologies were disappointing and puzzling.

In order to understand why the performance of our model was so low, and why neither the term propagation nor the WordNet enrichment technique provided us with any improvements, we did a small qualitative study of our data and the results that we had obtained.

The first thing we measured was the coverage between each ontology version and the documents in the query collection. Next, we did a closer inspection of the results to get an idea of how many of the labels in our gold standard did include terms that also were present in their associated document. If associated concept labels included terms that were not present in their associated document, even after term propagation or WordNet enrichment, it would also explain why the performance was low and why there was no significant improvements to the baseline.

The overall similarity between the ontologies we experimented on and the query collection is shown in table 4. We obtained these figures using the same vector model as we had used in our experiments. In this case we provided the model with the complete query collection as a single query to compare against the complete ontology. We adopted this method from Brewster et al.(Brewster et al., 2004) who describe this method in the framework of ontology evaluation for measuring the 'fit' between an ontology and a domain corpus it is suppose to model.

The figures in table 4 show that for all ontologies, there was a clear coverage of concept label terms in the query collection. Interestingly, the coverage of the propagated ontology was in fact smaller than for the original ontology, although only slightly. We were glad to see that our WordNet-enrichment technique did provide us with an ontology that more closely resembled the query collection.

The reason for propagated ontology having a similar coverage as the original ontology is not so surprising. The label terms in the propagated ontology are the same as those that describe concepts in the original ontology, and since the propagation technique did not add any *new* terms to the ontology, it did not provide us with an ontology which resembled our query collection more closely than the original ontology.

The figures in table 4 do not seem to explain why the performance was so poor for the experiments that we did. We therefore turned to the gold standard to see how well the label terms in our gold standard covered the terms in their associated documents. This would give us an indication of how well individual concept labels covered terms in our queries.

To clarify: what we would like is, of course, that each term in an associated label also is present in its respective document. A good example is the document 362680 displayed in section 4.1 and its associated concept labels we showed in section 4.2. In this example, each associated label includes terms that also frequently occur in the text. When we inspected the results for 362680, the model had accurately suggested all three correct concepts at position, 3, 4, and 14 in the ranked list:

```
...
31300000 Insulated wire
         and cable
28400000 Cable, wire and
         related products.
...
31330000 Coaxial cable.
```

However, we found that when we ran the experiments on the original ontology, 153 documents in our query collection did not include *any* of the terms in the labels with which they had been associated. E.g., document 171651 includes the following text: `"on the unique experiences of this leading company of greenhouse Climate and better crops".`

According to the gold standard, 171651 should be mapped to the concept 45211350 `"Multi-functional buildings"`.

Secondly, it seemed that the terms that the propagation and enrichment techniques had added the associated concept labels with, in a number of cases, simply were not present in the document. E.g., concept 45211350 `"Multi-functional buildings"` was enriched with `"the occupants of a building building"`. In this case, the only term introduced was occupant.

Also with the propagated ontology, cases like this could be observed. E.g., document 755728, originally associated with `"Beauty products"` and `"Perfumes and toiletries"`, included only the label term perfume. After the ontology had been propagated, the following terms were added to 755728's associated labels: toiletries, shaving, preparations, shampoos, manicure or pedicure, preparations, toilet, waters, hair, preparations, beauty, skin-care, antiperspirants, deodorants, make-up, preparations, oral, dental, and hygiene. Not a single one of these related terms were present in the document.

For cases like these, it is easy to explain why we observed only a small increase in performance of our model, after our ontology had been enriched or enlarged.

Further, for those cases where the enrichment or propagation technique had added terms to the associated concept label(s) and those terms were also *present* in the respective document, the study indicated that what we had added was *low frequency* terms. E.g., when the associated concept 29433000 `"Bending, folding, straightening or flattening machines"` had been enriched with

`"any mechanical or electrical device that transmits or modifies energy to perform or assist in the performance of human tasks machine"`,

only the term mechanical, occurred in the document and with a frequency of *one*. Again we could observe similar patterns when experimenting on the propagated CPV. E.g., document 14043 was originally associated to:

```
29474000  "Parts and accessories for
           metal-working machine tools"
29462000  "Welding equipment"
52000000  "Retail trade services"
74700000  "Cleaning services"
29423000  "Milling machines"
74230000  "Engineering services"
```

Only *one* of these label terms occurred in the document namely, engineering. The propagation technique then enlarged the associated labels above with 251 (unique) children terms, resulting in 360 associated label terms for this document. Measuring the coverage again, now six additional label terms could be found in the document (item, transport, process, support, control, and design). So, not only was just a small fraction (6/351) of the terms the propagation technique had added actually in 14043, in addition, all these terms occurred only once or at most three times in the document.

We concluded from this study that the texts in our query collection were simply too uninformative for our model to achieve good results. Although our ontologies seemed to model the business information domain well *overall*, there was too big of a difference between *individual* concepts and texts. The number of documents in our gold standard that did not include *any* of its associated concept label terms were 153 for the original ontology. Although we saw that these cases decreased as we enriched or enlarged the ontology, the tendency was that only few of the added concept terms were actually in the individual documents, and for those that were, instead, they were too infrequent anyway.

Another explanation for why no real improvement could be seen using the propagated ontology was that, by propagating the terms from children labels to all parents, the technique introduced these terms to a large number of other concept labels. This distributed label terms across large portions of the ontology, that in effect made the concepts more similar to each other. In fact, mapping the documents in our query collection on to the propagated ontology generated 10.000 more answers than when we mapped them to the original ontology.

A positive outcome however was that we did get confirmation that the WordNet enrichment technique did provide us with an ontology that more closely resembled the query collection.

It is important to note that we only enriched leaf concepts, and although leaf concepts make up the majority of the concepts, for this technique to have effect, not only must we have enriched the concepts with correct and useful terms, but also, the documents we are mapping need to be associated with these leaf concepts in the gold standard. We saw several cases were only a few of the associated labels for a document were leaf concepts. Similarly, since the term propagation only affects parent concepts, and leaf concepts are left unaffected and since they constitute the majority of concepts, it could explain why we saw only little improvement. As was true for the enriched concepts, for the propagation technique also to have a real effect, not only does the added concept terms need to be in the document, but the documents also needs to be associated with enlarged concepts (i.e., parent concepts).

## 9   Future work

To assess the pros and cons of our baseline method as well our other techniques, we need to do a much larger qualitative study than we did for these experiments. But before we do that, we need to collect texts that are more informative than those documents we currently have in our collection.

>From the small qualitative study we did, it is clear that terms describing the concepts in our ontology included few terms used in real business information texts. An appropriate next step will therefore be to enrich the ontology with terms from such real world business information texts.

The results we have reported here are based on exact matches. However, we have observed many cases where the model has either suggested a more general concept (parent) to a correct concept, but even more so a child concept to a correct concept. If the model suggests such closely related concepts, than it should count for something. In future versions of this system, we will regard cases like these as partially correct by giving them a penalty depending on their distance to the correct concept in the ontology.

## 10  Conclusions

In this paper, we have described a system that adopts the vector space model in the framework of automatically assigning concept labels to business information texts, by mapping these texts to a large ontology defining a wide range of products and services. We envisioned to task to be a difficult one, because of the number of concepts in the ontology and the sparse labels that describe them. However, the task proved to be more challenging than we had anticipated.

It became clear that the business information texts on which we tested our model, were of too poor quality for our task, something we simply could not do anything about, regardless of the experiment we conducted. Either the texts were too short (too uninformative) or included too much non-sense text. We tried several techniques for improving on the baseline, including the *reduction of concepts, enlargement of concept labels with related terms*, and the *enrichment of new terms* with the help of WordNet. We were able to show that the latter technique, by introducing many *non-present* terms to the ontology, did yield an ontology that more closely resembled the texts we tried to map overall, and that our improvement techniques did allow our model to achieve a higher accuracy. Still, the individual concepts labels in our enlarged and enriched ontologies included terms that rarely occurred in our queries.

To bridge the gap between the selective, generic vocabulary describing concepts in our ontology and the specific terminology used in online business information texts, in the future, we intend to develop an accurate method that instead enriches the ontology with such vocabulary.

## References

Ricardo Baeza-Yates and Berthier Ribeiro-Neto. 1999. *Modern information retrieval*. ACM Press, New York.

Christopher Brewster, Harith Alani, Srinandan Dasmahapatra, and Yorick Wilks. 2004. Data-driven ontology evaluation. *Proceedings of the 4th International Conference on Language Resources and Evaluation*.

Ben Choi and Xiaogang Peng. 2004. Dynamic and hierarchical classification of web pages. *Online Information Review*, Vol. 28, No. 2:139–147.

Ying Ding, Maksym Korotkiy, Borys Omelayenko, Vera Kartseva, Volodymyr Zykov, Michel Klein, Ellen Schulten, and Dieter Fensel. 2002. Goldenbullet in a nutshell. *Proceedings of the Fifteenth International Florida Artificial Intelligence Research Society Conference*, pages 403–407.

European Union and European Parliament. 2002. European union and european parliament. on the common procurement vocabulary (cpv). *Regulation (EC) no 2195/2002 of the European Parliament and of the Council*.

Christiane D. Fellbaum. 1998. *WordNet, an electronic lexical database*. MIT Press.

Svetlana Kiritchenko, Stan Matwin, and Fazel Famili. 2004. Hierarchical text categorization as a tool of associating genes with gene ontology codes. *Proceedings of the Second European Workshop on Data Mining and Text Mining for Bioinformatics (held at ECML-04)*, pages 26–30.

Yannis Labrou and Tim Finin. 1999. Yahoo! as an ontology: using Yahoo! categories to describe documents. *Proceedings of CIKM-99, 8th ACM International Conference on Information and Knowledge Management*, pages 180–187.

Ashwin Pulijala and Susan Gauch. 2004. Hierarchical text classification. *International Conference on Cybernetics and Information Technologies, Systems and Applications: CITSA 2004, Vol. 1.*, pages 257–262.

Soumya Raychaudhuri, Jeffrey T. Chang, Patrick D. Sutphin, and Russ B. Altman. 2002. Associating genes with gene ontology codes using a maximum entropy analysis of biomedical literature. *Genome Research*, 12(1):203–214, January.

Miguel E. Ruiz and Padmini Srinivasan. 1999. Hierarchical neural networks for text categorization. *Proceedings of SIGIR-99, 22nd ACM International Conference on Research and Development in Information Retrieval*, pages 281–282.

Gerard Salton, A. Wong, and C.S. Yang. 1975. A vector space model for automatic indexing. *Communications of the ACM*, 18(11):613–620.

Fabrizio Sebastiani. 2002. Machine learning in automated text categorization. *ACM Computing Surveys*, 34(1):1–47.

---

Kazuhiro Seki and Javed Mostafa. 2005. An application of text categorization methods to gene ontology annotation. *SIGIR '05: Proceedings of the 28th annual international ACM SIGIR conference on Research and development in information retrieval*, pages 138–145.

Aixin Sun and Ee-Peng Lim. 2001. Hierarchical text classification and evaluation. *Proceedings of ICDM-01, IEEE International Conference on Data Mining*, pages 521–528.

Martin Warin, Henrik Oxhammar, and Martin Volk. 2005. Enriching an ontology with wordnet based on similarity measures. *Proceedings of the MEANING-2005 Workshop*.

Andreas S. Weigend, Erik D. Wiener, and Jan O. Pedersen. 1999. Exploiting hierarchy in text categorization. *Information Retrieval*, 1(3):193–216.

Oxhammar: *Mapping product descriptions to a large ontology*

# The impact of phrases in document clustering for Swedish

**Magnus Rosell** and **Sumithra Velupiḷḷai**
KTH Nada
100 44 Stockholm
Sweden
{rosell, sumithra}@nada.kth.se

## Abstract

We have investigated the impact of using phrases in the vector space model for clustering documents in Swedish in different ways. The investigation is carried out on two text sets from different domains: one set of newspaper articles and one set of medical papers.

The use of phrases do not improve results relative the ordinary use of words. The results differ significantly between the text types. This indicates that one could benefit from different text representations for different domains although a fundamentally different approach probably would be needed.

## 1   Introduction

For document clustering one normally uses the vector space model to represent texts. It is based on the distribution of single words over the texts in a set. We have investigated the impact of introducing phrases in this representation for Swedish in different ways and in different domains. Our hypothesis was that phrases would improve results and that the improvement would be greater for the medical papers than for the newspaper articles as we believe that phrases carry more significance in the medical domain.

To calculate similarity between documents with respect to their phrases we use a word trie (in one set of experiments). This approach has a lot in common with the method presented in (Hammouda and Kamel, 2004). They show improvements in clustering results on web pages using phrases combined with single words, using other algorithms than we. Another related method is the Phrase-Intersection Clustering method which has been proven efficient on web pages (Zamir and Etzioni, 1998). It is based on word-n-grams rather than phrases.

## 2   Text sets

We have used a set of 2500 newspaper articles from KTH News Corpus (AB) (Hassel, 2001) and a set of 2422 medical papers from Läkartidningen[1] (Med). In Table 1 some statistics for the sets are given.

We need categorizations of the text sets for the evaluation. The newspaper articles have been categorized by the paper into five sections such as Economy and Sports etc.

The medical papers are categorized with The Medical Subject Headings (MeSH) thesaurus[2]. This thesaurus is (poly)hierarchical with a term and a unique code at each place in it. The terms are not unique and may occur at several places in the hierarchy. There are 15 *broad headings* at the top level.

---

[1]http://www.lakartidningen.se/
[2]http://www.nlm.nih.gov/mesh/meshhome.html

| Text Set | Categories | Documents | Words | Unique Words |
|---|---|---|---|---|
| AB | 5 | 2500 | 119401 | 5896 |
| Med | 15, 814 | 2422 | 4383169 | 26102 |

Table 1: Text Sets

Each paper has one or more terms from the thesaurus assigned to it. This categorization is very extensive, but also very hard to handle for clustering evaluation. Hence we have made four attempts to flatten and disambiguate it so that each paper belongs to only one of a set of non overlapping categories.

We have made three categorizations where we try to put each document into one of 15 categories corresponding to the 15 broad headings. The first, which we call General, is constructed by choosing the broad heading to which most of the MeSH-terms assigned to the paper belongs.

By choosing the broad heading under which the most specific term (the term deepest into the hierarchy) is found for each paper we have constructed the second categorization, which we call Specific.

Many of the papers have as one of the terms assigned to it one or several broad headings. In the third categorization we have chosen this (always one) as the categorization of those papers. The other papers are categorized using the same system as for our categorization Specific. We call this categorization Combined.

We have made a fourth categorization which we call Term. In this every paper is assigned the MeSH-term that has the highest frequency among the terms assigned to it. This leads to a categorization with 817 categories.

The categorizations General and Combined are those that seem most trustworthy. A paper may probably have a very specific term assigned without having its broad heading as the general focus (see Specific). Terms at different levels of the MeSH-hierarchy probably make up an unequal categorization (see Term).

## 3  Linguistics

We used the grammar checking program Granska[3] to extract nominal phrases from the texts and a stemmer (Carlberger et al., 2001) to stem all words. To prevent very similar but not identical phrases to be deemed unsimilar we removed stopwords within the phrases as well as from the single words.

Swedish solid compounds often correspond to phrases (or compounds) in other languages. We use the spell checking program Stava (Kann et al., 2001) to split them. An earlier study (Rosell, 2003) has proven this to improve clustering results for newspaper articles. We also try to represent the split compounds as phrases and try to split compounds within phrases (see Section 5).

## 4  Similarity

When calculating the similarity between two documents using phrases two natural alternatives are at hand. Either one chooses to deem phrases similar only if they are identical or one looks at the overlap of words between them. We have tried both. In the first case we have calculated the weight for each phrase in a document as the frequency of its appearance in that document multiplied by the sum of the idf-weight for the single words in it.

To find the overlaps of phrases in documents we have built a trie based on words for each document from the phrases appearing in them. Each phrase is put into

---

[3]http://www.nada.kth.se/theory/projects/granska/

the trie in its entire and with all but the first word, with all but the first two words, etc. In each node of the trie we save the number of times it has been reached. To calculate the overlap of phrases between two documents we follow all common paths in the tries and multiply relative appearances in each node weighted by the sum of the idf-weights for the words along the path.[4]

## 5  Representations

From the phrases and single words we built several different representations. Refer to Table 2 through this section.

Combining all the described possibilities (full phrases or overlap, using split compounds as phrases or not, and split compounds within phrases or not) we get eight different representations based on phrases. By combining[5] these with the ordinary single word representation with split compounds we get eight more. This gives 16 representations (representations 3 through 18 in Table 2). We also made the reference representation (only words, 1) and the representation where solid compounds have been split (2), giving in total 18 different representations.

Finally, for comparison we also try a random "clustering" (Rand) and in the evaluation we present the theoretical worst (Worst) and best (Best) possible results (see Sections 7 and 8).

## 6  Clustering algorithm

The clusterings have been made using the divisive algorithm Bisecting K-Means (Steinbach et al., 2000) which splits the worst cluster (i.e. largest) in two, using K-Means, until the desired number of clusters are reached. We have let the K-Means algo-

---

[4]Compare with Phrase-Intersection Clustering in (Zamir and Etzioni, 1998).

[5]We use equal weight on the two different representations. In (Hammouda and Kamel, 2004) they try different weightings.

rithm iterate ten times and for each split we ran it five times and picked the best split (evaluated using the similarity measure). Average results are calculated over ten runs to ten clusters for each representation.

## 7  Evaluation

As we compare different representations we use extrinsic evaluation measures that requires a categorization of the the same text set to compare with. Among the extrinsic evaluation measures that have been used for text clustering are *the purity* and *the entropy*. These measures are well suited for evaluation of single clusters, but for evaluation of whole clusterings *the mutual information* is better. (Strehl et al., 2000)

Consider a text set $N$ with $n$ texts. Let $C$ be a clustering with $\gamma$ clusters, $c_1$ through $c_\gamma$. By $n_i$ we mean the number of texts in cluster $c_i$ ($\sum_{i=1}^{\gamma} n_i = n$). Similarly, let $K$ be a categorization with $\kappa$ categories, $k^{(1)}$ through $k^{(\kappa)}$ and let $n^{(j)}$ denote the number of texts in category $k^{(j)}$.

The $\gamma$ by $\kappa$ matrix $M$ describes the distribution of the texts over both $C$ and $K$; that is $m_i^{(j)}$ is the number of texts that belong to $c_i$ and $k^{(j)}$.

The mutual information of clustering $C$ and categorization $K$ is:

$$MI(C,K) = \sum_{i=1}^{\gamma} \sum_{j=1}^{\kappa} \frac{m_i^{(j)}}{n} \log(\frac{m_i^{(j)} n}{n_i n^{(j)}}) \quad (1)$$

A theoretical tight upper bound is $MI_{max}(C,K) = \log(\kappa\gamma)/2$, the mean of the theoretical maximal entropy of the clustering and the categorization. By dividing the mutual information by this we get a normalized measure. (Strehl, 2002)

This normalization is theoretical and particular for each clustering-categorization-setting. We want to compare results on different such settings, with different text

---

| Repr. | Description | | | |
|---|---|---|---|---|
| Worst | The worst possible result | | | |
| Rand | Random partiton of the set | | | |
|  | – average for ten iterations | | | |
| Best | The best possible result | | | |
| 1 | Only words, stemming | | | |
| 2 | Only words, stemming | | | |
|  | and splitting of compounds | | | |
| 3 | P | PM | NSP | NSC |
| 4 | P | PM | NSP | SC |
| 5 | P | PM | SP | NSC |
| 6 | P | PM | SP | SC |
| 7 | P | POM | NSP | NSC |
| 8 | P | POM | NSP | SC |
| 9 | P | POM | SP | NSC |
| 10 | P | POM | SP | SC |
| 11 | P&W | PM | NSP | NSC |
| 12 | P&W | PM | NSP | SC |
| 13 | P&W | PM | SP | NSC |
| 14 | P&W | PM | SP | SC |
| 15 | P&W | POM | NSP | NSC |
| 16 | P&W | POM | NSP | SC |
| 17 | P&W | POM | SP | NSC |
| 18 | P&W | POM | SP | SC |

| Abbr. | Explanation |
|---|---|
| P | Similarity only between phrases |
| P&W | Similarity using both phrases and words |
| PM | Phrase-match |
| POM | Phrase-overlap-match |
| SP | Use splitted compounds as phrases |
| NSP | Do not use splitted compounds as phrases |
| SC | Split compounds within phrases |
| NSC | Do not split compounds within phrases |

Table 2: Representations

sets, having varying clustering complexity/difficulty. Therefore we need to normalize with regard to something else.

Since we want to know how much introducing phrases improve results we use the result from a clustering using only words as a reference. By comparing the results with this reference we take the complexity of the different text sets into account.

There are two simple and reasonable ways of normalizing the result using the word clustering result, $MI(C_{word}, K)$. We can divide the result by it:

$$MI_{word}(C, K) = \frac{MI(C, K)}{MI(C_{word}, K)}, \quad (2)$$

or we can divide the improvement by the maximum possible improvement from the word clustering result:

$$MI_{imp}(C, K) =$$
$$\frac{MI(C, K) - MI(C_{word}, K)}{MI_{max}(C, K) - MI(C_{word}, K)} \quad (3)$$

The first normalization is suitable when we have a decrease in performance. It puts the decrease in relation to the greatest possible decrease. The second normalization is suitable when we have an increase in performance.

## 8  Results

We present the results of our investigation in Tables 3 and 4. All values are average results over ten clusterings with standard deviation within parenthesis.

The first row of each part of these tables gives the results for the newspaper articles and the following the results on the medical papers compared to the different categorizations. In Table 4 we only give results for representations Term and General as the results for Combined, General and Specific are very similar.

The columns represent the different representations which were described in Section 2 and summarized in Table 2. In Table 3 we present the result for a random "clustering" (the average of 10 random partitions of the text set) and the theoretical worst and best possible results.

---

| | Measures | Worst | Rand | | Best | 1 | | 2 | |
|---|---|---|---|---|---|---|---|---|---|
| AB | $MI$ | 0.000 | 0.009 | (0.003) | 2.822 | 0.947 | (0.043) | 1.093 | (0.084) |
| | $MI_{word}$ | −100.0% | −99.0% | (0.3%) | 198.0% | 0.0% | (4.6%) | 15.4% | (8.9%) |
| | $MI_{imp}$ | −50.5% | −50.0% | (0.2%) | 100.0% | 0.0% | (2.3%) | 7.8% | (4.5%) |
| Combined | $MI$ | 0.000 | 0.038 | (0.006) | 3.614 | 0.407 | (0.016) | 0.415 | (0.010) |
| | $MI_{word}$ | −100.0% | −90.6% | (1.4%) | 787.9% | 0.0% | (4.0%) | 2.0% | (2.4%) |
| | $MI_{imp}$ | −12.7% | −11.5% | (0.2%) | 100.0% | 0.0% | (0.5%) | 0.3% | (0.3%) |
| General | $MI$ | 0.000 | 0.041 | (0.005) | 3.614 | 0.478 | (0.013) | 0.486 | (0.016) |
| | $MI_{word}$ | −100.0% | −91.5% | (1.1%) | 656.0% | 0.0% | (2.7%) | 1.7% | (3.4%) |
| | $MI_{imp}$ | −15.2% | −13.9% | (0.2%) | 100.0% | 0.0% | (0.4%) | 0.3% | (0.5%) |
| Specific | $MI$ | 0.000 | 0.038 | (0.005) | 3.614 | 0.396 | (0.010) | 0.397 | (0.017) |
| | $MI_{word}$ | −100.0% | −90.4% | (1.2%) | 812.6% | 0.0% | (2.6%) | 0.1% | (4.2%) |
| | $MI_{imp}$ | −12.3% | −11.1% | (0.1%) | 100.0% | 0.0% | (0.3%) | 0.0% | (0.5%) |
| Term | $MI$ | 0.000 | 1.450 | (0.008) | 6.498 | 1.850 | (0.023) | 1.868 | (0.018) |
| | $MI_{word}$ | −100.0% | −21.6% | (0.5%) | 251.2% | 0.0% | (1.2%) | 1.0% | (0.9%) |
| | $MI_{imp}$ | −39.8% | −8.6% | (0.2%) | 100.0% | 0.0% | (0.5%) | 0.4% | (0.4%) |

Table 3: Text Clustering Results (stdv)

| | Measures | 3 | | 4 | | 5 | | 6 | |
|---|---|---|---|---|---|---|---|---|---|
| AB | $MI$ | 0.067 | (0.020) | 0.071 | (0.017) | 0.086 | (0.024) | 0.080 | (0.032) |
| | $MI_{word}$ | −93.0% | (2.1%) | −92.5% | (1.8%) | −91.0% | (2.6%) | −91.5% | (3.4%) |
| General | $MI$ | 0.112 | (0.008) | 0.117 | (0.012) | 0.028 | (0.005) | 0.030 | (0.002) |
| | $MI_{word}$ | −76.6% | (1.7%) | −75.4% | (2.5%) | −94.2% | (1.1%) | −93.7% | (0.4%) |
| Term | $MI$ | 1.547 | (0.020) | 1.547 | (0.013) | 0.574 | (0.096) | 0.585 | (0.022) |
| | $MI_{word}$ | −16.4% | (1.1%) | −16.4% | (0.7%) | −69.0% | (5.2%) | −68.4% | (1.2%) |

| | Measures | 7 | | 8 | | 9 | | 10 | |
|---|---|---|---|---|---|---|---|---|---|
| AB | $MI$ | 0.095 | (0.020) | 0.150 | (0.024) | 0.071 | (0.021) | 0.058 | (0.010) |
| | $MI_{word}$ | −90.0% | (2.1%) | −84.1% | (2.5%) | −92.5% | (2.2%) | −93.9% | (1.0%) |
| General | $MI$ | 0.148 | (0.011) | 0.178 | (0.015) | 0.031 | (0.005) | 0.037 | (0.025) |
| | $MI_{word}$ | −69.0% | (2.4%) | −62.7% | (3.1%) | −93.5% | (1.0%) | −92.2% | (5.2%) |
| Term | $MI$ | 1.565 | (0.033) | 1.607 | (0.027) | 0.506 | (0.045) | 0.694 | (0.269) |
| | $MI_{word}$ | −15.4% | (1.8%) | −13.2% | (1.4%) | −72.6% | (2.5%) | −62.5% | (14.6%) |

| | Measures | 11 | | 12 | | 13 | | 14 | |
|---|---|---|---|---|---|---|---|---|---|
| AB | $MI$ | 0.820 | (0.051) | 0.809 | (0.057) | 0.946 | (0.078) | 0.919 | (0.100) |
| | $MI_{word}$ | −13.4% | (5.4%) | −14.6% | (6.0%) | −0.1% | (8.2%) | −3.0% | (10.6%) |
| General | $MI$ | 0.148 | (0.016) | 0.168 | (0.018) | 0.210 | (0.013) | 0.216 | (0.013) |
| | $MI_{word}$ | −69.0% | (3.4%) | −64.8% | (3.8%) | −56.0% | (2.7%) | −54.9% | (2.8%) |
| Term | $MI$ | 1.562 | (0.022) | 1.566 | (0.021) | 1.314 | (0.052) | 1.336 | (0.064) |
| | $MI_{word}$ | −15.6% | (1.2%) | −15.4% | (1.1%) | −29.0% | (2.8%) | −27.8% | (3.5%) |

| | Measures | 15 | | 16 | | 17 | | 18 | |
|---|---|---|---|---|---|---|---|---|---|
| AB | $MI$ | 0.746 | (0.090) | 0.734 | (0.063) | 0.954 | (0.063) | 0.940 | (0.061) |
| | $MI_{word}$ | −21.3% | (9.5%) | −22.5% | (6.7%) | 0.8% | (6.7%) | −0.8% | (6.4%) |
| General | $MI$ | 0.226 | (0.022) | 0.230 | (0.007) | 0.217 | (0.029) | 0.247 | (0.020) |
| | $MI_{word}$ | −52.8% | (4.5%) | −52.0% | (1.5%) | −54.7% | (6.1%) | −48.3% | (4.3%) |
| Term | $MI$ | 1.642 | (0.026) | 1.649 | (0.033) | 1.460 | (0.054) | 1.486 | (0.048) |
| | $MI_{word}$ | −11.2% | (1.4%) | −10.9% | (1.8%) | −21.1% | (2.9%) | −19.7% | (2.6%) |

Table 4: Results for Text Clustering with Phrases (stdv)

## 9  Discussion

When, in the following discussion, we refer to the results on the medical papers we consider the results on the categorization General (which is very similar to results on Combined and Specific). The results with respect to the categorization Term of the medical papers are a bit different than for the others. As we believe the other categorizations to be better we do not discuss this further.

To split *compounds* in the representation based only on words (representation 2 compared to 1) improve results when clustering the newspaper articles but not when clustering the medical papers. This may be because compounds in the medical papers would need a different analysis. We have also used a stoplist for certain words that should not be split based on other newspaper articles as described in (Rosell, 2003). An optimization for medical com-

---

Rosell & Velupillai: *The impact of phrases in document clustering for Swedish*

pounds here would perhaps improve results.

All variations of clustering using *phrases* performs worse than clustering using only words. Clustering performs worse when using only phrases (representations 3-10) than when using the combination of words and phrases (representations 11-18). Since clustering using words is superior the impact of phrases is diminished in the combined representations (11-18).

Looking at the *representations based only on phrases* (3-10) we see that results on newspaper articles are almost as bad as random clustering for all of them. The performance on the medical papers, on the other hand, is better than random clustering as long as we do not use split compounds as phrases. It is also better here to use the word trie representation (POM) rather than the simple phrase match (PM). In all this is an indication that phrases contain more information in the medical papers than in the newspaper articles.

For the *combined representations* (11-18) the results are much harder to analyze as the word representation is so much better than the phrase representation. The results on the newspaper articles are much better than on the medical papers here. This could be since the phrase representations do not contain as much information for the newspaper articles as for the medical papers and they thereby obscure the clustering to a lesser extent. Concerning the medical papers, all what is stated for the representations using only phrases holds, except that here it is not negative to use the split compounds as phrases (SP). For the newspaper articles there is even a great increase in performance when using the split compounds as phrases. This could be explained if the phrase representations using split compounds gives no information, which the results for representations 3-10 indicates. There is no reliable difference between the use of simple phrase match and the word trie representations for the newspaper articles as the standard deviation is very high.

No cases show any change in performance when splitting compounds within phrases (SC) or not. The reason for this could be beacause the amount of compounds within phrases is small.

It is important to bear the great *differences of the two text sets* in mind. The differences in results between them show that clustering works differently on corpora with different contents (i.e. medical text vs. newspaper text). However, this difference might as well to a great extent be explained by other things, such as the structure and size of the texts and the difference of the categorizations. The medical papers are much longer than the newspaper articles. This could in fact explain all of the differences between them regarding information found in the phrases and the compounds. The categorization of the newspaper articles is probably much better than our categorizations of the medical articles.

## 10 Conclusions and further work

Phrases do not improve clustering in Swedish. At least with the representations tried here. The impact of phrases is more obvious on the medical papers. Overlap match between phrases performs better than simple match. It seems to be bad to consider split compounds as phrases and it does not matter whether one splits compounds within phrases or not.

Splitting solid compounds for the ordinary word representation improves results for the newspaper articles and does not make results worse for the medical papers.

The results are very different for the two text types, the newspaper articles and the medical papers. Maybe one would need to develop different representations for different text types. The information found in the phrases of the medical papers could per-

---

haps be exploited using some other representation. But the same information might also be found in the ordinary representation using only words.

Our results are different from those presented in (Hammouda and Kamel, 2004). This is presumably, at least partially, because of differences between Swedish and English. Swedish solid compounds often correspond to phrases in English.

It could be interesting to try other variations of the representations using phrases presented here, but to really use the information that phrases contain relative to mere words a fundamentally different approach is probably needed. One interesting obvious extension of the present work is, however, to look at word-n-grams instead of phrases as these has proven useful in other works.

## Acknowledgements

Our thanks go to professor Viggo Kann for supervision, to VR (Vetenskapsrådet – the Swedish Research Council) for funding and to all participants in the project "Infomat" from KTH Nada (department of Computer Science and Numerical Analysis at the Royal Institute of Technology) and the department of Medical Epidemiology and Biostatistics (MEB) at Karolinska Institutet, both in Stockholm, Sweden.

## References

J. Carlberger, H. Dalianis, M. Hassel, and O. Knutsson. 2001. Improving precision in information retrieval for Swedish using stemming. In *Proc. 13th Nordic Conf. on Comp. Ling. – NODALIDA '01*.

K. M. Hammouda and M. S. Kamel. 2004. Efficient phrase-based document indexing for web document clustering. *IEEE Transactions on Knowledge and Data Engineering*, 16(10):1279–1296. Student Member-Khaled M. Hammouda and Senior Member-Mohamed S. Kamel.

M. Hassel. 2001. Automatic construction of a Swedish news corpus. In *Proc. 13th Nordic Conf. on Comp. Ling. – NODALIDA '01*.

V. Kann, R. Domeij, J. Hollman, and M. Tillenius, 2001. *Text as a Linguistic Paradigm: Levels, Constituents, Constructs. Festschrift in honour of Ludek Hrebicek*, volume 60, chapter Implementation aspects and applications of a spelling correction algorithm.

M. Rosell. 2003. Improving clustering of swedish newspaper articles using stemming and compound splitting. In *Proc. 14th Nordic Conf. on Comp. Ling. – NODALIDA '03*.

M. Steinbach, G. Karypis, and V. Kumar. 2000. A comparison of document clustering techniques. In *Proc. Workshop on Text Mining, 6th ACM SIGKDD Int. Conf. on Knowledge Discovery and Data Mining*.

A. Strehl, J. Ghosh, and R. Mooney. 2000. Impact of similarity measures on web-page clustering. In *Proc. AAAI Workshop on AI for Web Search (AAAI 2000), Austin*, pages 58–64. AAAI/MIT Press, July.

A. Strehl. 2002. *Relationship-based Clustering and Cluster Ensembles for High-dimensional Data Mining*. Ph.D. thesis, The University of Texas at Austin.

O. Zamir and O. Etzioni. 1998. Web document clustering: A feasibility demonstration. In *Research and Development in Information Retrieval*, pages 46–54.

# Chunking: an unsupervised method to find errors in text


**Jonas Sjöbergh**
KTH Nada
Stockholm, Sweden
jsh@nada.kth.se



## Abstract

We describe a method to use a chunker for grammar checking. Once a chunker is available the method is fully unsupervised, only unannotated text is required for training. The method is very simple, compare the output of the chunker on new texts to the output on known correct text. Rare chunk sequences that occur in the new texts are reported as suspected errors. By automatically modifying the chunk set to be more detailed for common verbs or prepositions more error types can be detected. The method is evaluated on Swedish texts from a few different genres. Our method can be used without modifications on any language, as long as a chunker is available for that language.


## 1   Introduction

In this paper we use chunking to mean dividing sentences into non-overlapping phrases. The sentence "The red car is parked on the sidewalk." could be chunked as "[NP The red car] [VC is parked] [PP on the sidewalk]" where NP means noun phrase, VC means verb chain and PP means preposition phrase. Chunking is a relatively well developed field of research. There are chunkers available for several languages that give good results, usually well over 90% accuracy.

We present a method to use a chunker for grammar checking purposes. Once a chunker is available no manual work is required by this method, only a reference corpus of unannotated text is needed.

Automatic grammar checking is traditionally done by manually writing rules describing different error types and then applying these rules to new texts. There are also methods based on statistics or machine learning. Our approach is similar to the method used by Bigert and Knutsson (2002). In essence, they use trigrams of part-of-speech (PoS) tags, comparing them to trigram statistics from a reference corpus. Any sufficiently unlikely trigram is flagged as a suspected error. A few refinements are used to deal with data sparseness, which otherwise lead to quite a few false alarms.

Our method is very similar, comparing chunk n-grams to statistics from a reference corpus. Using chunks gives longer scope, since each chunk can be quite long. It also detects other types of errors, since some error types do not affect the PoS level as much as the chunk level and vice versa. Since the number of chunk types is much lower than the number of PoS tags the data is less sparse. This means that there is less need to add modifications dealing with data sparseness. We instead modify our method in the opposite direction, by enlarging the chunk set automatically for common verbs and prepositions. This detects new error types.

## 2   Description of the method

Our proposed method is to run the chunker on a reference corpus with known correct text. This training step collects and saves a lot of statistics on what chunk sequences occur in normal language use. When a new text needs to be checked, simply run the chunker on the new text. If it contains chunk sequences that never occurred in the reference texts, these passages are marked as possible errors. It is also possible to use a higher occurrence threshold for accepting chunk the n-grams as correct, for instance if we suspect there to be a few errors in the reference texts.

The number of different chunk types is generally quite small. Since the reference corpus is automatically annotated, and the only requirement is that it should contain high quality texts, it can be very large. These two facts mean that we can get very good statistics even for quite long chunk sequences. This means that there are few false alarms, since even rare chunk sequences will normally be present in the reference corpus. In our evaluations even 5-grams of chunks give very few false alarms. There were less than 10 false alarms in 10 000 words, with slight variations between different genres.

While it is possible to use the method on long chunk sequences, it is probably better to use shorter sequences. Since there is no detailed error diagnosis available it is not that helpful to get an error report saying there is something wrong with a very long text sequence. Pointing out shorter sequences makes locating the error easier.

While the statistics collected are reliable and thus give few false alarms, there are also quite few correct detections. One example from our tests was 13 correct detections (and 1 false alarm) on data where other grammar checkers detected between 60 and 100 errors (but with more false alarms).

To detect more errors we can modify the chunk set, by automatically modifying the output of the chunker. If we are interested in detecting errors related to verb use we can substitute the chunk used for verb chains with the actual words of the chunk. So for the example "[NP The red car] [VC is parked] [PP on the sidewalk]" we originally get the trigram "NP-VC-PP". With the new modification we get "NP-is parked-PP". This allows detection of new error types, for instance wrong verb tense, as in "I want to went home" or "I thought he is nice". Similarly, if we want to find errors related to prepositional use we can do the same for preposition phrases. This detects errors such as "I arrived on Stockholm".

While this detects many new errors there are also negative effects. The number of chunk types is no longer small, but actually very large. This means that the statistics from the reference corpus is very sparse, and thus there are a lot of false alarms.

A better approach is to change only those verb chains or preposition phrases that are common, i.e. occur more than some limit number of times in the reference corpus. If the limit is high enough this works quite well. We still have reliable statistics (few false alarms, though higher than originally), but of course many correct detections are also removed.

For noun phrases our chunker produces additional information: is the noun phrase in definite or indefinite form, singular or plural etc. This information can be included in a similar way. Adding this to the chunk set enables us to detect errors such as "these are my the cars", but of course the statistics become more sparse again.

A nice property of our method is that it is simple to tune the number of alarms you get. If you want more alarms (usually both correct detections and false alarms), simply use longer chunk sequences or a lower limit for exchanging verb chains etc.

## 3  Evaluation

We evaluated our method on Swedish texts. As reference texts we used the Swedish Parole corpus (Gellerstam et al., 2000) (about 16 million chunks) and the KTH News Corpus (Hassel, 2001) (about 10 million chunks). We tested three different genres: newspaper texts, student essays and essays written by non-native speakers learning Swedish. All error reports were manually checked to see if it was a genuine error or a false alarm. The texts were not searched for unreported errors. Compared to other grammar checkers our method is outperformed by state of the art grammar checkers (using manually produced rules for error detection) but similar in performance to other statistical methods.

In the tests in this section we allowed chunk n-grams to span sentence boundaries, we changed the tag for common verb chains and preposition phrases to their corresponding word sequences and we used the extra information available for noun phrases. For chunking we used the output of GTA (Knutsson et al., 2003), which outputs the following chunk types:

- adverb phrase

- adjective phrase

- boundary (clause or sentence)

- infinitive phrase

- noun phrase

- preposition phrase

- verb chain

- outside of phrase (for instance punctuation or interjections)

Noun phrases can also be replaced with a tag indicating the type of noun phrase found, such as a genitive form or a definite and plural form.

Other grammar checkers have also been evaluated on these texts, and some results from those are also presented, in Tables 4, 5 and 6, to give an idea of how good our method is in comparison. The two best grammar checkers evaluated on these texts were the grammar checker in the Swedish version of MS Word 2000 (Arppe, 2000; Birn, 2000) and Granska (Domeij et al., 2000), which are both based mainly on manually constructed rules for different error types. These results were taken from (Sjöbergh and Knutsson, 2005) and reproduced here for convenience.

In Tables 1, 2 and 3 the results using different n-gram lengths and different limits for when to consider a chunk "common" are presented for three different genres.

The test genres was newspaper texts, essays by native speaker students and essays by second language learners. The newspaper texts were taken from the SUC corpus (Ejerhed et al., 1992), which contain almost no errors. The writers also have a very good grasp of the language and use many "advanced" language constructions. The student essays were taken from the written part of the Talbanken corpus (Einarsson, 1976). The essays are argumentative, discussing the views expressed in some other texts the writers have read, and they quote a lot from these texts. The second language learner essays were taken from the SSM corpus (Hammarberg, 1977). The language proficiency varies from writer to writer, some have studied Swedish for only a few months while some have studied several years. These essays are usually quite short.

Looking in the tables, it can be seen that the method is easy to tune to produce few or many error reports. The optimal choice is probably different for different users. Writers with a good grasp of the language using many varied constructions would likely use a very high limit

for "common" phrases, while users with limited knowledge of the language (and thus less productive use of their vocabulary) would benefit more from a lower limit. An experienced writer might also benefit more from reports of errors on long chunk sequences, probably being able to assess what is wrong and also capturing error types with longer dependencies. An inexperienced language user would probably be better served with a more precise diagnosis, i.e. use shorter n-grams, to understand what is wrong.

On newspaper texts there were almost no errors to detect. A reasonable performance level to choose on this genre for our method is perhaps 3-grams and the highest limit for "common" chunks. This gives one correct detection and two false alarms. No other grammar checkers were evaluated on this text, but on similar newspaper texts, also 10 000 words (which were not used for our method, since they turned out to be part of the reference corpus in our experiments), gave two detected errors and three false alarms for MS Word 2000, which was the best performing grammar checker on this genre. This is while not counting simple spelling errors, otherwise the best grammar checker was Granska which had 8 correct detections and 35 false alarms (no grammar checker had less than 35 false alarms when counting spelling errors).

The best performing grammar checker on essays written by non-native speakers was Granska, which detected 411 errors and made 13 false alarms, which is a lot more than our method detects, see Table 2. However, most of the 411 detected errors are simple spelling errors, which our method will generally ignore (since the chunker ignores them). If only grammatical errors and hard spelling errors (resulting in another existing word) are counted, the best performing grammar checker detects 118 errors, making 8 false alarms. Using 4-grams of chunks and a limit of 5 000 occurrences for "common" chunks, our method performs similarly, with 98 correct detections and 12 false alarms. MS Word 2000, which is tuned for high precision, detected 58 errors with only 3 false alarms on this text, not counting spelling errors.

There are very many errors in these essays, most of which were not detected by any of the grammar checkers. Since there are so many

---

errors and since even trigrams of chunks can span quite a lot of text, finding n-grams of chunks with errors in them might be thought to be too easy. While it is true that there are many errors in the texts, just pointing out random chunk n-grams does not perform that well. When checking 50 random chunk trigrams, 27 would be counted as correctly detected errors and 23 as false alarms. Our method performs better than this.

On the student essays MS Word 2000 detected 14 errors with 3 false alarms and Granska detected 31 with 13 false alarms. When including spelling errors MS Word detects 38 errors with 31 false alarms and Granska 48 errors and still 13 false alarms. A reasonable performance level for our method here is 24 correct detections with 13 false alarms, which is not so good.

Our method performs quite poorly on these essays. This is mainly caused by them differing a lot from the reference domain, while still using correct language constructions. The main problem is that there are a lot of "short quotes" which is rare in the reference texts and thus give rise to many unseen chunk n-grams. There are also longer quotes from "odd" genres, such as old bible translations and law books, which while not erroneous are not examples of the more common use of Swedish, and thus lead to more false alarms.

## 4 Discussion

Many of the unseen n-grams are caused by chunker errors, i.e. the unseen chunk n-gram is not the n-gram we should find. Usually the reason the chunker makes an error is because there is an error in the text, which means that this is not a problem. The method correctly signals an error, though the reason might not be the one we expect.

As mentioned regarding the poor performance on the native speaker student essays, our method has trouble with texts from domains that differ too much from the domains the reference texts come from. In general this is not a great concerns, since it is cheap to add more data to the reference texts. All we need is raw text, although with relatively few errors.

Increasing not only the number of domains covered by the reference texts, but also just increasing the size of the reference data is gen-

| N | Limit | Correct | False |
|---|---|---|---|
| 3 | 500 | 4 | 63 |
| 3 | 5000 | 2 | 7 |
| 3 | 50000 | 1 | 2 |
| 4 | 500 | 14 | 179 |
| 4 | 5000 | 6 | 52 |
| 4 | 50000 | 3 | 19 |
| 5 | 500 | 26 | 279 |
| 5 | 5000 | 17 | 144 |
| 5 | 50000 | 15 | 74 |

Table 1: Evaluation results on 10 000 words of newspaper texts, taken from the SUC corpus. There are very few errors in these texts, which leads to poor accuracy.

| N | Limit | Correct | False |
|---|---|---|---|
| 3 | 500 | 75 | 20 |
| 3 | 5000 | 24 | 2 |
| 3 | 50000 | 5 | 1 |
| 4 | 500 | 223 | 43 |
| 4 | 5000 | 98 | 12 |
| 4 | 50000 | 33 | 6 |
| 5 | 500 | 315 | 60 |
| 5 | 5000 | 199 | 27 |
| 5 | 50000 | 108 | 13 |

Table 2: Evaluation results on 10 000 words of second language learner essays from the SSM corpus. With many errors to detect, it is easy to get quite high precision. Most errors in the text go undetected, though.

| N-gram length | Limit | Correct | False |
|---|---|---|---|
| 3 | 500 | 26 | 47 |
| 3 | 5000 | 12 | 11 |
| 3 | 50000 | 6 | 1 |
| 4 | 500 | 93 | 138 |
| 4 | 5000 | 42 | 47 |
| 4 | 50000 | 24 | 13 |
| 5 | 500 | 174 | 233 |
| 5 | 5000 | 118 | 138 |
| 5 | 50000 | 68 | 69 |

Table 3: Evaluation results on 10 000 words of native speaker student essays from the written part of the Talbanken corpus. Frequent use of quotations leads to many false alarms.

*Sjöbergh: Chunking: an unsupervised method to find errors in text*

|                          | MS Word | Granska |
| ------------------------ | ------- | ------- |
| All detected errors      | 10      | 8       |
| All false positives      | 92      | 35      |
| Detected spelling errors | 8       | 6       |
| False positives          | 89      | 20      |
| Detected grammar errors  | 2       | 2       |
| False positives          | 3       | 15      |

Table 4: Evaluation of two state of the art grammar checking methods on proofread newspaper texts, 10 000 words. Table 1 shows our method on similar data.

|                          | MS Word | Granska |
| ------------------------ | ------- | ------- |
| All detected errors      | 392     | 411     |
| All false positives      | 21      | 13      |
| Detected spelling errors | 334     | 293     |
| False positives          | 18      | 5       |
| Detected grammar errors  | 58      | 118     |
| False positives          | 3       | 8       |

Table 5: Evaluation of two state of the art grammar checking methods on second language learner essays, 10 000 words. Table 2 shows our method on the same data.

|                          | MS Word | Granska |
| ------------------------ | ------- | ------- |
| All detected errors      | 38      | 48      |
| All false positives      | 31      | 13      |
| Detected spelling errors | 24      | 17      |
| False positives          | 28      | 0       |
| Detected grammar errors  | 14      | 31      |
| False positives          | 3       | 13      |

Table 6: Evaluation of two state of the art grammar checking methods on essays written by native speakers, 10 000 words. Table 3 shows our method on the same data.

erally a good idea. Since it is so cheap it is a good way to reduce the number of false alarms. False alarms are generally caused by rare language constructions being used, which is mitigated by a larger reference corpus. A larger reference corpus also gives a richer chunk set for a fixed limit on occurrences for "common" chunks, which can also lead to more correct error detections.

Our method detects many different types of errors. Some error types detected by our method are considered "hard" to detect by manually writing rules to detect them, and are thus not very well covered by traditional grammar checkers. This is one reason our method detected errors that no other evaluated grammar checker found.

The main error types detected by our method in these experiments was missing or erroneously placed commas, word order errors, spelling errors resulting in other existing words and using the wrong preposition for a certain verb. Other error types with fewer detections were verb tense errors, split compounds, missing words, missing sentence breaks, agreement errors, other inflectional errors, repeated words, unconventional use of fixed expressions and idioms and simply using a different word from the one intended (only from the learners).

Since our method detects many different types of errors but does not give a detailed diagnosis it is perhaps hard for a user to understand what is wrong. One way to mitigate this is to create different versions of the grammar checker. One version could for instance use the changing of chunk tags for verb chains and thus detect mostly verb related errors, while another might change the chunk tags for noun phrases and thus find noun related errors. They will likely all detect some error types related to chunk sequences in general, but those that only one version detects could be given a slightly more detailed diagnosis.

## 5  Conclusions

While our method did not perform as well as the best available grammar checkers it did produce useful results. The main strength of the method is that it is very cheap to use. All you need is a chunker and unannotated text.

Another strength of the method is that it is very easy to tune how many detections you want from the method. Usually both the number of correct detections and the number of false alarms are affected, so if you want to detect many errors and are prepared to accept more false alarms or if you want almost no false alarms at the cost of leaving some errors undetected, the same method can still be used.

Another strong point is that it detects errors that no other method detects and which are often hard to try to tackle with other methods. Together with the possibility to tune the method for very few false alarms means that our method can successfully be used in combination with other grammar checkers. With almost no new false alarms even quite few new detections can be useful, especially since it is so cheap to create a grammar checker using our method.

## Acknowledgments

We thank Viggo Kann and Ola Knutsson for contributing useful ideas and helpful suggestions.

This work has been funded by The Swedish Agency for Innovation Systems (VINNOVA).

## References

Antti Arppe. 2000. Developing a grammar checker for Swedish. In T. Nordgård, editor, *Proceedings of Nodalida '99*, pages 13–27. Trondheim, Norway.

Johnny Bigert and Ola Knutsson. 2002. Robust error detection: A hybrid approach combining unsupervised error detection and linguistic knowledge. In *Proceedings of Romand 2002, Robust Methods in Analysis of Natural language Data*, pages 10–19.

Juhani Birn. 2000. Detecting grammar errors with lingsoft's Swedish grammar checker. In T. Nordgård, editor, *Proceedings of Nodalida '99*, pages 28–40. Trondheim, Norway.

Richard Domeij, Ola Knutsson, Johan Carlberger, and Viggo Kann. 2000. Granska – an efficient hybrid system for Swedish grammar checking. In *Proceedings of Nodalida '99*, pages 49–56, Trondheim, Norway.

Jan Einarsson. 1976. Talbankens skriftspråkskonkordans. Lund University.

Eva Ejerhed, Gunnel Källgren, Ola Wennstedt, and Magnus Åström. 1992. The linguistic annotation system of the Stockholm-Umeå Corpus project. Technical report, Department of General Linguistics, University of Umeå (DGL-UUM-R-33), Umeå, Sweden.

Martin Gellerstam, Yvonne Cederholm, and Torgny Rasmark. 2000. The bank of Swedish. In *Proceedings of LREC 2000*, pages 329–333, Athens, Greece.

Björn Hammarberg. 1977. Svenskan i ljuset av invandrares språkfel. *Nysvenska studier*, 57:60–73.

Martin Hassel. 2001. Internet as corpus - automatic construction of a Swedish news corpus. In *Proceedings of Nodalida 2001*, Uppsala, Sweden.

Ola Knutsson, Johnny Bigert, and Viggo Kann. 2003. A robust shallow parser for Swedish. In *Proceedings of Nodalida 2003*, Reykjavik, Iceland.

Jonas Sjöbergh and Ola Knutsson. 2005. Faking errors to avoid making errors: Very weakly supervised learning for error detection in writing. In *Proceedings of RANLP 2005*, pages 506–512, Borovets, Bulgaria.

---

# DanPO – a transcription-based dictionary for Danish speech technology

**Peter Rossen Skadhauge** and **Peter Juel Henrichsen**
CMOL
Department of Computational Linguistics
Copenhagen Business School
Denmark
prs@id.cbs.dk and pjuel@id.cbs.dk

## Abstract

We present a new strategy for the creation of phonetic lexicons. As we argue, lexical resources for speech technology integration should be informed by transcriptions of spontaneous speech. We illustrate our strategy with examples from the dictionary DanPO (Danish Phonetic-Orthographic Dictionary) which is developed at the Center for Computational Modelling of Language (CMOL). For reference corpus we used DanPASS consisting of 57 recordings of task-oriented monologs, transcribed by professional and MA-level phoneticians using the Danish SAMPA phonetic alphabet. From the transcriptions, dictionaries and concordances were compiled, and these resources were merged with the (prescriptive) phonetic renderings of a standard Danish word dictionary of 87,000 lemmata. As an effect of the "transcription informed" strategy, DanPO is expected to significantly improve the success rate of automatic speech recognizers, as well as the naturalness of artificial voices. Furthermore, we devise an experimental strategy in order to evaluate the dictionary and further improve later versions.

## 1  Introduction

In this paper we present a novel approach to data-driven lexicography exploiting transcriptions of spontaneous speech as raw material. Our methods are being developed and tested in connection with our work on the Danish speech technological dictionary DanPO (Skadhauge and Henrichsen, 2005).

Formally speaking, DanPO (Danish Phonetic-Orthographic Dictionary) is an add-on to the general Danish language technological dictionary STO ("Sprogteknologisk Ordbase", "Lexical Database of Danish for Language Technology Applications", cf. (Braasch, 2003)). STO contains about 87,000 lemmata annotated with full inflectional and compound morphology as well as syntactic information (e.g. verb complement frames and semantic features). The STO dictionary was initiated by the Danish Ministry of Research. It was developed by researchers from a number of Danish universities, coordinated by the Center for Language Technology.

As a supplement to the STO dictionary, CMOL (Center for Computational Modelling of Language) is developing a phonetic computational dictionary DanPO. DanPO is distinct from a traditional paper-based phonetic dictionary in several ways:

- DanPO is generative, in the sense that any word or word form (including compounds) recognized in STO can be phonetically transcribed using the sound rules and inflectional information in DanPO.

- DanPO can be rendered as simple text files for easy embedding within speech technological products (e.g. artificial speech or automatic speech recognition).

- Our policy is 'open source', meaning that any party, be it private, institutional or commercial, will be allowed access to DanPO on friendly conditions (for a nominal fee).

- The phonetic transcriptions in DanPO are informed by actual transcriptions of spontaneous speech.

The DanPO project group consisted of two professional (computational) linguists and five student transcribers. It was functioning for about two years. The first release of DanPO is scheduled for October 2005. Several industrial partners are taking part in the development of DanPO as external evaluators.

The formal properties of DanPO are presented in section 2 below: its internal structure and its embedding in STO. In section 3, we motivate the "transcription informed" strategy that we have adopted, while section 4 contains a short status report for project DanPO. Section 5 describes development strategies for later versions of the dictionary. Finally, in section 6, we draw some (preliminary) conclusions.

## 2   Formal properties

The key design choices of DanPO are the following:

- Any word form recognizable or producible by STO must be recognizable or producible with the information in DanPO.

- The internal structure of DanPO must mirror the internal structure of corresponding STO parts as closely as possible.

- The phonetics for the majority of lemmata must be generated from existing resources, thus minimizing the need for phonetic hand-coding.

The main obstacle for obtaining parallelism between orthography and phonology is the mismatch between orthographic and phonological inflectional paradigms. Each lemma in STO is associated with at least one of 675 inflectional paradigms. The majority of these paradigms account for irregular and semi-regular inflection of minor categories of words. A few paradigms account for the inflection of all regular lemmata.

The correspondence between Danish phonetics and orthography is complex and irregular. Several distinctive phonetic features, such as stress, vowel length, and "stød" (a quick glottal contraction) are not fully predictable from orthography. Thus, we expect to have to account for a certain amount of mismatch between the structures of orthographic inflectional morphology and phonetic inflectional morphology.

The paradigm ORP0028 in Fig. 1 accounts for a class of common nouns, exemplified by "dag" (Eng.: "day"). The STO version of the paradigm covers 3485 lemmata:

The two exemplified subparadigms differ with respect to "stød" expressed by exclamation marks [!]. Nouns like "dag" [dz:] which bear "stød" in singular forms, fall into the paradigm of ORP0028.1, whereas nouns like "hest" [hEsd], (Eng.: "horse") which lack "stød", belongs to the paradigm of ORP0028.2.

In total, about 20 subparadigms express similar systematic phonetic differences between forms of the orthographic paradigm of ORP0028.

On the other hand, many of the phonetic subparadigms are similar across categories of orthographic paradigms. That holds for the orthographic paradigms which double final consonants, e.g. ("slot", "slottet", "slotte", "slottene", ...) and ("stop", "stoppet", "stoppe", "stoppene", ...), where the orthographic consonant duplication has no phonetic counterpart.

The phonetic notation of DanPO is derived from The SAMPA computer readable phonetic alphabet (Wells, 1997). The notation of suffixation corresponds to the "search-and-replace" mechanism for PERL (Wall et al., 2000) regular expressions in the following sense: Every suffix consists of a search string and a replacement string. Thus the suffixation can handle phenomena related to vowel length and "stød" of the vowel in the final syllable of the stem.

As an example, the imperative is the only form of the verb "tegne" [tAJn0] (Eng.: "draw") which contains a "stød" on the vowel. The pair of search string and replacement string defines the phonetic properties of the relevant subparadigm of the orthographic paradigm. In this case, the search string contains two subpatterns; the first pattern being a stem whose last vowel is a diphthong, the second being an optional syllable-final consonant. The replacement string returns the strings matched by the first and second subpattern with a "stød" [!] in between.

Search string:

```
(.+[\#V][\#S])([\#C]?)0
```

Replacement string:

```
\1!\2
```

#V is the set of vowels, #S is the set of sibilants, and finally #C is the set of consonants.

The subpatterns (in parentheses) match [tAJ] and [n] respectively, which are reproduced by the "duplication" strings [\1] and [\2]. This

Figure 1: Sample paradigms of STO and DanPO

**A STO paradigm (**ORP0028**)**

```
ORP0028:dag:NOUN:COMMON:SINGULAR:INDEFINITE:NOMINATIVE::
ORP0028:dag:NOUN:COMMON:PLURAL  :INDEFINITE:GENITIVE  ::es
ORP0028:dag:NOUN:COMMON:SINGULAR:DEFINITE  :GENITIVE  ::ens
ORP0028:dag:NOUN:COMMON:PLURAL  :INDEFINITE:NOMINATIVE::e
ORP0028:dag:NOUN:COMMON:PLURAL  :DEFINITE  :NOMINATIVE::ene
ORP0028:dag:NOUN:COMMON:PLURAL  :DEFINITE  :GENITIVE  ::enes
ORP0028:dag:NOUN:COMMON:SINGULAR:DEFINITE  :NOMINATIVE::en
ORP0028:dag:NOUN:COMMON:SINGULAR:INDEFINITE:GENITIVE  ::s
```

**Corresponding DanPO sub-paradigms**

ORP0028.1 **(899 lemmata)**

```
NOUN:COMMON:PLURAL  :INDEFINITE:GENITIVE  ::[0s]
NOUN:COMMON:SINGULAR:DEFINITE  :GENITIVE  ::[!0ns]
NOUN:COMMON:SINGULAR:INDEFINITE:GENITIVE  ::[!s]
NOUN:COMMON:PLURAL  :DEFINITE  :NOMINATIVE::[0n0]
NOUN:COMMON:PLURAL  :INDEFINITE:NOMINATIVE::[0]
NOUN:COMMON:SINGULAR:DEFINITE  :NOMINATIVE::[!0n]
NOUN:COMMON:PLURAL  :DEFINITE  :GENITIVE  ::[0n0s]
NOUN:COMMON:SINGULAR:INDEFINITE:NOMINATIVE::[!]
```

ORP0028.2 **(331 lemmata)**

```
NOUN:COMMON:PLURAL  :INDEFINITE:GENITIVE  ::[0s]
NOUN:COMMON:SINGULAR:DEFINITE  :GENITIVE  ::[0ns]
NOUN:COMMON:SINGULAR:INDEFINITE:GENITIVE  ::[s]
NOUN:COMMON:PLURAL  :DEFINITE  :NOMINATIVE::[0n0]
NOUN:COMMON:PLURAL  :INDEFINITE:NOMINATIVE::[0]
NOUN:COMMON:SINGULAR:DEFINITE  :NOMINATIVE::[0n]
NOUN:COMMON:PLURAL  :DEFINITE  :GENITIVE  ::[0n0s]
NOUN:COMMON:SINGULAR:INDEFINITE:NOMINATIVE::[]
```

generates the imperative form [tAJ!n] from the stem.

DanPO also enlists lemma-specific compound-formation properties ("glue elements"), such that the dictionary accounts for productive compound morphology.

## 3 Compliance with the spoken language idiom

Since DanPO is aimed at speech technology, including speech recognition, we needed to ensure the descriptiveness of the dictionary. Therefore we engaged in a cooperation with the DanPASS project (Grønnum, 2005) lead by Dr. Nina Grønnum (Dept. of Linguistics, University of Copenhagen).

The main goal of the DanPASS project (Danish Phonetically Annotated Spontaneous Speech) has been the establishment of Korpus Spontan-Tale (Corpus Spontaneous-Speech) consisting of 57 short monologues (19 speakers performing 3 distinct tasks including a map-guidance task). Each recording was made in the echo free room of Eksperimental-Fonetisk Laboratorum (Experimental Phonetic Lab), and the recordings are of a very high acoustic quality. All recordings were transcribed in a SAMPA-compatible sound alphabet by two phoneticians in parallel. A third phonetician was consulted for each discrepancy found in the two parallel transcription corpora. Spontan-Tale contains about 25,000 tokens annotated with prosodic markup.

Based on the SAMPA-transcription an orthographic-phonetic concordance is derived. In Fig. 3 three selected concordance entries are shown covering some of the types appearing in Fig. 2.

Orthographic-phonetic combinations with few occurrences (C<4) are annotated with transcription references for easy proof reading.

Highly frequent words usually exhibit multiple pronunciation forms and therefore have many alternative entries. An example is the multi-purpose pronoun "der" (there/that) which occurs in 15 phonetic variants, some much more frequent than others. Depending on the grammatical function, "der" is typically pronounced as either (A) or (B), cf. Fig. 3.

(A) is preferred for the expletive use of "der" while (B) is typically used as a locative. When

Figure 3: Sample from the orthographic-phonetic concordance

**overgardin**

| 1 | 'ÅwágAdi:!n | [m_013_h,t=208] |

**hedder**

| 3 | heD!á | [m_013_k,t=266] |
| | | [m_014_k,t=101] |
| | | [m_033_h,t=11] |
| 2 | 'heDá | [m_014_k,t=251] |
| | | [m_016_h,t=187] |
| 5 | 'heD!á | |
| 46 | heDá | |

**der**

| 1 | deR | [m_019_h,t=145] |
| 49 | 'deR! | |
| 1 | de:!R | [m_021_k,t=22] |
| 4 | dV | |
| 35 | 'dA | |
| 10 | 'da | |
| 2 | dER! | [m_033_h,t=117] |
| | | [m_033_h,t=137] |
| 1 | 'dæR | [m_031_g,t=115] |
| 4 | deR! | |
| 1 | 'de:!R | [m_021_k,t=150] |
| 1 | d@ | [m_007_g,t=41] |
| 1 | dæR | [m_031_g,t=48] |
| 223 | dA | |
| 1 | dER | [m_033_h,t=150] |
| 116 | da | |

---

*Legend*

Each record is indexed by the orthographic form (e.g. "hedder"). Phonetic entries have three fields:

1. no. of occurrences,

2. phonetic representation,

3. transcription references [*filename,time-ref*] (optional)

---

Figure 4: Pronoun "der": prototypical phonetic forms

| mode | vowel | accent | stød | prototype |
|------|-------|--------|------|-----------|
| (A) | [A]*or* [a] | no | no | [dA] |
| (B) | [e] | main | yes | ['deR!] |

---

Figure 2: Sample from corpus Spontan-Tale (monologue *m_013_h*)

```
SAMPA: sV   'adAed       'Åwá gA di:!n  va    'sV dn, nå:D sV   'heD!á
EnOrt: så   ,er der  et ,overgardin  + hvad s,ådan  noget så   h,edder =
Gloss: then is   there an upper curtain    what such     stuff  then is-called
Trans:  "then there is an upper curtain or whatever it's called"
```

> *Legend*
>
> SAMPA = transcription using Speech Assessment Methods Phonetic Alphabet
> EnOrt  = Orthographic rendering enriched with prosodic information (eg. [+] =
>            pause, [=] = hesitation with phonation, ['] = stress)
> Gloss  = English lexical equivalents
> Trans  = English translation
> Observe that segmentations in SAMPA and EnORT are sometimes in conflict.

such grammatically dependent variation can be detected, multiple phonetic forms are allowed in DanPO.

In general, more frequent phonetic variants are preferred over less frequent, everything else being equal. As explained, in cases where the variation is correlated with the grammatical context, two (or more) alternative phonetic forms are introduced in DanPO and annotated with the according selectional restrictions.

Observe that despite the prototypicality of forms (A) and (B), many other pronunciations of "der" are actually encountered (cf. Fig. 2). Much care must be taken in the selection of prototypical pronunciations for introduction in DanPO. The process of validating preliminary linguistic hypotheses by consulting the transcription files is indeed a labor-intensive one.

Nevertheless, as we argue, there are good reasons to go descriptive. Relying on traditional prescriptive sources (such as dictionaries or linguists' intuitions) is highly risky. The authors of this paper have often found our personal judgments — even of our own pronunciation — to be misleading. Here we present but a single example. According to one of the major pronunciation dictionaries of Danish (Hansen, 1990), expletive "der" (cf. Fig. 3) is pronounced [dæR], [dA], or [dV] (in that order). Likewise, the locative "der" is ['dæ:!R], ['de:!R] or ['dæR!] (in that order). These pronunciations come close to our own when e.g. presenting "der" to a foreigner.

As the reader may wish to verify (or rather falsify) in Fig. 3, this provides a very poor description of "der" as occuring in actual speech. Only one of the six dictionary forms has any sig-

nificance in the transcriptions, viz. [dA], while the remaining five forms cover just 6 out of 450 occurrences, or 1.3three dictionary forms accounting for only one single occurrence. As it seems, Danes do not speak by the book.

## 4   Status and prospects

At the time of writing, the DanPO dictionary contains 87,104 lemmata and morphological information capable of generating 766,474 inflected forms (plus an infinite number of compounds), each of which associated with a phonetic form. Of these, about 1000 are derived using transcription informed phonetics (TIP), as exemplified in section 3 above (lexeme "der"). The remaining phonetic forms are generated using standard phonological rules and methods including traditional hand-coding.

One thousand TIP based phonetic forms may not seem a lot. However, recall that spoken language — especially as occurring in informal situations — recycles the same word types to a much larger extent than is typical for the written genres. Compare e.g. the frequency distribution of two Danish corpora covering spoken language (informal conversations) and written language (newspaper articles), respectively. Each corpus consists of 1,335,000 word tokens (Henrichsen, 2002).

Observe that just 30 word types are needed to cover about half of the transcription corpus while almost 200 types are needed f a similar coverage of the newspaper texts. We have reasons to believe that other languages — maybe all? — show similar distributional patterns (e.g. (Allwood and Henrichsen, 2005), (Leach et al., 2001)).

---

Figure 5: Word type distribution for spoken and written language

| Rank | Spoken lng.cov. | | Written lng.cov. | |
|---|---|---|---|---|
| | Count | Freq. | Count | Freq. |
| 1–10 | 380,599 | 28.5% | 277,161 | 20.8% |
| 1–20 | 549,283 | 41.1% | 412,762 | 30.9% |
| 1–30 | 671,223 | 50.3% | 473,882 | 35.5% |
| 1–100 | 940,834 | 70.5% | 618,383 | 46.3% |
| 1–200 | 1,046,036 | 78.4% | 696,591 | 52.2% |
| 1–1000 | 1,197,670 | 89.7% | 876,435 | 65.6% |

A lexicon containing 1000 TIP entries is thus expected to provide TIP based coverage of about 90% of the words occuring in typical ordinary speech.

## 5 Evaluation, experiments and further development

The heterogeneous status of the dictionary makes it relevant to compare different versions of lemmata and full forms in a systematic way. This would make it possible to judge the quality of the sources in order to choose the direction which development of phonetic dictionaries should take.

As an example, one particularly intriguing lemma (or set of lemmata) is the homograph "der", which has the following phonetic representations in DanPO:

**Normative annotation**  [d2A]

**DanPASS transcriptions**

| Freq | SAMPA | DanPO |
|---|---|---|
| 45 | 'deR? | [d2eR!] |
| 33 | 'dA | [d2A] |
| 234 | dA | [dA] |
| 100 | da | [da] |

**"Editor's choice"**  [d2A]

The lemma occurs very differently whether pronounced in stressed or unstressed versions. The manual editor suggests the normative choice. We plan on conducting systematic naturalness judgements of phrases containing lemmata with alternative phonetics.

Furthermore, we suggest that segments, frequency (F0) contours, and segmental durations be refined by use of the Segment Editor developed by Peter Rossen Skadhauge. The Segment Editor, whose main functionality is depicted in Fig. 6, facilitates editing of the segmental quality, duration and frequency for every segment in an utterance. Segments may be inserted, changed, or deleted at random places in the utterance. Since frequency (F0) is shown as horizontal sliders, the graphical picture of all the frequency sliders may be seen as an intonation curve for the utterance, which may be altered by adjusting the sliders individually.

The example shows the state of the editor just having loaded a raw phonetic sequence corresponding to the text "Der er ikke noget at gøre ved det".

The Segment Editor may be used to facilitate improvement of utterance synthesis in the following ways:

- Experts' hand-tuning of parameters

- Informants' hand-tuning of parameters by negotiation.

We are going to set up experiments where informants negotiate parameter values for determination of optimal rendering of synthesis. These parameters may, in turn, be used as a basis of machine-learning intonation patterns for spoken language.

## 6 Concluding remarks

The first version of DanPO is finished. Judgments of DanPO's potential for speech technological improvements are preliminary, but have shown the DanPO lexicon to significantly improve the naturalness of the Danish Synthetic Voice (Henrichsen, 2004). In a pilot experiments, we shall present a panel of native speakers of Danish with samples of synthetic speech in two variants, with and without TIP based versions of DanPO, keeping everything else unchanged, such as lexical content, fundamental frequency contour, timing, and voice quality.

## References

Jens Allwood and Peter Juel Henrichsen. 2005. Swedish and Danish, spoken and written language - a statistical comparison. *International Journal of Corpus Linguistics*, 10(3):367–399.

Anna Braasch. 2003. Sto: A lexical database of Danish for language technology applications. *elsnews*, 12(3), Autumn.

Nina Grønnum. 2005. Danish phonetically annotated spontaneous speech. http://www.cphling.dk/~ng/danpass.html.

Figure 6: The Segment Editor

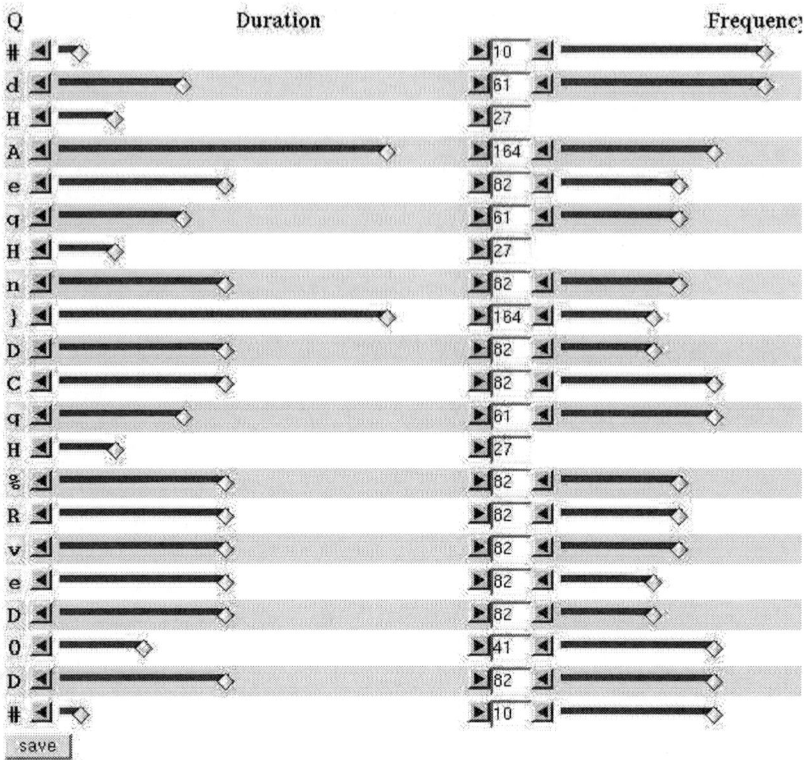


Peter Molbæk Hansen. 1990. *Dansk Udtale.* Gyldendal, Nordisk Forlag.

Peter Juel Henrichsen. 2002. Some frequency based differences between spoken and written Danish. In *Gothenburg Papers in Theoretical Linguistics*, volume 88.

Peter Juel Henrichsen. 2004. The twisted tongue. tools for teaching Danish pronunciation using a synthetic voice. In Peter Juel Henrichsen, editor, *Copenhagen Studies in Language,* volume 30, pages 95–111. Copenhagen Business School Press.

Geoffrey Leach, Paul Rayson, and Andrew Wilson. 2001. *Word Frequencies in Written and Spoken English.* Longman.

Peter Rossen Skadhauge and Peter Juel Henrichsen. 2005. Danish phonetic-orthographic lexicon. http://www.id.cbs.dk/~prs/danpo.

Larry Wall, Tom Christiansen, and Jon Orwant. 2000. *Programming Perl.* O'Reilly, 3rd edition, July.

J. C. Wells. 1997. Sampa computer readable phonetic alphabet. In D. Gibbon, R. Moore, and R. Winski, editors, *Handbook of Standards and Resources for Spoken Language Systems.* Mouton de Gruyter, Berlin and New York. Part IV, section B.

# Functionality in grammar design


**Anders Søgaard**
Center for Language Technology
University of Copenhagen
Njalsgade 80
DK-2300 Copenhagen, Denmark
anders@cst.dk

**Petter Haugereid**
Dept. of Lang. and Comm. Studies
Norwegian University of Science
and Technology, Dragvoll
NO-7491 Trondheim, Norway
petterha@hf.ntnu.no



## Abstract

The implementation of the Scandinavian Grammar Matrix gave rise to a number of methodological and theoretical discussions about the desiderata for a formal theory of natural language grammar. In this paper, a strong hypothesis of *the functionality of grammar* is presented. Functionality is imposed on constraint-based grammars, on their lexicons and on the grammars themselves. It is demonstrated how this radically reduces complexity, i.e. the recognition problem is in ptime. Certain aspects of the hypothesis are motivated by methodological and psycholinguistic considerations too. The implementation employs underspecification techniques, type inference and some amount of constructional specification.


## 1   Credits

Our joint work was supported by the Scandinavian Network of Grammar Engineering and Machine Translation (NorFa) and conducted at various institutions: Bremen Universität, Copenhagen Business School, Göteborg Universitet, and the Norwegian University of Science and Technology in Trondheim. In the weeks and months spend at these institutions, we benefited from discussions with a number of people, incl. Lars Ahrenberg, Felix Bildhauer, Dan Flickinger, Lars Hellan, Per Anker Jensen and Stefan Müller.

## 2   Introduction

We begin with a text-book definition of a mathematical function:

*In mathematics, a function is a relation, such that each element of a set is associated with a unique element of another (possibly the same) set.*

It is in this sense we will speak of functionality. The next preliminary step is to bring to mind how natural language grammar is often defined as "a finite set of computable functions on signs". If functionality is understood mathematically, many interesting consequences can be derived from this definition. In fact, it turns out that this is a very strong hypothesis about the nature of natural language grammars; a hypothesis few (if any) grammatical frameworks pursue in full.

In this paper, we are interested in two different applications of functionality. Functionality is implemented at two levels of natural language grammar, so to speak; the lexicon and the grammar itself. In other words, the lexicon is designed such that a unique phonological string is associated with a unique lexical entry. Similarly, the grammar only produces one, possibly underspecified, analysis per unique string.

The structure of the paper is simple. In the next section, the computational and methodological advantages of functionality are demonstrated. It is shown that the recognition problem of fully functional (and off-line parsable) constraint-based grammars is in ptime, compared to the NP completeness results of Berwick (1982) and Trautwein (1994) for off-line parsable, but non-functional constraint-based grammars without lexical rules. The reader may suspect that by imposing this functionality constraint on the lexicon, complexity is merely moved from the lexicon into the rules. This can be avoided in constraint-based grammar formalisms with typed feature structures. The relevant mechanisms are illustrated by a discussion of the syntax of the prenominal field in Mainland Scandinavian. The discussion focuses on distribution, modification and quantification. The next section presents an approach to argument structure under this kind of functionality. Since the lexicon (in the worst case) only contains sound-meaning pairs and closed class items, argument structures are inferred in syntactic composition. Some possible objections to functionality are mentioned that all relates to ambiguity, and a novel argument that (some) natural languages are non-context-free is given. The last section briefly discusses the role of syntax as perceived here in a system of natural language understanding. All data is from the Scandinavian Grammar Matrix (Søgaard and Haugereid, 2005); see www.cst.dk/anders/matrix/main.html.

## 3 Complexity of constraint-based grammars

Of the set of constraint-based grammar formalisms (patr, lfg, ...), our interest lies with those formalisms which employ typed feature structures, e.g. lkb-hpsg (Copestake, 2001) and other computational variants of hpsg. It is a common feature of constraint-based formalisms that they combine a generative-enumerative backbone with a model-theoretic perspective on well-formedness of structures described in terms of some feature logic. The model-theoretic perspective tells us that the set of well-formed strings of a grammar with principles $\pi$ is the strings for which the generative-enumerative backbone generates analyses that satisfy $\pi$. The most common backbone is a context-free grammar. Consequently, a *typed* constraint-based grammar is a tuple $\mathcal{T} = \langle\langle\{\tau_1, \ldots, \tau_n\}, \sqsubseteq\rangle, \pi, \mathcal{C}\rangle$, where $\langle\{\tau_1, \ldots, \tau_n\}, \sqsubseteq\rangle$ is a partial order on a set of typed feature structures $\{\tau_1, \ldots, \tau_n\}$.

**Definition 3.1.** A context-free grammar is a tuple $\mathcal{C} = \langle C, s, W, R, L\rangle$ where $C$ is a finite set of categories (feature structures), $s \in C$ is the distinguished start symbol, $W$ is a finite set of words, $R \subseteq C \times C^*$ is a set of grammar rules, and $L \subseteq C \times W$ is a lexicon.

Consider only grammars for which $\epsilon \notin L(\mathcal{G})$, in which all rules are unary or binary, and in which no cyclic unary extensions are possible. This is an *off-line parsability* constraint. Call an off-line parsable context-free grammar

a cfg$^-$. In constraint-based formalisms, off-line parsability ensures the decidability of recognition, e.g. Johnson (1988). Call a cfg$^-$ with a functional lexicon a cfg$^-_{lx}$.

**Definition 3.2.** A cfg$^-_{lx}$ is a tuple $\mathcal{C} = \langle C, s, W, R, lx\rangle$ where $C$ is a finite set of categories (feature structures), $s \in C$ is the distinguished start symbol, $W$ is a finite set of words (and $\epsilon \notin W$), $R$ is a set of binary grammar rules, and $lx : W \longrightarrow C$ is a lexicon. $\mathcal{C}$ is off-line parsable.

cfg$^-_f$ is the subset of cfg$^-_{lx}$ where each string in the language receives exactly one parse, i.e. there is a function $f : \sigma \longrightarrow \tau_s$ for every grammatical string $\sigma$ s.t. $\tau_s \sqsupseteq s$.

Three classes of grammars are now defined. The classes have different properties. For instance, a non-functional lexicon means multiple input for the combinatory parsing procedure, since the lexical resolution results in a disjunction of possible inputs. Consequently, if $l$ is the number of lexemes associated with a string of $n$ length in the language of cfg$^-$ and cfg$^-_{lx}$, then if the complexity of cfg$^-_{lx}$ is $c$, the complexity of cfg$^-$ is $(l - n)c$.

Trautwein (1994) shows that a restricted version of constraint-based hpsg, roughly the off-line parsable fragment corresponding to cfg$^-$ in lkb-hpsg with no lexical rules, is NP complete. The standard NP hardness proof for constraint-based formalisms relies on a translation of the 3sat problem into the feature logic. The correspondence depends on assignments, i.e. $g : \phi \longrightarrow \perp/\top$ translates into $L \subseteq C \times W$, truth preservation, i.e. reentrancies, and preservation of satisfiability. In other words, "the ability to have multiple derivation trees and lexical categorizations for one and the same terminal item plays a crucial role in the reduction proof" (Berwick, 1982). The standard proof does not apply to a cfg$^-_f$ constraint-based grammar. It is thus natural to ask if there is a tractable (ptime) parse algorithm for constraint-based grammars with restricted backbones, i.e. cfg$^-_f$?

Since weak subsumption of typed feature structures (without disjunction or negation) is polynomial (Dörre, 1991), the recognition problem of cfg$^-_f$ constraint-based grammars with simple typed feature logic, say $\mathcal{T}_f$, is also in ptime.

**Theorem 3.3.** *The recognition problem of $\mathcal{T}_f$ is in* ptime.

*Proof.* This follows immediately from the polynomial nature of satisfiability in standard feature logic where unification is defined wrt. weak subsumption. □

$\mathcal{T}_f$ provides a tractable, but very restrictive grammar formalism. Since it is a trivial task to write a tractable grammar formalism, the next sections are devoted to demonstrating the *adequacy* of $\mathcal{T}_f$. First, however, let us briefly address the psychological plausibility of a strong functionality hypothesis.

Functionality has vast consequences for the lexicon. For instance, any open-class lexeme must be underspecified with respect to syntactic category, if there is a remote possibility that at some point it is used in the clothings of two different syntactic categories. Since this is very likely for most open-class items, the functional lexicon generally underspecifies open-class items for syntactic categories. The intuition is that the closed-class items coerce the open-class items into nouns, verbs and adjuncts in syntactic composition.

Functionality is thus falsifiable and is open to psycholinguistic evidence that the lexicon includes category information at the grammatical level, i.e. that the verbal and nominal associations cannot be reduced to the ontology of the referents. A recent article by Collina et al. (2001) reviews the literature on the lexical organizations of (what functions as) nouns and verbs.

It is often remarked in the literature that agrammatic patients experience greater difficulties in the production of verbs that in the production of nouns. Syntactic and semantic explanations of this category specific deficit have been proposed. Some influential studies have reported that dyslexics showed *no* category dissociation when presented with nouns and verbs of matched imageability and frequency. Such a claim supports our view of the lexicon. The dissociation comes from ontological concerns and language use. Similar studies have proposed that patients' performance reflects an object-action distinction. This again supports our view of the lexicon. Collina et al. (2001) show that there is a relational noun deficit too, i.e. argument structure or relationality is important for the performance of agram-

matic patients. If the deficit is in fact due to argument structure or (ontological) relationality seems an unsettled issue. See Borer (2005) for more linguistic and philosophical arguments for a functional lexicon.

## 4   Linearized modification and quantification

The prenominal field in Mainland Scandinavian comes in the following set of configurations:

(1)  (a)  Quantifier$^?$ ≪ Demonstrative$^?$ ≪ Possessive$^?$ ≪ Numeral$^?$ ≪ (Adjective$^*$) ≪ Noun$^?$

 (b)  alle disse mine fem røde bamser ('all these my five red teddybears')

The point is that all constituents are optional, but the order is fixed. The configuration of the prenominal field can be analyzed in two ways, roughly. The first analysis is a right branching analysis, while the other bundles the prenominal elements one way or another; cf. Neville (2003). A conventional cfg posits 10 rules to account for (1). Since the category labels in the cfg backbone of an hpsg are feature structures, complexity moves from the rules into the lexical entries. Conventionally, the hpsg Specifier Head Schema and Modifier Head Schema are used to collapse the 10 rules into two, e.g.:

$$(2)\quad \mathrm{X}''\left[\mathrm{spr}\,\langle\rangle\right]\longrightarrow \boxed{1}\mathrm{Y}''\left[\mathrm{spec}\,\boxed{2}\right]+\boxed{2}\mathrm{X}'\left[\mathrm{spr}\,\langle\boxed{1}\rangle\right]$$

The schema subsumes both the right branching and the bundling approach. Interestingly, they seem to be equally complex, roughly. The complexity does not come from the number of rules now, but from the number of lexical entries. This is easily illustrated. If no specifier phrase is assumed, only one constituent can function as the specifier of the noun phrase, but since – according to (1) – the specifier can be of any category licensed in the prenominal field, a demonstrative pronoun, for instance, must be listed as both a specifier and a non-specifier. On this right branching analysis, the total number of lexical entries for our five word fragment in (1b) is 11. On the bundling analysis, the number is 9.

If type inference is exploited, it is possible to clean up this redundancy. In addition, the approach can be extended to adjuncts. Crucially, the type hierarchy below is employed:

(3) 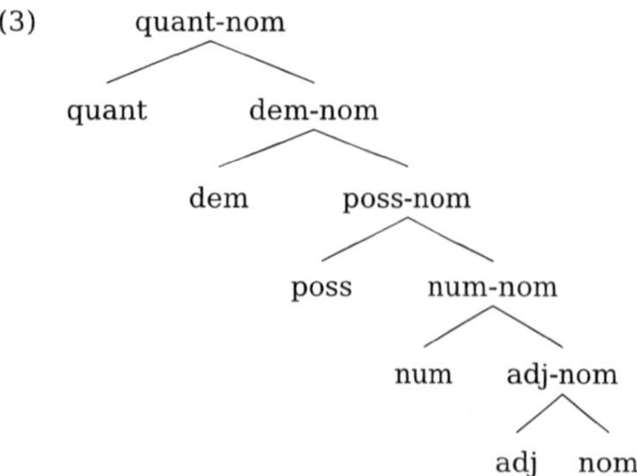

Introduce now some feature $\beta$ s.t. a prenominal type $\alpha_i$ constrains the type it combines with (to the right) to be of type $\beta(\alpha_i) = \alpha_j$. The appropriate constraints are easily implemented relative to the type hierarchy, e.g. $\delta(\text{quant}) =$ dem-nom, $\delta(\text{dem}) =$ poss-nom, etc. The exceptions to this systematic behavior are easily added, e.g. the constraints imposed by articles and definite inflections. Søgaard and Haugereid (2004; 2005) describe how this account of the prenominal field fits into a general account of the distributional syntax of Mainland Scandinavian noun phrases.

Since there is no way in (1) to know which elements introduce quantification and determination, our setup calls for a constructional account of such phenomena. Our solution is to basically treat quantification and determination as agreement phenomena. Consider, for illustration, the givenness hierarchy of the Scandinavian Grammar Matrix: (The type names and their model-theoretic interpretation are introduced in Borthen and Haugereid (to appear).)

(4) 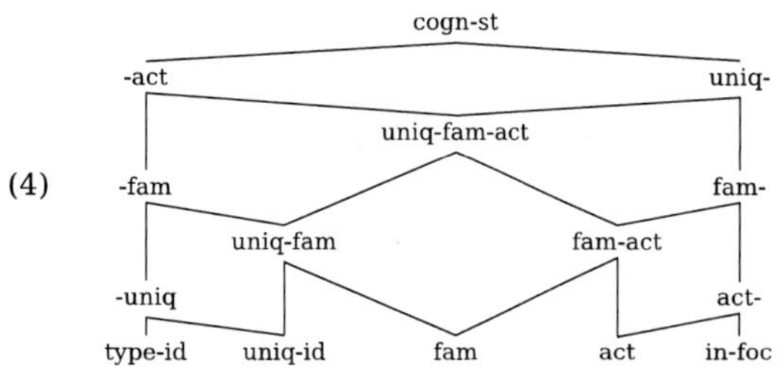

The intuition here is that while the givenness value of a nominal percolates up the noun phrase tree, it is forced down this hierarchy in search of the greatest lower bound of all the prenominal constituents' givenness values. At the constructional level, i.e. the mother node of the noun phrase, an actual givenness predication is then inserted. Similarly for quantification.

The constructional approach is not just an artefact of our design, motivated only by efficiency, but results in a linguistically more adequate treatment of quantification and determination, we claim. Our arguments for a constructional account of quantification relate to floating quantifiers, measure phrases (Søgaard and Haugereid, 2004), number agreement and anaphora resolution (Søgaard, to appear). Our arguments for a similar account of determination relate to the behavior of light pronouns and bare singulars (Borthen and Haugereid, to appear), and declension, vocatives and specification in logical form (Søgaard and Haugereid, 2004; Søgaard and Haugereid, 2005).

The conceptualization of grammar that is proposed here is quite simple: A grammar determines word order (by partial orders), agreement (by unification) and linking. Linking is discussed in the next section and is more configurational than the "linearized" structure of the prenominal field. The linearized structure is found in Mainland Scandinavian with modification more generally. Consider also the distribution of adverbs, e.g. in the Danish *Nachfeld* (Nimb, 2005):

(5)   Manner or free adverbs* ≪ Predicative adverbs* ≪ Bound adverbs* ≪ Free adverbs*

## 5   Underspecification of argument structure

Åfarli (2005) claims that verbs in a language like Norwegian can have five different argument frames, an intransitive, a transitive, a ditransitive, a resultative and a ditransitive-resultative frame. These frames are illustrated in (6-10). Åfarli also points out that some verbs ('danse' *dance*) are found with all these frames.

(6)   *Marit  grubler.*
Marit  ponders
'Marit ponders.'

(7)   *Marit  kasta  steinen.*
Marit  threw  stone.def
'Marit threw the stone.'

(8)   *Marit  innvilga  oss  lånet.*
Marit  granted  us  loan.def
'Marit granted us the loan.'

(9)   *Marit  la  arket  på  bordet.*
Marit  put  sheet.def  on  table.def
'Marit put the sheet on the table.'

---

Søgaard & Haugereid: *Functionality in grammar design*

(10) *De      puster    oss   dårlig   ånde    i*
     they   breathe   us    bad      breath   in
     *ansiktet.*
     face.def

     'They breathe us bad breath into our face.'

Haugereid (2004) suggests to encode linking information in the syntax rather than in the lexicon, using a neo-Davidsonian semantics and letting valence rules introduce relations which identify the relation between the main event and the index of the argument. Consequently, a arg1-rule, an arg2-rule, etc., and a set of single-valued features (arg1, arg2, etc.) were introduced. It is described below how this leads to a satisfactory account of Åfarli's valence frames. Ergatives and null-verbs are also treated as frames. For expository reasons, resultative frames are omitted here.

It is assumed that phrases which mark the outer boundary of a clause (like the head-filler phrase) constrain the verb projection to have *minus* link types as values of the valence features. In (11) it is shown how the arg1 feature of the head daughter has a *arg1–* value, the arg2 feature has a *arg2–* value and the arg3 feature has a arg3– value.

(11)

$$
\begin{bmatrix}
\text{\textit{head-filler-phrase}} \\
\text{synsem | non-local | slash } \langle\,!\,!\,\rangle \\
\text{h-dtr | ss}
\begin{bmatrix}
\text{loc | cat | val}
\begin{bmatrix}
\text{arg1 | link } \textit{arg1–} \\
\text{arg2 | link } \textit{arg2–} \\
\text{arg3 | link } \textit{arg3–}
\end{bmatrix} \\
\text{non-local | slash } \langle\,!\,\boxed{1}\,!\,\rangle
\end{bmatrix} \\
\text{non-head-dtr | synsem | local } \boxed{1}
\end{bmatrix}
$$

When a valence rule applies, it changes the *minus* link type in the mother to a *plus* link type in the head daughter as shown in Figure 1. For example, the arg1-rule changes the *arg1–* type in the mother node to *arg1+* in the head daughter.

The tree in Figure 1 shows how information about which valence rules have applied, ends up in the verb word. The verb word will now unify the linking types (13). In the case of *Avisen leser Marit* ('The newspaper Marit reads'), the types *arg1+*, *arg2+* and *arg3–* are unified. The type hierarchy of linking types in (12) then ensures that we get a transitive frame *arg12*.

(12)

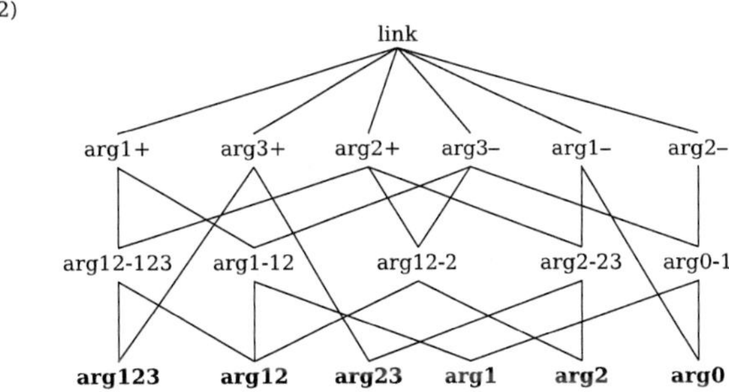


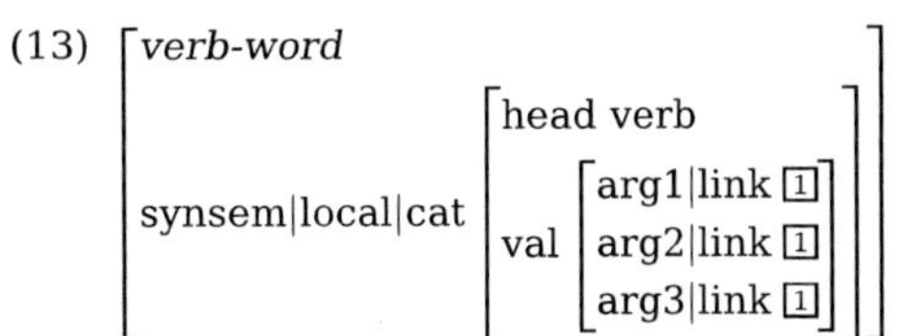


(13)

$$
\begin{bmatrix}
\text{\textit{verb-word}} \\
\text{synsem|local|cat}
\begin{bmatrix}
\text{head verb} \\
\text{val}
\begin{bmatrix}
\text{arg1|link } \boxed{1} \\
\text{arg2|link } \boxed{1} \\
\text{arg3|link } \boxed{1}
\end{bmatrix}
\end{bmatrix}
\end{bmatrix}
$$

Open class lexemes can be underspecified, e.g. *smile* in (14). This makes it possible for the same lexical entry to enter all kinds of argument frames, and it can be the input of a verb word inflectional rule as well as a noun word inflectional rule. The head value *open-class* is compatible with *adjective, noun* and *verb*.[1]

(14)

$$
\begin{bmatrix}
\text{\textit{open-class-lxm}} \\
\text{phon}\langle\text{"smile"}\rangle \\
\text{ss | loc}
\begin{bmatrix}
\text{cat | head } \quad \textit{open-class} \\
\text{cont | rels } \langle\,!\,[\text{pred "smile-rel"}]\,!\,\rangle
\end{bmatrix}
\end{bmatrix}
$$

If one on the other hand wants to stipulate that a verb like *burn* can be both agentive-transitive and ergative, one can do that by giving it an *intermediate* link type like *arg12-2* in (12). That will make the lexical entry compatible with the *arg12* frame, which is the active version of the transitive verb, and the *arg2* frame, which is the ergative frame.

## 5.1 Ambiguities

The obvious question if one wants to maintain a functional grammar, is how to represent natural ambiguities? Our answer is equally obvious: underspecification. The technicalities are not always straight-forward, however. This is the main concern of a grammar writer, as we see it, to construct adequate type hierarchies. The hierarchies are supposed to reflect all sorts of

---

[1] Selection of a direct object of a certain case, for instance, is still possible, since unary relations subsume binary and ternary ones. Consequently, the type hierarchy can be used to enforce, say, a dative direct object, but only in the case there is one.

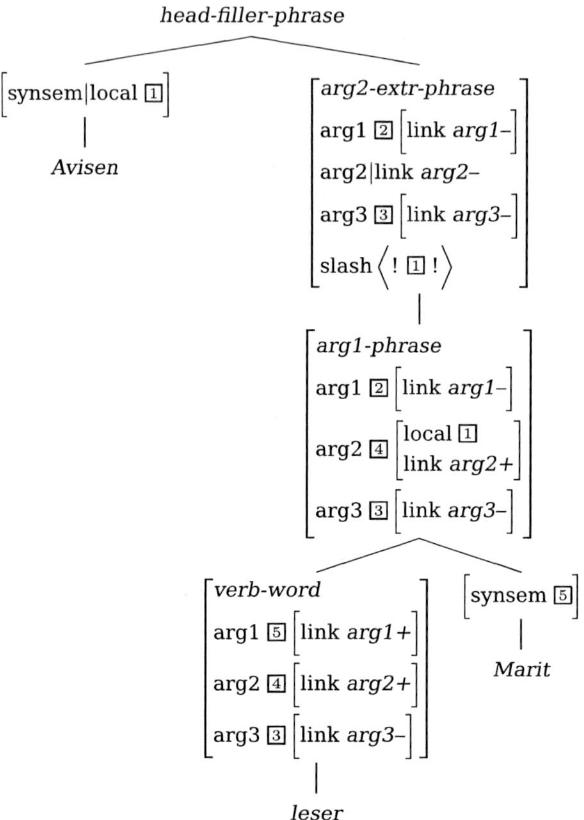

Figure 1: *Avisen leser Marit*, one reading.

generalizations, e.g. in the Scandinavian Grammar Matrix the type hierarchy directly encodes cross-linguistic generalizations. On the other hand, a type hierarchy must also provide an underspecified type whenever it is relevant to obtain functionality in the language-specific component.

The analysis in Figure 2 obviously subsumes the analysis in Figure 1 when the complements are unmarked. Consequently, if no further restrictions are imposed, *Avisen leser Marit* would result in three parses, two specified ones and the underspecified analysis in Figure 2. How is this avoided? (15) presents a rather complex alternation of the encoding of case to account for similar ambiguities with scrambling in Western Germanic, but in Scandinavian it is actually a lot easier, since only pronouns are case-marked. Consequently, the specified rules only apply to pronominal complements. The underspecified rule of course has more specified subtypes, so that the placement of sentence adverbials, for instance, can coerce a particular reading.

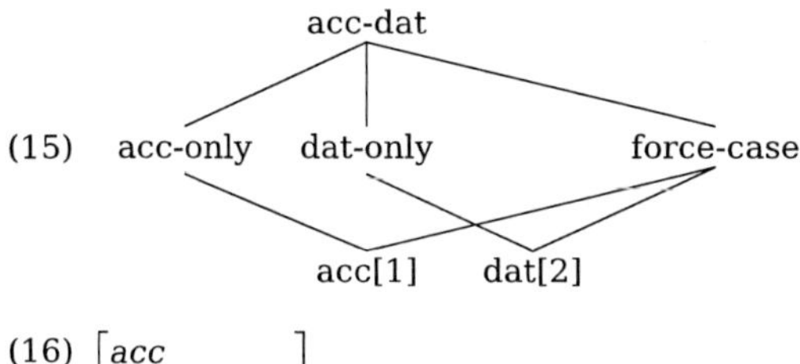

$$(15)$$

In (15), acc[1] is an abbreviation of (16). The case types are lexically declared, e.g. proper names are specified to be case-type = 3, but only in rules that enforce case by force-case case-type values are relevant, i.e. proper names are still compatible with acc-only and dat-only. The specific arg1- and arg2-rules are thus incompatible with proper names and most common nouns, i.e. an underspecified rule combines verbs and their non-case-marked complements. However, the underspecified phrase can be further specified by context (e.g. the position of sentence adverbials in Danish). This is why it is important that non-case-marked nominals are still compatible with acc-only and dat-only. In this way, functionality is maintained, since the case types are incompatible.

A third alternative, and perhaps a more elegant one, is to stipulate one underspeci-fied rule with an underspecified valence-type, which subsumes a hierarchy of different valence types. The valence type can then be further specified by its context. So, for instance, if the rule applies for the first and only time, and the verb is agentive, the valence type will be forced into an arg1-val. This of course complicates the type hierarchies somewhat, but the underspecified rule seems rather elegant.

Similarly, attachment ambiguities must be addressed. This issue is ignored here, though, since the topic is already covered in the literature, e.g. Chrysmann (2004). A more serious problem would be functor-argument ambiguities, but it is not clear to us if such actually exist (at least not if punctuation is said to serve as sentence type classifiers).

## 5.2 Another argument for non-context-freeness

The feature logic of lkb-hpsg of course extends the expressivity of context-free grammars. Some evidence for the non-context-freeness of natural languages, i.e. that there are constructions in natural language that cannot be generated by a context-free grammar, has been presented, for instance by Shieber (1985). If functionality, in our sense, is found to be a realistic requirement for models of natural language grammar, another argument for non-context-freeness can be made. The reason is that certain context-free languages are inherently ambiguous, i.e. there is no context-free grammar that can derive all the strings of one of these languages unambiguously. Consider, for instance, the two languages $L_1 = \{a^n b^n c^m | n, m > 0\}$ and $L_2 = \{a^n, b^m, c^m | n, m > 0\}$. Any grammar that generates $L_1 \cup L_2$ is inherently ambiguous (Sudkamp, 2005). Such a language translates into a natural language where you have (i) case-marking, (ii) SVO and OVS constructions, and (iii) nominative objects. In Mainland Scandinavian, only the two first requirements are satisfied. Constructions with nominative objects are attested in other languages, however, and include the Icelandic copula construction (17) and various constructions in Korean, e.g. with verbs of direct perception (18):

(16) $\begin{bmatrix} acc \\ \text{case-type } 1 \end{bmatrix}$

(17) *Hún   spurði   hvort      sá*
    she    asked    whether    the.nom
    *grunaði            væri               örugglega*
    suspected.nom   was.3sg.subj   surely

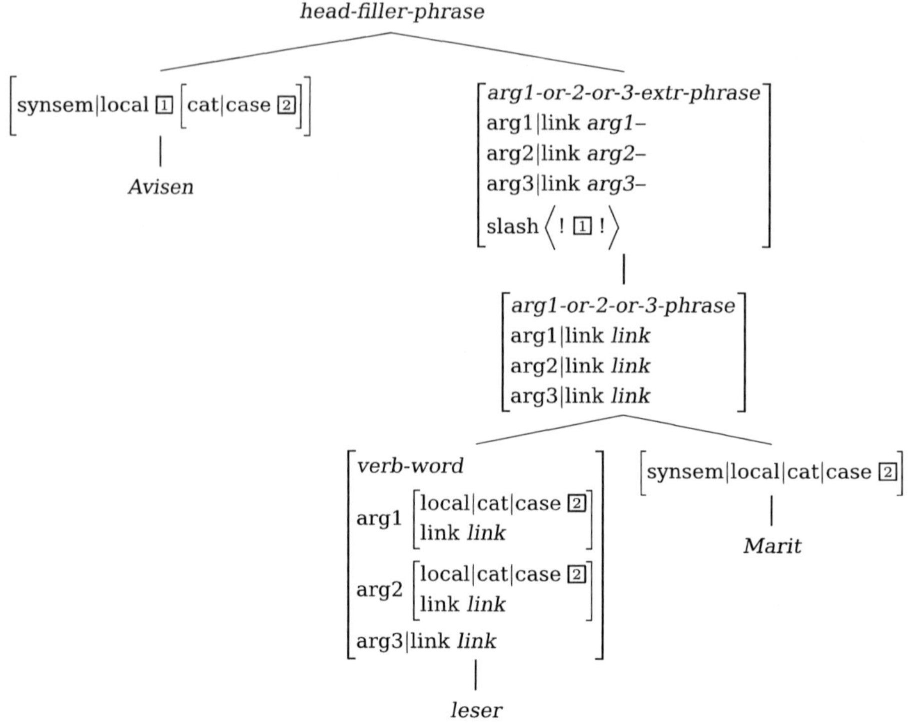

Figure 2: *Avisen leser Marit*, underspecified.

þú.
you.sg.nom

'She asked whether the suspect surely was you.'

(18) *Minwu-ka    umak-i/*ul     tulli-ess-ta*
     Minwu.nom   music.nom/*acc  hear.pst.decl

'Minoo heard the music.'

Icelandic also satisfies (i), obviously, and (ii). In Korean, (ii) is paralleled by the co-existence of SOV and OSV constructions (SOV is canonical). Such SOV-OSV ambiguities are also found in West Germanic subordinate clauses. Consequently, both languages are non-context-free, if natural language grammar is fully functional.

## 6   Parsing, generation and inference

What are the consequences of functionality for a natural language processing system? The amount of underspecification complicates the type declarations considerably, and the information addressed by the syntactic component should thus be as limited as possible. Selectional restrictions, anaphora resolution and ellipsis, for instance, are treated in terms of *in-ference.* On our view, grammatical composition is interfaced with two inference components, a monotonic and a non-monotonic one. The monotonic component performs highly efficient, taxonomic inferences which are to some extent subconscious. The studies of Søgaard (to appear) and Hardt (to appear) suggest that preliminary model generation also takes place at this step of natural language processing and is in fact crucial to the resolution of anaphora and ellipsis. The non-monotonic component is conscious higher-order cognition and performs more complicated pragmatic accommodation.

Is there functionality, is it a relevant notion, in these components? The distinction between the monotonic component and the non-monotonic one is important here. On our view, the non-monotonic component is clearly non-deterministic. This is evidenced by the relative freedom of thought. The monotonic component, however, is believed to be deterministic, and for each logical form it outputs a unique structure or model. In Konrad (2004) and Søgaard (to appear), this is the *locally minimal* model.

Generation can not be made functional in lkb-hpsg. This requires some method for underspecification of phonological strings. Some of this relates to word order, but also, for instance, to homographs. A separation of linear precedence from immediate dominance may allow some underspecification of word order, but novel techniques must be invented to underspecify the phonology of a lexeme. This may be an interesting technical challenge, but it is far from certain that it has any empirical value. It is very unclear, at least to us, if natural language generation is in fact functional and monotonic.

## 7  Computational resources

In the first report of the Scandinavian Grammar Matrix (Søgaard and Haugereid, 2004), a broad coverage noun phrase grammar was presented. It covered various word order phenomena, agreement, double articulation, superlatives, secondary modification, coordination, genitival possession, quantifying nouns, pseudopartitives, partitives, comparatives, compounds, postnominal possession and postgenitival quantification. The report came with a test suite. The functionality ratio of the noun phrase fragment of the Scandinavian Grammar Matrix was relatively low. The test suite consisted of 138 sentences covering the phenomena just listed. Four sentences were assigned two readings, and one sentence was assigned three readings. The rest of the sentences which were grammatical, were assigned only one parse. The functionality ratio is not perfect, however. So we realize it is not an easy task to obtain a fully functional grammar, but we conjecture that this is a realistic goal and a sound objective for grammar engineers.

In addition, Petter Haugereid is currently finishing an implementation of a considerable fragment of Norwegian which employs a high degree of functionality. It also relies on the principles for underspecification of argument frames and syntactic categories presented here. A preliminary version of the grammar is available from Petter's website; see the link from the website of the Scandinavian Grammar Matrix. The topological approach sketched in this paper is extended in a Danish grammar that Anders Søgaard is now working on. Some preliminary work on a new formalism, designed to implement functionality in a more direct way, has also begun.

## 8  Conclusions

This paper discussed various aspects of functionality in grammar design. It was shown how a typed feature structure grammar can, however complicated this task is, implement a strong functionality hypothesis. It was shown that such a grammar is also learnable and, apparently, quite realistic. Some fragments with a functionality ratio close to one has already been written for Mainland Scandinavian as part of the Scandinavian Grammar Matrix project. These fragments were written in lkb-hpsg. It is uncertain if other formalisms implement a strong functionality hypothesis, but it was shown that if the adequate grammar is functional, natural language is not context-free.

## References


Tor Åfarli. 2005. Do verbs have argument structures? Unpublished manuscript, Norwegian University of Science and Technology.

Robert C. Berwick. 1982. Computational complexity and lexical-functional grammar. *American Journal of Computational Linguistics*, 8(3–4):97–109.

Hagit Borer. 2005. *Structuring sense*, volume 1. Oxford University Press, Oxford.

Kaja Borthen and Petter Haugereid. to appear. A grammar component for referential properties of nominals. *Readings in Language and Computation*.

Simona Collina, Paola Marangolo, and Patrizia Tabossi. 2001. The role of argument structure in the production of nouns and verbs. *Neuropsychologia*, 39:1125–1137.

Ann Copestake. 2001. *Implementing typed feature structure grammars*. CSLI, Stanford, California.

Jochen Dörre. 1991. Feature logic with weak subsumption constraints. In *Proceedings of the 29th annual meeting on Association for Computational Linguistics*, Berkeley, California.

Daniel Hardt. to appear. Natural language inference as triggered submodel search. In *The 18th International Florida Artificial Intelligence Research Society Conference*, Clearwater Beach, Florida.

Petter Haugereid. 2004. Linking in constructions. In Stefan Müller, editor, *Proceedings of the 11th International Conference on Head-Driven Phrase Structure Grammar*, Stanford.

Mark Johnson. 1988. *Attribute-value logic and the theory of grammar*. CSLI, Stanford, California.

Karsten Konrad. 2004. *Model generation for natural language interpretation and analysis*. Springer, Berlin.

Anne Neville. 2003. Danish pre-nominals as specifier heads. In *Proceedings of Scandinavian Conference of Linguistics 19*, Tromsø, Norway.

Sanni Nimb. 2005. *Danske adverbier mellem leksikon og syntaks*. Ph.D. thesis, Center for Language Technology, Copenhagen, Denmark.

Stuart Shieber. 1985. Evidence against the context-freeness of natural language. *Linguistics & Philosophy*, 8:333–343.

Anders Søgaard and Petter Haugereid. 2004. The noun phrase in mainland scandinavian. In *The 2nd Meeting of the Scandinavian Network of Grammar Engineering and Machine Translation*, Gothenburg, Sweden.

Anders Søgaard and Petter Haugereid. 2005. A brief documentation of a computational hpsg grammar specifying (most) of the common subset of linguistic types for danish, norwegian and swedish. In Henrik Holmboe, editor, *Nordisk Sprogteknologi 2004*, pages 247–256. Museum Tusculanum, Copenhagen.

Anders Søgaard. to appear. Model generation in a dynamic environment. In Takashi Washio, Akito Sakurai, Satoshi Tojo, and Makoto Yokoo, editors, *New frontiers in artificial intelligence*. Springer, Berlin.

Thomas Sudkamp. 2005. *Languages and machines*. Pearson, Boston, Massachusetts, 3rd edition.

Marten Trautwein. 1994. The complexity of structure sharing in unification-based grammars. In *The 5th Computational Linguistics in the Netherlands*, Entschede, the Netherlands.

# Optimizing the finite-state description of Estonian morphology

**Heli Uibo**

Institute of Computer Science
University of Tartu
J. Liivi 2-339, Tartu 50409
Estonia
`heli.uibo@ut.ee`

## Abstract

The research on modeling the Estonian morphology by finite state devices has been influenced mostly by (Koskenniemi, 1983), (Lauri Karttunen and Zaenen, 1992) and (Beesley and Karttunen, 2000). We have used lexical transducer combined with two-level rules as a general model for describing Estonian morphology. As a novel approach we can emphasize the application of the rules to the both sides of the lexical transducer – both to the lexical representation and to the lemma. In the paper the criteria of optimality of the finite-state description of a natural language morphology and the means of fulfilling these criteria are discussed on the example of Estonian – a language with very rich and complex morphology. Other builders of finite-state morphological transducers may profit from the ideas proposed.

## 1 Introduction

During the last 25 years the finite-state approach has been the most fruitful one in the field of computational morphology. A morphological finite-state transducer describes the correspondence between word forms and their morphological readings (lemma + morphological features) as a regular relation, or a correspondence between two languages. In the simplest case the morphological transducer is a lexical transducer, on the upper side of which are primary forms concatenated with appropriate morphological information and on the lower side – word forms. Each path from the initial state to a final state represents a mapping between a word form and its morphological reading. The morphological analysis can then be understood as the "lookup" operation in the lexical transducer, whereas synthesis – the "lookdown" operation ((Beesley and Karttunen, 2003). The lexical transducer can be composed with rule transducer(s) that convert lexical representation to surface representation, using either two-level (Koskenniemi, 1983) or replace rules (Karttunen, 1995).

The finite-state description of Estonian morphology has been built up, lead by the principles of the two-level morphology model (Koskenniemi, 1983). The model consists of a network of lexicons and a set of two-level rules. The two-levelness means that the lexical representations of morphemes are maintained in the lexicons and the task of two-level rules is to "translate" the lexical forms into the surface forms and vice versa. The lexical forms may contain information about the phoneme alternations, about the structure of the word form (morpheme boundaries) etc. The model is language-independent, but for the different languages the balance between rules and lexicons can be different. The network of lexicons is good for agglutinating languages like Finnish (Koskenniemi, 1983), Turkish (Oflazer, 1994) and Swahili (Hurskainen, 1995), where word forms are built by concatenation of morphemes. Two-level rules are convenient to handle single phoneme alternations. We will show how we have described the Estonian morphology by the means of finite-state devices and discuss the occurred problems and their solutions.

## 2 Estonian morphology

Estonian is a highly inflected language – grammatical meanings are expressed by grammatical formatives which are affixed to the stem instead of using prepositions. In some cases the analytical forms – adpositional phrases – can be alternatively used (Table 1, but there is often a style difference. According to a more detailed analysis the stem consists of word root and derivational affixes and formative – of features and endings.

Table 1: Inflected forms of a noun and the corresponding adpositional phrases

| Case | Word form | Adpositional phrase | Translation |
|---|---|---|---|
| nominative | raamat | - | book |
| genitive | raamatu | - | book's |
| partitive | raamatut | - | book (object) |
| illative | raamatusse | raamatu sisse | into a book |
| inessive | raamatus | raamatu sees | in a book |
| elative | raamatust | raamatu seest | out of a book |
| allative | raamatule | raamatu peale | onto a book |
| adessive | raamatul | raamatu peal | on a book |
| ablative | raamatult | raamatu pealt | from a book |
| translative | raamatuks | - | (become)a book |
| terminative | raamatuni | kuni raamatuni | up to a book |
| essive | raamatuna | raamatu kujul | as a book |
| abessive | raamatuta | ilma raamatuta | without a book |
| comitative | raamatuga | koos raamatuga | with a book |

Based on the morphological behavior, there are three morphological word classes in Estonian:

- nouns (declinables) – substantives, adjectives, pronouns and numerals;

- verbs (conjugables);

- uninflected words (indeclinables) – adverbs, adpositions, conjunctions and interjections.

Nouns have 14-15 cases in singular and plural, there are often parallel forms in plural. Verbs have four moods (indicative, conditional, imperative, quotative), four tenses (present, imperfect, present perfect and past perfect), two modes (personal and impersonal), two voices (affirmative and negative), three persons and two numbers (singular and plural). There is no gender distinction in Estonian.

Derivation is mostly done by suffixing:
*kiire* (Adj) 'quick' – *kiiresti* (Adv) 'quickly'
*õppima* (V) 'to learn' – *õppimine* (N) 'learning'

For compounding the concatenation of stems is used. The pre-components of compound nouns can be either in singular nominative, singular genitive or in some cases in plural genitive case. Only the last component of an Estonian compound is declinable.

The word forms in Estonian are constructed by the following morphological processes:

- Agglutination – concatenation of morphemes, whereas morphemes are clearly distinguishable

  a) declination: *probleemi + de + ta = probleemideta* 'problems' – 'without problems';

  b) conjugation: *ela + ksi + me = elaksime* 'live' – 'we would live';

  c) derivation: *rahu + lik = rahulik* 'peace' – 'peaceful';

  d) compounding: *all + maa + raud + tee = allmaaraudtee* 'subway' ("underground railway").

- Flexion – morpheme having the same meaning changes its shape in different grammatical forms, e.g. *tuba : toa* 'room' sg nominative : sg genitive;

- Suppletivity – the forms in the paradigm come from absolutely different stems that historically have been words with similar meanings, e.g. *minema : lähen* 'to go : I go', *hea : parem* 'good : better', *üks : esimene* 'one : the first', *kaks : teine* 'two : the second';

- Analyticality – multi-word forms

  a) verb forms with auxiliaries, e.g. *oli tehtud* 'had been done', *on söönud* 'has eaten';

  b) chain verbs, e.g. *hakkab olema* 'will be', *paneb põlema* 'switches on';

  c) phrasal verbs, e.g. *alla kirjutama* 'to sign';

  d) idiomatic expressions, e.g. *jalga laskma* 'to escape';

  e) adpositional phrases, e.g. *laua peal* 'on the table', *metsa sees* 'in the forest', *minu järel* 'after me'.

- Reduplication – the repetition of the stem (sometimes in a slightly varied shape).

This phenomenon occurs in some descriptive adverbs and adjectives only, e.g. *kilin-kõlin* 'jingle-jangle', *kimpsud-kompsud* 'bundles', *siiruviiruline* 'striate', *pilla-palla* 'higgledy-piggledy', *sahker-mahker* 'hugger-mugger'.

---

Uibo: *Optimizing the finite-state description of Estonian morphology*

## 3 Finite-state morphology of Estonian

The morphological phenomena in the Estonian language have been divided between rules and lexicons as follows:

- The rules of phonotactics, different stem flexion types and morphological distribution have been formalized as two-level rules (An example is given on Figure 1.

- The rules of morphotactics have been described in the network of lexicons.

- The stem final alternations have been divided between lexicons and rules.


Figure 1: "b,d,g,s deletion"

```
"b,d,g,s deletion"
  GC:0 <=> V: _ V: $:;
```

(The symbol $ marks the weak grade and GC is the set of gradating consonants.)


The network of lexicons was designed after the morphological classification of Ülle Viks (Ülle Viks, 1992) which is based on pattern recognition. This classification is compact and oriented for automatic morphological analysis. It contains 38 inflection types – 26 for nouns and 12 for verbs. 84 words (including most of the pronouns) are handled as exceptions. There is a branching inside some noun types according to the stem final vowel in our lexicon. The lexicons of inflection types (noun types 01-26 and verb types 27-38) contain a number of linked lexicons. The first group generates the stem variants, the second group locates the stem variants in paradigm and the third builds the base forms and their analogy forms.

Noun declination, verb conjugation, comparison of adjectives, productive derivation and compounding have been implemented, using the continuation lexicons. Agglutinative processes occuring by declination of nouns and conjugation of verbs have been described by three layers of lexicons (cf. Figure 2):

1. continuation lexicon for each inflection type (lexicon 10_NE-SE-S). There are references to these lexicons from the root lexicons of word classes (Substantive, Verb, Adjective, etc.).

2. allocation of stem variants in the paradigm (lexicons An_SgN, An_SgG ... An_PlP_id)

3. adding of grammatical features and endings (lexicons Cases_1 and Cases_2)


The finite-state description of Estonian is a little unbalanced – the network of lexicons plays the major role, but Viks's type system allows to reuse the automatic inflection type detection module developed for this particular system.

The Estonian finite-state morphology has been implemented using the XEROX tools LEXC, TWOLC and XFST. There are 45 two-level rules. The network of lexicons covers all the inflection types. The stem lexicon contains ca 2500 most frequent word roots, based on the frequency dictionary of Estonian (Kaalep and Muischnek, 2002). Additionally, the network of lexicons include ca 200 continuation lexicons, which describe the stem final changes, noun declination, verb conjugation, derivation and compounding.

## 4 Optimizing the finite-state description of Estonian

The question could arise, in which sense should the finite-state description be optimal. We can consider it from the point of view of efficiency (computer) and maintainability (human).

- Time- and space-complexity of the resulting transducer should be minimized. It is important, although nowadays the processor speed and amount of operative memory are not any more so critical resource than in 1980s.

- The system of lexicons and rules should be not only machine-readable, but also human-readable and easy to update. Everybody who has tried to build a system consisting from both lexicons and rules knows how complicated it might get to update the rules and lexicons, if the system is not reasonably structured.


This is always to some extent a subjective matter which phenomena to describe by the means of rules and which by using lexicons. As an objective matter, productivity is the key issue here. We have to be aware, how productive are the rules that participate in the word inflection, derivation and compounding processes. If the rule is absolutely productive then it is easy

---

Figure 2: Linked lexicons describing the agglutinative processes in noun morphology

```
LEXICON Substantive
! Root lexicon of substantives
hobu 10\_NE-SE-S; ! horse
LEXICON 10\_NE-SE-S
! Inflection type for 3-syllable words
! ending in -ne.
:ne An\_SgN; ! Stem variant -ne
            ! (nominative stem)
! continue from the lexicon An\_SgN.
:se AnŽ\_SgG; ! Stem variant -se
             !(genitive stem)
! continue from the lexicon An\_SgG.
:s An\_SgP\_t; ! Stem variant -s
             ! (consonant stem)
! continue from the lexicon An\_SgP\_t...
:s An\_PlG\_te; ! ... or from the lexicon
             ! An\_SgN.
:se An\_PlP\_id;
LEXICON An\_SgN
+Sg+N:0 GI; ! sg nominative +
            ! optional stress particle -gi.
Compound; ! precomponent of a compound
LEXICON An\_SgG
+Sg+G:0 GI;
+Sg:0 Cases\_1;
! Singular cases are built from the
! genitive stem.
+Pl+N:+d GI;
Compound;
LEXICON An\_SgP\_t
+Sg+P:+t GI;
LEXICON An\_PlG\_te
+Pl+G:+te GI;
+Pl:+te Cases\_1; ! Plural cases are built
                  ! from the consonant stem
                  ! + plural feature -te.
LEXICON An\_PlP\_id
+Pl+P:+id GI;
+Pl:+i Cases\_2; ! short plural
LEXICON Cases\_1
! Case endings from illative to comitative
+Ill:+sse GI;
+In:+s GI;
+El:+st GI;
+All:+le GI;
+Ad:+l GI;
+Abl:+lt GI;;
+Trl:+ks GI;
+Ter:+ni GI;
+Es:+na GI;
+Ab:+ta GI;
+Kom:+ga GI;
LEXICON Cases\_2  ! Cases illative
                  ! ...translative
+Ill:+sse GI;
+In:+s GI;
...
+Trl:+ks GI;
```

Figure 3: Lexical representation of stem variants of the word *jõgi* 'river'.

```
         jõgi
jõG=i    jõe
         jõge
         jõkke
```

to formalize either as a rule or a part of the network of lexicons. For example, for regular stem changes we have applied the "many in one"-solution – all the possible stem variants are encoded as a single lexical entry in the root lexicon, using lexical symbols (morphophonemes) that correspond to different phonemes on the surface (Figure 3). Stem internal and phonologically caused stem final changes are handled by lexical symbols. Two-level rules state the legal correspondences between lexical and surface phonemes, depending on the current morphophonological context.

As an example of regular non-phonologically caused stem changes once again consider Figure 2 to see how non-phonologically caused stem final changes e.g. hobune : hobuse : hobust (horse sg nom, gen, part)have been described using continuation lexicons.

Exceptions always cause problems and often lead to inelegant solutions in the language description. Extreme exceptions should be certainly listed in the lexicon. But how to handle the semi-productive morphotactic and phonological rules? We have to choose between introducing lots of new lexical features which trigger the rules and are hard to memorize and writing lots of small lexicons which are linked between themselves and change the network of lexicons to a "spider's net". Beesley and Karttunen (2003) propose a more convenient solution from the human viewpoint – flag diacritics, but it has its own drawback – we can lose in system's efficiency by using it.

Building the finite-state description of Estonian we tackled the fact that it was especially the network of lexicons which got too complicated to maintain. The problems with the rules had more to do with efficiency and they have been solved in rather early stages of the system's development. Therefore, we concentrated on the optimization of the network of lexicons.

---

Uibo: *Optimizing the finite-state description of Estonian morphology*

Based on our experience we could give to the builders of finite-state lexical transducers the following recommendations:

1. Avoid redundancy in lexicons.

   For example, substantives and adjectives decline similarly, but behave differently as regards to derivation, compounding and comparison processes. However, this can be a compromise between the size and readability.

2. Split up the lexicon into the system of linked lexicons logically.

   One should follow the rules of morphotactics; it is better if the morphemes are not split into smaller parts. This principle can be followed quite naturally for completely agglutinative languages. In the Estonian language, however, the boundary between the morphemes is often blurred, e.g. in the word form *anti*'was given' (the lemma is *and/ma*)the phoneme *t*is "shared" between the stem and formative .

3. Use meaningful lexical forms.

   A good example here is the description of Estonian consonant gradation (Trosterud and Uibo, 2005)where we denote the gradating consonants with corresponding uppercase letters. However, there is a problem with deletion of the phoneme s which can occur as a result of stem internal consonant gradation but it can also be dropped from the stem end in some other inflection types. We have chosen to denote the disappearing s in both cases by uppercase S, but as a consequence the contexts in the S:0 rule come from substantially different sources (Figure 4).

4. Keep the number of lexicons reasonable.

   The general principle is to try to use rules instead of lexicons as much as possible.

5. Minimize the size of root lexicons.

   This is done by avoiding stem doubling in inflection, derivation and compounding and also by unknown word guessing using the phoneme patterns as regular expressions for productive inflection types where the inflection types is unambiguously determined by the phonological shape of the stem.

Figure 4: Rule: Deletion of stem internal and stem final s.

```
S:0 <=> Bgn V [C+] (GC:GCstr) V:  _ StemEnd;
! küngas-künka
        Bgn V GC:GCstr C V _  StemEnd;
! kobras-kopra
        Bgn V  _ (V) \%$:; ! käsi-käe
        Bgn V V s  _ V \%$:;  ! kauss-kausi
                where GC in  (G B D K P T )
! set of gradating consonants, except for S
                GCstr  in  (g b d k p t )
! corresponding strong grade phonemes
            matched;
```

## 5 A step towards better readability and reduction of lexicon size – two-levelness extended

One step towards better readability, satisfying the requirements 3 and 5 from the previous section is our novel idea to use the two-level representation also for **lemma stems** in the root lexicons. We will take a closer look at this approach.

The majority of Estonian verbs are subject to productive derivation processes. The problem arised with the verbs with weakening stem flexion, for which the base form (supine) is in the strong grade (*lugema*'to read'). The morphological information for the derived word form, outputted during morphological analysis, should contain the derived base form, which is sometimes in the weak grade (*loetav* 'one that is being read', *loetud* 'read (finished)', *loetu* 'one that has been read'*).

The lexical transducer picks up the strong-grade stem and the word class V (verb), but finding a derivational suffix from the word form, it might turn out, that it is a substantive or an adjective with weak lemma. The initial solution was to include the verbs with weakening stems into root lexicons three times – once into the root lexicon of verbs and in both strong and weak grade into the root lexicon of verbal derivatives (Figure 5).

We have found a helpful solution to the weak grade verb derivatives problem: to extend the two-levelness to the left side of the lexical transducer (to the lemma). The approach has been applied for verbs with stem flexion (Figure 6).

Figure 5: Derivation from verb roots: storage consuming solution
LEXICON Verb
lugema+V:luGe V2;

LEXICON Verb-Deriv
loe VD0;
luge VD1;

Figure 6: Derivation from verb roots: a better solution
LEXICON Verb
luGe V2;

As a result, the productive verb derivatives do not require three, but only one record in the root lexicon. To get the lemma in the surface form, stem flexion rules have to be applied onto the left side of the lexical transducer. The resulting morphological transducer of Estonian can be formulated as follows:

$$((LexiconFST)^{-1} \circ RulesFST_1)^{-1} \circ RulesFST,$$

where LexiconFST is the lexical transducer, RulesFST is the rule transducer (the intersection of all the two-level rules) and

$$RulesFST_1 \subset RulesFST$$

is the intersection of stem flexion rules. The operations used are composition and inversion. More about the extension of two-levelness in Uibo (2005).

The percentage of verbs is about 15 % among the 10000 most frequent words of written Estonian (Kaalep and Muischnek, 2002). Consequently, after the extension of two-levelness the number of records in root lexicons would decrease ca 23 %. The testing and lexicon extending cycle will go on, as the present coverage of the lexicon is about 30 % only.

## 6   Conclusion and future work

We have given an overview of the finite-state description of Estonian morphology and pointed out the criteria of optimality of the description from the point of view of both efficiency and maintainability of the system. These criteria have arised from the practice. The present finite-state description of Estonian is far from being perfect yet, but we have the ideas how to reorganize the system to improve first of all its human-readability.

We can bring forth the following strengths of the finite-state approach:

- The two-level representation is useful for the description of the Estonian stem internal changes, especially because the stem flexion type does not depend on the phonological shape of a stem in the contemporary Estonian any more.

- The network of lexicons, combined with rules, having effect on morpheme boundaries, naturally describe the morphotactic processes.

- The lexicons are useful for describing the non-phonologically caused stem end alternations.

- Due to the possibility to compose finite-state transducers we can use an economic solution for modelling productive verbal derivation: we have extended the two-levelness partly to the upper side of the lexical transducer – to the lexical representations of the lemmas of forms productively derivable from the verb roots. The proposed approach may be applied in describing the morphology of languages, where the word stems are subject to change during productive derivational processes.

There are some open problems for which we know in the best case a theoretical solution:

- How to guess the analysis of unknown words? The idea that has so far tested only on a very limited lexicon is to have a root as a regular expression (e.g. CVVCV) in the root lexicon for each productive inflection type.

- The balance between productivity and lexicalization – how complex is it to describe partially productive derivation types by minilexicons and continuation links (instead of including the derivatives into stem lexicons as independent stems)? Which derivation types to consider productive enough? Which are the formal features that could be used to handle some processes in derivation by rules?

- How to constrain the overgeneration of compound words? The idea is to apply the semantic features. An alternative idea is to use weighted finite-state transducers trained on the corpus data.

- To include the finite-state component into practical applications? The most interesting idea in this perspective is to work on fuzzy information retrieval that is tolerant to misspellings and typos.

## 7 Acknowledgments

The research on finite-state morphology of Estonian has been supported by the Estonian Science Foundation grant No. 4605 (2001-2003). Our thanks also go to Kimmo Koskenniemi, Lauri Karttunen, Kenneth Beesley and Trond Trosterud for encouraging discussions.

## References

Kenneth R. Beesley and Lauri Karttunen. 2000. Finite-state non-concatenative morphotactics. In *Proceedings of SIGPHON-2000. 5th Workshop of the ACL Special Interest Group in Computational Phonology*, pages 1–12, Centre Universitaire, Luxembourg.

Kenneth R. Beesley and Lauri Karttunen. 2003. *Finite State Morphology*. CSLI Studies in Computational Linguistics. CSLI Publications, Stanford, USA.

Arvi Hurskainen. 1995. Information retrieval and two-directional word formation. *Nordic Journal of African Studies*, 4(2):81–92.

Heiki-Jaan Kaalep and Kadri Muischnek. 2002. *Eesti keele sagedussõnastik (The frequency dictionary of written Estonian)*. University of Tartu Press, Tartu.

Lauri Karttunen. 1995. The replace operator. In *Proceedings of the 33rd Annual Meeting of the Association for Computational Linguistics. ACL-95*, pages 16–23, Boston, Massachusetts.

Kimmo Koskenniemi. 1983. *Two-level Morphology: A General Computational Model for Word-form Production and Generation*. Publications of the Department of General Linguistics, University of Helsinki. University of Helsinki, Helsinki.

Ronald M. Kaplan Lauri Karttunen and Annie Zaenen. 1992. Two-level morphology with composition. In *Proceedings of the 14th conference on Computational linguistics*, volume 1, pages 141–148, Nantes, France.

Kemal Oflazer. 1994. Two-level description of turkish morphology. *Literary and Linguistic Computing*, 9(2):137–148.

Trond Trosterud and Heli Uibo. 2005. Consonant gradation in estonian and s?mi: two-level solution. In *Inquiries into words, constraints and contexts: Festschrift in the Honour of Kimmo Koskenniemi on his 60th Birthday*, CSLI Studies in Computational Linguistics ONLINE, pages 136–150. CSLI Publications.

Heli Uibo. 2005. Finite-state morphology of estonian: two-levelness extended. In *Proceedings of Iternational Conference Recent Advances in Natural Language Processing. RANLP 2005*, pages 580–584, Borovets, Bulgaria.

Ülle Viks. 1992. *A Concise Morphological Dictionary of Estonian*, volume 1. Eesti Teaduste Akadeemia, Keele ja Kirjanduse Instituut, Tallinn.

# Rigorous dimensionality reduction through linguistically motivated feature selection for text categorization


**Hans Friedrich Witschel** and **Chris Biemann**

NLP department
University of Leipzig
Augustusplatz 10–11
DE-04109 Leipzig
{witschel,biem}@informatik.uni-leipzig.de



## Abstract

This paper introduces a new linguistically motivated feature selection technique for text categorization based on morphological analysis. It will be shown that compound parts that are constituents of many (different) noun compounds throughout a text are good and general indicators of this text's content; they are more general in meaning than the compounds they are part of, but nevertheless have good domain-specificity so that they distinguish between categories. Experiments with categorizing German newspaper texts show that this feature selection technique is superior to other popular ones, especially when dimensionality is reduced substantially. Additionally, a new compound splitting method based on compact patricia tries is introduced.


## 1 Introduction

The task of automatic text categorization can be divided into two fields of research: first, appropriate features have to be selected for representing documents. Second, the actual classification algorithms have to be developed and applied to the previously generated feature vectors. Most of recent research has been devoted to the latter task.

In this paper, however, we argue that in text categorization, feature selection is absolutely crucial for the quality of classification results. Moreover, many applications require a drastic reduction in dimensionality, i.e. it is rarely possible or desirable to use the full set of terms occurring in a given document. Moreover, differences between feature selection algorithms become more visible as dimensionality is reduced (which is somewhat trivial because, when using the full set of available features from a text, all algorithms will have equal performance). We therefore consider feature selection for text categorization a good evaluation method for indexing algorithms that aim at very compact document descriptions.

As indicated by (Sebastiani, 2002), there are two possibilities of dimensionality reduction: selecting a subset of the existing terms or generating a set of synthetic terms, e.g. by using clustering or Latent Semantic Indexing (LSI). In this paper, an instance of term selection will be discussed.

It should be noted however, that the notion of "term" or "feature candidate" can be understood in various ways: in a bag-of-words model every string surrounded by whitespace will be considered a term – with the possible exception of so-called stop words. Alternatives are possible: as we will propose, compound constituents can also form a feature candidate set as well as phrases (multi-word units) or arbitrary character n-grams. Each method for generating a set of feature candidates can be individually combined with different selection methods for reducing its size.

In the following, we wish to make two major contributions:

- First, we introduce a new algorithm for feature selection that is based on shallow linguistic knowledge and especially designed to rigorously reduce dimensionality.

- Second, we support the findings of (Yang and Pedersen, 1997) who have shown that different algorithms for feature selection behave quite differently when the number of features is reduced significantly.

The rest of this paper is organized as follows: The following section introduces some related work, in section 3 the actual feature selection techniques that we want to compare will be discussed. Section 4 will detail one of the linguistic processing techniques that we used (namely compound splitting), sections 5 and 6 will describe the experiments that we conducted and section 7 concludes.

## 2  Related work

### 2.1  Statistical feature selection

Most approaches to feature selection rely on pure statistics. Normally a bag of words approach for representing documents is used together with these methods, i.e. all words (i.e. one-word units) from a text are used as feature candidates, regardless of their syntactic function (part-of-speech) or other linguistic characteristics. The only "linguistic" operation that is widely performed is the removal of so-called stop words (functional words) by predefined lists.

One of the simplest of these methods is selecting terms with medium to high *document frequency* (DF), i.e. ones that occur in many documents. However, terms with *very high* DF are normally excluded as stop words. A vocabulary that consists of terms with a medium to high DF is likely to cover a large portion of the collection, i.e. it is probable that each document contains at least one term from this vocabulary even if its size is reduced substantially. DF scores are used by e.g. (Ittner et al., 1995) or (Yang and Pedersen, 1997).

Some more sophisticated statistics are based on information-theoretic measures that select terms, the distribution of which is strongly biased towards documents from one single category (i.e. terms that occur in documents of one category but *not* in others). Examples for these measures include the $\chi^2$ measure (cf. e.g. (Yang and Pedersen, 1997; Galavotti et al., 2000)), information gain (Lewis, 1992; Larkey, 1998) or mutual information (Dumais et al., 1998; Larkey and Croft, 1996). This is only a very small fraction of all the research that has been carried out in that direction.

In a comparative study that evaluated many of the most popular statistical approaches, (Yang and Pedersen, 1997) surprisingly found DF to fall only very slightly short of the other,

more sophisticated methods. Mutual information even performed significantly worse than DF. This means that the benefits of information-theoretic measures for feature selection in text categorization are somewhat arguable.

### 2.2  Linguistic methods

Linguistic methods for generating feature candidates have been applied in the past, but most efforts in this direction have concentrated on phrasal features: often noun phrases (identified in different ways – statistically or linguistically) are used as feature candidates (cf. e.g. (Lewis, 1992; Tzeras and Hartmann, 1993)). Different phrasal indexing approaches have led to different results, but most research in that direction found that the use of (noun) phrases as features does *not* improve classification accuracy because

> "an indexing language consisting of syntactic indexing phrases will have more terms, more synonymous or nearly synonymous terms, lower consistency of assignment (since synonymous terms are not assigned to the same documents), and lower document frequency for terms" (Lewis, 1992).

This has led to the general conclusion that linguistic feature selection methods should not be further explored.

Approaches that try to use linguistic information – apart from the identification of noun phrases – have therefore not attracted much attention. An example of such an approach can be found, however, in (Junker and Hoch, 1997), where the use of part-of-speech and additional morphological term characteristics is proposed: both of them were found to improve classification results on OCR and non-OCR texts.

As far as part-of-speech information is concerned, only nouns, adjectives and verbs were admitted as features in their experiments and morphological analysis comprised stemming and compound analysis. Parts of compounds were permitted as additional feature candidates (similarly to our hybrid strategy, see below) and mutual information was then applied as a statistical term selection method on this candidate set. (Junker and Hoch, 1997) also found character n-grams to be good features (namely 5-grams), showing approximately equal performance to the use of the linguistic methods mentioned above.

The overall feature selection process in (Junker and Hoch, 1997) was similar to the one we are going to present in this paper, with the important difference that we are going to combine morphological analysis with a local statistical filter – instead of using the (global) mutual information measure – and use compound parts as the *only* feature candidates for describing texts.

## 3　Linguistically motivated feature selection

### 3.1　Preliminary thoughts

What should good features for text categorization look like? First, they should be specific of their domain or category – words or units that appear uniformly in texts throughout all categories are very ill suited for distinguishing between categories. This is the idea behind many of the statistical approaches introduced in the last section: measures like mutual information or $\chi^2$-tests aim at extracting "category-specific" features.

On the other hand, the selected vocabulary must cover as many documents as possible, i.e. each document should contain at least one term from the vocabulary. When reducing dimensionality through term selection techniques, however, documents must be described by only very few terms. This poses a serious problem: if terms are very specific, they are unlikely to cover a large portion of the document collection. Selecting terms with high document frequency has been proposed exactly for this reason: when reducing the size of the vocabulary significantly, the terms that we leave over must be general enough to cover the majority of all documents. This is also why weighting terms by TF/IDF is probably a bad idea: it prefers terms with high IDF, i.e. ones that occur in very few documents.

To summarize: good features for text categorization should be category-*specific*, but *general within* that category or domain.

The use of linguistic – or more precisely, shallow syntactic and morphologic – criteria that we propose is based on the intuition that some syntactic categories have a larger fraction of content-bearing elements than others. We especially focus on nouns and noun compounds because they tend to be more content-bearing and less ambiguous than verbs or adjectives.

More specifically, the parts of a compound noun (especially its head) have a more general meaning than the whole compound: "Saft" (juice) is more general than "Orangensaft" (orange juice). Therefore, compound constituents that appear frequently in many (different) compounds of a text tend to be good indicators of the text's *general topic*. Moreover, parts extracted from noun compounds are nearly always free morphemes or even words, i.e. they can appear in a text by themselves. They are thus also informative index terms when inspected by humans.

The approach that we will describe subsequently does not examine the distribution of compound parts throughout categories, i.e. it will not assure that they appear in feature vectors of only one category. Instead, a local feature selection technique using within-category frequencies will be used. We will see in the experiments that this is sufficient because compound parts are not only general but also specific of the topic that the documents cover: they yield surprisingly good classification results, especially at very low dimensionalities.

### 3.2　Feature Selection using compound constituents

The approach that we propose is based on syntactical as well as morphological knowledge: in a first step, common nouns are extracted by using a part-of-speech (POS) tagger and their frequencies are calculated. Thereafter, all these nouns are passed to a tool designed to split compounds into their constituents (see section 4). Whenever this tool produces two or more parts, i.e. whenever we find a true compound, a count for each of these parts is incremented by the frequency of the compound that contains it.

When regarding compound constituents and their counts as feature vectors, we can reduce dimensionality as follows: The whole set of positive training instances for each category is treated as one large document and compound parts are extracted from this text as indicated above. Then, we can select the X most frequent compound parts from each category as an indexing vocabulary. The feature vector for a single text is computed by generating the list of all compound parts contained in both the compounds of this text and in the indexing vocabulary.

Splitting compounds is obviously restricted to languages which use one-word compounding, such as German, Dutch, Japanese, Korean and all Nordic languages. However, the same idea can in principle be applied to English as well: again using a part-of-speech (POS) tagger, it is possible to extract noun phrases that match POS patterns like N N (two successive nouns, e.g. "information retrieval") from texts. These often correspond to compounds in one-word compounding languages and their constituents can be treated in the same way as suggested for compound parts above.

## 4   Compound splitting

For setting up a compound splitting component, it is clearly desirable to use a machine learning approach: We would like to train a classifier using a set of training examples. In application, this classifier uses regularities acquired in the training phase to split compounds that have not been necessarily contained in the training set.

Generally, there are two ways to design a generic compound splitter: one is based on training on all possible breakpoints and using letter n-grams to both sides as features, e.g. used by (Yoon, 2000). Another way is to memorize possible prefixes and suffixes of compounds and match them during classification, a methodology conducted by e.g. (Sjöbergh and Kann, 2004). While n-gram splitters are capable of reaching comparatively high accuracy scores with small training sets, affix splitters need more training data but handle exceptions more naturally.

Here, we present an affix compound splitter that uses Compact Patricia Tries (CPT) as a data structure, which can be extended to function as a classifier on affixes of words.

### 4.1   Classification with Compact Patricia Tries

A trie is a tree data structure for storing strings, in which there is one node for every common prefix. The number of possible children is limited by the number of characters in the strings. Patricia tries (first mentioned in (Morrison, 1968)) reduce the number of nodes by merging all nodes having only one child with

their parent's node. When using the structure for a string-based classification task, redundant subtrees and strings in leaves longer than 1 can be pruned, resulting in a structure called Compact Patricia Trie (CPT).

For classification, the sum of the weights for all classes in a subtree is stored with the string in the respective node. For example, in the CPT depicted in figure 1c), the prefix "Ma" has the class "m" associated with it three times, whereas the class "f" was seen only once with this prefix. Confidence of a node for a class C can be calculated by dividing the weight of C by the sum of the weights of all classes. Figure 1 shows an example, for thorough discussion on CPTs see e.g. (Knuth, 1999).

The CPT data structure possesses some very useful properties:

- the upper bound for retrieving a class for a word is limited by the length of the word and independent of the number of words stored in the CPT. When using hashes for subtree selection and considering limits on word lengths, search time is O(1).

- the number of classes for the classification task is not limited.

- when there is only one class per word, CPTs reproduce the training set: when classifying the previously inserted words, no errors are made.

- words that were not inserted in the CPT nevertheless receive a morphologically motivated guess by assigning the default class of the last matched node (partial match)

CPTs as classifiers can be put somewhat in between rule-based and memory-based learners. For unknown words, the class is assigned by choosing the class with the highest confidence in the node returned by a search. Nevertheless, CPTs memorize exceptional cases in the training set and therefore provide an error case library within the data structure.

### 4.2   Compound splitting with CPTs

Germanic compound nouns can consist of an arbitrary number of nouns or other word classes. A segmentation algorithm must proceed recursively, splitting the noun into parts that are split again until no more splitting can be performed. Segmentation can be done from the front and

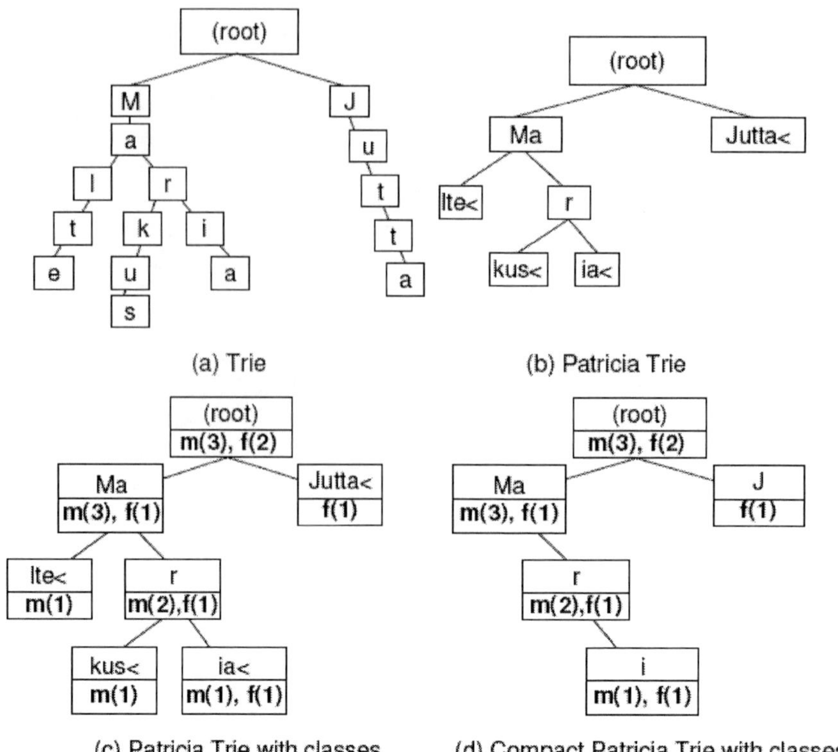



Figure 1: From Trie (a) to Patricia Trie (b,c) to CPT (d) for the classification of first name genders. m denotes male, f denotes female. Note that 'Maria' can be both.

from the end of the word. According to this, two CPTs are trained: One that memorizes at which position – counting from the beginning of the word – a split should be performed, and another one memorizing the break points in counting characters from the end of the word. The training set not only consists of known compound nouns, but also of all sub-compound nouns. Table 1 illustrates the training examples for both CPTs as obtained from the compound *Dampf//schiff//fahrt(s)//gesellschaft* (German lit: steam//ship//trip//society). The numbers indicate the position of the break points, the optional string part is used to denote possible interfixes (linking elements) that are inserted for phonological reasons, e.g. the (s) in table 1.

Now we have two classifiers predicting segmentation points on the basis of words. These classifiers either utter a proposal or respond "undecided" when confidence for the deepest retrieved node is too low. During segmentation, the following heuristics were applied:

- *Case 1*: both CPTs agree on a segmentation point - segment at this point

- *Case 2*: one of the CPTs is undecided - segment on the other's proposed point

- *Case 3*: the CPTs disagree: believe the CPT that reports the highest confidence

- *Case 4*: both CPTs are undecided or predict segmentation points out of word bounds: do not segment.

Evaluating the compound splitter using the Korean Compound noun training set of (Yun et al., 1997) with 10-fold cross-validation, we achieved an F-value of 96.32% on unseen examples and 99.95% on examples contained in the training set. The reasons for not perfectly reproducing the training set lies in the incapability of the approach to handle ambiguous splits (e.g. Swedish *bil+drulle* (bad driver) vs. *bild+rulle* (film roll)). These cases, however, do not play a major role in terms of frequency and can be handled by an exception list.

---

| word | rule in prefix CPT | rule in suffix CPT |
|---|---|---|
| dampfschifffahrtsgesellschaft | 5 | 12 |
| schifffahrtsgesellschaft | 6 | 12 |
| fahrtsgesellschaft | 5s | 12 |
| dampfschifffahrt | 5 | 5 |
| dampfschiff | 5 | 6 |
| schifffahrt | 6 | 5 |
| dampf | 5 | 5 |
| schiff | 6 | 6 |
| fahrt | 5 | 5 |
| gesellschaft | 12 | 12 |

Table 1: Compound constituents of *Dampfschifffahrtsgesellschaft*

For our experiments described in the next section, we used a German training set that was automatically constructed using a large corpus. Manual evaluation showed that more than 90% of segmentations are correct for compounds with at most 4 constituents.

## 5  Experimental setup

We conducted some experiments with a German newspaper corpus consisting of 3540 texts from 12 different subject areas using an implementation of Multinomial Naive Bayes from the Weka package[1] with 10-fold cross-validation. Experiments with other classifiers showed the same effects and are therefore omitted. We built three sorts of indexing vocabularies:

- *Compound parts:* For each category, the set of positive training instances was concatenated to form one single text and the parts occurring in many compounds throughout this text were extracted together with their frequencies.

- *Common nouns:* From the preliminary phase of our shallow linguistic analysis, we retained the set of common nouns, together with their frequencies. We used the same form of building the final feature set on these candidates, namely selecting the highest ranked nouns from each category.

- *DF:* A bag of words model without any linguistic knowledge, using document frequency (DF) for feature selection (which (Yang and Pedersen, 1997) have shown to

---

[1] http://www.cs.waikato.ac.nz/%7Eml/weka/

behave well when compared to more sophisticated statistical measures, see section 2). Terms with medium to high DF were chosen in this method: the ones with *very high* DF (stop words) were first removed. Thereafter, terms with low DF were pruned in order to arrive at the different vocabulary sizes.

Finally, we implemented a *hybrid* strategy, combining nouns and compound parts, again selecting the most frequent items (nouns *or* compound parts) from each category.

## 6  Results

By varying thresholds, we produced results for different numbers of features. Figure 2 shows the classification accuracy for our three different feature selection techniques as a function of the indexing vocabulary size.

These results show that all algorithms perform similarly when using 1000 or more features (somewhat over 80% precision). When reducing the number of features drastically, however, the performance of the DF-based algorithm and the one with common nouns drops much faster than that of our compound part extraction.

When using as little as 24 features (i.e. only two from each category), DF term selection and common nouns both produce an accuracy of just around 35%, whereas when using compound parts, we obtain a precision of nearly 60%. This difference of performance can be understood when looking at the selected features: Table 2 shows the indexing vocabularies of size 24 for nouns and compound parts, detailing the

---

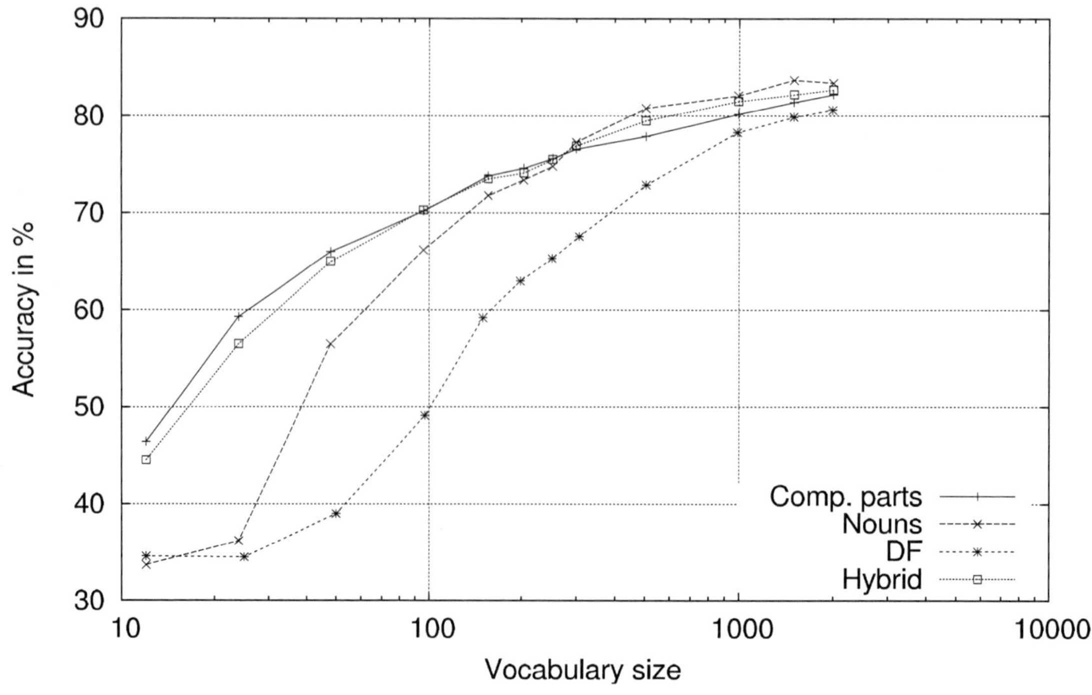


Figure 2: Classification results as a function of vocabulary size

features contributed by each of six (from 12) categories. Translations are – if necessary – given in brackets.

| Category | Comp. parts | Nouns |
|---|---|---|
| Auto (*cars*) | auto (*car*) motor | Auto (*car*) Jahr (*year*) |
| Erde (*earth*) | tier (*animal*) meer (*sea*) | Jahr (*year*) Tier (*animal*) |
| Geld (*money*) | gebühr (*fee*) studie (*study*) | Student Euro |
| Mensch (*man*) | zelle (*cell*) stoff (*substance*) | Jahr (*year*) Mensch (*man*) |
| Reise (*travel*) | stadt (*city*) berg (*mountain*) | Jahr (*year*) In (*in*) |
| Studium (*studies*) | schul (*school*) uni (*university*) | Student Jahr (*year*) |

Table 2: Top 2 features selected for six of the twelve categories by the *Nouns* and *Comp. parts* strategies

As we can see, the two most frequent nouns from the category "Job und Beruf" (job and profession) were "Jahr" (year) and "SPIEGEL" (the name of the magazine we built the corpus from). These occurred in many other categories

as well. The two most prominent compound parts for the same category were "arbeit" (job) and "beruf" (profession) which is very specific to that domain (but, of course, also very general *within* that domain). This shows that compound parts are not only general but also domain-specific.

When using many features, however, the algorithm that uses common nouns performs slightly better than the one using compound parts. This suggests that the high generality of compound parts is at some point outperformed by the higher specificity of nouns. The hybrid strategy, combining compound parts and common nouns yielded good results but was still slightly inferior to using only nouns in the high dimensionality regions.

It would be interesting for future work to investigate if the statistical approaches like $\chi^2$-tests or information gain could further improve the results of the *Compound parts* strategy, e.g. in the higher (i.e. medium) dimension regions.

## 7 Conclusions

In this paper, some shallow linguistic techniques for feature selection were proposed and applied to text categorization. One of these

– namely the use of frequent compound constituents extracted from compound nouns – produces features of high "within-category" generality and acceptable domain-specificity.

All in all, we have been able to show two things: first, when reducing dimensionality substantially, there are notable differences between different feature selection algorithms. Second, we have built a selection algorithm that beats other approaches substantially when using a very low number of features.

This shows that although linguistic methods for feature selection have not been widely used in the past, it might be a good idea to so in the future, especially when dimensionality has to be reduced significantly.

## References


S.T. Dumais, J. Platt, D. Heckermann, and M. Sahami. 1998. Inductive learning algorithms and representations for text categorisation. In *Proceedings of CIKM-98*, pages 148–155.

Luigi Galavotti, Fabrizio Sebastiani, and Maria Simi. 2000. Experiments on the use of feature selection and negative evidence in automated text categorization. In *Proc. of ECDL '00*, pages 59–68.

D. J. Ittner, D. D. Lewis, and D. D. Ahn. 1995. Text categorization of low quality images. In *Symposium on Document Analysis and Information Retrieval*, pages 301–315.

Markus Junker and Rainer Hoch. 1997. Evaluating OCR and Non-OCR Text Representations for Learning Document Classifiers. In *ICDAR '97: Proceedings of the 4th International Conference on Document Analysis and Recognition*, pages 1060–1066.

Donald Knuth. 1999. *The Art of Computer Programming. Volume 3: Searching and Sorting.* Addison-Wesley, Reading, Massachusetts.

Leah S. Larkey and W. Bruce Croft. 1996. Combining classifiers in text categorization. In *Proc. of SIGIR '96*, pages 289–297.

Leah S. Larkey. 1998. Automatic essay grading using text categorization techniques. In *Proc. ofSIGIR '98*, pages 90–95.

David D. Lewis. 1992. An evaluation of phrasal and clustered representations on a text categorization task. In *Proc. of SIGIR '92*, pages 37–50.

D. Morrison. 1968. Patricia- practical algorithm to retrieve information coded in alphanumeric. *Journal of ACM*, 15(4):514–534.

Fabrizio Sebastiani. 2002. Machine learning in automated text categorization. *ACM Computing Surveys*, 34(1):1–47.

Jonas Sjöbergh and Viggo Kann. 2004. Finding the correct interpretation of swedish compounds - a statistical approach. In *Proceedings of LREC-2004, Lisbon, Portugal*.

Kostas Tzeras and Stephan Hartmann. 1993. Automatic indexing based on bayesian inference networks. In *Proc. of SIGIR '93*, pages 22–35.

Yiming Yang and Jan O. Pedersen. 1997. A Comparative Study on Feature Selection in Text Categorization. In *ICML '97: Proceedings of the Fourteenth International Conference on Machine Learning*, pages 412–420.

Juntae Yoon. 2000. Compound noun seqmentation based on lexical data extracted from corpus. In *Proceedings of the 6th Applied Natural Language Processing Conference*.

Bo-Hyun Yun, Min-Jeung Cho, and Hae-Chang Rim. 1997. Segmenting korean compound nouns using statistical information and a preference rule. *Journal of Korean Information Science Society (KISS)*, 24(8):900–909.

**Association for Computational Linguistics**
209 N. Eighth Street
Stroudsburg, Pennsylvania 18360

ISBN 978-1-5108-3518-4